Praise for Jeanine Basinger's

I DO AND I DON'T

"Authoritative and perceptive. . . . Crammed with summaries and analysis of films from the past one hundred years, *I Do and I Don't* brilliantly demonstrates Hollywood's abiding ambivalence about the institution of matrimony." —*The Wall Street Journal*

"An insightful account of how films have represented wedlock, both holy and unholy, through the years. . . . Basinger has a gift for zeroing in on tantalizing details that bring a visual medium to readable life." —*USA Today*

"Lively. . . . Knowing and illuminating. . . . Hollywood movies of the studio era were not, as Basinger takes pains to point out, produced by naifs. Many of them convey sophisticated references to sexual intercourse, prostitution, even homosexuality—if you know how to interpret them. That some of us still do is often thanks to popular scholars like Basinger. . . . Hilarious, spot-on." —*Salon*

"Basinger [is] one of the great film gurus. . . . An exhaustive survey of its subject. . . . Basinger is wonderfully insightful, and her witty asides made me laugh out loud. . . . Ultimately Basinger makes a fine case for the place of marriage movies in particular and American moviemaking in general."
—Judith Newman, *The New York Times*

"Where Basinger's book is most useful is in helping us see the thematic and structural patterns that unite such movies with scores of others. Where her book is most provocative is in suggesting the ways in which marriage movies both reflect and shape our attitude toward marriage itself." —*The Washington Post*

"[Basinger's] writing is strong, the vision clear. . . . The amount of titles discussed and revisited are staggering. . . . Informative and witty. . . . Deft." —*Slant Magazine*

"A spikily opinionated voice congenial to a diverse readership: barbed observations for the casual fan and a hog heaven of footnotes for the tenure-track cineaste." —*San Francisco Chronicle*

"Thanks to her impeccable research and thoroughly entertaining prose, Basinger provides a take on matrimony that is never less than fascinating. Nimbly moving through history, she illustrates the lengths to which Hollywood has gone in order to make the institution of marriage exciting enough to attract audiences looking for escapism. . . . A riveting lesson in history and pop psychology, one that will appeal to film buffs of just about every stripe, not only those interested in happily ever after." —*Entertainment Weekly*

"Breezily written, aggressively researched. . . . Basinger manages to map out the terrain of the world of marriage that movies cover with the skill of an experienced cartographer who isn't afraid to stop and enjoy the view once in a while." —*Milwaukee Journal Sentinel*

"[An] entertaining take on how the silver screen has portrayed wedded bliss and wedded misery. . . . The main pleasure here is Basinger's explication of how the movies and stars of the studio system years made all this work. . . . Fascinating, fact-filled." —*Kirkus Reviews*

Jeanine Basinger

I DO AND I DON'T

Jeanine Basinger is the chair of film studies at Wesleyan University and the curator of the cinema archives there. She has written nine other books on film, including *A Woman's View: How Hollywood Spoke to Women, 1930–1960*; *Silent Stars*, winner of the William K. Everson Film History Award; *Anthony Mann*; *The World War II Combat Film: Anatomy of a Genre*; and *American Cinema: One Hundred Years of Filmmaking*, the companion book for a ten-part PBS series.

ALSO BY JEANINE BASINGER

I DO
AND
I DON'T

JEANINE BASINGER

I DO

AND

I DON'T

A History of Marriage in the Movies

VINTAGE BOOKS
A DIVISION OF RANDOM HOUSE LLC
NEW YORK

FIRST VINTAGE BOOKS EDITION, MARCH 2014

Copyright © 2012 by Jeanine Basinger

All rights reserved. Published in the United States by Vintage Books,
a division of Random House LLC, New York, and in Canada by
Random House of Canada Limited, Toronto, Penguin Random House
companies. Originally published in hardcover in the United States by
Alfred A. Knopf, a division of Random House LLC, New York, in 2013.

Vintage and colophon are registered trademarks of Random House LLC.

Frontispiece: Myrna Loy and William Powell in *After the Thin Man*,
married but not domestic

The Library of Congress has cataloged the Knopf edition as follows:
Basinger, Jeanine.
I do and I don't : a history of marriage in the movies / Jeanine Basinger.—
First edition.
pages cm
Includes bibliographical references and index.
1. Marriage in motion pictures.
2. Marriage in popular culture—United States. I. Title.
PN1995.9.M3B37 2012
791.43'655—dc23   2012036283

Vintage Trade Paperback ISBN: 978-0-8041-6974-5
eBook ISBN: 978-0-307-96222-5

Author photograph © Bill Burkhart
Book design by Iris Weinstein

www.vintagebooks.com

Printed in the United States of America

This book is dedicated to the man I married
at a Justice of the Peace office in Saratoga Springs
on September 22, 1967.

O the wo that is in marriage!

The Wife of Bath

CONTENTS

ACKNOWLEDGMENTS

I have always been fortunate in having superb family, friends, colleagues, and students who have supported my efforts in everything I've attempted. There are many to thank. At Wesleyan University, I have the best fellow film faculty anyone could want, superb sounding boards one and all: Steve Collins, Lisa Dombrowski, Scott Higgins, Leo Lensing, Marc Longenecker, Katya Straub, Jacob Bricca, Krishna Winston, and Wesleyan's President, Michael Roth. Everyone who works around me, Joyce Heidorn, Sal Privatera, Joan Miller, and most especially and most exceptionally, Lea Carlson, deserve thanks. The list of former students who contribute ideas to my work would be endless, but for this book I'll single out Jeffrey Lane, Sammy Wasson, Eric Lichtenfeld, Joss Whedon, Paul Weitz, Miguel Arteta, Eric Levy, David Kendall, Ed Decter, Domenica Cameron-Scorsese Frenzel, Owen Renfroe, and especially Jeremy Arnold, who also did amazing photo research. I always find great conversations about anything to do with movies from old friends such as Leonard, Alice, and Jessie Maltin; Richard Schickel, Annie Schulhoff, and Richard Slotkin. For this particular book, both Molly Haskell and David Thomson gave me great advice on the pitfalls of attempting to write about marriage, and Clint Eastwood provided thoughtful insight into unusual "married" relationships in our conversations about his film *J. Edgar*. I thank Ron and Howard Mandelbaum and Buddy Weiss of Photofest, and Maxine Fleckner Ducey at the Wisconsin Center for Film and Theater Research for their research efforts, deep knowledge of film history, and intrepid location of stills, and Robert Osborne of TCM provided both insight and access to *Seventh Sin*. Many thanks go to all the people at Knopf who contributed to this book: the talented and sensitive designer, Iris Weinstein; the scrupulous and patient production editor, Kevin Bourke; the brilliant jacket designer, Carol Carson; the indefatigable Roméo Enriquez; and eager editorial assistant Dan Schwartz.

As ever, I thank (and thank again) my editor, the fabulous Bob Gottlieb, who has never been anything but patient with me (and my lack of a computer), and who always asks the key question at the key moment. His ability to find exactly the right film (*Flavor of Green Tea Over Rice*) or the right television show (*Friday Night Lights, Borgen*) to make the right point is simply amazing. And he's funny, too.

For my family goes an extra truckload of thanks, since this project took much support from everyone: my husand, John; my daughter, Savannah; my granddaughter, Kulani; and my son-in-law, Rob (who had to help with computers). From one and all I received good ideas, encouragement, and the reassurance that "I do!" can still be a viable form of the marriage story.

AUTHOR'S NOTE

This is a book about marriage in the movies, and yes, I am married. I have been for forty-five years, and to the same saint of a guy. When we first announced we'd wed, his friends gave it five minutes, and mine about ten. Yet here we are, forty-five years later, long after most of them have hit the divorce courts at least once. (Somebody once told me, "You two are like one of those movie marriages where he's a cowboy and she's a fashion designer and the whole audience knows it's never gonna work, but the movie claims it will.")

In writing this book, I am doing something unfashionable. I am describing stars and stories and business strategies, and I am not analyzing sociological and cultural influences, discussing psychoanalytical theory or the differences between the male and the female gaze. These things are all worthwhile pursuits, but this book is an overview of how commercial movies told the story of marriage, and how they used it to draw audiences into the theater. The book is descriptive, historical, and personally speculative. It's about what the average person saw and heard at the movie theater. Nothing more and nothing less. It's written in plain language, and it just tries to describe what was *there* up on the screen over a few decades of American life. It is not heavily footnoted (except with personal asides), but it is carefully researched. In presenting it, I am well aware that scholars won't think it's scholarly enough, and general readers will think it's too scholarly. It's a book for people who like movies and want to share a conversation about them.

This book does not represent how I teach my film classes: it's a book about *content* rather than a formalist examination of movie aesthetics. I chose to do this because in watching marriage movies, I felt that they were pitched at the audience's own level of experience more closely than any other type of movie I had seen. These movies *were* about content. They were talking to an audience who knew the subject, knew the subtext, knew the reality. I think this is one of the reasons that the topic of marriage in the movies, unlike the American West, horror, melodrama, combat, crime, and others, has not yet captured the full attention of academia. There are books on romantic comedy, and books on runaway brides, and Stanley Cavell's well-respected book on comedies of *re*marriage, but very little on marriage itself.

Cavell's book uses a series of celebrated screwball comedies from the 1930s and early 1940s to discuss the well-known characteristics of the genre but also to use the films to ask philosophical questions: What is a marriage? Is marriage merely habit? If the habits aren't working, should the marriage be broken up? And what are the habits that American popular culture encourages audiences to pursue? Cavell discusses the transformative process of marriage between a man and a woman, and he uses recognizable film-studies issues such as the way movies begat movies, how they always refer to each other (concepts of film genre study), and how movie stars become real to viewers as a persona they carry from film to film. Cavell translates philosophical issues onto popular Hollywood comedies. He understands that people who went to the movies experienced them as a conversation carried from film to film, a conversation that influenced the way American filmgoers thought, felt, and responded to life. Cavell's thoughts are beautifully expressed, and his appreciation of the films he writes about is deep and joyous. My book differs in one simple way: he uses movies to think about philosophy; I use them to think about movies.

I have already written about certain movie marriages in *A Woman's View: How Hollywood Spoke to Women, 1930–1960,* so I did not redescribe any of those films, some of which, such as *Week-end Marriage, Roughly Speaking,* and *I'll See You in My Dreams,* are significant. I also had to select which other movies to write about, and there were many choices. This means that some movies with interesting marriages aren't discussed: *The Arrangement, Dust Be My Destiny, So Goes My Love, Come Live with Me, Cinderella Jones, Good Sam, Next Time We Love, She Married Her Boss, There's Always Tomorrow* (both versions), *The Letter, Written on the Wind, Seems Like Old Times, The Enchanted Cottage, The Stratton Story, Such Good Friends, Hot Blood, Home from the Hill, Wild Is the Wind, Invitation, My Foolish Heart, Walls of Jericho, Mr. Skeffington, Craig's Wife* (and the remake, *Harriet Craig*), *I Married a Monster from Outer Space, Illicit, Ex-Lady, Woman in Hiding,* aspects of Preston Sturges's films, and countless others. As I completed this book, a new interest in marriage seemed to be surfacing after a period of time in which the institution had become almost anachronistic. I hope that new interest will carry over to this book, and into a willingness to hear through these pages what older movies had to say about the subject.

"Marriage," said Eddie Cantor, long wed to his Ida and the parent of five daughters, "is not a word. It's a sentence."

INTRODUCTION

Once upon a time, I decided to write a book about marriage in the movies, and I had no idea that might prove to be a problem. Both Molly Haskell and David Thomson told me it would, but I didn't listen. I had even been warned about it by filmmakers. (Frank Capra said, "Embrace happy marriage in real life, but keep away from it onscreen.") I had read research in which executives such as Sam Briskin, RKO's production chief, complained about the married couple in John Ford's *The Plough and the Stars*: "Why make a picture where a man and woman are married? The main thing about pictures is love or sex. Here you've got a man and woman married at the start—who's interested in that?" I didn't pay any attention. I just wanted to write a book about marriage in the movies.

I started out by asking friends and colleagues to tell me their favorite marriage movies. In almost every case, they stared at me blankly and had no answer. A few imaginative souls came up with the *Thin Man* series or *The Awful Truth*, but that was about it for the suggestion pile. Of course, the *Thin Man* movies and *The Awful Truth* aren't really marriage movies; they have marriages in them, but that doesn't make them marriage movies. *The Thin Man* is about a detective who solves murders. He has a wife and she tags along, looking extremely chic, and the two of them are utterly charming together whenever they cohabit the screen. But the movies are not about marriage per se; they are about who murdered whom while other guests at the table were dining on breast of guinea hen. As for *The Awful Truth*, it's a delightful screwball comedy in which a married couple gets divorced in the first few minutes and spends the rest of the movie romping around and insulting each other until they fall in love all over again. There's no domesticity on display.

In short, no one came up with a list of real marriage movies for me. But why? Why weren't people bombarding me with titles, the way they'd always done with every other subject, whether I wanted them to or not? I knew perfectly well that movies told stories about marriage. Starting my research, I read the original reviews of hundreds of movies in *Variety* and *The New York Times* and combed through my extensive collection of vintage movie posters, magazines, pressbooks, and reviews from the era of the studio system.

The first thing that struck me came as a surprise. In plot terms, there were relatively few sound movies that were *only* about the state of being married. And even though fan magazines such as *Photoplay* ran monthly columns ("Brief Reviews") designed to give readers a quick reference guide to plot types, there was no generic category designated as "marriage movie" ("domestic drama" sometimes, but never "marriage movie").*

This advertising practice was consistent. The September 1939 issue of *Photoplay* indicates how clearly (and easily) the guidelines worked: *Dodge City* (western); *Bridal Suite* (madcap comedy); *Big Town Czar* (gangsters); *Clouds Over Europe* (mystery); *Back Door to Heaven* (social-message picture); *Confessions of a Nazi Spy* (propaganda); and *The Wizard of Oz* (musical fantasy). (*Variety* also identified movies by type. *As Husbands Go* [1930] was "a drawing room comedy-drama.") In these columns, any movie built around a big-name star was identified as such ("a Shirley Temple film" or "the latest Deanna Durbin"), or even as imitative of a successful star ("a Sonja Henie film without Henie"). Sometimes movies were defined by other movies ("kind of a *Mr. Deeds*" or "another *Informer*," because *Mr. Deeds Goes to Town* was a box-office hit and *The Informer* was an Oscar winner). But there was no "marriage movie," and advertising conformed to this practice.

For example, the 1951 film *Close to My Heart* is a marital soap opera in which a husband (Ray Milland) has a serious conflict with his wife (Gene Tierney) over adopting a child. Magazine ads feature a large picture of Milland and Tierney, his lips hovering over hers in a hot embrace. Shown full-face, Milland looks suave and handsome, and Tierney, in profile, looks willing and submissive. The tag line says, "This thing called love . . . and the wonderful things it makes happen . . . There's the best reason in the world for everybody to see this picture: it's great and makes you feel great!" Nobody's doing the dishes, taking out the garbage, changing any diapers, or mentioning "marriage." Down in the corner, however, there's a very small photo of Tierney holding a baby. Beside it runs the line: "We're not going to tell you how Danny fits into this picture . . . Let's simply say that he's one of the reasons that moviegoers of every age, everywhere, have taken *Close to My Heart* close to their hearts." Looking at this ad, potential ticket buyers would inevitably focus on the hot-looking

---

* Sometimes "marriage" would appear in a title as a joke or to suggest something slightly racy or intriguing: *He Married His Wife*, but such a film was usually a screwball comedy. Sometimes "husband" or "wife" would be used in a title for sexual innuendo. For *My Favorite Wife*, there were "two blazing brides—and only one blushing!"

Milland and Tierney. As to that kid hovering way down in the corner—why is *he* there? Are Milland and Tierney by any chance married? The ad writers are not going to be the ones to tell us.

Movies about married couples were almost without exception sold as "love" or "romance" instead of "marriage." Romance was the motion-picture cash cow, but any kind of misdirection would do. In *The Homestretch* (1947), a couple marry outside their own class backgrounds and suffer for it. ("Your kind of romance!" said the poster.) In *Over 21* (1945), a middle-aged pair struggle with the changes World War II brings to their marriage. ("Theirs is the kind of fun that makes the world go round!") *An Innocent Affair* (1948; also known as *Don't Trust Your Husband*), starring Fred MacMurray and Madeleine Carroll, tells a discouraging tale of imagined infidelity, but it was sold as "a saucy, glossy comedy." In *Rachel and the Stranger* (1948), in which William Holden purchases and weds an indentured servant (Loretta Young), the story was marketed as "an unusual pioneer picture"; and when a postwar GI (Holden again) and his youthful, pregnant wife (Jeanne Crain) can't find housing or enough money to live on in *Apartment for Peggy* (1948), the movie ads claimed that the story had "humor, wisdom and sentiment." No mention of marriage woes and pressures. Even *Pitfall* (also 1948), a film noir in which a husband (Dick Powell) strays, shoots a man, and messes up his relationship with his wife, was disguised as "a strong domestic drama."

Alfred Hitchcock's Oscar-winning Best Film, *Rebecca* (1940), based on Daphne du Maurier's famous book, featured an unlikely marriage, a possible murder, and a mansion haunted by an ex-wife. Ads told would-be audiences that the film was about "a man . . . a young girl . . . gloriously in love . . . a great dramatic romance." *The Very Thought of You* (1944) was a World War II release starring Dennis Morgan and Eleanor Parker, a tender story of the problems a young couple encounter when they marry after a brief courtship just before he ships out. The film conveys an honest wartime sadness that adds up to a depressing portrait of a dysfunctional American family, but the ads trumpeted happily: "Want to see one great big honey of a picture about Rookies and their Cookies? . . . Here's a screenful of huggin' and kissin' where every hug and kiss feels like it's meant for *you*! Want to have some—what we mean—fun?" Perhaps the ultimate in deception in movie advertising was for *Madame Curie* (1943). Boasting the presence of "the romantic stars of *Mrs. Miniver*" (Greer Garson and Walter Pidgeon), the prevue trailer describes the wedded union of the Nobel Prize–winning scientists Pierre and Marie Curie as "a strange journey into the unknown . . . the love story of the most exciting woman of her day." No mention of radium, science, or the Periodic Table of Elements.

Even when the subject was implied in the film's title, the ads misdirected.

Father Takes a Wife (1941) is a story of a wealthy older man (Adolphe Menjou) who weds a famous actress (Gloria Swanson) over the objections of his grown-up children. "There's glamour on the screen again because Gloria's back!" the advertising campaign claimed. The film was categorized as "romantic comedy" and variously described as "hilariously amorous . . . about two lovebirds . . . a screaming comedy." *Marriage Is a Private Affair* (1944), starring Lana Turner, was dubbed "a wartime romance" in movie review columns, though it's actually the story of a hasty wartime marriage that goes on the rocks. The sales poster featured a very large (and beautiful) drawing of the luscious young Turner at the peak of her new stardom. Under her name in giant letters is the film's title in a smaller type. The tag line says, "It's So Romantic!" and a corner box notes Lana's thirty-five costume changes.*

When a movie really absolutely *was* a marriage film and nothing else, the advertising still skirted the issue. The 1940 movie *Penny Serenade*, starring Irene Dunne and Cary Grant, is the story of a marriage gone on the rocks; it's a marriage movie if there ever was one. Yet *Photoplay* labeled it "a romantic love story . . . a Dunne-Grant co-starrer." The original sales trailer made for a Clark Gable/Myrna Loy/Jean Harlow film about marriage, *Wife vs. Secretary* (1936), also totally avoided its main subject. "In this gay story of love and laughter," says the copy, "which one did he choose?"—there's no mention of the fact that he'd already chosen one of them several years before the story began. *Wife vs. Secretary* was sold as "an ultra modern story about three people in love."

Reading about these movies, and noting how they avoided the label "marriage," I remembered back to when I worked in a small-town movie theater in the early 1950s. We showed up at 5:45 p.m. to pop the corn, vacuum the rugs, lay out the candy bars, set up the ticket machines, and prepare to open the house at seven. My job was always to answer the phone and wrangle the twenty or so chatty calls about that night's "show" (as we called it). Nobody needed to ask what time the feature started. It had been starting at 7:30 p.m.—in boiling heat, torrential rain, and below-zero cold—for well over twenty-five years. Callers had only two questions: "Who's in the movie?" and "What kind of movie is it?" They weren't hard to answer. All I had to do was nail down the star (Betty Grable = songs, legs, and Technicolor) or the genre (western = horses, guns, and cowboy hats) and I was home free. Stars and stories were all I needed to know.

As I thought about those days and those conversations, I realized that there

---

* The poster uses "marriage" in its title at a time (during World War II) when the audience was particularly concerned about its sanctity, with men overseas and wives left behind at home. The ad images ignore it for the bigger sales appeal of its star and her wardrobe.

was one word I had never used in explaining or selling a movie: "marriage." I never described a "show" as a "marriage movie." What's more, neither did anyone else. I didn't remember—then or now—anyone claiming they'd just seen the latest "marriage movie" or "the best marriage movie ever made."

Why would everyone—in both the movie business and the audience—want to avoid the label "marriage"? Marriage was presumably everybody's business. People were either born into one, born outside of one, living in one, living outside of one, trying to woo someone into one, divorced from one, trying to get divorced from one, reading about one, dreaming about one, or just observing one from afar. For most people, it would be the central event—the biggest decision—of their lives. Marriage was the poor man's trip to Paris and the shopgirl's final goal. At the very least, it was a common touchstone. Unlike a fantasy film or a sci-fi adventure, a marriage story didn't have to be explained or defined. Unlike a western or a gangster plot, it didn't have to find a connection to bring a jolt of emotional recognition to an audience. Marriage was out there, free to be used and presented to people who knew what the deal was. Perfect!

But evidently not so perfect. Capra and Briskin and the movie ad men were onto something. Marriage, after all, was the known, not the unknown: the dull dinner party, not the madcap masquerade. It was a set of issues and events that audiences knew all too well offscreen. Unlike the wide-open frontier of the western, offering freedom and adventure, or the lyrical musical, with its fantasy of release through singing and dancing, or the woman's film, with its placing of a marginalized social figure (the woman) at the center of the universe, or the gangster movie, with its violent excitement and obvious sexual freedom, the marriage film had to reflect what moviegoers already had experienced: marriage, in all its boredom and daily responsibilities.

Although marriage seemed at first glance to be a natural movie story form, I began to realize that it wasn't that easy to deal with. Indeed, even on the simplest level, a marriage story was a screenwriter's nightmare. Telling the story of a marriage meant somehow being able to unlock a secret—the vast mystery that explains what She sees in Him and why He should put up with Her. Such a movie had to show what happens when a couple close their doors at the end of the day and the unexplained dynamic between them—partly about sex, which couldn't even be shown—would unfold. And there were bigger problems. When most marriages go downhill, it's because the partners, for whatever reason, have begun to turn against each other. Screenplays, therefore, had to make a marriage kill itself—and then find a way to rush in with some trumped-up emergency, wipe the blood off, and resuscitate it.

Marriage was both a rigid social contract and a state of mind. When turned into a movie, its goals became restrictive and evasive. They were hard to quantify and demonstrate. "Happiness" may seem like a straightforward goal for a story's characters, but only if they're moving toward it, not when they're supposed to be already there. Happiness is no easier for a film to define and pursue than it is for an individual in real life. Unlike a war film, a marriage film couldn't win. Unlike a woman's film, it didn't offer an adventure or experience of freedom that most women couldn't achieve in real life.

Worst of all, marriage had no story arc. It just went on, day after day, month after month, year after year. Marriage took time, and movies had no time to give to it.* A good movie was usually a story in a hurry—good pacing being one of its best characteristics. Marriage took years to develop and mature. Novels could be written about marriages, and plays could crystallize their tensions into significant scenes of dialogue; but movies . . . what were movies to do in ninety minutes?

In *The Power of Myth*, Bill Moyers interviews Joseph Campbell about marriage: "What is marriage? . . . It's different from a love affair . . . When people get married because they think it's a long-time love affair, they'll be divorced very soon, because all love affairs end in disappointment." In the movies, all love affairs supposedly ended in marriage, which by Campbell's definition meant all movie marriages would begin in disappointment. If we stayed in our seats, we'd be let down. Since marriage was the "You stayed in your seats, you fools" variation of a love story, what could moviemakers do with their fundamental problem: telling an entertaining story about disappointment and failure? It was obvious that to tell such a story—and to give it oomph, get it out of the house, as it were—a problem would have to be created that might threaten, destroy, undermine, question, or somehow subvert the status of wedded bliss. Mates would have to die. Houses would have to burn down. Wars would have to sweep over cozy and secure little worlds. Lovers would have to fall out, and new lovers would emerge. Children would have to disappear, never appear; die or run away. Was any of this going to be entertaining? Perhaps . . . if set to operatic music, or justified by literary credentials. Or goosed up by costumes and settings, fortified by star power. But the bottom line for the business was apparent: in a movie that told the story of the recognizable workings of a marriage, the problem that motivated the plot might upset audiences, because it might depict the circumstances of their own lives too negatively to be entertaining. A marriage movie would have to sell disappointment to be credible—

---

* "People are married by time," says Frank Morgan to his wife of many years (Spring Byington) in 1942's *Vanishing Virginian*, "not by the marriage vows."

and would then have to demonstrate how that same disappointment was bogus and restore order.

And there was more than disappointment to think about. American movie-goers liked action—some kind of forward movement that glued them to their seats. They liked the chase, not the capture. They preferred the excitement of solving a problem to the smug satisfaction of a dubious solution. From the very beginning of the silent era, audiences responded happily to physical complications: runaway trains and cars, dancing bears and charging bulls, exploding cookstoves, sinking ships, and marauding crooks. In a slapstick comedy, everybody had to go on the run to resolve little daily problems. They would run and run and run—and then fall into the water, or off a cliff, or out of a car, or just into the bushes, after which the fun was over. The End. This "run for fun" was not unlike a romantic quest for a life partner, in which case the ending could be called the happily-ever-after tradition. After some charming romantic shenanigans, the couple could fall not off a cliff, but into love—and that "fall" would clearly imply the next step: marriage. But nobody needed to *see* the marriage. After the fall, the fun was over. Time to go home.

The romantic-chase movie, whether comedy or drama, reached fulfillment with the capture of the desired love. It was boy meets girl, boy gets girl. Finis. Courtship—defined as a forward-moving romantic romp—provided endless variations and was about winning, not losing, and most of all about finishing and resolving. This became the traditional bargain Hollywood made with audiences, and it was an arrangement most audiences were happy to accept. And why not? Did anyone want to imagine that Ilsa and Victor Laszlo's plane would crash? That they would divorce? That Captain Renault would step on a land mine and Rick would go back to America and open a hot-dog stand in Jersey? Of course not. Everyone wanted to leave them all in a glamorous fog on the Casablanca tarmac, hat brims pulled down low, morals ramped up high, no future necessary.*

It was quite another thing to keep the fun going into the other half of the equation—the married part. It was a bigger challenge to keep the magic alive after the couple said "I do," to keep the story from turning into a very bitter and disillusioned "I don't." A movie about marriage—not a movie about the quest for love that could lead to marriage—was automatically in opposition to the terms of the romantic-moviegoing bargain.

---

* All film historians know that "the Hollywood happy ending" was only one part of the complex outpouring of movies from the studio system. It's an oversimplification to imagine that's all there was, but the romantic escapist movie fit the pattern.

I began to understand why "marriage" was not a term that was used to lure audiences into theaters. A tale about marriage was a story form in which film-makers could not easily dictate an escapist path. It was the dangerous business intersection where moviemakers and the moviegoing public faced off as equals. A poet wrote that to an ordinary housewife, the darkness of the movie theater was "the fur she could afford"—but what if the story was about the rabbity old thing she brought in with her? Any housewife might accept that she wasn't ever going to get the jewelry, the yacht, or the champagne seduction. She'd know it was too late to "meet cute" with Jimmy Stewart, thrill to a moonlight coupling with Clark Gable, or undergo a lively wedding process with Cary Grant. She understood she'd never dance with Fred Astaire, her feathers floating slowly to the floor around his feet. She was willing to buy those dreams anyway, because accepting the con was worth it. But what if a movie tried to convince her that a perfect world of happily-ever-after was true? It was hard to know what the customer wanted when you were selling her a product she had already bought.

For audiences, marriage was like Mom and apple pie, a signpost to their own reality in the way that churches, stores, streets, fur coats, fireplaces, and roving cattle could be. Such things located audiences in time and space. Marriage said, "Something you know is here, something you've experienced." For anything believably exciting to happen, it was best used only as an end goal and kept offscreen; otherwise, the leading man and woman were locked into their positions, already defined in their sex lives, their romantic lives, and their relationships. Popular movies wanted to lead men and women to one another—also to salvation, Europe, outer space, the Wild West, parts unknown, and possibly to hell and back, but really to one another. Such quests suggest to an audience that there is more for them in life—another, better quest if they are already married, or something fabulous if they're not. *More*: that's what movies always offered the public. It could be more in terms of adventure, romance, heart-break, money, satisfaction, wardrobe, whatever—but something more. It was that something more that American movie audiences went to the movies to get. And because of that something more, the business of moviemaking found it a better idea to sell love rather than marriage and never to call the marriage movies they made what they actually were.

The sense of marriage as a problem did, though, become a much-discussed issue *inside* many movies. All through film history, then and now, there's a constant yammering about marriage, and not much of it is positive. A book could be constructed out of nothing but quotes about marriage that were uttered in movies. "Marriage," says Robert Benchley in *Janie Gets Married* (1946), "is being locked in a boxcar with a mad horse." In *Living on Velvet*

(1935), Kay Francis realizes she wants a solid, simple home life (in her furs and jewels) but has married a footloose airplane pilot. "Same old story," she muses: "young romantic girl marries a man in order to reform him." Rosalind Russell in *Craig's Wife* (1936) thinks that's a good plan: "No man's born ready for marriage. He has to be trained." In *Latin Lovers* (1953), Ricardo Montalban says that if he tells his fiancée everything, "once we're married, there'll be no surprises." His uncle (Louis Calhern) tells him, "Believe me, once you *are* married, there never are." In *Boom Town* (1940), Claudette Colbert wears an apron in a cheap shack in a Latin American oil field and muses about her married life: "Happiness doesn't come easy. I've learned that." Playing Andrew Jackson's wife, Rachel, in *The Gorgeous Hussy* (1936), Beulah Bondi thoughtfully puffs on her corncob pipe and informs Joan Crawford, "Marriage ain't a party dress. You gotta wear it mornin', noon, and night." When handsome architect Robert Young starts spending all day with his chic client Mary Astor in *Claudia and David* (1946), he snaps at his jealous young wife, "Do you think marriage means the end of all other human contact?" Danny Thomas begs his wife (Doris Day) in *I'll See You in My Dreams* (1951), "Please, please let me make *one* decision . . . a man's gotta be a man in his own house . . . Stop running my life!" Even unmarried characters yak about it. *Road to Singapore* (1940) opens with Bob Hope and Bing Crosby all set to begin the first of their seven successful road trips. They're on a ship's deck, watching a seaman's wife give him a quick embrace, grab his pay envelope, and tuck it safely into her blouse. "There you are, Josh," says Hope. "That's married life for you." Crosby replies, "You know, if the world was run right, only women would get married."* This opening dialogue was a surefire joke, designed to grab the audience and make it love the two carefree, rootless heroes. As they watch a sailor wheel a baby carriage, surrounded by his nagging wife and three other kids, Crosby warns Hope, "Let that be a lesson to you."† Hope and Crosby give the male view; and a radiantly Technicolored Rita Hayworth sings the female variation to not one, but two, leading men (Larry Parks, Marc Platt) in *Down to Earth* (1947): "I want to marry the two of you . . . I will have a man for lovin' / And a man to fix the oven too / One with endurance / the other with plenty of life insurance." Marriage, as Hollywood understood it, was clearly a problem, as articulated by the venerable Judge Hardy in *Judge Hardy and Son* (1939). (The

---

* Comedy dialogue about marriage is often shockingly misogynistic. In *Women Are Like That* (1938), a character sagely advises that where men went wrong was that "society made a mistake when it separated women from goats and took the women into the home."

† This *Singapore* dialogue was typical, and a real crowd-pleaser. Knock marriage, everyone will get the joke—but later on, sell love (Dorothy Lamour) and keep hope alive.

Hardy series was famous for its "man-to-man" talks between father and son, the judge portrayed by Lewis Stone with Mickey Rooney as his youngest, Andy.) Calling marriage "the biggest responsibility a man can undertake," the judge offers Andy his definitive observations: "In all the relationships between a man and a woman, both before and after marriage, it's one series of adjustments after another with each other in which each one must adjust their whims to the other's liking and help each other realize what will prevent friction." Andy's response? "Dad, you don't make marriage sound like any picnic."* Playing the dully married title character in *H. M. Pulham, Esq.* (1941), Robert Young summed it all up: "When you come right down to it, why does anyone marry anyone?" The answer comes from one of a group of convicts in *You and Me* (1938): "Some chump ate an apple once and the rest of us chumps have been gettin' cramps from it ever since . . . regular."† And as for the romantic notion that the perfect mate awaits out there somewhere in the ozone? When Katy Jurado (in 1956's *Trapeze*) tells Burt Lancaster, "Someday you'll find the right woman and get married," he wastes no time in snapping back, "*Nobody* finds the right woman." The story of marriage was discussed in popular art forms as a failed enterprise, with everyone seemingly in agreement on the issue. The popular song "Makin' Whoopee," written in 1928, had lyrics that laid out a plot progression for the average marriage. At first "he's" a happy groom, and "she's" another bride; they're off on a sunny honeymoon and then ensconced in "a little love nest." Soon enough, she's "neglected" and he's "suspected." There's no money, and in the divorce court he finds out he'll owe more alimony than he earns. He thinks it'll be cheaper to keep her, and that's what he gets for "makin' whoopee." It's the story of a marriage set to music, infused with comedy, but all too accurate in its sense of doom, all too familiar in its story. Who would want to pay money to see it acted out in all its discouraging detail?

The challenge to movies was to find a way to link the desire for marriage—or the desire to escape marriage—directly to the audience in a way the audience

---

* Later, Andy tells the truth: "All's I ever get out of you are these man-to-man talks."
† These disparaging remarks have not disappeared from movies. Characters continue to tell us it's a dreary and frustrating business. In Woody Allen's celebrated *Annie Hall* (1977), a couple are interviewed separately as to how often they have sex. The man complains, "Hardly ever. Three times a week." His wife rolls her eyes and says, "Constantly! I'd say three times a week." In the distinguished literary movie *The Last Station* (2009), Count and Countess Tolstoy tear at each other viciously. When the countess (a superb Helen Mirren) becomes overly tragic, the count (Christopher Plummer) yells, "You need a Greek chorus!" Even in a movie aimed at the young-adult audience, marriage is savaged. In 2010's *Percy Jackson & the Olympians: The Lightning Thief*, the young heroes adventurously cross the river Styx to find Hades yelling to his wife, "Persephone! What's taking you so long? Get over here!" She coldly replies, "Or what? I'm already in Hell." It's a definitive statement on many marriage movies.

wanted to experience it. As a business, Hollywood concerned itself with what it termed "audience values." When questioned about the über-stardom generated by her dramatic and unusual beauty, Joan Crawford once famously commented that if audiences wanted to see the girl next door, they'd go next door and not out to the movies to spend their hard-earned money. A lot of things might be said about Crawford (and they have been), but no one ever suggested she didn't understand what the Hollywood game was all about. For her, the studio system and its business practices were a college education, and she was an A-plus student. She knew movies needed someone like her—someone who wasn't living down the street, someone to lure them into the theater. Crawford knew that no matter how much money she made or how much jewelry she bought, she was still a highly paid shill created to help fulfill what Hollywood euphemistically called "audience values." In his book *Irving Thalberg: Boy Wonder to Producer Prince*, Mark A. Vieira quotes the famous MGM producer as calling "audience values" the "most important element in a motion picture script." Admitting that the concept was difficult to define, Thalberg added that without these elusive qualities "no picture has audience appeal or greatness. I might say that almost without exception, every great picture has audience values." "Fulfilling the audience's values" sounded noble, but it was only camouflage for what they really meant: "picking the public's pockets."

The movie business always tried to find a way to please as wide an audience as possible. As early as 1927, writing in a book entitled *Building Theater Patronage: Management and Merchandising*, J. F. Barry and E. W. Sargent reminded readers that "photoplays cannot be made with only one type of audience in mind. Nor can they be made for any particular community . . . In fact, in every photoplay there are different highlights which when brought to the attention of different groups or different classes of the community . . . can be selected around which to build an advertising campaign."

In selling their movie dreams, Hollywood studios understood that the best way was to connect as directly as possible to the audience's real-life experience, and then draw them up and out of it and into a dream world. First, the friendly reality . . . then the luxurious escape hatch. Start with a poor little girl working in a department store or a box factory—preferably some "poor little girl" like Joan Crawford. Take her out of that store upward and onward to furs, jewels, penthouses, caviar, champagne, and Clark Gable. (Now you're talkin' audience values!) Marriage could be used that way. It could be disguised, reshaped, broken, and rebuilt, put to other purposes. Hollywood didn't throw away anything useful, and it always searched for the positive. The marriage story might be a challenge, but wasn't it also a useful, ready-made direct link to the audience—that "built-in" connection to "audience values" the business was always looking for? Couldn't it function like the horror film, by showing us all the bad and scary things, and then making them go away?

Marriage *was* a given, a kind of freebie for movie stories. The ghost of marriage hangs over all kinds of films. What did Shane, the lone cowpoke, ride away from? A marriage, with a home and a family. What did men in combat think about, talk about, and write home to? The wives and marriages they had left behind. What was a no-no for an on-the-run gangster, because it would finally trip him up? Marriage. And what, of course, was the goal of all romantic comedies, and dramas? Marriage, marriage, marriage.

Marriage was out there, ready to be used. But what could the marriage movie do for audiences that was positive? To entertain them, reassure them, lift them up and away? To motivate them to buy tickets? What could be its purpose? Satirization of an institution everyone knew was flawed but needed to sentimentalize anyway? A few shared laughs over a set of restrictions that had been set by society and agreed on? The killing of the contract through death, murder, train accidents—anything that could suddenly liberate a married person to move to another genre? What?

Because marriage was a finish line, not a starting place, it made a good background for *other* types of stories. It could be a supporting player. It served with distinction as a tragic backdrop for stories about deaths of children and mates, and wives driven by poverty into prostitution. It was effective representing the stable household that the roving western hero could not (or would not) attain, and explaining stolid characters like Andy Hardy and George Bailey, who were products of traditionally defined "happy marriages, normal households." It was highly suitable for true-life biographies. These stories were gender-flexible. Émile Zola writes, Mrs. Zola hands him a dish of pie. Madame Curie titrates, Monsieur Curie hands her a petri dish. Audiences could see that men like Zola and Louis Pasteur were able to do what they did because they were happily married, and Marie Curie could discover radium because she was *Madame* Curie, with a convenient, Nobel Prize–winning husband (until he got absentminded, the way husbands do, and walked in front of a carriage and got run over).

Marriage could be used like a chemical element. It could stand alone, merge with another element, lie dormant inside other elements, or become part of an alloy involving the combination of many elements. Its property—a marriage certificate that never changes—can be transposed into something else by such catalysts as history, society, and emotional recklessness. It is a status that can appear anywhere, at any time, in any film. It was like characters such as doctors, or settings such as kitchens, or actions such as driving a car. Doctors can be doctors (in medical films) or subjects for biopics (*Dr. Ehrlich's Magic*

Bullet), or love interests (in both versions of *Magnificent Obsession*). They can also be western heroes (*The Hanging Tree* and *My Darling Clementine*) or war heroes (*The Story of Dr. Wassell, Homecoming, Battle Circus*), or comic heroes (*M*A*S*H, People Will Talk, The Disorderly Orderly*). Kitchens can appear in screwball comedies (*My Man Godfrey*), westerns (*The Man Who Shot Liberty Valance*), melodramas (*Imitation of Life*, 1934 version), gangster movies (*The Public Enemy, The Godfather*), and many others. Driving a car—or a wagon, or a stagecoach, or a mule, or a spaceship—is ubiquitous, and the point is that some kinds of characters, settings, and actions are so adaptable that they can literally go anywhere. Marriage is like that.

Whenever a marriage movie came onscreen, it could ask a series of questions that audiences could clearly recognize as issues in their own lives. Who wears the pants in the marriage? Did you choose the right mate? Are your values the same? Do you have enough money or too much money? Are you keeping your marriage vows? Does your mate "understand" you? Do your in-laws interfere? Do you get along on a daily basis? Can you trust each other? Can you deal with pressures that fall on you that are outside your control? Did you marry outside your class? Do you want a divorce?

Having concluded that marriage in the movies was that damned elusive Pimpernel, I began watching the films anyway—films across decades, across different genres, and with different tones of voice (drama, comedy, musical). I watched a constant stream of movies that were either about marriages or had marriages somewhere in them. At the end of three years of screenings, I summed up the basics I had learned:

1. Writing about marriage in the movies *was* indeed a problem.

2. There *were* movies that were strictly about the condition of being married, but there weren't many of them, and there were fewer and fewer as film history advanced.

3. The film business *was* consistent in almost never labeling a movie a "marriage" film, and it avoided the word as much as possible in all forms of advertising unless it could be made comic or eroticized.

The bottom line was that the marriage movie was a difficult story to both tell and sell, because to find dramatic purpose, it had to become negative about itself in a positive way. It had to both link to and escape from reality, and it had to remember that the audience already knew its secrets.

The business didn't trust it, audiences didn't really want it, but marriage could never be ignored. It was everywhere and nowhere, the genre that dared not speak its name, the ghost that hung over the happy ending of every romantic comedy. As a subject, it existed to be achieved (jolly comedy, great love story), destroyed (death, murder, tragedy), or denied (divorce). If it was achieved, the movie was over. If it was destroyed, it was no longer there, gotten rid of and abandoned once and for all. If it was denied, it was only temporarily shelved (for some fun) and could be reassuringly restored. The more I studied it, the more I realized that although marriage was indeed a very difficult topic to locate and identify in movies, its history was an example of how audiences and filmmakers influenced each other, reflected each other, and defined each other. It was a problem because at its core it contained a contradiction. "I do," it said—and also "I don't." I decided that it was the very contradictions and complexities of the marriage film that made it worth writing about.

PART ONE
THE SILENT ERA

In the silent-film era, movies told the story of marriage straightforwardly, as a familiar situation—and audiences cheerfully accepted it as such. The idea that marriage might be unappealing at the box office, or perhaps a depressing plot development, didn't seem to exist in the same way it did later, in the studio-system years. Silent-film makers presented marriage as something audiences could and would recognize, and therefore enjoy seeing on the screen. In embracing the subject, they had available current history, past history, imaginary history . . . different tones, attitudes, moods . . . myriad events and characters . . . the works. Although it was a rigid or fixed social event, marriage could still be used flexibly. It could be the main event, the comic relief, or the tragic subplot. And, of course, it could always be linked to the surefire box-office concept of love.*

Unlike in later decades, many silent movies openly carried the concept in the title: *The Marriage of William Ashe* (1921); *The Marriage Maker* (1921); *Man, Woman, Marriage* (1921); *The Marriage Chance* (1922); *Married People* (1922); *The Married Flapper* (1922); *The Marriage Market* (1923); *Marriage Morals* (1923); *The Marriage Cheat* (1924); *Marry in Haste* (1924); *Married Flirts* (1924); *The Marriage Circle* (1924); *Marriage in Transit* (1925); *Marry Me* (1925); *The Marriage Whirl* (1925); *Married?* (1926); *Marriage License* (1926); *The Marriage Clause* (1926); *Marriage* (1927); *Married Alive* (1927); *Marriage by Contract* (1928); *Marry the Poor Girl* (1928); *The Marriage Playground* (1929); and *Married in Hollywood* (1929); etc. And this doesn't include titles with the words "bride," "groom," "wife," and "husband."†

The marriage film found its basic definition in the silent era, and had no trouble doing so. Why would it? All anyone had to do to tell a story about mar-

---

* It is a supreme irony that moviegoers could be conned into believing in romance that led to happy endings in one kind of movie, and then be shown that what came after the happily-ever-after was pretty awful . . . and yet still be conned all over again into believing that the awfulness could be fixed, made new, and restored to the point of the original happy ending. (And, of course, be conned even further into going to more romantic comedies.)

† Most of these films are actually romantic comedies. A few are melodramas, which magazines and reviewers broke down into a more specific type ("comedy-melodrama," "society melodrama," "domestic melodrama," etc.). Not all are actually marriage movies about domestic travails, and none were labeled as marriage movies.

riage was to present a couple in love, get them married in the first scene (or open with them already married), set them up in a home of some sort, give them a recognizable problem, make the problem worse, and then resolve it. Couple, situation, problem, resolution: this is the pattern silent audiences saw and embraced, and their responses to it were clear. They would laugh at it. Or they would cry over it. Silent films were a beautiful art, and they were never simpleminded, but many of them often presented marriage in a basic mode, happy or sad. They went bipolar: raucous comedy or stark tragedy.

Both types could be shaped into cautionary tales. The comedy version provided audiences with release as they laughed at their own problem in a safe form, and the tragic one warned them things could be much, much worse. In other words, the pattern for stories about marriages was simple enough: Was it going to be a yes or a no version? Was it "I do" or "I don't"? Would it divert or warn?

This "bipolar" approach to the basic setup (couple, wedding, home, problems) was a useful business discovery. It was one thing to treat marriage as a joke—that was predictable. The really significant thing was to accept it as a failed enterprise. Once it became clear that viewers had no trouble accepting the idea that marriages could turn into problems, that romance could fail, movies could show marriage as a disappointment without offending married couples. Up there on the screen, marriage didn't have to be sacred. Entering a movie theater apparently was an absolution. Long before they had arrived in their seats, boy had met girl, boy had got girl, and boy had married girl. *That* part was over, and they apparently felt it was now okay for all hell to break loose on the screen. Nosy neighbors, hideous in-laws, naughty children, snotty and ungrateful children, interfering children, lost children, kidnapped children, crippled children, evil children. Uppity cooks, oversexed maids, lippy gardeners, and butlers with more class than their employers, because, lord knows, you just couldn't get good help. Adultery, competition, bankruptcy, arson, death, murder, and suicide. Incest. War and plague. Earthquakes and typhoons and a household of terrible furniture never fully paid for.* Marriage on film could be a world of woe, all the direct result of merely saying two words: "I do." Marriage could be—and was—accepted as a hangover, the "after" of the happily-ever-after.

The hilarious comedy version was common in two-reelers, where lampoon-

---

* In the sound era, not all the problems were predictable. Pets could start talking, aliens take over the PTA, and atom bombs reduce husbands or wives to miniature size (quite a challenge for the sex life).

One of filmdom's first (and funniest) mismatched married couples: Fatty Arbuckle and Mabel Normand in *He Did and He Didn't*: how tight will she (should she?) tie that bow?

ing marriage had great appeal for audiences. For filmmakers, it was an easy shorthand with which to connect to what men and women knew—and get them to laugh about it. In particular, Mack Sennett comedy shorts made use of marital conflicts between two incompatible mates. (Bring on the rolling pin and the mother-in-law jokes!) The mockery of marriage liberated everybody—audiences, who roared at what they recognized, and moviemakers, who rolled freely over its sacredness in all directions. Two great examples from Sennett star the wonderful team of Fatty Arbuckle and Mabel Normand, talented clowns of the silent era. In 1915, Fatty and Mabel made two gems, *That Little Band of Gold* and *Fatty and Mabel's Married Life*. In the former, an entire romantic comedy is neatly wrapped up with one single title card: "A Kiss, A Pledge, A Ring." (So much for the meet-cute.) Immediately following, after the marriage, trouble arrives. Another title card says it all: "And now she waits for him." A few frames later, she's being told "Your husband is sipping wine with a strange woman"—and suddenly it's "all over but the alimony." Mabel's mother is very helpful in this brief but eloquent scenario. With no need for a title card, she is seen clearly mouthing the traditional words "I told you so" to Mabel when Fatty begins to misbehave.

Fatty and Mabel's Married Life, a self-labeled "farce comedy," lays out what would always be a typical conflict in movies about marriage: the man goes out to work, and the woman is left home alone. When he comes back at night, he sits and smokes his cigar, and she has nothing to do but sew. Progress in their relationship is depicted by Mabel getting mad and throwing things and by Fatty falling down a lot. In the end, the police arrive and the neighbors are shocked. Crammed into the brief two reels of running time are such further developments as kisses and promises, mistakes and misunderstandings, apologies and accusations, tears and laughter—not to mention some gunfire, an organ grinder, and a monkey. All these things are pretty much what will become the basic elements of the marriage movies of the future, only with more gunfire and no organ grinder. (The monkey stays in the picture.)

Even comics such as Buster Keaton and Harold Lloyd, who created their own specific and original universes on film, used wretched marital behavior as basic material. In *Spite Marriage* (1929) Keaton becomes the victim of a sophisticated stage actress (Dorothy Sebastian) who marries him only after she's been jilted, hence the film's title. Keaton, a pants presser by trade, is then stuck with a tantrum-throwing bride who gets dead drunk on their wedding night and creates an awful scene in a nightclub. In *My Wife's Relations* (1922), Keaton is yoked to an unloving Polish wife who has four huge and horrible brothers who constantly torment him physically and mentally and, despite everything, hilariously. Keaton is, in fact, a kind of house slave.* Things change when the brothers mistakenly think Keaton's inherited a fortune. "He's rich," one grouses. "Now we'll have to be nice to him." Another brother is more cerebral: "Let's murder him first and then kill him." When it came to marriage, Keaton's character was snakebit. He and his new bride are happy in *One Week* (1920), but when they try to work together and assemble their little prefab house, nothing goes right.

Harold Lloyd made a charming two-reeler called *I Do* in 1921, in which he and his beloved surreptitiously elope, never realizing that her parents, who are dying to get them married, are facilitating their sneaky actions all the way. Lloyd's best film about marriage is feature-length: *Hot Water* (1924). As the movie begins, the audience is treated to the following title card:

> Married life is like dandruff—it falls heavily upon your shoulders—you get a lot of free advice about it—but up to date nothing has been found to cure it.

---

* Keaton had learned all too well offscreen what it meant to be married to domineering in-laws. He was unhappily wed to Natalie Talmadge, the third sister to the powerful star actresses Norma and Constance. All three daughters were under the very firm thumb of their formidable mother, Peg.

As the plot gets under way, Lloyd's character says no matter what he'll never exchange his freedom for marriage, but bang! He spots the lovely Jobyna Ralson, and his life is suddenly defined as: "A honeymoon—then rent to pay." Lloyd has to support not only his wife but also her hideous family: a lazy lout of an older brother, a Dennis-the-Menace younger one (an artist with a pea shooter), and one of film's most horrific mothers-in-law, played by Josephine Crowell. Crowell is described as having "the nerve of a book agent, the disposition of a dyspeptic landlord, and the heart of a traffic cop." (And what's more, she sleepwalks.) Lloyd earns a living for the sponging brood, runs their errands, puts up with their insults, and endures comic interludes that include his struggle to bring a live turkey home on a crowded streetcar as well as a terrifying ride with the family in his new automobile ("the Butterfly Six"). With help from his in-laws, the car is totaled.

The Keaton and Lloyd films are very funny, but if you described the events happening onscreen to a blind man, he'd probably weep. Most silent comedy presented marriage as hell. What made it work was that although the movies were saying "marriage is a disaster," they were also winking and adding, "but it's *our* disaster." The comedy was empathic. It touched on issues that plagued ordinary people—in-laws, money, infidelity, misunderstandings—and exaggerated them into comic excess. There was a jaunty quality to the horror, an almost jolly sense of shared entrapment, with an underlying agreement that it may have happened to you, but it's happened to all of us. The slapstick marriage comedy of the silent era had camaraderie on sale, and audiences bought it happily.

The wonderful thing about such rollicking cartoons was that although they were about marriage, you didn't have to be married to enjoy them. They were just funny, with a wide appeal. Inside the brief twenty minutes of comic chaos was a solid honesty: kitchens, sofas, rocking chairs, dining tables, and bedrooms. Ordinary things such as furniture and mealtimes were juxtaposed with exaggerated details and unexpected twists. Marriage was marriage, with its daily routines, but added to it would be a round of burglaries, a monstrous mother-in-law, a set of misunderstandings, a matched pair of incompatible desires (he wants to smoke and read, she wants some excitement), and hand-to-hand combat with rolling pins, humidors, and frying pans—and a monkey. It was the marriage film made both comic and active, a marriage on its feet, up and running.

The cautionary-tale approach became the most typical of the marriage-movie plots. It could warn about any sort of topical problem; it maintained current morality; and it provided an opportunity to get around censorship or prudery by punishing whatever sin it decided to depict. Best of all, it reassured audiences. It showed them their troubles, but put them to rights. Its canny pattern of establishing normalcy (and proper values), following with a visual depiction of sinful behavior (pushed as far as the movies dared to go), and concluding with a restoration of the original family values, became the golden mean of marriage movies.

An example of the cautionary tale as a high-stakes drama is Cecil B. De-Mille's 1915 version of *The Cheat,* starring Fannie Ward and Sessue Hayakawa. *The Cheat* teaches audiences that there is passion out there, and danger, and delicious exotic "otherness"—but suggests they should experience it only at the movies, for the sake of their own flesh and the safety of their families. *The Cheat's* social-butterfly wife is the treasurer of a charity, and when she wants to buy some expensive clothes she can't afford, she uses the charity's money to gamble on Wall Street. She loses. Unwilling to admit her indiscretion to her straitlaced husband, she accepts a loan from a "rich Oriental" (Hayakawa) in return for her "affections." Her husband then unexpectedly (and conveniently) earns the same sum of money on his own, more successful speculations and gives it to his wife to spend as she wishes. When she happily takes the money to Hayakawa to cancel their arrangement, he calls her a "cheat." To make his point, he spectacularly burns his brand on her naked shoulder, marking her as his property because he "bought" her. She then does what a silent-film woman is supposed to do: she shoots him. Unfortunately, her husband shows up and is arrested for the crime.

This tale of a cheating wife whose flesh gets burned is beyond cautionary. It is an outright warning, and it's far more effective than it sounds. (A brief plot description cannot do full justice to the movie.) Hayakawa is exotic, and overtly presented as a sexually exciting Asian male. (He was reviewed in *Variety* as "the best Japanese heavy man that has been utilized in this fashion.") The movie suggests that whereas the wife's misuse of funds is unacceptably naughty indeed, her sexual excitement is thoroughly understandable. She's a bored woman wed to a husband *Variety* describes as "one of the milk and water sop sort of husbands who really doesn't know enough to assert himself as master of his own ménage." Their marriage is correctly upper-class, but dull. The "loan" and the "arrangement" are alluring—hot stuff for the times—and anyone can understand why the wife falls under the almost hypnotic control of her exotic lover. DeMille's use of editing to connect his lovers across time and space, as well as for the presentation of a sense of psychological space, is considered an important moment in his career as well as in the development of film language.

Audiences embraced *The Cheat.* It was a cautionary tale that struck close to

The story of marital lies, potential infidelities, and disasters represented by *The Cheat* was so popular, the movie was made three times between 1915 and 1931. DeMille's 1915 prototype, with Sessue Hayakawa and Fannie Ward . . .

. . . was remade in 1923 with Pola Negri and Charles de Roche . . .

. . . and resurrected for a sound version in 1932 with Tallulah Bankhead and Irving Pichel.

home. Flesh branding they may not have experienced, but dull husbands they knew. *The Cheat* was so popular that it was remade twice, in 1923 with Pola Negri and in 1931 with Tallulah Bankhead.* Since the audience knew what was required by the rules of marriage, the same basic story could be repeated with slight adjustments to reflect changing morality. In the 1923 version, Pola Negri's would-be lover was no longer Asian, only a "fake Hindu prince." The racial elements were totally abandoned. In 1931, Bankhead merely got a scoundrel, played by the lackluster Irving Pichel. Instead of being from an exotic culture, Pichel was "just back from the Orient," a traveler to mysterious areas, rather than a mystery. What was directly connected to an audience's sense of morality and racism in 1915 had been toned down in 1923. By 1931, the film openly treated the material as dated, as if women were branded weekly around the old small-town campfire. (*Variety* said, "Something of an ancient complexion clings to the story.") The villain no longer has the power to hypnotize a naïve wife into submission—he just chases her around some cavernous sets as if he were trying to get a prom date. (With Bankhead playing her, who was to believe in her innocent inexperience?) And yet the film did well, because its fundamental excitement lay in a wife daring to be unfaithful but learning her lesson—which was a lesson for everyone. Some things went out of style, but caution was always smart.

An excellent example of the silent era's "cautionary tale"—a prototype both tragic and comic—is D. W. Griffith's aptly named 1928 feature *The Battle of the Sexes* (a remake of his own earlier 1914 version). In this film (which carries the credit "personally directed by D. W. Griffith"), the opening title card warns the audience: "The Battle of the Sexes—always being fought—never being won." Jean Hersholt plays a very successful businessman (he's just made over $250,000 on a single deal). He has a loving family: a son, a daughter, and a loyal wife. They are rich, happy, and fully satisfied with their marital and familial existence. The first scene establishes their domestic harmony in detail. Hersholt arrives home as everyone prepares to celebrate his wife's birthday. This good woman (Belle Bennett) is modest, softly lovely, somewhat stout, and frankly middle-aged. The son (William Bakewell) and daughter (Sally O'Neil) seem to have nothing to do except stand around and adore their mom while she unwraps a cornucopia of lavish gifts: a crystal candy dish, a leather manicure set, French perfume, an expensive silken shawl. Then Hersholt, a jolly man, pulls a little surprise. "Mama . . . my coat . . . hang it up," he instructs.

---

* DeMille's version is still an involving movie for today's modern audience, and all three versions made money.

Without a moment's hesitation, even though it's her birthday celebration, Mom dutifully hops up and goes to get the coat. Out of it falls a stuffed rabbit, and inside the rabbit is her secret gift from her husband: a diamond bracelet.

Candy dishes! Stuffed rabbits! Diamond bracelets! This is marriage as everyone knows it should be or wants it to be or dreams it will be. Mom makes a wish as she bends down to blow out the candles on her cake: "I wish that life could go on like this forever." But Mom fails to snuff all the candles, and audiences know a bad omen when they see one. Trouble is coming. The trouble actually lives in the same building, right down the hall: Phyllis Haver. She's a bottle-blond jazz baby, and she read about the $250,000 deal in the newspaper.

A story about infidelity unfolds, confirming an audience's real-life knowledge about what might go wrong in a marriage, as well as giving them a glimpse of licentious freedom. When Hersholt lets loose after years of pent-up good husbandship, he *really* lets loose. Happily drunk in a raucous nightclub, he playfully pulls on Haver's tight blond curls, one at a time, slowly rolling up a fifty-dollar bill in each of them. His pleasure in this openly sexy behavior—and any audience's understanding of its excitement—is used later when a hideous quarrel erupts between Bennett and Hersholt—in front of their children. Bennett confronts Hersholt with his infidelity, but he just doesn't care: the sexual freedom (which viewers have seen) is too appealing to him after all these years. Mom weeps as she looks at a photo from their wedding day . . . and the kids stand around helpless, appalled, frightened, lost.

Although it actually *is* a movie about marriage, *The Battle of the Sexes* is labeled a "domestic drama" in the American Film Institute catalog of movies from 1920 to 1930. It might equally have been listed as a "domestic comedy," as there is a great deal of humor throughout, well mixed into the tragedy. The finale becomes a bedroom farce. Hersholt's daughter comes to Haver's apartment to confront and, if necessary, shoot her (a popular solution in silent movies). Haver has to hide the girl when her other lover, Don Alvarado (playing a drunken lounge lizard), shows up, and then he has to be hidden in the same room when Hersholt arrives. The inevitable misunderstandings occur, the inevitable doors open and close, and Daddy thinks the lizard is his daughter's lover. Daddy spanks her, while she cries out, "I have as much right to be here as *you* do!" Daddy presents the double standard of the day, saying, "That's different. I'm a *man*." But, reaching out to the full audience, both men and women, the next title card provides an unexpected response: "Yes . . . well . . . *I'm a woman!*" No one has any answer for this, and the film suddenly ends happily at next year's birthday party for Mom, everyone reunited, Dad once again dull, Mom still plump, and the kids relieved to be feeling secure.

The Battle of the Sexes taught a straying man his lesson. A loyal wife was rewarded for her virtue and devotion. But there had also been some red-hot fun while Phyllis Haver shimmied around on the sidelines with fifty-dollar bills in her curls, and bonbons and Jean Hersholt in her lap. The movie used what the audience knew was real (infidelity happened), didn't deny them some honest emotion about it (people got hurt), showed them a little escapist glamour (nightclubs and diamond bracelets), lifted them up to a final catharsis (shed a few tears over poor Mom and the kids and the wedding photo), and then brought it all home. It was a cautionary tale that sent audiences out the door happy and reassured—but suitably titillated.

These cautionary marriage tales were popular from the very beginning of the feature-length movie in the teens and throughout the heyday of silent films in the 1920s. In particular, marriage was a topic that movies used to showcase the great female stars of the era. In *Panthea* (1917), Norma Talmadge cemented her stardom by portraying a wife who sacrifices herself to exile in Siberia so her husband can get his opera produced. In 1920, in a film cleverly titled *Yes or No*, she played both a rich wife and a poor wife who are neglected and tempted by men who promise to pay them the attention they're due. (The rich wife gives in to the adultery and is jilted, but the poor wife soldiers on and is rewarded when her husband invents the washing machine and she "gets everything.") Norma Talmadge also played wives in *The Wonderful Thing* (1921), *Secrets* (1924), and *The Lady* (1925). Her sister Constance appeared successfully in 1922's *The Primitive Lover*, in which she's a wife dreaming of a caveman-type lover instead of her own meek husband. When she goes to Reno for a divorce, the husband is galvanized to follow and fight for her, turning himself into the man of her dreams. Gloria Swanson was *My American Wife* (1923), and Pola Negri's American debut film, *Bella Donna* (1923), was the story of a woman who walks out on her British husband for an Egyptian tycoon. (Negri is later spurned by this lover and ends up staggering around in the sand, threatened by tigers and jackals.) In *Flesh and the Devil* (1927), Garbo played a faithless wife who pays for her sin by falling through the ice wearing a spectacular fur coat. Even male stars couldn't escape marriage plots. Valentino was an adulterous husband in *Blood and Sand* (1922), and the victim of an aggressive female seducer (Nita Naldi) in *Cobra* (1925). (Before succumbing, he chokes out, "Aren't you forgetting your husband is my best friend?")

Eleanor Boardman, a major star of the silent era who is far lesser known today, starred in a classic example of the popular marriage movie: *Wine of Youth* (1924). Well directed by King Vidor (who was wed to Boardman from 1926 to 1932), the film tells the story of three generations of women: grandmother, mother, and daughter, each named Mary, each young and approaching marriage, and each played in turn by Boardman.* The three episodes take place in 1870, 1897, and the early 1920s. The grandmother and the mother both desire marriage, and are depicted using their feminine wiles to achieve that goal. The third Mary, in contrast, is a flapper. She's modern, and she's not at all sure she wants to be tied down. She wonders why anyone would want to be a wife, but she has two ardent suitors (Ben Lyon and William Haines), so she decides to try them out on a camping trip. Like most flappers, she can't live up to her own new morality. After an attempted seduction by Haines, she flees homeward, only to find her parents quarreling horribly when she'd always imagined them to be blissfully wed. She becomes hopelessly disillusioned and vows never to marry. However, her stressed-out mother faints; the husband erroneously believes she's poisoned herself, and he suddenly realizes how much he loves her. The young Mary decides their love is real after all and accepts the quiet, more considerate suitor (Lyon) rather than the more aggressive and sexy one (Haines). The comfortable pattern of the plot was reassuring, but Vidor's visual presentation was unafraid to put real teeth into the downside of marriage, to give the questions credibility.

Silent marriage movies were sometimes slightly silly in their concepts (tigers in the desert), but never in their conviction. They had the ability to reach out to audiences with offers of hope and escape, followed by the "punishment" and return to normalcy that marks the cautionary tale. They were successful; and as a result, so many were made that cynicism about the idea surfaced in critical reviews. *Restless Wives* (1924) was chided for having "hardworking husbands, bridge-playing wives, and other conventionalities." Dismissive comments on *Yesterday's Wife* (1924; "nothing new") and *Flapper Wives* (1924; "nothing new in the story") confirmed that the audience was being subjected to formula. Sometimes there were warnings (*A Wife's Romance* [1923] was "not for the family") and sometimes real praise (*The Marriage Circle* [1924] was "a master piece of direction by Lubitsch . . . a strikingly amusing comedy"), but on the whole, the reviewers were onto the game very early. Audiences, as usual, went to see what they wanted to see.

As the silent era moved forward and movies became a primary form of mass entertainment, comedy and caution endured as ways to use marriage. A new twist was added: spectacle (or the "clothes, sex, and furniture" development). Marriage was something audiences wanted in life, but too many of them already had it, so onscreen it needed a little perking up—some glamour, some pizzazz. Spectacle came in two forms: European sophistication (sex

---

* *Wine of Youth* was based on a successful stage play, *Mary the Third*, by Rachel Crothers.

without consequence) and American consumerism (sex with cautionary consequence—and lots of fancy furniture). These types are well represented in the
films of Ernst Lubitsch and Cecil B. DeMille.

Lubitsch was the master of sexy silent-movie marriages in the sophisticated
European version, champagne to DeMille's hearty ale. Lubitsch was clever at
removing threat from marital problems; that is, he moved temptation off Main
Street and over to Paris. Over there, his films seem to say, married couples
allow temptation through the door, and you may watch it happen. Over there,
you're safe—forget about caution. There's a kind of freedom from guilt in a
Lubitsch marital comedy. Everyone is essentially too well mannered for chaos
to occur. Lubitsch was sly (as was DeMille), and his movies typically showed
reconciliation at the end. *The Marriage Circle*, one of his best, has a happy marriage threatened by a visit from the wife's sexually predatory friend, who tempts
the husband. The possibility of infidelity causes both the husband and wife to
become more aware of their own sexuality, and in the end they become sexier
together, wised up as they are, and even happier. Lubitsch's films have great
style and fashion. He put top hats on the men and jewels on the women. Everyone wore fur, rode in chauffeured cars, and sat on great furniture. Lubitsch
linked marriage to European manners, clothing, and art deco glamour.

Cecil B. DeMille also brought glamour to the cautionary tale, especially
in his four marriage masterpieces: *Old Wives for New* (1918), *Don't Change
Your Husband* (1919), *For Better, for Worse* (1919), and *Why Change Your Wife?*
(1920).* DeMille was very canny. With a title like *Why Change Your Wife?*, he
didn't waste any time putting up the safety net. He used a set of opening title
cards to denounce divorce, in case anyone should misunderstand. And then
he proceeded to interest everyone in the topic by having his leading man and
woman do it—and divorce was a scandalous choice at that time.

In fact, Cecil B. DeMille might easily be called the Father of the American
Movie Marriage. It's DeMille who used the fundamentals of marriage for a
specific and personal cinematic purpose. He gave the marriage movie goals.
He elevated the couple and their home into wealth way beyond the audience's
wildest ideals, but remembered to ground their problems in the ones anyone
could have. He linked their broken dreams to escapist living conditions, then
shattered their security, and ultimately restored it by reminding them that
what those people up there on the screen did was not for them out in Peoria.

* In his excellent book on Cecil B. DeMille, *Empire of Dreams*, Scott Eyman labels these
films "comedies of divorce" that anticipated the works of Lubitsch. He adds, "DeMille
started his comedies where most directors end them . . . with marriage. They all take
place after the glow has worn off and the partners are growing bored with each other."

Don't Change Your Husband warns Cecil B. DeMille's movie, but Gloria Swanson takes a look at Lew Cody anyway . . .

. . . and in *Why Change Your Wife?* Thomas Meighan learns the hard way that Gloria Swanson was the right one all along. Different husbands, different titles, but the same Swanson, same DeMille, same message.

Cecil B. DeMille defined the silent marriage movie, as in *For Better, for Worse*, with Elliot Dexter and Swanson. *Motion Picture News* said Swanson's marital troubles "fairly make the heart cry out."

DeMille united comedy, caution, and clothes . . . and he nailed down the pattern of serenity, chaos, and restored order that wouldn't be abandoned by marriage movies for decades to come. The "upper-class" marriage threatened by sin—featuring very well-dressed protagonists living in ritzy digs—became one of the wily director's story trademarks. DeMille eroticized marriage; ironically, he commandeered its holy state for purposes of sin.

DeMille's skills as a filmmaker enabled him to sketch out what was happening between two people in a marriage with simple visual shorthand. He needs only two shots in *The Affairs of Anatol* (1921). The audience sees the feet of the husband tapping impatiently as he waits for his wife to make breakfast, followed by a shot in which the audience sees the feet of his wife—being given a pedicure by her maid. This definition of their marriage is swift (two shots), unexpected (using a pedicure for a punch line), prophetic (the couple have different goals), amusing (audiences always laugh), and a full definition of where they are in their marriage (in trouble). It has a wonderful economy. But DeMille was also a master of visual excess. Against a background of lavish sets, with bathrooms as big as Rhode Island and beaded and feathered costumes, he would have his married characters stray . . . and stray . . . and stray just a tiny bit more. After they had fully enjoyed straying, and everyone in the audience had enjoyed watching them stray, DeMille's movies would remember to punish the sinners, reminding everyone that sinning was not going to lead to a happy ending outside of a Cecil B. DeMille movie. If you want sin, said DeMille (and you apparently do), go to a DeMille movie. Participate without consequences. Because his protagonists were usually married, and because it was made clear they were wrong to stray, and because everyone was distracted by costumes and sets, DeMille managed to get away with a lot.

DeMille's portraits of well-heeled marriages in trouble were perfect for luxury-hungry moviegoers of the silent era. They came partly to view the goods on display. His movies starring Gloria Swanson set a high tone of sophistication, presenting a soignée heroine who was definitely not a Victorian virgin. She was, after all, a married woman. Swanson's wives were fabulously dressed, jeweled to the gills, and out on the town ready for something to happen. A woman like the one Swanson portrayed was exciting to the (possibly) bored men in the audience, and very liberating for the women. The DeMille Swanson is always juggling two challenges: her husband, and what to wear. The key question in her world is clearly presented onscreen as a title card in *Male and Female* (1919). "Why shouldn't the Bath Room express as much Art and Beauty as the Drawing Room?" The audience is allowed to decide its own answer, but after viewing Swanson stepping down into a bathtub the size of a small

Swanson, again with Thomas Meighan, ultimately became tired of her DeMille marriage movies and opted to move on, despite the luxury she was surrounded with in *Male and Female.*

swimming pool filled with bath salts and rose petals, attended by two maids and surrounded by art deco luxury, their answer was likely to be a heartfelt "It should!" DeMille's presentation of marriage as a setting for idealized homes, clothes, travel, and a lifestyle of luxury had a major historical influence that is still seen on modern screens.*

The press campaign for *Don't Change Your Husband* indicates how the DeMille marriage movie was really designed more for spectacle than for caution: "Gorgeous gowns, beautiful women and a startling story of married life. Cecil B. DeMille has done it again. He put married life in a show window, with all its heart aches, misunderstandings—with all its joy and genuine beauty." The gowns and the women and the shocks get top billing. The campaign suggested theaters stress the film's spectacle and glamour and remember to "go the limit." The campaign should be designed to appeal to "everyone married or thinking about getting married or against getting married." In other words, marriage was not necessarily what would put them in the seats; it was just as likely to be the gowns and the spectacle.

In his personal life, DeMille became a sort of marriage guru. The movie

---

* Movies like 2008's *It's Complicated* link stories about married and divorced couples to an upper-middle-class vision of glamour, largely through the presentation of astonishingly appointed homes.

magazines of the era carried interviews such as the one written by Adela Rogers St. Johns that appears in a 1920 *Photoplay*. In the article, " 'What Does Marriage Mean?' As Told by Cecil B. DeMille," the director gave St. Johns his views on marital infidelity (a subject, many said, on which he was an expert), suggesting that "if a woman has the mental strength to stand the gaff, her husband will always come back to her . . . if she just has the moral poise to weather his yieldings to the beast within."*

Because DeMille's titillating portraits of marriage managed to hide sex behind a conformist cover-up, they were wildly popular with audiences and inspired imitations. *Fig Leaves* (1926) is a perfect example of the DeMille-ish comedy. Directed by Howard Hawks (in an early effort), designed by William Cameron Menzies, with gowns by Adrian, *Fig Leaves* has three major characteristics of the DeMille marriage movie: a sequence set in ancient times (cave days), marital discord (over clothes), and a great emphasis on luxury (a "Color by Technicolor" fashion show). *Fig Leaves* opens in the days of cavemen, in which "the Garden of Eden was the only fashionable part of town." The hero (Adam, played by George O'Brien) gave his rib "to learn the quaint old sport of matrimony." His wife, Eve (the beautiful Olive Borden), is "one of the few brides who never threatened to go home to mother." Charmingly anachronistic, à la *The Flintstones, Fig Leaves* shows O'Brien reading the morning newspaper (a hunk of granite), with stories like "There's Bad Blood Between Cain and Abel," an announcement of "Mastodon Races Today," and an ad that suggests "Try Forbidden Fruit—an Apple a Day Keeps the Doctor Away."

Adam is contented with his life, but Eve has three problems: "I haven't a thing to wear, I haven't a thing to wear, and I haven't a thing to wear." She spots "a wonderful bargain in fig leaves" in the paper, but her husband angrily informs her that "ever since you ate that apple you've had the gimmes—first it was twin beds and now it's clothes." Imitating DeMille—and simultaneously satirizing him—the movie makes use of the basic male/female "we're stuck with one another" personages of the original married couple, Adam and Eve, who here are a 1920s version of Blondie and Dagwood. When the image fades from cave days to present time, Adam becomes a plumber, but Eve's still a

---

* DeMille's favorite star of his marriage/divorce movies, Gloria Swanson, was a similar spokesperson for the female side of the discussion. In the December 1919 issue of *Motion Picture*, in an article entitled "Gloria Swanson Talks on Divorce," she told American women: "I not only believe in divorce, but I sometimes think I don't believe in marriage at all . . . After all, marriage is just a game. The more elastic the rules, the less temptation there is for cheating. I think that divorce should be made more easy, instead of more difficult. Yes, I believe in divorce as an institution." Swanson, aged twenty at the time, definitely proved she meant it: she married six times and divorced five.

housewife who wants more clothes. ("Woman hasn't changed a bit," says the title card.) Eve's girlfriend (Phyllis Haver) gives her dubious advice—"Get all the pretty clothes you want regardless of Adam"—while a title card solemnly informs the viewer that "in all probability the Serpent in Eden was really another woman." Adam's male friend isn't much more helpful. He advises Adam on how to handle women: "Treat 'em rough, but don't kill 'em. You might want 'em for somethin' someday."

Fig Leaves is fast-paced and charming. When Eve is struck by a car owned by a big-name fashion designer ("She loitered in front of my motor, but I'm not angry"), she is offered a job as a model; Adam objects. It's the traditional "No wife of mine will ever work." Eve models anyway without her husband's knowledge, until he accidentally sees her parading around in her skivvies. The crisis of the film is put directly onto the screen in a clearly stated dialogue exchange between Adam and Eve, an exchange that every audience member could understand. It's all about clothes. "You didn't give them to me," says Eve, "so I went out to earn them. That's every woman's right." Adam fires back: "And every man's right is to respect his wife and not have her parading around half-naked! You wanted clothes? You cared more for them than you did for me. Very well, Eve, you keep the clothes." He stalks out, but within minutes everything is resolved. "Please, Adam, I'm sorry. I've learned my lesson. I know that clothes don't mean everything." *Fig Leaves* takes marriage to its roots, the conflict between Adam and Eve, and gives it a DeMillian problem—gorgeous clothes designed by Adrian and displayed on beautiful women in glorious Technicolor. Then it puts temptation in its place; a cautionary tale, but with a soupçon of irony. The end returns an audience to cave days. "Cain and Abel are having a slaying party," says Adam. "Oh, but I haven't a thing to wear!" responds Eve.

By the end of the silent era, some standards and traditions involving movie marriages had been established. It had become obvious that audiences liked to sit in the dark and observe marriages they would never have—sexy, rich, glamorous, exotic—and that they were willing to be cautioned, warned, and made to suffer for the experience. They were willing to pimp marriage out as an excuse to see clothes and furniture and places they would never see any other way.

Comedy, caution, and clothes—all these were molded into audience-pleasing movies about marriage. The 1920s marriage movie was a movie about what it meant to a man or a woman to be married. The state of being married was central to the plot. (The movie had to stay, as it were, in the family.) The stories were hermetically sealed, linked directly to the condition of the marriage; even if it was set in Borneo or against a political struggle, it was nevertheless still the story of a marriage and nothing else. Borneo and politics were background settings, decorations, or bonuses added on for variety.

The silent era also located the fundamental attitudes that would endure for marriage stories: an "I do" movie in which happiness would dominate, and an "I don't" in which tragedy would prevail. Equally importantly, the movies of the 1920s found the handle on how to keep from offending any audience members who wanted to believe in the sanctity of marriage: establish happiness and destroy happiness, but always restore happiness. Along the way, show viewers something new, something beautiful, something sexy (if you can get away with it), and something escapist. Throw in some spectacle—a fur coat and a swan-shaped bed.

By 1929, the silent-film movie marriage was a set piece, smoothly operating in a beautifully produced film such as *Wild Orchids*, starring Greta Garbo. When the audience first meets the married Garbo, she is not the languid woman most people associate with her. She's animated, excited, and alive. Married to one of those ubiquitous older movie millionaires (Lewis Stone, in this case), Garbo has just had the wildest ride of her life as their chauffeur recklessly races the couple to their departing ship. (The film opens with the defining call: "Hold the ship! The Sterlings are on their way!" Thus we learn of Stone's wealth and importance: ships are held for him.)

This opening sequence, very brief, cleverly tells viewers important news: Garbo is married. She is youthful, full of life and humor, and craves excitement. Her husband, however, is older, calmer, and super-wealthy. And they are on their way to "inspect his plantations in the Orient." "The Orient" was then, and has always been, the place American women go to find weird sex in the movies. On board ship, in fact, Garbo will encounter "sex" in a 1920s-style physical form: Valentino clone Nils Asther. Garbo stumbles across Asther as he is beating one of his servants in the hall outside his stateroom. This heats Garbo up for future inappropriate meetings between them. Heat ("the everlasting heat") is, in fact, the theme of *Wild Orchids*. Asther explains to Garbo that she wears "cold orchids" but that in his country (Java) "the orchids grow wild" because of all the heat. "The East," he tells her, "is a country of the senses." While Garbo and Asther flare nostrils and exchange smoldering glances, Stone pursues his business interests. Thus, the movie carries out the established pattern of silent-movie marriages: orchids, Javanese dancers, pulsating heat, a wife who wants to make love, a husband who wants to make another business deal . . . and a man who represents sexual freedom, with a slight touch of kink

A formula for marital trouble: *Wild Orchids*, with the older Lewis Stone and the young and glamorous Greta Garbo. Stone, from his twin bed, reaches out to his wife . . .

. . . gives her a chaste peck "good night" . . .

. . . and falls asleep, leaving her awake and full of longing, soon to be really awakened on a trip to the exotic Orient, where the heavy scent of "wild orchids" will tempt her.

thrown in. The plot is essentially that of *The Cheat*, but without any money being owed. In the end, all the heat (Garbo and Asther all wrapped together in the moonlight) cools down. Garbo and Stone sail home and back to normalcy.

This pattern might be called the "rich and strange" approach, well designed for the poor and ordinary. It can be seen to be clearly in place by the sound era in one of Alfred Hitchcock's earliest films, suitably entitled *Rich and Strange* (1932). A young married couple live in very modest circumstances in London. The husband is overtly dissatisfied with his lot. Riding home on the crowded subway, he sees an ad in a newspaper that asks him directly, "Are you satisfied with your present circumstances?" He knows he is not. The audience knows he is not. The idea is that they probably are not, either, so empathy is established. The husband arrives home, finding his cheerful little wife seated at her sewing machine, making herself a dress. She, unlike her husband, is totally contented, and thus a touch of hope for their future is established: at least one of them is happy. Noting that he's grumpy, the wife suggests the solution that the entire international film business hopes will be the chosen one: why don't they go out to the pictures that evening? His reply sounds like the clarion call of the unhappy mate. "Damn the pictures . . . I want some life! Life, I tell you! I want some of the good things in life! Money!" Immediately following this outburst, in the magic way of movies, the postman arrives with the news that the husband's wealthy uncle has decided to give them all his money so they can have some adventures while they are young.

There can be no more overt announcement of what the marriage movie was designed to do by the end of the silent era. As an audience sat watching in their theater seats, they were sold a series of lies. Now you have some money. Now you can leave your boring situation. Now you can have some adventures. Now you can escape your disappointment. And so they do, for "now." Onscreen appears the quote from *The Tempest* that gave the movie its title: "Doth suffer a sea change into something rich and strange." The surrogate movie couple take a sea voyage, and a great deal happens. New clothes. New friends. Excitement. Seduction. Theft. Imprisonment. Shipwreck. Rescue. And, finally, a return home, back to their little flat, both united and now willing to live their own lives as they know them, dedicated to loving each another and maintaining their marriage. And for the perfect honest touch, as the movie ends they begin bickering. The compatibility of their incompatibility has been restored. In a sense, they *did* go out to the movies, as their experience is exactly the one their audience has had.

PART TWO
DEFINING THE MARRIAGE MOVIE
IN THE STUDIO SYSTEM

S ilent movies had successfully defined a purpose for the marriage film: comedy, caution, spectacle, a little sail-away into something rich and strange, but also as something that would, in the end, take viewers back to where they were in the first place. Marriage evolved on the movie screen and found success by going home. Everything about this seems clear, even simple. And yet after the silent era, marriage, the one thing that audiences really understood and had personal knowledge of, turns out to be one of the most elusive and confusing topics to tease out of motion-picture history. In the sound era, marriage is everywhere, all over any kind of plot or setting or genre or star vehicle. It's Nick and Nora Charles. Judge and Mrs. Hardy. Tarzan and Jane. Bluebeard and all his short-lived companions. Pierre and Marie Curie. The Barkleys of Broadway. The Tuttles of Tahiti. Mr. and Mrs. Bridge. The Dodsworths. And more than one Mr. and Mrs. Smith. It's in the west, it's in the east. Outer space, Transylvania, the frozen north, ancient Rome, modern New York, and Gopher Prairie, Minnesota. Couples are happy, unhappy, old, young, and alien. They're vampires and they're Communists and they're doctors and they're lawyers. Marriages, all kinds, all shapes and sizes, are everywhere in the movies, yet nobody thinks to call one of them "a marriage movie." Not then and not now. To write about the unnamed marriage movie, I first searched out films in which the plot was clearly *about* the state of being married, observing the way the stories were told and finding the strategies the studios used with which to vary them.

Despite the fact that no one I asked could remember any sound that were only about marriage, and despite the business practice of trying to pretend they didn't exist, there *are* movies purely and utterly about marriage. They tell the story of domesticity . . . and nothing else. They are honed in. Their purpose is not so much to amuse or warn or provide spectacle—although they often do those things—as to reflect directly the circumstances of marriage in a recognizable form. The world they depict is the world of two people cohabiting, with or without family, but cohabiting under the pressure of a bargain they made with each other—a restrictive bargain that induces pressure. And thus a story of some sort, but a story narrowly focused on those same pressures and that same social bargain. As a result, a second purpose emerges: reassurance. "It's all right," say these movies; "it will be all right." Stick with your bargain, and bad things will not happen. There will be no floods, fires, plagues, earthquakes, illnesses, or disasters like the birth of triplets. Nothing could be much more ironic, in that in order to make audiences believe this, bad things are made to happen. There *are* floods, fires, plagues, earthquakes, illnesses, and plenty more. The suffering will be worth it, says the marriage film, because in the end you will find you have love. You won't be alone. Thus the marriage film is one of Hollywood's most shockingly blatant forms of contradiction, and a great example of how audiences liked to be lied to about things they knew from their own lives.

To reassure everyone that married domesticity was a useful and rewarding enterprise, the movies needed a careful manipulation of narrative structure. It was all in the screenplay. The movie either told the story of a marriage in the popular moving-forward, active mode (young couple get married, things go wrong, all ends well) or they told it backwards as a flashback (everything has gone wrong after a young couple got married and things have so far not ended well). The first is the "I do" form, often, but not always, a comedy; and the second is the "I don't," which is the story of a divorce. These two forms were the main strategies found to present stories of marriage in movies.

There is a fine line to be drawn in actually defining a film as a pure marriage movie, because it is necessary to locate the difference between a movie that contains a marriage or uses a marriage as a background and a movie that is very specifically created to define marriage as an onscreen world. Just having a marriage in the story doesn't make a film a "marriage movie." If it did, two famous Oscar-winning films of the 1930s would be marriage movies, which they aren't. Both *Gone with the Wind* (1939) and *The Good Earth* (1937) are full of marital issues and have plenty to say about the subject if we'd care to focus on it while we're watching the North defeat the South and the locusts eat half of China. *Gone with the Wind* is, in fact, a grab bag of mismatched wedding pairs. Melanie and Ashley are devoted to each other, but possibly passionless; they marry because their families expect it. Scarlett and Rhett marry because they are loaded down by their obsessions, but they barely like each other. She wants the security of his money, and he just wants her. Scarlett's parents were married across class lines, and Emmie Slattery and Jonas Wilkerson represent a cheap, shotgun example of a similar principle, having married on the sex-first-pay-later plan. Widows and old maids in the plot are defined primarily by their marital status, as is Belle Watling, a husbandless madam (with a son in military school) who makes her living off the needs of married men. The heroine, Scarlett O'Hara, is a rule breaker, and the rules she rails against are those by which women are supposed to comport themselves in marriage.* Nevertheless, GWTW is not really a marriage movie. It's a movie about a willful heroine during the Civil War in America, and what happens to people in her world when the Old South is destroyed. (Some of those people just happen to be married.)

The Good Earth, based on a best seller by a Nobelist in literature (Pearl S. Buck), tells an epic story about the lives of two peasants, Wang Lung and his wife, O-Lan. The film opens with their marriage and ends with her death, and during its running time the couple experience many marital woes: deep poverty, in-law problems, the death of a newborn child, and adultery.† But their marriage is really the background for a story about the nation of China, war and politics, and the importance of the land to its peasants. (That same importance of land was also featured in GWTW.) The issues of *The Good Earth*, like those of GWTW, are larger than an individual marriage. The settings are historically real, and the purpose of each film is higher, going beyond the parameters of its basic married relationship.

A simple question to ask in order to decide whether a film is fundamentally about marriage is this: Could the characters undergo the same story line if they were *not* married? Would the focus be the same? *Gone with the Wind* would still be a film about a willful female in the Civil War and the changes to the Old South, and *The Good Earth* would still be about war and Chinese peasants, even if their main characters never married. The subplots might not be as interesting, but the events could go forward.

Leave Her to Heaven (1945) is an example of how to draw the line. It's a disturbing story about a writer (Cornel Wilde) who marries an exotic beauty (Gene Tierney) shortly after he meets her. (Their marriage ceremony isn't seen onscreen.) They become man and wife approximately 34 minutes into the film, which has a total running time of 110 minutes. Their marriage officially ends about one hour after it begins, because Tierney kills herself, setting up her death to implicate her supposed rival (Jeanne Crain) as a murderess. (Seventeen minutes of film story follow after her death.) Since nearly a full hour of the running time of *Leave Her to Heaven* is focused on an unhappy marriage between Wilde and Tierney, why isn't it a marriage movie?‡ It *is* grounded in

---

* For Scarlett O'Hara, marriage is not much more than a career move. She weds her first husband to cover her embarrassment about losing Ashley, and her second to pay off the taxes on Tara. She marries Rhett for everything he can give her. In the novel, Rhett was actually her fourth husband.

† "Hunger for the lips of lotus," as explained in the trailer.

‡ Today it is often labeled film noir, even though it was shot in glorious Technicolor rather than black-and-white. In its own day it was "melodrama."

Leave Her to Heaven doesn't show domesticity between Gene Tierney and Cornel Wilde. It's all about obsession, desire, and murder.

a bad marriage, and it's that marriage that brings on doom; but *Leave Her to Heaven* isn't *about* marriage—it's about obsession and evil. Audiences never observe domestic bliss. The movie opens up in present time—the bulk of the story is told in flashback—as Wilde arrives to board a boat that will take him to his lake retreat. He has just been released from prison. He is not introduced to audiences as a married man, or a happy man, but as a man who has been in prison. It is *his* story that will be told, *his* character that will be explained. Why did he go to prison? Why is he alone? Is he a good man or a bad man? These are not marriage-movie issues.

It is only in the return to the past that the audience learns about the "her" in *Leave Her to Heaven*, and she is definitely not a role model for wives. No sympathy is ever intentionally created for her at any point. She murders Wilde's crippled brother (by sitting in a rowboat and watching him drown) and aborts her own child (by throwing herself down the stairs in a negligee and satin pumps). Why? She doesn't want to share Wilde with anyone. She wants him all to herself. She's not interested in finding a way to balance their individual needs. In other words, this is a noirish melodrama that *uses* marriage in order to present a tale of suicide, obsession, and extremely bad female behavior— downright unwifely, in fact. Gene Tierney doesn't become obsessive just because she marries Cornel Wilde. Marriage doesn't make her selfish and evil; she was already that way. Marriage counseling isn't going to help her. Her character soars past the boundaries of everyday behavior into a delicious hyped-up hysteria (it's a fabulous movie!). The film could present its story of a jealous woman who behaves irrationally even if Wilde never married Tierney. Except for the scene in which she aborts her unborn child ("I hate the little beast"), most of the same events could take place with minor adjustments to the plot.

Secrets (1933), starring Mary Pickford and Leslie Howard, on the other hand, *is* a marriage movie, done with a deft referential shorthand that indicates audiences were familiar with the format.* Pickford, who has the larger role in the film (as fits her legendary status), plays a daughter of wealthy southerners who, against the wishes of her parents, boldly elopes with the penniless Howard, who takes her west in a covered wagon. Told in flashback from the point of view of their happy old age, in which Howard has just retired from a successful political career, the elopement is by default endorsed and justified.

The story of Pickford and Howard's long marriage is boiled down to its main events: their elopement, their fight for survival (including living through the death of their first child), and his infidelity. In fact, the movie has only three extended scenes: the elopement, played as romantic comedy; the long and difficult struggle in the wilderness, played as tragedy and a triumph of courage and heroism; and an extended ballroom scene set at a gala celebrating Howard's campaign for the governorship. The latter provides costumes, glamour, a little sex, and some spectacle for viewers. These three key episodes are glued together by montages that fill in the full story "behind the scenes," as it were: their actual wedding, their arduous journey west, their long fight to build their business into extended wealth, the birth of their additional children, his successful rise into politics, etc. None of these are seen in detailed presentations, just in montages that speedily impart the information.

Secrets only has time for basic marriage issues: love (the elopement), union (the wilderness), and trouble (his adultery). The infidelity comes out of nowhere: an audience has seen Howard previously as a devoted, faithful, and almost worshipful husband to Pickford. At the big ball scene, a dark-haired, dark-eyed "Spanish woman" (code for madam or prostitute) suddenly arrives and confronts Pickford. Pickford is stoic (her lot in life). When she's told that her husband has promised his mistress he'll marry her if Pickford will let him go, she says calmly, "In that case, I will release him." She calls her husband into the room and brings him up to speed. Seemingly a bit annoyed, Howard tells his mistress flat out that he has no intention of marrying her, and that's

---

* In fact, it is a remake of one of silent star Norma Talmadge's greatest hits, made in 1924 and also called *Secrets*. Both versions are well directed by Frank Borzage.

Leslie Howard and Mary Pickford elope in *Secrets*,
a sound remake of a silent film starring Norma
Talmadge. The story of how over the years their union
survives troubles from all directions makes *Secrets*
a pure marriage movie.

that. (The movie assumes that audiences understood star power—there would
be no leaving Pickford.) After the "Spanish woman" slinks off, Howard decides
he needs to confess to his wife. Pickford says not to bother: she has known all
along—not only about this particular woman but also about "all the others."
It's news to Howard (and also to the audience). He's crushed, but Pickford
instructs him on what to do and say: "I know you want to tell me that none
of this meant anything . . . I was always the one you loved." After a return to
the present in which the old couple steal their butler's car to drive away for
an adventure together, another "elopement," their young and eager faces are
superimposed over their aged ones. Once again, they're back in their covered
wagon, full of youth and optimism—and love.

    Secrets knows the audience knows its story—the story of a marriage. It also
demonstrates how movies work that story: key in on the romantic couple, ennoble their struggle, select one problem, and resolve it. *Secrets* is almost minimalist. (It could have been titled *Secret*.) No details are needed for the full story

because everyone knows what it is. Affirm, question (sort of), reaffirm, and resolve, with a glamorous overlay of ballroom costumes and souped up with some western excitement. *Secrets* proves that an entity that could be called the "marriage movie" did exist, but *Secrets* was labeled a "historical saga" and a "love story" in ad campaigns and industry house organs.

As movies became American vernacular, a code of images emerged: the subtle presentation of the exotic "other woman" in *Secrets* shows clearly how movies could imply what they wanted an audience to understand.* A couple who kissed passionately, followed by a cut to fireplace flames—or fireworks—or waves crashing on the shore—were understood to be going beyond the kiss when the camera discreetly moved to those flames, those explosions, and those waves. The audience got it. It was subtext.

There is no comprehension of Hollywood and its product without the realization that planned subtext is not a modern, after-the-fact discovery or interpretation. Hollywood was run by canny men who came out of salesmanship and poverty, and who had a desire to get more, get better, get up to the top of the heap—to win. Dissembling was something they understood. Stifled by censorship pressure, eager to attract and hold on to the very widest possible audience, moviemakers shrewdly hinted, covered up, misdirected, double-talked, and became vague. They'd show what they wanted to show in the way they wanted to show it, and then deny it in dialogue if necessary. Underneath every movie story runs another story, and it often contradicts or questions the one on the surface. This skill was very useful in tales involving marriage, particularly in the years of strict censorship. It allowed movies to deny love and still confirm it, to indicate sex but never show it, and to say marriage was hell but we should all want and respect it.

The great director Frank Borzage used subtext regarding marriage in *Mannequin* in 1937. The film starred Joan Crawford (as a girl from ye olde box factory) and Spencer Tracy (as a shipping magnate). It is a story of love, failed love, new love, new failed love, and, finally, love triumphant. Along the way there are marriages. First there's the wretched marriage of Crawford's parents, in which the mother slaves away in the kitchen and her unemployed husband calls for his supper. The mother (Elizabeth Risdon) tries to tell her daughter that marriage plans don't always turn out the way you think they're going to ("Make a life for yourself"), but Crawford still weds her irresponsible beau (Alan Curtis).

---

* American viewers learned to "read" design: a small town had one kind of street, a western settlement had another, and a big city yet another. Sets on back lots were labeled this way: "Western street," "New York City block," "small-town residential street," etc.

At their wedding supper can be observed how eloquently Borzage creates subtext by using close-ups of three faces: Crawford's, Risdon's, and Tracy's.

The supper ("eleven 85-cent dinners") is held in a Hester Street Chinese restaurant (run by a man named Horowitz). Crawford's beautiful face is radiant, tear-stained with joy. (People sometimes forget what a truly beautiful young woman she was.) Her close-ups show a tremulous happiness, a deep pride in her new status as wife, and an utterly unshakable belief in her future and her husband's love. (He just sits by looking handsome.) In contrast, her mother's face is a mask of grief. She is tight-lipped, and she looks away from her daughter and the festive table and tries not to show that she knows only too well how short-lived this joy is going to be. The third close-up is of the wealthy Tracy. He only happens to be in the restaurant, having visited the poor neighborhood to attend a meeting of the longshoreman's union. When he spots Crawford's face (in her close-ups), his own close-up reveals desire, loneliness, appreciation, yearning, a sense that watching such bliss happen will be his only portion in life. (He's the audience surrogate.) Tracy pays for the dinners as his gift to a happy bride and groom, largesse from afar, the gratitude of a lonely man for his glimpse of their joy.

A triangle is present onscreen through these close-ups, which are also three contradictory statements on love and marriage. From the mother (no belief or hope) to Crawford (belief and hope) to Tracy (belief but no hope), the camera establishes for a viewer an explanation of three characters. It also simultaneously affirms the joy of romantic love and undercuts it. Crawford's mother will turn out to be right: the new husband *is* a cad who leaves his bride in the lurch. Crawford then goes out on her own to "make a life for herself" and meets the wealthy Tracy, who marries her. Crawford makes a transition from hope to no hope to new hope as she *really* finds what she only thought she had. Tracy gets what he thought he'd never have, but in the plot also loses it when he thinks Crawford has betrayed him. When they are reunited, a new belief, a new hope provides the audience with an escapist dream ending. *Mannequin* illustrates the perfect Hollywood strategy for marriage films: reality needs to be somewhere in the picture, to affirm the audience's knowledge, so that when tragedy occurs, they really want to believe they can be lifted out of it. This goal was achieved partially through cinematic strategies: in the case of *Mannequin*, the effective use of close-ups.

Only rarely would the marriage film try to tell audiences directly, with no subtext, something that married couples know but not everyone wanted articulated: marriage and romantic love are not the same thing. David Lean's 1949 British movie *The Passionate Friends* (called in the United States *One Woman's Story*) clearly states that point. Based on a novel by H. G. Wells, the story concerns the inevitable triangle of wife, husband, lover. Director Lean superbly manipulates time, presenting a movie involving flashbacks, memories, and present tense—all effectively mixed—to demonstrate how an unresolved love from the past can dominate a woman's emotions. The story is the tale of a young couple who fall in love in 1930: Ann Todd and Trevor Howard. "Will you always love me, Mary?" he asks. "Of course," she confidently replies. "I shall never love anyone as much as I do you." Later, however, she throws in a little P.S. "I want to belong to myself." It's not so much that she doesn't want to belong to him, but more specifically that she doesn't want to be *owned* by her passion for him. She ditches him for Claude Rains, an older, richer, and quieter love. She's a modern variation of the Cathy character from *Wuthering Heights*: she makes the choice of security, comfort, and station, eschewing the wilder passion of the Heathcliff option.

Nearly a decade later, in 1939, Todd and Rains (now wed) attend a New Year's Eve ball at which Howard and his new girlfriend are also present. Todd and Howard are drawn together but behave politely and introduce their mates to each other. Howard's girl asks him about Todd's husband. Howard explains that Rains is a banker, and terribly rich, and that was "the sort of life Mary wanted." Predictably, however, while Rains is conveniently away on one of those numerous business trips rich men make so their wives can get into trouble, Todd and Howard begin a passionate affair, rekindling their youthful love. Ultimately, they are found out when they don't go to the theater to see a musical—ironically called *First Love*. When Rains goes to check up on them, he hears the merry song lyrics "East love or west love, my first love's the best love." Afterwards, the three face off. Rains is tough. Todd is upset. Howard is direct and honest. In other words, Rains dominates, Todd vacillates, and Howard tries to do the right thing. The next day, Howard receives a note from Todd breaking off their relationship (for the second time). Howard visits Rains to argue over it, and it is in this scene that an onscreen articulation about marriage vs. romance occurs. Rains boldly, strongly, irritably tells Howard to go away and give up on Todd:

> You say you love Mary. You may love her, but you don't know her as I do. Our marriage has been very successful until now. It's based on freedom . . . and understanding . . . and a very deep affection. It's a marriage both Mary and I wanted. Your love is the romantic kind. The kind that makes big demands. Nearness . . . longing . . . fulfillment . . . and priority over everything else. That isn't the kind Mary really wants, although you almost persuaded her it was. Don't you see that you two together are dangerous?

Ann Todd wants wealth and security from marriage in *The Passionate Friends*, so she marries Claude Rains . . .

Rains firmly explains that the romantic dream of marriage must be abandoned for any marriage to work. Although Howard says, "It's a cold, bloodless, banker's point of view," he nevertheless *does* go away and make a happy marriage of the Rains/Todd type for himself. When Todd and Howard are accidentally yet again united years later, after World War II, they spend a platonic afternoon on a picnic, climbing the Alps, and both agree they are now happier, better people. (Howard has married the woman he'd brought to the New Year's ball, and they have a son and a daughter.) Todd and Howard part friends.

In *The Passionate Friends* lies the problem of the marriage movie: like Todd and Howard, it has to abandon the romantic dream. Thus it becomes a "cold and bloodless banker's" event, and moviegoers are human beings who want a little heat, a little passion, a little escape, and a lot of romantic drama. It's what they pay for, and what they have to have. They want to hear the words "I shall never love anyone the way I do you" and have it mean something. They want the eternal flame . . . for ninety minutes. They want to believe the Gypsy.*

Made for Each Other (1939), directed by John Cromwell and starring James

---

* Another movie that states ideas coldly about marriage is James Whale's *One More River* (1934), starring Colin Clive and Diana Wynyard, based on John Galsworthy's last novel. Clive says marriage is nothing but a mixture of "mutual interest and desire," and that the desire will fade but the mutual interest can become stronger. He turns marriage into a long-term business deal (and uses this as his excuse to beat his wife when she falls in love).

. . . but she can't resist temptation when her former lover, Trevor Howard, re-enters her life.

Stewart and Carole Lombard, is the very best classic example of the sound-era, studio-made, pure marriage movie, designed to be "realistic."* It can clearly be defined as an "I do!" version of a story that has no purpose other than entertaining audiences with a story focused totally on marriage. The union of its protagonists, Jane and John Mason, is the film's central event. All story elements are linked directly to it. *Made for Each Other* is not a film about how society views the Masons' marriage, or how war has separated them, or how they have worked together side by side to discover radium and win the Nobel Prize. It's just a story about their marriage. Episode by episode, it presents viewers with the ordinary things that can grind a young couple down: money problems, in-law interference, boredom and disappointment, dashed dreams, parenthood, bad luck, and the inevitable unpaid-for furniture.

Made for Each Other, however, was *sold* as a love story, not as a story of marriage. Across the top of a full-page ad in *Movie Mirror* in April 1939 runs the word "HEARTBREAK!" The copy says: "The heartbreak of two young people in love . . . facing the world with song in their hearts . . . Laughter . . . Melo-

---

* *Made for Each Other*, a late 1930s product, shows how sound marriage movies, while still remaining glamorous with stars and wardrobes, nevertheless stepped down and away from the 1920s marital spectacle in an attempt to be more realistic and thus closer to the audience's experience. These movies differ from the glamorous screwball comedies and sophisticated "divorce" movies of the era.

drama . . . and Carole Lombard in a brilliant transition from comedienne to dramatic star!" Marriage is not mentioned. The illustration presents Stewart and Lombard kissing in profile, looking very glamorous and sexy. Lombard is the bigger star and is given pride of place in the copy. Oh, and down in a corner is a small photo of a baby with a toy. No one's eye is directed there.

At first glance—and certainly at this point in their careers—Stewart and Lombard might seem to be inappropriately paired. Lombard, who was married to Clark Gable, had been in movies since 1924.* She was every inch a star. Stewart had been in movies for only four years, and although he had moved into top billing and had sixteen films in the can, he was not yet the huge star he was going to become and certainly not the legend we know him as today.†(Stewart and Lombard made only this one film together.) Stewart in retrospect was better matched with Jean Arthur, a down-to-earth gal, not a sophisticate, or with June Allyson, his all-American female counterpart. At this stage of his career, prior to *Mr. Smith Goes to Washington*,‡ *The Philadelphia Story* (1940), or any of the movies of his postwar career, Stewart seems too young for Lombard, too innocent. Lombard (at the peak of her glamour) appears much more sophisticated and experienced. (Alas, she didn't age onscreen for us; she died in an air crash in 1942.) Lombard had arrived at this 1939 established presence from a long line of other kinds of roles. Like most stars in old Hollywood, she had labored to find her most believable onscreen persona. Although today we may not think of her as the right person to play "little wife" roles, she had actually been previously cast that way in such movies as *Virtue* (1932), *No Man of Her Own* (1932), and *Swing High, Swing Low* (1937). (One of the reasons she didn't get stuck in the category was that her wifely roles usually had a little wrinkle in them. And that was how Hollywood figured out that Lombard was best cast as a screwball: the little wrinkle was the part she did best.)§

---

* Although Lombard actually made a movie in 1921, it was 1924 when she began her career in earnest.
† Stewart's first film was *The Murder Man* in 1935. He played a fledgling reporter and was billed ninth.
‡ *Made for Each Other* was released on February 10, 1939, *Mr. Smith* on October 16, 1939.
§ In *No Man of Her Own*, Lombard played a mousy librarian (!) wed to Clark Gable, an unreliable heel. In *Swing High, Swing Low*, a musical, she suffered while her husband (Fred MacMurray) became an alcoholic. And in *Virtue*, a pre-Code movie, she weds taxi driver Pat O'Brien without his realizing she's been a prostitute. No punches are pulled about this occupation. She's not called a "dance-hall girl," a "model," or a "nightclub hostess"; as she herself later admits to O'Brien, "I picked men up on the streets." As the movie opens, Lombard is being run out of town, and since the "town" is New York City, that's quite impressive. (One of the cops advises her, "Buy yourself a hot-water bottle.") Lombard had also played a nun, a nurse, and a schoolteacher on her way to stardom.

The pairing of Lombard and Stewart in *Made for Each Other* nevertheless works precisely *because* of their clashing styles. The audience can look at them and wonder why they are together. The hint of a mismatch brings on a touch of worry—*are* they right for each other? Will their marriage make it? Of course, no one who has ever been to the movies imagines for one minute that a movie called *Made for Each Other* is going to end with them *not* being made for each other. The fact that they are not a perfectly simpatico star pairing works within the plot, adding another layer of uncertainty.

Made for Each Other announces itself specifically as a marriage movie in its credits. (By this time the audience has already spent its money.) The first image onscreen is a marriage license. Under the empty column marked "Bride," Carole Lombard's hand writes her name, and under "Groom," James Stewart's writes his. These signatures (autographs, really) are immediately followed by their star-power names turned into large block type that reads: "Carole Lombard and James Stewart in *Made for Each Other*." When the credits are completed, a title card informs the audience that "greater New York has a population of 7,434,346, among the least important of whom is . . . " and the image fades into a page from the Manhattan telephone directory. A spotlight searches the crowded page for one lone name, finally locating it: "Mason, John H., Atty." This swift and eloquent opening states clearly to an audience that the hero of the film will be an ordinary man, not unlike them, and his story will be individual and personal, one to which they can directly relate. It has also stated clearly that it will be the story of his marriage to Carole Lombard. The visual shorthand is specific.

John and Jane Mason have gotten married unexpectedly over a weekend, never having met previously. Their story is a cleverly structured script that moves the couple forward across a series of events, each one of which presents them with a problem to be solved, and each problem directly connected to the state of marriage. First, Stewart must tell his boss (a crotchety Charles Coburn) that he is married. "It happened rather suddenly," he explains to the disbelieving (and disapproving) Coburn. "I saw her standing there . . . She had a cinder in her eye . . . We knew the moment we looked at each other." "Did you?" interrupts Coburn. "Last year there were nearly half a million divorces in this country." The audience is asked to recognize Coburn as the voice of cynicism, but also as the cold air of realism. (Who knows what skeptics spoke up before their own nuptials?) Viewers know their job is to expect trouble in the plot, but mainly to endorse the lovely screwball "meet-cute" that Stewart just sketched for them—the street-corner cinder in the eye. After all, they saw *that* movie, or certainly one very much like it, and it might easily have starred Stewart or

Lombard. The marriage movie knows its sources, and it knows which references to make to hook the audience.

It's important that viewers never see the Stewart/Lombard courtship. This makes *Made for Each Other* a pure marriage film, since there can be no suggestion that it's in any way a romantic comedy in the usual terms of that genre. Although the movie has romance (married) and comedy (screwball), the denial of the courtship period—the repression of the romantic-comedy plot—is key to the film's definition of itself.*

Facing Coburn is not easy for Stewart, but the next episode pits him against an even tougher foe: his mother. This crafty dame (well played by Lucile Watson) has no plans to let go of her meal-ticket son. She knows a problem when she sees one, and she sees one in the shape of Carole Lombard. As the three of them politely sip tea in the apartment Stewart and his mom share, Stewart can't find the right moment—or the right words—to break his out-of-the-blue news. As he stammers and hesitates, growing more and more uncertain, he begins to refer to Lombard (sitting eagerly at his side) as his new "girlfriend." The bride picks up on this and becomes very alert, ready for what's coming. Mom starts to grill her: who are her people, and what is she doing with herself, and why did she leave Boston to come down here right after just meeting Stewart on a weekend? "She was taking a course in journalism," offers Stewart, adding weakly, "but gave it up." "Oh?" says Mom, who then advises Lombard to go back to Boston at once and keep on with the journalism, to have herself "a good career." Not one to lose track of the direction they're trying to go, Lombard spars back, "Isn't marriage a career unto itself?" Mom, now knowing she must bring out the heavy artillery, fires full-bore: "Oh, yes. Indeed, indeed. Marriage is a business, a very serious business. A partnership in the strictest sense of the word. *And* one must prepare for it. So many things to learn. That's why one mustn't *rush* into it . . . No reason for Jane to develop into a household drudge." Hearing this, Lombard wastes no more time: "We're married," she states flatly, finishing her opponent off. Mom immediately collapses, pulling her best defense: "My heart!"

---

* The romantic comedy was a movie staple in the 1930s. It was meat-and-potatoes filmmaking, a form that Hollywood could practically do in its sleep. The system had the writers, it had the stars, and it had the chops. For a period of time, it was one of the easiest types of movie they could make, whereas today it's apparently the most difficult challenge for moviemakers. Alas, they keep on trying. Romantic comedies today are called "romcoms." This is perhaps the explanation of why they are no good: we can't even bring ourselves to say the two words. We have no faith in either category, much less the unification of the two. The "romcom" is just about what its name suggests: something truncated, cut down, and therefore diminished. "Romcom" implies a little bit of love but not too much, and a little bit of comedy, but not too much ("not too much" being all they can give).

One image says it all: newlywed Jimmy Stewart looks nervous. He forgot to tell his mom (Lucille Watson) that he unexpectedly married Carole Lombard. Mom's reaction speaks for itself and Lombard wonders how things are going to work out. That's the basic plot of *Made for Each Other.*

This early scene demonstrates clearly that Stewart will be caught between his two women. They will loathe each other from day one. Since it's too late to send Lombard packing, Mom pretends to accept the marriage ("What's done is done"). She plays on Stewart's genuine love and Lombard's essentially good nature to secure her position, wangling an invitation to live with them. In these two funny yet serious opening confessional episodes, the young couple, clearly in love and happy with each other, are forced to tell their news to two key people in their future, his boss and his mother, both of whom disapprove and would be happy to see the marriage undone. At no time have events (or even conversation) strayed from the central issue of marriage—or into anything the audience wouldn't find familiar.

As the film moves forward, each episode (all of which are well written, well performed, and grounded in easily recognizable events) is introduced by some type of formal institutional image: a document, a newspaper headline, a building title, an office door. Each of these images sets up and defines a particular domestic crisis that the couple will have to face: competition at the office, a pregnancy test, a hospital crisis, etc. The movie will grow darker as it progresses. The problems will escalate in importance and in danger to their happiness. Lombard and Stewart will begin to live out a series of disappointments and disasters.

The first disappointment is a delayed honeymoon. Immediately after they board the *Normandie* in blissful excitement, Stewart is summoned back to the office for an emergency that will keep them in New York. If he wants to hold his job, and advance to a junior partnership, he has no choice but to give up their European honeymoon trip.

Moving forward in time, the young couple, still optimistic and hopeful, still happy together, are seen hosting a dinner party in their new apartment. The guests will be his boss, the boss's daughter (who everyone, including her but excepting Stewart, thought would be the person he'd marry), his chief rival at the office (the smarmy Carter, who has half of Stewart's abilities), and, of course, his mother, who lives with them. This episode is written as a comedy, but inside it lies a dark streak of frustration and misery. Both Lombard and Stewart are frantic and under pressure. Lombard wants everything to be perfect so she'll be an asset to her man. Stewart is anticipating that his boss will announce a new junior partnership, and although he has no reason to believe it won't be him, he's very nervous. Mom, of course, is busily running the household, giving the maid orders that directly contradict those Lombard has given ("Dear, I was only trying to help"). With a tense couple, an angry maid, and an interfering mother-in-law, the film sets the stage for disaster—and delivers it. After the guests arrive, Coburn is ungracious and demanding. His daughter (who yawns throughout the proceedings) means to punish Stewart for dumping her. His rival intends to sit by and let everything crash in flames. Mom is Mom, and Lombard works too hard at hostessing. The maid, who has announced she's quitting but will see the party through until exactly 9 p.m., serves dinner as if it were an army drill. On the stroke of nine, wearing her coat and hat, she marches into the dining room and demands what they owe her: twelve dollars. Lombard doesn't have any money, so while Stewart runs around the apartment trying to scratch twelve dollars together, Coburn announces he's giving the junior partnership to the unworthy Carter.

This extended dinner party is the first fully developed portrait of the young couple's married life. As the scene unfolds, it cleverly—without undue attention—defines a host of problems: in-law trouble, lack of money, servant issues, rivalry at work, and, in particular, a deep, confidence-shattering disappointment for the hardworking Stewart. The scene ends with him pulling himself together to graciously, generously, and sincerely toast the elevation of his rival—even though they've run out of wine, another flaw in their plans for the evening.

Made for Each Other then picks up speed with a series of events: Lombard becomes pregnant; the baby is born and brought home to an apartment now overcrowded with Mom, parents, and baby paraphernalia; a never-ending parade of unhappy maids comes and goes; debts pile up; more arguments occur between the tired and beleaguered Lombard and the endlessly interfering mother-in-law. These events are directly connected to marriage and home life, a parade of common problems faced by couples of the day. Events move unceasingly downward out of comedy into frustration and disappointment, finally reaching a scene in which Stewart comes home drunk after attending his college reunion (class of '28). He was once voted Most Likely to Succeed, but his classmates have now passed him by. Lombard, still believing in him, nevertheless tells him the truth: he lets the office take advantage of him, and he needs to stand up to them. Believing totally in her capable husband, Lombard tries to give him the spine to ask for a raise, which he truly deserves. She eggs him on—but in a supportive and confident manner. She's right in every way, but when he finally manages to blurt out his request to Coburn, everything goes wrong, and he's asked to take a pay cut instead. Stewart is broken by this disappointment. "I let you down," he tells Lombard. The happy young man we first met is near tears, lost and ashamed. He has wanted to give his wife a fur coat and a home in the country, the two blue chips of the Hollywood marriage game. "You're all I want," she replies.

After the drunk scene and the pay cut, the movie has set the stage for the final crushing defeat of a young couple and their starry-eyed hopes for marriage. The scene takes place on New Year's Eve. Mom has a terrible cold, blowing her nose and sniffling, and Lombard is complaining that she has passed it on to the baby. Stewart and Lombard are all dressed up and lookin' good (especially Lombard, in silver lamé). They are going out, but their destination is not a happy one. Stewart's rival, the ghastly Carter, is coming to pick them up for a party in which they know he's going to announce *his* engagement to the boss's daughter. When a former maid (she was number fifteen, and the only one they liked, but they had to let her go for financial reasons) brings them a charity basket from her new employer's kitchen, it's the last straw. The film explodes into open quarreling among all three key participants—Lombard, Stewart, and Lucile Watson.

The mastery of the presentation is impressive as the three main characters in *Made for Each Other* shift focus, drop pretense, and openly turn on one another. From the moment Charles Coburn cynically told Stewart about the nation's divorce statistics, this marriage has had a question mark in its subtext. The quarrel scene doesn't tell an audience anything they don't already know, onscreen and off-, and it doesn't refute anything they've seen and observed in both places. It confirms their familiarity with trouble and disappointment.

Stewart's mother is bitter. She's old, has no home of her own, and has lost her son to Lombard, whom she resents. Lombard is genuinely angry with her situation. She has to do all the cooking, cleaning, mothering (to both mate and child), and she's also caught between her mother-in-law and her husband. Mom criticizes everything Lombard does, but the unhappy and disappointed Stewart isn't strong enough to do anything about it. All three have had it—and all three let go on each other, no sides taken. Finally Stewart yells, "I can't stand it anymore!" and stomps out. After a stunned moment, Lombard grabs her coat and follows. As she catches up to him on their apartment stairs, she cries out in despair, "Oh, Johnny, what's happened to us?"

"What's happened to us?" is a key question always asked by the true marriage movie. *Asking* it was what the audience needed, and it's obviously a main purpose of the form. It no doubt echoed the thoughts of many couples in the audience, and the fears of many others, maybe even the happy ones. It was a question for which the movies had no answer other than "Get your coats and go out to a movie with Stewart and Lombard"—a movie that could perhaps in some way reassure them or at least make them feel that if the beautiful people like the ones onscreen had troubles, no wonder they and theirs were experiencing the same.

Asking the question—but resolving its problem with no real answer—was the modus operandi of the marriage movie. Every marriage movie comes to its question of "What happened to us, Johnny?"—which is followed as quickly as possible by a resolution reaffirming the couple's marriage. If the film is a tragedy, the spark to reunite will come from some shared disaster; and if it is a comedy, it will come from some hilarious revelation or tricky device. These sparks, given what an audience has lived with for ninety minutes, need to be conflagrations; but marriage films close down their plots rather suddenly, emphatically, with inexplicable reunions grounded in some imagined need for everyone to go home with the concept of marriage intact. The party's over. The teacher has returned to the room.

Following the quarrel scene, *Made for Each Other* moves Lombard and Stewart to the inevitable decision that their marriage doesn't work. This is a moment of delicate balance, in which the audience must believe in the trouble but not let go of the belief that their stars can fix it and live happily ever after. Standing on the stairs, the couple decide to just go out on the town for New Year's Eve and to hell with everything. They're then suddenly seen at a glamorous party, with noise and merriment all around them. If you walked in on *Made for Each Other* at this point, you would see two very beautiful people inside what might appear to be a classic example of Hollywood escapism: balloons, music, tuxedo and lamé, star power looking at star power across a night-club table.

There is almost always a moment in a "realistic" Hollywood marriage film in which the movie will suddenly reveal itself as not all that realistic. It's a shift into a different visual universe, as in TV's *Buffy the Vampire Slayer* when her evening's date suddenly gets those wavy lines upside his nose, and fangs sprout on his teeth. (No wonder the best-looking guy in school asked you out! He wants to drink your blood!) In *Made for Each Other*, the fangs appear at the New Year's Eve party. Lombard and Stewart, their marriage in shambles, their lives going nowhere, both feeling trapped and disillusioned, are suddenly in the middle of a riotous celebration. Lombard is shown in radiant close-up, her backlighting perfect, her hair blonder than blond, her makeup natural yet glamorous, her corsage fresh, and her lamé sparkling away. Her huge eyes and perfect bone structure are on full display. Across from her, the young Jimmy Stewart—noble, exuding intelligence and integrity—makes a decision. "Maybe the whole thing's been a mistake," he says. He outlines the issues: he's gotten into debt, gotten nowhere at the office, and—here comes the kicker—he's made a *household drudge* out of *her*! Just as he points this out, the film cuts to a close-up of Carole Lombard. She sparkles, she radiates, and she's dressed like a million bucks. Household drudge? As the film brings the audience to the low point of what they might feel, have felt, or fear they may be going to feel about marriage—the moment of maximum honesty—the images pull a viewer out of truth and sharply back into glamour, a shaky form of reassurance. "I've made a household drudge out of you" indeed.

Carole Lombard, aglow with glamour, is supposed to be believed as a house-hold drudge, and that's Stewart's solemn explanation of why they must part. Because of her drudge-ism, he can no longer hold her to their marriage contract. Well, why not decide to believe it? The leads are snatching a New Year's Eve out for themselves, just as the couples in the audience are doing the same thing at the movies. When the film gently reminds viewers that they *are* at the movies, it's also reminding them that they're in on the game. (As they said on *Seinfeld*, "Not that there's anything wrong with that.") The movie has done its job. It's told a believable story of a marriage between two young people who didn't really know each other and who moved too quickly toward a perma-nent union. Things have gone wrong, and they're stuck. Okay, that's enough of that. *Made for Each Other* needs to wrap it up, put all the broken pieces back together, and send everyone home. It needs to move toward its inevitable "I still do."

Just as Stewart and Lombard decide to give up because of their little problems, they get a *big* one. Word comes to them at the party that their baby is dying of pneumonia. (Mom and her damned cold—escalated by plot.) Stewart has to confront Coburn and demand money to have a special serum flown in (through a blizzard—nothing is easy here), and suddenly Coburn turns into a swell fella who helps them out. Their baby is miraculously saved, Stewart is made a junior partner, and the marriage is repaired. Even Mom goes all human in reaching out to Lombard, feeling guilty about having given her cold to the baby. (To help an audience digest this, Lombard diagnoses what's been wrong with the old bat: "Why, you're lonely!")

Jane and Johnny Mason are "realistic." Two lovely stars play the couple, and the story humorously delineates recognizable problems that could confront any marriage, topped off by a highly improbable crisis that can easily resolve those same problems. It's both discouraging and reassuring. This pattern of pretense toward honesty, capped off by exaggerated resolution, was the "I do" marriage movie pattern. Affirm, question, reaffirm, and resolve. Destroy a marriage in order to reassemble it as a form of glamorous reassurance.

A similar story was released only a few months later, in early 1940, verifying the format. *We Who Are Young* was designed as a vehicle in which MGM could showcase two young performers they were hoping to develop into stars: Lana Turner, on the brink of stardom, and John Shelton, just on the brink. A cross between Robert Taylor in looks, Robert Walker in youthfulness, and Dennis Day in lack of leading-man gravitas, Shelton never became a star, though he would appear in such films as *Dr. Kildare Goes Home* (1940) and *The Time of Their Lives* (1946).

We Who Are Young (like *Made for Each Other*) begins by telling the audience that there are lots of people out there and that this movie will be about the ordinary ones. A voice-over says: "This is the city of New York, the biggest sprawl of men and masonry on the face of the earth. Her feet in the dirt, her head in the sky. Seven and a half million people live here side by side. The righteous and the unrighteous. Every week two thousand of them are born . . . Day in and day out, stories leap from the front pages of a million newspapers. Important people, as any editor can tell you, make better copy, and yet . . . " etc., etc.

Like *Made for Each Other*, *We Who Are Young* shows no prior onscreen relationship, no romantic courtship. When the movie begins, Turner and Shelton are standing in front of a judge, speaking their vows. When they go to a hotel for their wedding night, they tell each other their dreams. "I'm gonna lick this town," Shelton says. He'll get a better job . . . a car . . . clothes for her, maybe a fur coat. (The fur coat was an enormous status symbol during the 1930s, '40s, and '50s.) Turner says, "If we really make money, I'd like to take a trip." She also wants "a little house . . . trees around." The audience is also allowed to hear their secret thoughts—the unshared information—through voice-overs. He thinks: "This is serious. This is for life. I've *got* to get ahead and I've got to make some money. Gosh, she's so beautiful! *My* wife." She thinks: "Tomorrow we go back to work, but tonight is our honeymoon. It's just as I always hoped it would be . . . How did I ever get him? . . . Gosh, he's so handsome!" Out loud she solemnly says to him, "I'm going to try to be a good wife."

The opening immediately establishes their inexperience, that they've been drawn together by surface looks and (just like Lombard and Stewart) have no real knowledge of each other. Shelton's dreams are big. He is driven to succeed, and his need to achieve is related to himself as much as to his marriage. Turner's dreams are smaller, more domesticated, and she is far more practical in thinking about tomorrow instead of a long-range future. But they are married, and their marriage is like the one from *Made for Each Other* minus the live-in mother-in-law. There's an uncaring boss who doesn't appreciate what a good person he has in Shelton. There are furniture payments that lead to debt. There's a pregnancy that comes along too soon. There's financial trouble when Turner gets fired because the company finds out she and Shelton are married, and they don't hire married couples. ("A man who gets married should be able to support his wife," says the boss. "And with millions of men out of work, it isn't right for married women to take their jobs.") In the end, though, these issues blow away. Like *Made for Each Other*, the movie was designed to connect directly to realistic marital problems and then easily resolve them with a sudden change of direction. Turner gives birth to twins, a boy and a girl, while Shelton is offered, not one, but two excellent jobs. "This is the city of New York," the voice-over solemnly intones. Films such as *Made for Each Other* and its cheaper counterpart *We Who Are Young* demonstrate the basic marriage movie in its forward, most optimistic variation.

Proving the format could endure—that it *was* basic—twenty-eight years after *Made for Each Other*, in 1967, an allegedly more sophisticated and modern marriage movie was released. *Two for the Road* starred Audrey Hepburn and Albert Finney as Joanna and Marc, two characters inside an intelligent and complex script (written by Frederic Raphael). *Two for the Road* could easily be the story of John and Jane Mason from *Made for Each Other*, or even Blondie and Dagwood, if either of those two couples had been rich, well dressed, and casual about their wedding vows. Although there are differences between *Made for Each Other* and *Two for the Road* regarding sex, fashion, and automobile design, the films tell the same story underneath. Despite its shaky morality, slick surface, and open ending, *Two for the Road* is a traditional "I do" marriage movie. It's a very shaky form of "I do"—a kind of "Well . . . I kinda do"—but it *is* an "I do."

Made for Each Other was a movie grounded in two places: Jimmy Stewart's workplace (his domain) and his apartment (the domain of Carole Lombard—and, sadly, his mother). The film was released at a time when couples married, moved into a home, and had children while the man tried to climb the ladder of success. If they went anywhere, it was out to a New Year's Eve party. (Stewart and Lombard didn't even make it to their honeymoon.) *Two for the Road* is set in the world of the Sexual Revolution. There is no real need for the couple to be married or build a home together. It takes place literally on the road, with the couple driving in different cars over shifting time frames. It never once depicts the home base in which the couple actually live. They are always travelers and visitors, never dwellers. Their domicile is their car; and although it provides them with constant mobility, nothing ever really changes for them. They argue but stay together. Their progress is strictly economic and their change only geographic.

Two for the Road has a highly sophisticated cinematic presentation, and is well directed by Stanley Donen. The couple journey backward and forward in time, revealing how their relationship grew and how it changed, and ironically asking the same question that *Made for Each Other* asked: "When did it all start to go wrong?" ("What happened to us, Johnny?"). *Two for the Road* is a film shaped by editing, and transitions are made by lines of dialogue and images that violate temporal honesty. For instance, the young Finney and Hepburn are hitchhiking, but no one stops to pick them up. As an audience hears them vow that when they are rich and have a car, they will absolutely pick up every hitchhiker they see, the image moves them forward in time, their car now zooming past a young couple with their thumbs extended. Hepburn and Finney don't even consider stopping.

Two for the Road's story is told in six major time units, which are overlapped and juxtaposed for ironic comment. By removing all transitions and indications of change and by juxtaposing time frames ironically, the movie speaks cinematically about what happens in a marriage: as time passes, it gets edited and loses its original frame of reference. Each time frame is marked by a trip to Europe and a traveling format. First they don't have a car . . . then they ride in someone else's station wagon . . . then they have a secondhand green MG that dies on them . . . then they upgrade to a natty little red sports car . . . and in the end, they're secure inside a very expensive white Mercedes convertible. The cars—as well as Hepburn's clothes and hairdos—mark, not only the passage of time, but also the constant upgrading of their financial and social status. In chronological order, the time frames are:

1. Hepburn and Finney first meet as college-aged travelers, she with a musical girl group on its way to a European festival, traveling in a VW minibus, and he on a hitchhiking journey through Europe to see "buildings" (he's an architect). All the other girls get chicken pox, so Hepburn and Finney set off alone and fall in love.

2. Wed for two years, they undertake a car trip through France (in a big American station wagon) with Finney's former girlfriend (Eleanor Bron), her obnoxious husband (William Daniels), and their truly horrible little daughter.

3. They undertake a low-budget camping vacation, driving through Europe in an old green MG. They're struggling financially and live in a basement apartment in London (which the audience never sees). During this journey, the car catches on fire and they meet an older French couple (Claude Dauphin and Nadia Grey) who will become their sponsors. Hepburn tells Finney she is pregnant with their first child.

4. Finney, now working for Dauphin and loving his success, is obsessed with his career. During this time frame, Hepburn is seen mothering their daughter, Caroline, while Finney often has casual affairs. His focus is on the upward trajectory of his career.

5. Finney and Hepburn reach a plateau of success, but Hepburn is lonely and neglected—though very well dressed. She embarks on a serious affair with a dapper Frenchman, and Finney is shocked and possessive. They reconcile.

6. Finally, in the "present tense" of the film, in which the story opens, Finney and Hepburn, rich and bored and in their marital rut, have loaded their expensive car onto an Air Ferry and are traveling to the fancy party Dauphin is giving to celebrate his new home, built by Finney. Caroline has been left behind with her nanny. This story unit begins and ends the movie—which means it begins and ends with an argument.

The story of the marriage between Audrey Hepburn and Albert Finney in *Two for the Road* is summed up: she pushes to make things go forward and he takes it easy with cigar and map.

Two for the Road qualifies as an updated example of the traditional marriage movie because it begins with Finney and Hepburn already wed and arguing about their situation. The first sound is of wedding bells, as they drive past a local ceremony and peek out at the newlyweds. "They don't look happy," says Hepburn. "Why should they?" counters Finney. "They just got married." This "present time" journey introduces the audience to a motif that will be repeated: Finney always loses his passport, and Hepburn always has to keep track of it for him. (He never remembers she'll have it.) In other words, he needs her, and she looks after him. As they drive, their voices are heard on the sound track: "You haven't been happy since the day we met, have you?" she asks him. "There was a time when you were happy to go on a trip with me," he replies. Hepburn looks out the window of the Air Ferry and down below sees the cheaper channel ferry chugging along. On that boat is their youth—and the movie begins its back-and-forth movement across their lives together, and the development of their relationship, which is seen to be problematic from the very beginning. The young version of themselves met on that ferry—when, in fact, he first lost his passport and she first found it.

In 1967, *Two for the Road* has no need to protect the sanctity of marriage.

It does not shy away from asking out loud serious questions like "Do you want a divorce?" It is full of frank unhappiness. "You don't give me everything I want . . . you give me everything you want to give me." In the early time slots, Finney constantly maintains "I've no intention of getting married." Married people, he says, fight about money and sex, and "that's marriage for you." After they wed, Hepburn feels forced to take care of their child by herself, and Finney reminds her, "*You* were the one who wanted a child." He says things went wrong between them "when the sex stopped being fun and became official. Sex isn't personal anymore." Although Hepburn has an affair and complains constantly, she is more mature than Finney. At one point, she tells him that Caroline's on the phone. "Caroline who?" he asks, forgetting it's his own daughter. Finney thinks he's clever—he does Bogart imitations—but he's selfish, career-obsessed, and unfaithful. (There's an implication that among his numerous affairs might be one with Dauphin's wife, but a specific one with a blonde he casually picks up on the road is depicted. As the audience watches this flirtation and its ultimate outcome, the bedroom, he's heard in voice-over in a loving and duplicitous letter he writes to Hepburn, marking him as a real cad.)

Unlike *Made for Each Other*, *Two for the Road* has no simple resolution. The film ends with a sequence in which, at the swinging party at Dauphin's house, one of the guests tells another couple to look at Hepburn and Finney: "If you can be as happy as those two over there . . . and have a marriage like theirs . . . " The audience is asked to realize that a happy marriage is not only elusive but probably also an illusion. Back in the car, their natural habitat, Hepburn and Finney discuss their ongoing topic: their marriage. "What would you do if we got a divorce?" "Cry." They go over their tired old issues, and he says he just can't accept "that we're a fixture . . . that we're married." She tells him to stop thinking, and kisses him. "I love happy endings," she says, as they prepare to make love. The next day, at the end of the movie, they're seen driving up to a border check. "You have to admit it," she tells him, "we've changed." Except they haven't: he can't find his passport; she has it. "Bitch!" he says to her. "Bastard!" she responds.

Two for the Road is the story of a marriage in a world in which marriage has grown unnecessary, featuring a couple adrift internationally in a world of easy money and sex. It's too late for a marriage movie to tell a straightforward story in which everything can be changed by a plot event such as the death of a child. The cinematic format of *Two for the Road*, using editing across varying time frames, strengthens the fundamental idea of their marriage. A marriage story—for a 1967 audience—can no longer be simple and, thus, linear. Hepburn and Finney do love each other, but all their initial vows and promises have been broken. The old romantic notions about marriage are now unsophisticated. Male and female roles have changed. But for an audience's sake, the couple will soldier on. There's no resolution for this couple, only more confusion and uncertainty, and probably more affairs . . . and, ultimately, another new car, another road to drive, another journey across time. These two will always be on the road. And yet the movie shows, if constructed chronologically, a story of love and marital happiness established, destroyed, and, if not fully reassembled, at least maintained. The purposeful question—"What happened to us?"—has been asked.

The movie ends ambiguously, but only because it is the more modern way for a movie on this topic to conclude—but is it really any more ambiguous for a viewer than *Made for Each Other*? An audience of 1939 was leaving the theater without a real-life easy solution such as the one the screenplay provided for Lombard and Stewart. The constant marital discussions that Hepburn and Finney indulge in, questioning everything, seem honest, but they, too, are cover-ups, not unlike the new job for Jimmy Stewart. Both films are pure marriage movies, and both show how filmmakers made such stories both discouraging and uplifting, so that viewers could recognize in them what they knew to be true about marriage.*

The story of Hepburn and Finney's marriage is not one in which they are preparing to divorce and are looking back on the "What happened?" It's one thing to tell a story about a marriage by moving it forward through time, showing characters encountering difficulties and either solving them or becoming lost in them, or even to mix up time for ironic juxtapositions; it's quite another to tell a marriage tale by *beginning* with a scene in which a couple have definitely already decided to divorce and then showing the audience *why* this decision was made by turning backward in time. The divorce format (the "I don't" variation) sets up higher stakes, because the story begins at a point of unresolved crisis. The focus in the first method is positive, moving a story forward through happiness and across trouble toward a solution. In the second format, the story presents divorce as the solution already chosen and, thus, a darker situation. What the movie then *explains* is the negativity. On the positive side, a divorce film gives the audience a temporary release, an opportunity to fix blame, and the sense that serious marital troubles are common, but even when a film refutes the divorce at the end, it still has to visualize seri-

---

* In *Two for the Road*, the couple are unquestionably remaining together. The ambiguity lies in whether they will continue to do so.

ous problems to get where it's going. Audiences begin by viewing the relationship as a failure, becoming alert to little problems and differences that appear onscreen, less inclined to believe the love scenes or the promises made. Even if the divorcing couple reconcile, the viewing experience is shaped by negative forces. Audiences receive two different messages, and the successful pattern of "affirm, question, reaffirm, and resolve" is challenged. It is reconstituted as "question, affirm (in past tense), resolve, reaffirm." It's a difficult form to make work despite its initial honesty. It works against itself.

American movies never actually endorsed divorce. The June 13, 1934, Production Code guidelines did not mention the word, but did dictate (under the category of "Sex"): "The sanctity of the institution of marriage and the home shall be upheld." This gave movies quite a bit of wiggle room. It was the tradition for canny motion-picture makers to shape marriage as sad, doomed, and threatened from many directions, but able to be brought back to life at the end to, evidently, respect the "sanctity" of the institution.

Despite the Production Code, Hollywood movies didn't avoid divorce, or worry about audiences being offended by it. When, for complicated plot reasons, Fred Astaire is forced to marry Ginger Rogers in *Shall We Dance?* (1937) and needs to extricate himself from the union as quickly as possible, he asks a justice of the peace, "What are the grounds for divorce?" The reply is terse: "Marriage." And, as far as the movies go, that's pretty much it. To obtain the desired goal of divorce, first one marries. It's Hollywood logic: the goal of marriage is divorce, but they didn't have to endorse it or even actually show it onscreen—they just had to wink at the audience about it. Everyone understood.

Three movies illustrate the "I don't" version of the marriage movie (which is really a divorce movie): *Chicken Every Sunday* (1949), *Payment on Demand* (1951), and *The Marrying Kind* (1952). *Chicken Every Sunday*, based on a best-selling memoir which was also a popular play, stars Celeste Holm and Dan Dailey in a story about a husband full of pie-in-the-sky financial schemes that never pan out, who's supported by his hardworking and practical wife. *Payment on Demand*, with Bette Davis and Barry Sullivan, tells of a hard-driving, manipulative wife who pushes her more laid-back husband to the top. *The Marrying Kind* is the story of an ordinary couple (Aldo Ray and Judy Holliday) struggling to make a go of things. *Chicken* (a light comedy) tells an audience that Holm is right; *Payment* (a serious drama) says Davis is wrong; and *Marrying Kind* (a seriocomedy) says that it's nobody's fault either way. Significantly, all three films come out the same place in the end: the divorcing couple decide to stay together. All three are told in flashback.

Chicken Every Sunday is a fairly benign divorce movie, whose message, like those of "I do" movies, is reassuring. The story concerns a turn-of-the-century couple living in Tucson, Arizona. It opens up on the leading lady, Celeste Holm, striding purposefully down a dusty street, a grim look on her face. As she passes a group of men who obviously know her, one of them asks the question the audience also wants answered: "I wonder what's the matter with her?" The camera follows as Holm enters a building and goes directly upstairs and into a lawyer's office. Her very first words as a character are "I just can't stand it anymore, Charlie. And I don't want any advice. I want a divorce." Charlie refuses her, pointing out that her husband is one of his closest friends. Holm storms out and goes down the hall to a younger lawyer, who's new in town. He agrees to accommodate her wishes, but asks her, puzzled, what the grounds would be. "Nonsupport" is her curt answer. She walks to the window, looks out, and begins to narrate her story as the audience is taken back in time to her wedding day . . . and told her marriage story.

Twenty years previously, Celeste Holm wed Dan Dailey. At the time of their marriage, they'd already known each other for four years, and she had ample time to learn all about him. One of the things she learned was his irresponsibility with money. "If you don't throw it away," she tells him, "you give it away." Even though he's currently (and only temporarily) vice-president of the bank, he's had to "borrow money to pay the minister." Holm's voice-over narration tells viewers that her own attitude toward money is very different. As a child, she suffered because her southern parents owned a plantation that never really became profitable. Her family never really knew if the land was theirs or the bank's, and this shaped her personal goals for marriage: "I want security. I've wanted it all my life."

This immediately raises a key question: why, then, for heaven's sake, is she marrying Dan Dailey? She already knows he can't manage money, and subtle dialogue references indicate he's also had plenty of other women in his life.* Her character married for the wrong reasons. This establishes Holm as a strong connective figure to women in the audience, and the movie is built around her.

The flashback story of the union between Holm and Dailey unfolds cheerfully, as if there's really nothing for an audience to worry about. This is largely due to the presence of Dailey, who's better known as a song-and-dance man, partner to Betty Grable in a series of Technicolor musicals. Dailey found a solid stardom by playing charming cads who underneath it all were really good guys. He brings this positive persona to his role as Holm's unreliable husband—with

---

* Later, we'll hear that after years of marriage he's finally become too old to "climb the mountains" to find the attractive girls on the other side.

another actor, the balance of happiness might have been seriously impaired. What an audience *sees* in Dailey is a loving husband, a caring father, and a loyal friend to everyone in town . . . who just also happens to be totally irresponsible with money and who continually hatches a series of harebrained schemes that don't pan out. There's his hotel, his laundry, his streetcar line, his creamery, his general store, his theater, his hospital: all bear his name, but someone else took them over to make them work after he was forced to give them up. He's earned no financial reward from any of them.

The couple's family survives because Holm takes in boarders. She's a fabulous businesswoman, slowly expanding the size of their house one room at a time (one room for each of his crazy failures). She keeps cows, chickens, geese—whatever it takes to make a buck. Slowly, she pays off their mortgage. It's this mortgage that initiates the movie's opening marital crisis. On the very day she has finally paid it off and planned a celebratory party at which she'll burn the deed, Dailey has gone into the bank behind her back and mortgaged their home again. Furthermore, he's hocked all their furniture, and the man who will reclaim it is planning to arrive that night during the party. (Furniture is always a big deal in the marriage movie. Owning it and losing it are the wife's equivalent of the stock-market crash.)

By most women's standards, Dailey is a pretty awful husband. He lies to his wife and has never earned a steady living, leaving her to scrimp and save and scrub and cook and keep the family solvent. However, as the movie plays out, the audience is asked to see such events as really quite charming ("Isn't all this fun?"). The impending divorce introduced at the beginning is ignored, and viewers watch hilarious boarders, a loving couple, happy children (including a teenage romance for the daughter), and a town full of camaraderie and supportive friends. The most successful thing about *Chicken Every Sunday* is its portrait of a devoted couple: in other words, it's a divorce movie that sells *love.* Except for a few sweetly remarked oh-no-you-don'ts from Holm to Dailey about spending on some new financial scheme, there's no real tension and anger between them. (There's also a strongly implied sexual chemistry, which endures over the passing years.) By the time the movie returns to present tense—where viewers rediscover the possible divorce, the new mortgage, and a set of furniture about to be reclaimed—it's a jolt to be back behind the eight ball. The film has signaled the audience every step of the way that everything will turn out okay—and, in fact, it soon will. The furniture is taken away . . . but brought right back. Why? Because all of Dan Dailey's male friends have chipped in to pay off his loan. When Holm asks why, the men carrying back the tables and chairs tell her simply, "Jim's an old friend of ours."

Celeste Holm and Dan Dailey start out happy in *Chicken Every Sunday* . . .

In the end, the starring couple, Holm and Dailey, directly tell the audience the simple and reassuring things about marriage that they wanted to know. Dailey goes first. All his life he'd been looking for Easy Street, and it was "right in front of him all along." (His wife, his meal ticket, paved his way to Easy Street: he didn't have to work, because she did.) When it becomes Holm's turn, she tells her daughter that "house and furniture meant security to me" but she's learned her lesson: she now knows that security is two people loving each other, "willing to go through anything together. With that kind of security, you've got everything. Without it, you've got nothing." (Nothing *is* what she's got.) Holm tells her daughter, newly engaged, that she hopes she'll be "as happy as your father and I have always been." The reunited couple embrace, and it's The End.

The plot sounds silly and the movie trivial, yet it's not so easy to dismiss *Chicken Every Sunday*. It was a successful book, a successful play, and a highly successful movie (a top box-office draw of 1949–50). Its ability to gloss over a lifetime of struggle for a woman married to an unreliable man was reassuring to audiences, both men and women, because it was a movie that lightened these issues, making taking in boarders sound like a zany romp. It justified irresponsibility, endorsing it as charming, loving, and the source of deep friendships. Above all, it suggested love would make everything turn out all right. Love would burn the mortgage. The success of *Chicken Every Sunday* shows how a marriage movie couched as a divorce movie could reassure everyone

. . . and end up older, wiser, and burdened with financial troubles.

that a bad deal wasn't all *that* bad . . . if it could be turned into a romantic comedy selling *love*.

The little-known Bette Davis vehicle *Payment on Demand* (also known as *The Story of a Divorce*) begins in an alleged marital heaven: a beautiful home with a circular driveway, a uniformed maid to answer the door, a lavish interior loaded with antiques, and the lady of the house (La Davis herself) floating down a grand staircase in a long dress and plenty of jewels, a fur draped casually over her arm. Davis plays the wife of a highly successful man, one who has given her everything, including children. She is proud and happy. However, when hubby (Barry Sullivan) arrives home that day, he flatly tells her, to her great surprise, "I want a divorce." He refers to their situation as "the whole meaningless mess" and warns her that "all your platitudes aren't going to make it right." She replies in a traditional Davis manner: she slaps him.

The "divorce" conversation that opens *Payment on Demand* is a clear depiction of how two people can see their marriage in completely different ways. The movie endorses the *argument*. Davis feels that she and her husband have everything that matters. She states firmly that she has always believed they have "a good marriage." Her husband, however, says that their marriage is lost, what they had is gone, and they are bored with each other. From this point onward, the movie shows the audience two levels of story: the advancing tale of the divorce, as the couple move closer and closer to the end of their union, and the flashback story of how their marriage collapsed. The moving forward/

moving backward format is headed toward a moment of final confrontation, in which an audience is led to believe that there is no way this couple can ever reunite (although, in the end, they do).

The marriage portrayed in *Payment on Demand* shows two people with two different levels of ambition and two different definitions of success. Their goals are not—and never really were—in sync. Davis wants money and success, and to get away from the farm life she was born into. Sullivan would prefer to live in the country, and he doesn't want to play the social game in the city. Like so many movie husbands, however, he is easily manipulated and follows the directions Davis lays out for him. Unbeknownst to Sullivan, she cheats his business partner, eliminating him from their lives. Later, the wife (Jane Cowl) of his city boss tells Davis: "You are a ruthless climber, aren't you? You'll climb, maneuver, do whatever's necessary . . . step over anyone to help him, won't you?" That, in fact, is the story of their marriage. Davis drives, Sullivan rides along.

After Sullivan asks for a divorce, Davis refuses to believe her marriage is over. She tells her daughters that their father "will get over it." Trying to keep busy, she joins her divorced female friends at lunch. (They say, "Welcome to the sisterhood.") When she finally grasps that things *are* finished (he has fallen in love with another woman), Davis turns ugly. The film's most honest (and horrifying) moments come during the property-settlement scenes with their lawyers. (This stark honesty probably reflects the grim knowledge clearly gleaned from personal experience in the highly divorced film business.) "Marriage does not provide security," states Davis, demanding a trust fund for both daughters. She rejects 50 percent of everything as her share, asking for 100 percent. She's vicious and demanding, but he says it's worth it to get rid of her and exit his miserable marriage. He just wants to walk away, and learns that to do so he will have to give her everything.* (Earlier he's said, "You hate people who aren't strong and successful, don't you?" and she has yelled back, "Without me you'd be nothing!")

Davis finds out what her life as a divorced woman will be when she takes a cruise and visits Jane Cowl, who is now living in an island paradise. Cowl's cohabitant is Arthur, a young man who she claims is writing a history of the island "in iambic verse." "Arthur is my protégé," she explains; but later she

---

* As Warren William, a divorce lawyer, says to a man in *Smarty* (1934): "In marriage, when you leave before the final curtain, you get no privileges." Originally titled *Hit Me Again*, *Smarty* was a dubious marriage comedy about spousal abuse. The pressbook suggested theater owners should sponsor newspaper contests in which local moviegoers could write up their own experiences of abuse—"but make 'em funny."

breaks down and tells Davis the truth. "At first I had a dog . . . then an old widower . . . then a lady companion . . . now I have Arthur. I don't know what I'll have next . . . It's a bad thing to be lonely . . . When a woman starts getting old, time can be the avalanche and loneliness a disaster." Needless to say, Davis arrives home for her daughter's wedding a greatly sobered woman.

The film's inevitable denial of its own presentation happens when Sullivan and Davis attend the wedding. The groom and his family represent everything Davis had hoped to move away from: an ethnic group with no money. The Polanskis are happy and full of the simple joy that only movie ethnicity can represent. (We're poor, we're loud, we eat salami, but we're happy.) The groom's mother, Mrs. Polanski, is presented as a frankly older woman, neither chic nor glamorous—the subtle implication being that this is the proper way for wives to be. She advises the young couple that "life is stones as well as flowers . . . nothing's all happy." Davis comes unhinged by all this wisdom and wedding cake, and after the youngsters fly off, she breaks down and weeps. When Sullivan takes her home, she tells him of her loneliness without him. "I didn't know how much a part of you I was." At this moment, the movie has arrived at the false reunion of a couple the audience has just been told have absolutely no chance of making their marriage work because of their fundamental differences, outside pressures, and deeply rooted misunderstandings. "Joyce," says Sullivan to Davis, "if we tried again, do you think we could find what we had in the beginning?" Since the audience has been shown that what they had in the beginning was based on lies, the suggestion seems improbable; but the husband tells his conniving wife, "I want you back, Joyce." He is as alone and lonely as she is. The woman he had loved in a genuinely caring and sharing relationship (Frances Dee) has left him because of pressure exerted by Davis. (Threatened with the revelation of their affair, Dee moves on because of her "job at the university.") Davis plays a big scene: "Are you sure you don't just pity me . . . I owe you something, David . . . Be sure . . . Don't decide tonight." After telling him that tomorrow, or even the next day, will do, she adds, "I'll be waiting." It's the Scarlett O'Hara resolution. Sullivan has lost everything—money, home, lover, status, confidence—but he has not, apparently, lost Davis.

There is a demented quality to *Payment on Demand*, the sense that audiences were forever to be denied marital happiness . . . that the only divorce they could have was a flashback that would then be refuted. Hollywood cleverly granted divorce for its audiences for about fifty cents a ticket, but figured this was the only type of divorce they could afford. *Payment* also shows them a marriage that made every mistake in the book and still survived. However fake,

The ending of *Payment on Demand* (originally called *The Story of a Divorce*) finds Bette Davis and Barry Sullivan divorced, standing on the threshold of their former home, poised for a shaky reconciliation. Will they reunite? Yes, but should they?

it *was* reassuring because it contained a raw honesty inside. As the youngest daughter (Betty Lynn) says: "Funny things happen to married people sometimes. They start to hate one another."

The Marrying Kind is one of the more honest portraits of an average marriage that have been told onscreen. Everything about it—its sets, its costumes (even with the "gowns by Jean Louis" credit), its location shooting in New York City and surrounding areas—is grounded in reality. Its script, by Ruth Gordon and Garson Kanin, carries a brother-and-sister relationship to their more sophisticated, upbeat marriage movie, *Adam's Rib* (1949) starring Katharine Hepburn and Spencer Tracy. The married couple of *Marrying Kind*, Judy Holliday and Aldo Ray, are a Hepburn and Tracy for the masses. Holliday, an extraordinary talent and presence on film, managed to be the perfect embodiment of an ordinary woman. A little too plump, a tad less than chic, and with just the hint of the "dumb blonde" about her,* she was nevertheless capable of elevating an average female into a noble creature not only to be sympathized with, but also admired. Aldo Ray, who was introduced to moviegoers in the film, was a likable, lumpkin Spencer Tracy. He was big and solid, with a

---

* She was anything but: known for her high IQ and ability to learn lines quickly.

raspy voice, and he seemed to be a kind and loving man whose big-bear body would be a secure place for a woman to seek haven. The movie business had so much confidence in Ray's future stardom that *Marrying Kind* carried not only a special credit ("Introducing Aldo Ray") at the front end, but also an unusual tribute at the finale. After "The End" appeared, Ray's image appeared again onscreen with the caption "You have just seen our New Personality, Aldo Ray. Please watch for his next picture."*

The Marrying Kind also bears a strong parallel with another marriage film, King Vidor's 1928 masterpiece, *The Crowd*.† Both couples marry with great optimism after relatively short acquaintances, and both feel the pressure of money problems. Both bank on a big dream coming true, and both husbands lose their way when financial burdens overwhelm them. Both men are pictured working as cogs in a big American business machine: Aldo Ray in the post office, and James Murray, the hero of *The Crowd*, in an office. Both women, Holliday and Eleanor Boardman, give up work to make a home for the family. Both movies are stories of marriages between ordinary people, and both aim for honesty in the storytelling process. Both speak of recognizable pain—the death of a child. Both reaffirm the marriage at film's end, with the couple reunited, but with the sadness not taken away or made light of.

The Marrying Kind begins at the New York Domestic Relations Court with two "arguing" sounds: the cacophony of divorcing couples yelling at each other overlaid by Mendelssohn's Wedding March. This ironic juxtaposition says much, but also sets both the essentially comic tone of the movie as well as the cinematic style it will maintain: show an audience the opposite of what character narration claims, a visual denial of verbiage.

As the story begins, Holliday and Ray are divorcing, and *Keefer vs. Keefer* is next up on the court docket. They tell the judge they are a hopeless case: "Ours is not a sick marriage. It's a dead one." It's six p.m., the end of the day, and the judge (significantly, a woman) says she'd like to hold their case over for the next morning. Then, as she gathers herself to leave, she sits down to talk to the Keefers. "I don't do this very often," she tells them, and explains why: her husband

---

* Ray had previously appeared uncredited in two 1951 movies; and billed as Aldo DaRe, he also had small roles in *My True Story* (1951) and *Saturday's Hero* (1951). He was nevertheless treated as an unknown for *Marrying Kind*. He later achieved a stardom of sorts in *Pat and Mike*, war films, and tough little noir movies. Sadly, just as he emerged, the studio star system was beginning to collapse, and he also developed personal problems, so he never became a big name. As a cult figure, however, he's greatly respected for his unique qualities as an "ordinary American guy."

† *The Crowd*, while not told in flashback and not a "divorce" movie, represents the late silent era's move toward the emerging sound format for marriage movies.

doesn't like her to get home too late. Three things are indicated by this woman: she postpones because she has a hunch about them (and we all know about female intuition); she's happily married, putting her husband before her court schedule; and Holliday and Ray's story is both typical and atypical.

The judge asks the Keefers to tell her about their marriage. "How did you meet?" They immediately disagree: "It was just a pickup," he says, and "It was *not!*" says she. As they narrate, the audience is taken to the past to learn their story. As events unfold, working back and forth from the past to the present, each past segment is triggered by specific questions from the judge and introduced by contradicting narrations and opinions by Holliday and Ray. Cleverly, the audience is shown how wrong they are about their marriage. As each one describes an event ("I got a frosty hello"), viewers see the opposite (a warm welcome). The couple argue over their memories, and it's clear that their basic problem is that although they both remember the same events, they don't see them the same way.

Holliday and Ray are an average couple akin to Stewart and Lombard in *Made for Each Other.** They live in a small apartment, and he works for the post office. She has given up her former secretarial job at his request, so they have a limited income after their two children are born. Their troubles were small in the beginning—or so they say. "The way it all started . . . " they tell the judge, was with "little things." They answer incorrectly when a quiz show calls their house, and lose the much-needed prize. When they save up for a big anniversary night out, his sister and her husband (the designated babysitters) show up drunk, so they can't go. Most of all, when Ray has a brilliant idea—"Slide-Airs," a ball-bearing roller skate—they can't get financial backing, although later on, someone else patents the idea and makes a fortune. Nothing goes right for them, and the pressures of bills and children give Ray a hideous nightmare (shot on location in New York City's main post office).

None of this, however, is *really* the problem. "Are you saying that not getting rich broke things up?" asks the judge. When they deny this, she probes, asking Holliday, "What did you want out of marriage?" ("What I didn't get.") "What makes you incompatible?" ("Being married to one another.") What's really destroyed the Keefers is finally revealed in a brilliant scene, a flashback that moves from a tone of comedy and joyous camaraderie to one of desperate tragedy: their son drowns on a family picnic. One year ago, they finally admit, their family of four took off for a little holiday excursion to a lake. Happy and relaxed, they laugh and eat and talk. When their son runs off to swim with

---

* *The Marrying Kind* is essentially *Made for Each Other* told in flashbacks.

friends, Holliday picks up her ukulele and begins to play and sing, "How I love the kisses of Dolores . . . ay yi yi, Dolores." As she lazily strums, behind her the audience sees action, and increasing agitation. Holliday is reclining, so only the legs and feet of other picnickers are observed running by, first in one direction, then in another, and then in a terrible, confused frenzy, until word is brought: "Joey!" Their son is dead.

In the return to present time, Holliday collapses in racking sobs, and Ray brings her a glass of water. "What's the use?" he asks, and then he, too, cries. "I don't know how we lived through it. Maybe we didn't." Holliday, an ordinary woman unable to articulate her grief with any eloquence, says, "I got all tired out."

The Marrying Kind doesn't shirk its dark side, or pass over it lightly. Unlike some "flashback/divorce" films, it continues in a downbeat mood for significant minutes. One of the most honest parts of the film involves the role of the little daughter who is left behind. She has tantrums and wakes up screaming. When she enters the kitchen to find her parents quarreling over breakfast, she makes them sit down and sing their "good-morning song" with her. A dejected and discouraged Holliday and an impatient and distracted Ray sing along, while their daughter, with an almost demonic look, *forces* togetherness on them:

> *Good morning to you,*
> *Good morning to you,*
> *We're all in our places*
> *With sunshiny faces,*
> *And this is the way*
> *We start a new day.*

It's an insane re-enactment of an earlier, happier shared moment, and a ghastly comment on a happy 1950s family breakfast scene.

There is more tragedy to come. Walking to work, Ray sees a street vendor selling toys and stops to buy one for Joey, forgetting he's dead. Shocked when he realizes what he has done, he crosses the street in a daze and walks in front of a truck. The resulting hospitalization, and required upstate rehab (for one month), is the couple's undoing both financially and emotionally. Holliday is forced to go to work, something Ray hates. Worst of all, after he's finally home, her former boss has died and left her a sum of money: $1,284.63. Over this small bequest, which triggers Ray's jealousy and sense of inadequacy, they quarrel . . . and quarrel . . . and end up in divorce court after seven years of

The Marrying Kind reverses the formula of *Chicken Every Sunday*.
Aldo Ray and Judy Holliday start out already in the divorce court
with Judge Madge Kennedy . . .

marital commitment. The marriage in *The Marrying Kind* breaks up over surface issues (money, in-laws, broken dreams, competition over earning power)
and one deeply ingrained tragedy that has made it impossible for them to continue to be with one another.

In the end, Aldo Ray admits that Holliday's boss, as it turned out, had left
the same sum of money to fifty-five other girls ("And thirty-five men," adds Holliday). The judge, not pushing her luck, says, "You've had hard times . . . but
good ones, too. We'll finish you up tomorrow morning." When she leaves, she
tells the docket clerk to remove their names ("Scratch *Keefer* for tomorrow")
for good luck: she has a hunch. The Keefers are left behind to talk things over,
and they decide that maybe it's a good thing for a married couple to realize
that all the things they have taken for granted—the happiness they expected
the day they wed—could disappear. "Maybe it's a good thing to know it's possible" you may end up in divorce court: that's the marriage message for the
audience. If you're aware you might break up, you may be more careful; you
may work harder at making your marriage work. Ray and Holliday ask each
other what would happen if they reconciled. "I would certainly try," says Ray,
and "I would too," says Holliday. As they leave the building together, the clerk
is removing their names from the divorce roster.

The Marrying Kind is a particularly intelligent depiction of a married couple
who are shattered by an unexpected blow, but who have enough commitment

... and through flashbacks the audience is returned to their wedding day to search for what went wrong.

to keep going. What is not stated, but can be inferred, is that a couple like Ray and Holliday, with limited means and limited futures, really need to hold on to each other, because this is all they have and all they will have in life. Viewers are asked to get little things into perspective, because this couple, who faced something terrible, have now survived. (If they can do it, you can, too!) This is the traditional role for both the marriage movie and the divorce movie: tell the audience to keep on going. "I do, and I don't, but I do"—that's the story of the American marriage movie.*

Sometimes an "I don't" marriage movie uses the flashback format (the doom mode), but stops the marriage, not with divorce but with death. *The Last Time I Saw Paris* (1954) is such a movie, and it is a dreary film. One of the reasons it's so dreary is that it presents an *almost* honest portrait of a malfunctioning marriage. The "almost" caveat is due to its essentially fake soul, the epitome of what most people think of as a bad Hollywood melodrama. It stars Van Johnson and an awesomely beautiful young Elizabeth Taylor as an unhappy couple trying to figure out what they want out of life (and marriage) in a post–World War II Paris scene. Based on the F. Scott Fitzgerald short story

---

* Movies often overtly articulate the need to fight for a good marriage. In *B.F.'s Daughter* (1948), for instance, an unhappy wife (Barbara Stanwyck) is lectured by her best friend (Margaret Lindsay) on the subject: "Marriage is an investment. It's easy to quit, but it's better to fight . . . Lots of marriages aren't the way they say in books . . . but still . . . they're worth fighting for." She was talking directly to the audience.

"Babylon Revisited," it has, underneath its oversimplified gloss, an honest set of bones. Fitzgerald, after all, knew Paris and knew marital disaster. The film version trades on cheap sentiment, and after killing off Taylor, quickly resolves such issues as Johnson's alcoholism and lack of success. Taylor dies because she forgot her house key—absentmindedness as a source of death.*

The Last Time I Saw Paris begins with Johnson, sober and successful, the author of a fine novel, as he returns to Paris from America to try to recover custody of his daughter (who apparently has not aged while he was away and who remembers him and everything they did together perfectly clearly). His sister-in-law, sternly played by Donna Reed, refuses to give him his child until her husband (George Dolenz) lectures her and she gives in.

Although the average filmgoer doesn't live in Paris, has not had an unexpected oil well come in, and probably can't identify with the high living onscreen, he *can* recognize two people who get out of sync with each other and don't know what to do about it. In particular, they can recognize the genuine self-loathing and anger put onscreen by Van Johnson in a scene in which he arrives home at eight a.m. after spending a night on the town with the glamorous Eva Gabor. He sneaks in, and as he climbs the stairs, he acts out both halves of a marital quarrel he hears in his head. He alternates between a mocking tone for himself and a nagging one for Taylor. He lets himself tell her, "I'm sick and tired of your sitting around those crummy cafés, day and night, the darling of every phony, petted by writers who don't write, adored by painters who don't paint." He hears her respond, "What do *you* write? Interviews with useless, sloppy women!" He criticizes her for jumping into fountains and "lapping up" all the liquor in Paris, but she counters with "Why don't you ask me *why* I drink, *why* I jump into fountains?" He concludes with "That's right— blame me, blame me." When he reaches their bedroom, and has worked himself into a rage, he sees his oblivious wife sound asleep in bed. He's ready to fight, and she doesn't even realize he's been out all night. Sleepily she sits up. "Morning, darling," she says.

Johnson's "argument" with himself spares an audience the actual argument, giving it a new performance twist and taking the worst sting out of it by mak-

---

* She arrives home in the wee hours after a night of partying, and there's a wet, soggy snow all over the ground. Standing outside in her blazingly red evening gown (with matching wrap), she pounds on the door to be let in, but Johnson has passed out drunk on the stairs inside. Forlorn and believing herself to be deliberately rejected, Taylor staggers off in the slush in her little red (also matching) high heels, contracting pneumonia the way one always does when one gets wet in the movies. (Movie rain and snow are lethal, and that's a fact.) Taylor dies, looking radiantly healthy, in a French hospital bed, while Johnson sobs at her side and they pledge their love for one another all over again.

ing it comic. However, it has delineated days and days of offscreen behavior for both main characters. She's carousing while he works, but his work is taking him nowhere. He's embarrassed by her behavior, but she has nothing else to do with herself. He's finally taken a leaf from her book and stayed out all night. She hasn't even noticed. This marriage may have all the glamour of Paris and the expatriate life, but it's recognizable by the smallest-town couple as doomed, really doomed.

What *The Last Time I Saw Paris* puts onscreen is hopeless, so much so that it is possible to believe that a deathbed reconciliation is the only kind that would work for this couple. They don't divorce each other—but only because one of them dies as another way out. The death relieves the pressure—and provides a form of reaffirmation through his sobriety and embrace of parenthood.

Both the "I do" and the "I don't" approach to the marriage movie tell the same story, of course: they are about failed dreams, hopes, and love. Both maintain the patterns of destroy-and-rebuild. Both are equally false, equally true. Box-office returns don't really endorse either mode. Between 1930 and 1966, very few of the twenty to twenty-five top-grossing movies could be labeled as being about marriage or divorce specifically and exclusively.* Lack of financial success in a big way, consistent over time, caused Hollywood to begin to make fewer and fewer marriage movies.†

The "I do" and "I don't" variations of the pure marriage movie worked, but they tied the leading man and woman down. Since the real bread-and-butter for the motion-picture business was always a romantic love story, it was inevitable that movies would be made that would find a way to play with marriage: to keep its available sex, and yet create a reason why a married couple couldn't have it. Not being allowed to have sex created the essential frisson of the romantic comedy: the leading man and woman dying to make love, but unable to do so. The movie could take a couple to the edge and let them hover there while the audience shared the excitement. (This is probably why the

---

* Among the good moneymakers: *Dodsworth* (1936), *Swing High, Swing Low* (1937), *The Women* (1939), *Woman of the Year* (1942), *Claudia* (1943), *Random Harvest* (1942), *Mr. Skeffington* (1944), *Without Love* (1945), *Life with Father* (1947), *Cass Timberlane* (1947), *When My Baby Smiles at Me* (1948), *Clash by Night* (1952), *Come Back, Little Sheba* (1952), *The Long, Long Trailer* (1953), *Ten North Frederick* (1958), *Please Don't Eat the Daisies* (1960), *Strangers When We Meet* (1960), *Midnight Lace* (1960), *Days of Wine and Roses* (1962), *The Thrill of It All* (1963), *What a Way to Go!* (1960), and *Send Me No Flowers* (1964).

† Numbers matter here. Hollywood made and/or released between five hundred and seven hundred features per year in the glory days of the studio system. We're talking relative numbers in comparison to other, more popular story forms: westerns, musicals, romantic comedies, etc.

"romcoms" of today don't work: there's no need for anyone *not* to have sex. It's a real screenwriting challenge.)

In most romantic comedies, the big question is: Would the boy really get the girl? Could he and she sort out their basic misunderstandings and make it to the altar? By working a clever variation on this question, a marriage movie *could* be turned into a variation on the romantic comedy. A story could be told in which a couple had *already* gone to the altar for some crazy reason— something unpredictable, catchy, funny. They were married . . . but not really. They could have sex . . . but not really. Creative screenwriters found two useful plot strategies for this: the "without love" marriage and the "Oops! We're not really married" variation. The resulting films are disguised romantic comedies, but they maintain the basic pattern of "affirm, question, reaffirm, and resolve" indigenous to the marriage movie, and thus confirm that the subject of marriage in the movies was defined cinematically in a specific way. A *Photoplay* review of the "without love" pretend-marriage movie *The Doctor Takes a Wife* (June 1940) imagined the story conference that thought up the idea: "We can have 'em married . . . and still *not* married . . . so the romance will keep."

The "without love" marriage sounds ridiculous, but it wasn't all that hard to sell. Lots of movie marriages are entered into for a dubious premise.* The "without love" scenario just had to come up with some credible reason—the need to escape, a cash reward, an inheritance, a misunderstanding, a voluntary substitution—for a couple to agree to marry. They would forge a bargain in which they would cohabit but not have sex because theirs would be strictly a business arrangement. (This is a subliminal form of divorce, an acceptable form in days in which divorce itself was socially unacceptable.) In *Hired Wife* (1940), Rosalind Russell marries her boss (Brian Aherne) to save him from a tax problem. In *The Lady Is Willing* (1942), obstetrician Fred MacMurray agrees to marry actress Marlene Dietrich so she can legally adopt a baby she finds on her way home one day (just lying out in the street, it seems). What does MacMurray get out of it? Financing for his laboratory experiments—plenty of equipment and lots of rabbits.†

---

* Men apparently are drawn to marrying women who are going to die soon (*Dark Victory* [1939], *Embraceable You* [1948], and *Invitation* [1952]), sometimes for financial gain, but mostly out of the goodness of their hearts, and only occasionally for love.

† "Without love" movies also include *Next Time I Marry* (1938), with Lucille Ball, and *I Married a Doctor* (1936) and *Rachel and the Stranger* (1948), both with Loretta Young. In *Honeymoon for Three* (1941), Ann Sheridan merely pretends to be her boss's (George Brent) wife so he can conduct his dalliances without consequence. (Sheridan will arrive at just the crucial moment to save him from the altar.) In *Pillow to Post* (1945), Ida Lupino is a traveling saleswoman who needs accommodations during wartime. Since there's a

What a "without love" marriage purported to do was give an audience their boy-meets-girl situation in a fresh way. Husband had to "meet" his wife under new circumstances: husband meets wife; husband gets wife, even though, strictly speaking, he'd already got her. What made such a concept interesting was that the main object of any courtship—marriage—was already accomplished. What had not been achieved was the fundamental accepted action of marriage: sex. Thus the "without love" marriage movie found a clever way to heighten the need for sex, increasing the audience's sense that it was available at any minute, just waiting to happen. (Hollywood's ability to inject sex into a frame in which no sex was allowed was always remarkable.) It also found a way for marriage to be romanticized.

The "without love" marriage movie was often disappointing because it was actually a romantic comedy under pressure. A classic example actually called *Without Love* (1945), starred Katharine Hepburn and Spencer Tracy. It was only the third pairing of the two, but they already were fully at ease in each other's company. The movie was based on a play by Philip Barry that Hepburn had done on the stage with Elliott Nugent as her leading man. On stage, the action was written to serve Hepburn's talents (Nugent wasn't her equal in star power). On film, however, the events skew toward Tracy, who had the larger box-office appeal of the two.* The film opens up on Tracy as he seeks a place to live and work in Washington, D.C., during the crowded wartime years. Tracy portrays a successful scientist—and Hepburn is the daughter of another. (Paging Dr. Freud!) In fact, Hepburn had met Tracy's own father "right here in my father's house" when she was a girl. Thus a connection is established for the couple: their fathers were respectful friends, companions, fellow scientists. This background legitimizes the reasons Hepburn and Tracy decide to marry. Others emerge: he needs a lab assistant in his work and she is experienced, and "there's a war on," which was a well-established motivation in World War II movies.

Without Love qualifies as a marriage movie because its main focus is on

---

housing shortage, people will only rent to servicemen and their wives, so she has to find a guy (William Prince) to pretend to be her husband. In *Guest Wife* (1945), Dick Foran lends his wife (Claudette Colbert) to his best friend (Don Ameche) because Ameche's boss requires his employees to be married. The oddball "without love" format is still with us: consider Sandra Bullock's box-office smash *The Proposal* (2009), in which a tough boss (Bullock) hires one of her employees (Ryan Reynolds) to marry her so she can get her visa renewed.

* Tracy appeared on the lists of top ten box-office draws every year from 1938 to 1942, reappearing in 1944, 1945, 1946, 1948, 1950, and 1951. Hepburn never appeared on such lists at all during the golden age of Hollywood; her first appearance was in 1969.

questions about marriage: why one marries; if one should remarry when widowed; what makes a good marriage; how couples can work together; who makes a good marriage partner. (It answers none of those questions.) An audience is presented with a relatively appalling series of events that suggest that as long as you're not in love with your mate, you'll be fine. Hollywood apparently couldn't easily reconcile love and marriage.

Neither Tracy's nor Hepburn's character wants love, but for very different reasons. Hepburn's character has, according to her friends, not cracked a smile in years. Although she was once married, her husband is dead. She spends most of her time in the country. She lives alone, eats alone, rides alone, and, naturally, sleeps alone. Tracy is a scientist focused on science. He only trusts "facts." He doesn't want love because it's "a sickness." He fell in love once, but she was "bright and gay and shallow . . . lived for parties . . . a witch on a broom." He describes their relationship as a "supremely joyless affair."

Tracy has had the worst of it, and it's made indirectly clear that he knows it was his sexual attraction to "Lila"—which still exists—that turned his otherwise sensible life upside down. He met Lila in Paris, and there is a subtle hint that staying away from that city might be a good plan for people who want to keep their feet on the ground. Hepburn's marriage, on the other hand, is right out of a romance novel—and just as false. She was twenty, and he was twenty-two. "He was everything," she says, and for two years ("but a lifetime, really") they lived an idyllic marriage. At least that's how she remembers it. Ever since he was thrown by his horse and killed, she has deified his memory.

The first inexplicable thing that happens is the marriage itself. Hepburn announces she's been "thinking" and proposes to Tracy. He looks suitably dubious, but she explains that there must be "another basis to a good and happy marriage besides love." Ever the practical scientist, he asks bluntly, "And what would that be?" Her response is eloquent: "Things shared in common. Honesty, say, and courage and . . . humor . . . free of the jealousy, the possessiveness, the misery, the exacting, the demanding . . . You'd have companionship . . . and the independence you prize . . . and you could *work*. We could both work." She will assist him as he tries to invent the oxygen mask that will "win the war."

Tracy's opinion? "It would never work." But when he hears Lila is in town, he accepts Hepburn's offer, thus blowing his credibility as a clear-thinking scientist. (He also sleepwalks and plays "Clair de lune" on the piano late at night.) After they make their deal and shake hands on it, Hepburn says, "There's just one thing, though . . . I could never . . . never—." Tracy cuts her off: "Madam. You would never have to give that a thought." Thus, the issue of sex is clarified for the viewer. And in case we doubted them, we have to suffer through a

The "without love" variation of the marriage movie is represented by a film appropriately titled *Without Love*, starring Spencer Tracy and Katharine Hepburn as a married couple facing up to the rules of their decision.

sequence in which Tracy sleepwalks into Hepburn's bedroom and climbs into her bed while she is off getting her hot water bottle ready for the night. We watch her throw him out. (The movie doesn't trust the audience to believe they actually wouldn't have sex, so it makes sure we *see* them not have it. Obviously, Hollywood understood its audience: who could, indeed, really believe in this concept?)

Although it has attempted to deny marriage and reconstitute itself as a boy-gets-girl romantic comedy, *Without Love* puts an audience through the wringer. Suddenly (but not suddenly enough) it all goes south when a sophisticated European male (Carl Esmond) arrives on the scene. Such men in movies were either capons (Erik Rhodes in *The Gay Divorcee*, 1934), initiators into the pleasures of sex (Rossano Brazzi in *Summertime*, 1955), evil seducers (Vittorio Gassman in *War and Peace*, 1956), or men like this one, whose purpose is strictly plot motivation. When Hepburn and Tracy visit her Virginia country home, Esmond turns up in the neighborhood. Soon he and Hepburn are out buggy riding, reciting T. S. Eliot to each other ("April is the cruellest month"). In most movies, it's a rule that shortly after people start quoting poetry, something ghastly is going to happen. In *Without Love*, it's simple and predictable: Esmond kisses Hepburn, awakening her sexually.

Unfortunately for him, Hepburn's awakening is not aimed in his direction but in Tracy's. When she realizes she loves him and tries to stir him alive, everything goes wrong between them. (She tries poetry on him, once again reciting T. S. Eliot, which the movie obviously believes inspires men to kiss with abandon. Alas, Tracy is immune.) The desire to be a romantic comedy, to deny marriage while showing an ideally paired "married" couple, has gone out of control. Here we have the news this movie delivers: theirs was a perfect marriage as long as they weren't in love; as long as they were emotionally disconnected.

The conclusion seeks, as Hollywood films so often do, to refute this message. Hepburn dresses up as Lila (whom the audience has never seen but has heard way too much about) and romps about the room in feathers, waving a cigarette holder. (Hepburn has trouble being honestly silly in an exaggerated female way without indicating she doesn't believe in her own performance.) She can't clarify whether she is mocking Lila or trying to *be* Lila, and Tracy appears as confused as the audience. The only way to reconnect to "audience values" is to go where audiences will always go: to sex as a solution. Once again, Tracy walks in his sleep.

While trying to find a clever and appealing new way to tell a marriage story, *Without Love* accidentally undermines the idea of marriage and unfortunately doesn't do much for "love," either. As long as there is no jealousy, no rivalry, no competition, no family, no children—and, of course, no sex—a "marriage" is heaven. Add in anything human, turn the relationship away from professionalism to passion, and there is no possibility of it working. That is what we *see* onscreen, and the movie relies on a sleepwalking gimmick to change that fact.

One of the more curious strategies of the marriage movie that tries not to be a marriage movie is the plot in which the couple are "divorced" by accident of fate. All of a sudden, two people find out they're not really married. Oops! These stories don't care much about the why: the judge was an impostor, the documents were never filed, or the ceremony took place in Mexico—where, in film terms, nothing can be eaten, digested, or trusted, and even if you manage to get back across the border alive, whatever you brought out will immediately break down on you. The only "why" of the "oops" plot that matters is the one in which the couple ask themselves the traditional questions of the marriage movie: Why are we still married? Do we really want to be? And what has happened to us? This "oops" variation is a freebie escape, or yet another safe form of divorce, even though the titillating "we've been living in sin" issue automatically dictates a finale of remarriage. Nevertheless, the issues of what is wrong with marriage are laid comfortably bare.

"We're not married" plots are almost always comedies. (Censorship issues made it necessary for Hollywood to deflect any serious discussions of sex without benefit of clergy. This worked best in a comic bedroom farce.) Films that used the "we're not married" plot included Alfred Hitchcock's 1941 *Mr. and Mrs. Smith,* with Carole Lombard and Robert Montgomery, and 1951's *Let's Make It Legal,* with Claudette Colbert and Macdonald Carey; but one that neatly sums up all the issues is cleverly called *We're Not Married.*

We're Not Married (1952) has a simple, jaunty format: five couples receive a letter stating the facts. Victor Moore, playing a slightly fuddled example of nepotism, interpreted his becoming a justice of the peace to mean that he could start marrying people as soon as he got the letter appointing him. From Christmas Eve to his official starting date of New Year's Day, he jumped the gun and married six couples with the dithering support of his equally silly wife (Jane Darwell). Two years and six months later, his error has been discovered. Why? Well, what else? One of the six couples has decided to get divorced. Adopting a "let's keep this simple and low-key" attitude, the state merely mails out a form letter to the other five couples, informing them, "We are compelled to tell you that you are not married."

"We're not married!" each of the couples cries out. Yes indeed. And then the five stories are told:

• Ginger Rogers and Fred Allen married only for career reasons. Theirs is a "without love" marriage, an arrangement that allowed them to snag a successful radio show called *Breakfast with the Glad Gladwyns,* because if they weren't married, they wouldn't be hired. Two years later, they're rich and successful, pretending not only to be married but also to have a three-year-old daughter. They chatter happily away on the air, never speaking to each other otherwise. Their relationship is nothing but a series of product placements disguised as a real-life marital conversation.

• David Wayne and Marilyn Monroe have a real baby, but no real domestic life. Wayne cooks, babysits, and waits for Monroe as she pursues the Mrs. Mississippi beauty-queen title. Monroe, not yet the name star she would become within months, parades on runways while Wayne, clutching the kid, stands by and watches.

• Paul Douglas and Eve Arden, remembered as a couple who were "talking incessantly" as they wed, are now well-to-do Long Island

Oops! *We're Not Married* is the news for five couples two and a half years after their wedding day. For Ginger Rogers and Fred Allen, who united only to snag a job as a married couple on radio, it's pretty much "who cares?" . . .

. . . but Marilyn Monroe and David Wayne (with James Gleason) shift her out of the *Mrs.* America pageant into the *Miss* America contest, while he tends to the baby either way . . .

. . . Eve Arden and Paul Douglas stopped communicating years ago so why discuss anything now . . .

. . . but Zsa Zsa Gabor, who was trying to divorce Louis Calhern for his money, gets a rude shock . . .

. . . and Mitzi Gaynor and Eddie Bracken (with Harry Harvey) face a real crisis: she's pregnant and he's shipping out the next day . . . the race is on to correct their problem with a hasty re-wedding.

suburbanites who neither speak directly to each other nor bother to listen if the other should speak. "The Book-of-the-Month Club came today" is the biggest news they share.

• Zsa Zsa Gabor and Louis Calhern live in Dallas. He's a rich oil man; she's a young and nubile beauty who hoodwinked him into marriage. She has just set him up in a "love nest" with another woman so she can sue him for divorce and take him to the cleaners financially.

• Eddie Bracken is a professional soldier; his wife, Mitzi Gaynor, is newly pregnant. He's just learned he's shipping out immediately, so theirs is a time-pressure dilemma.

Taken as a whole, these five little plots illustrate five marriage problems: the "without love" marriage; the career role reversal involving control; the death of communication and onset of marital boredom; the money matter; and, of course, what happens when you have sex. These mini-plots are almost akin to the old silent two-reelers in which marriage is lampooned.

In *We're Not Married*, four of the five "oops" marriages are happily resolved. Allen and Rogers just remarry—after all, what difference does it make? Monroe shifts out of the Mrs. Mississippi pageant into the Miss Mississippi pageant—a career upgrade for her—and Wayne still stands by with the kid. Douglas thinks about his possible new freedom, but realizes it would cost him a fortune if he started dating again. He burns the letter. Gaynor and Bracken, with the help of the United States Army, manage to get remarried in time to give their kid a name before Dad's ship sails. Only Gabor and Calhern join the actual ranks of the divorced. Taking advantage of the "oops" factor, Calhern tells Gabor at the very last minute that she's out of luck because "we're not married," and now that he's learned the truth about her, they never will be. Looking at the statistics of the film, two of the original six couples ended up divorced—or about one in three, which was the national average at the time.

Hollywood probably thought that many couples in the audience would welcome a letter from Victor Moore, because the "oops" movie was popular. It was the Great Escape. Audiences apparently liked to see a couple split up for no reason of their own, a hand-of-fate divorce. Clearly, judging by the box office, audiences were responsive to (as well as curious about) what getting out of marriage might mean. It was an attractive idea—wake up one morning and a letter from someone you don't know tells you that you're free. Hollywood was happy enough to learn that audiences might like divorce better than they liked marriage. Many people in Hollywood, after all, felt the same way.

Another interesting strategy for presenting a pure (or honest) form of marriage was used when the subject was moved off-center and out of the spotlight. It was an excellent supporting player. As such, it usually had a character actor's schtick: it was wacky (Ma and Pa Kettle); it was idealized (the Hardys) or glamorized (Nick and Nora Charles). Hollywood played with marriage, dropping it into the mix here and there for a laugh or a heart tug or a warning. Keeping marriage on the screen as a secondary player kept it familiar, kept it fresh, kept it as a touchstone—but also kept it at a distance. As any typical movie story progressed, a marriage of some sort—usually hideous—might pop up, like a little yoo-hoo to the audience, a sort of visual drive-by. These "drive-by" marriages are a way of acknowledging the condition without either dealing with it fully or treating it as an idyllic state. Such scenes are escape valves and act as reminders of reality for audiences. The fact that these scenes are often brutally honest indicates that *they* were the marriage stories that Hollywood understood. In fact, when it came to showing what *didn't* work—and making it funny—Hollywood knew how to get it right and almost always did so from the very beginning.

These little marriage reminders often appear in screwball comedies, and almost always present a short vignette of a quarreling couple. For instance, in *It Happened One Night* (1934), Claudette Colbert and Clark Gable, two relatively unacquainted characters from completely different backgrounds, can easily, hilariously fall into an improvisation of a "typical" married couple at a motor court. Colbert and Gable come from opposite ends of the social scale, but they both know what a bad marriage looks and sounds like. She whines and cries and accuses. He snarls and complains and threatens. Inside the romance of *It Happened One Night* lies a cruel but amusing glimpse of what "happily ever after" could bring.

In *The Awful Truth* (1937), Irene Dunne discovers her husband (Cary Grant) has lied to her about going on a business trip to Florida. The implication is that he stayed around the city, having a high old time, and resorted to lying under a suntan lamp for his alibi before going home with a load of oranges (which turn out to be from California). Dunne has already found out "the awful truth," and she lays a trap for him. They quarrel, and she decides to divorce him, immediately calling her lawyer. The audience is shown this well-dressed, older man in his lavish home as he speaks to Dunne on the phone. He takes a condescending tone to what he obviously sees as "the little woman" in one of her "female" moods, and tries to jolly her out of her plan for divorce. He speaks slowly, as if she isn't very bright: "Now, now, my dear." As he speaks, his own wife appears in the background. A somewhat Wagnerian figure, she is neither beautiful nor chic, and she is clearly angry at him. She interrupts the call to tell him to come to dinner. He pays absolutely no attention to her. "As I was saying, Lucy," he tells Dunne, his tone highly conciliatory, "marriage is a beautiful thing, and when you've been married as long as I have, you'll appreciate it, too." His wife has, in her turn, also paid no attention to him, carrying right on with "Your food is getting ice cold. You're always complaining about your food. How do you expect me—?" The lawyer interrupts her, very angry, covering the phone so Dunne cannot hear: "Will you shut your big mouth? I'll eat when I get good and ready, and if you don't like it, you know what you can do! So *shut up!*" Then he turns back to the telephone, his voice once again patient, soothing, gently reassuring. "Lucy, darling. Marriage is a beautiful thing." The film immediately cuts to a divorce court.

In the multiple-character story *Dinner at Eight* (1933), Jean Harlow and Wallace Beery have a great scream-out in her boudoir ("You big lug!" "Oh, yeah?"). He's old and overweight, and she's young and greedy. The only thing they have in common is their vulgarity. She married him for money, and he married her for sex, and they both know it. They are hilarious, and deeply frightening. They are, however, supremely united in their social climb. When they realize the proposed dinner invitation has something for both to gain, they suit up together. Beery puts on the Ritz with his tuxedo and top hat, and Harlow breaks out her backless lamé and white furs. They soldier forward like the couple they are not, because the "dinner at eight" gives him the business connection he wants and puts her silver slipper in the social door. They sweep into Billie Burke's dinner party in a dubiously united marital front, ready to do battle together if they have to. There's a naked honesty in their unified purpose.

Perhaps the most perfect example of the short little "yoo-hoo" marriage is the famous breakfast-table sequence in *Citizen Kane* (1941). In a brief six minutes, Charles Foster Kane and his beautiful society bride, Emily, enact a full marriage story from start to finish, and it's one any audience can recognize. As Joseph Cotten narrates in left-screen foreground, the nursing home he lives in fades out, to be replaced by a deep-focus image of the youthful and happy Kanes. Cotten says, "After the first couple of months, she and Charlie didn't see much of each other . . . except at breakfast. It was a marriage just like any other marriage."

The story of this "marriage just like any other marriage" then advances in six scenes across time through the use of swish pans. It begins with the young Kanes in lavish evening clothes, just coming home from a ball. Charles Kane is resplendent in tuxedo, and Emily softly feminine in a shoulderless gown, graciously pouring tea. He is her "waiter," bringing her a little dish of something, grandly sweeping a napkin over his arm, stooping to plant a loving kiss on her head and then sitting down within touching distance beside her. Obviously young and deeply in love, they cannot take their eyes off each other. They murmur, their dialogue overlapping in unison, mingled in their eagerness to tell each other what they are thinking and feeling. She's saying she's never stayed up this late, and he's telling her, "You're beautiful . . . you're very, very beautiful." As she begins to make little protests to deny his compliments, he continues to reiterate how beautiful she is. She says, about the lateness of the hour, "I don't know what the servants will think." He replies, "They'll think we enjoyed ourselves. Didn't we?" She responds with sweet petulance, "I don't see why you have to go straight to the newspaper," and he admonishes her with "You should never have married a newspaperman. They're worse than sailors . . . I absolutely adore you." Looking truly lovely, her bare shoulders reflecting candlelight, she delicately introduces the topic of bed: "Charles, even newspapermen have to sleep." Easily persuaded, and looking totally smitten, he says, "I'll call Mr. Bernstein and have him put off my appointments until noon." She smiles. "What time is it?" he asks. "Why, I don't know," she replies. "It's late." Grinning somewhat lasciviously, he says, "It's early," and leans in close to her. All audiences can read this charming love scene correctly.

However, a swish pan suddenly takes the viewer rapidly forward in time to a different view. Mrs. Kane is now wearing a negligee and speaking from her end of the table in a bored, rather arch tone with which she clearly means to spank her husband in a correctly wifelike manner: "Charles, do you know how long you kept me waiting last night while you went to the newspaper for ten minutes? What do you do at a newspaper in the middle of the night?" In a glamorous dressing gown, lighting his pipe at his end of their long table, Kane sardonically replies, "Emily, my dear, your only co-respondent is the *Inquirer*."

The next swish moves ahead to Mrs. Kane looking peeved, dressed primly for the day. Her tone is clearly disapproving: "Sometimes I think I'd prefer a rival of flesh and blood." Mr. Kane has obviously heard this before and doesn't care, concentrating on his breakfast. "Emily, I don't spend *that* much time on the newspaper." (A few brief lines of dialogue then lay out what is obviously a familiar morning quarrel over politics.)

Swish again, and this time Mrs. Kane is haughty, superior, and condescending. There's real coldness in her as she tells her husband, "Mr. Bernstein sent Junior a most incredible atrocity yesterday, Charles. I simply can't have it in the nursery." Her spouse is controlled but angry: "Mr. Bernstein is apt to pay a visit to the nursery now and then." "Does he have to?" "Yes." It's firm and it's grim.

The next swish has her saying, "Really, Charles, people will think—" He cuts her right off, no longer interested in anything she says or feels: "—what I tell them to think!"

In the last swish to the final scene in the story of their marriage, Mrs. Kane is seen pointedly reading the rival newspaper, the *Chronicle*, looking up to see if Mr. Kane notices. He glances up from his *Inquirer* but doesn't care. He ignores her, engrossed in his own world and his own ideas.

As the Kanes fade out of the image and are replaced by the nursing home once again, the film's narrator asks Cotten: "Wasn't he in love with her?" Cotten responds simply, "He *married* for love."

Each of the six swish pans moves Charles and Emily Kane forward in time to show how a change has taken place in their marriage: a growth in animosity and a diminishment in communication. The table grows longer, so they sit at greater distance; instead of being together in the same frame, they are cut apart. Their attitudes sharpen, their naturalness disappears, and their attire indicates they no longer sleep together. She becomes more formal with him, and he becomes ruder to her. The story of their marriage from start to finish is depicted through the cinematic use of swish pans, settings, lighting, costuming, performance, and dialogue. The issues for this kind of marital problem are clearly demonstrated: his dedication to work, her stuffiness, and their different backgrounds (she is from high society, he is nouveau riche).

Citizen Kane is not a marriage movie, but if its breakfast-table sequence were expanded, with all the gaps between swishes filled in, it *would* be, because its goal is to tell the story of the marriage between Charles and Emily Kane. It certainly asks, "What happened to the Kanes?" Welles and his filmmaking team knew their little marriage would be fully understood by an audience that was living between the gaps. It is a full marriage movie miniaturized: affirm and destroy, but don't reassemble.

Another short vignette, not unlike the breakfast scene in *Citizen Kane*, occurs as the climax of *The Lady Eve*. Henry Fonda plays a hapless groom who, on his wedding night, is forced to listen to his con-woman bride (Barbara Stanwyck, posing as "Lady Eve") suddenly reveal her former life of lovers, husbands, and various amorous adventures. Under the skillful writing and direction of Preston Sturges, the "story" plays out through an extended montage of the speeding honeymoon train, screeching train whistles, whirling train wheels, Fonda's appalled face, and Stanwyck's nonstop verbalization (never heard by the audience). Clackity-clack, clackity-clack. An audience watches the disintegration of a marriage unfold in quick time, as Fonda is observed moving from a mood of blissful romance and sexual anticipation toward the inevitable finale of a bad marriage: disillusionment, disappointment, and the grasping of the knowledge that the person you wed with such optimism is not who you thought she was. It's hilarious and horrible, a combination of elements often seen in marriage movies, and it's also efficient.

The marriage vignette as a background to a larger story is not always comic. Movies that directly address other issues often contain honest small portraits of marriages. In *Watch on the Rhine* (1943), based on Lillian Hellman's successful play, Bette Davis and Paul Lukas play a devoted couple who have faced the horrors of Nazism and the oncoming war in Europe. In the movie version (for which Lukas won 1943's Best Actor Oscar), their relationship palpitates in every frame. Davis, once a wealthy Washington, D.C., young lady, now knows what hardship is in every definition of the term, but she has never questioned her choice in marriage, never doubted her husband's nobility, and never let him down when he needed her to sacrifice. For his part, he is grateful, and values her character. They work in perfect unison. Every look they exchange speaks volumes. Davis's loyalty and devotion to her husband are heartbreaking. (Those who think she could only play a strident diva should look at this low-key performance, in which she totally harnesses her star power to serve Lukas. A lot of his Oscar was due to her cooperative performance.) Theirs is a model movie marriage in a time of international stress.

A lifetime of complications and commitments is expressed simply through one final scene between Ida Lupino and Robert Preston in *Junior Bonner* (1972). The movie is far from a marriage film—it's a modern story of a former rodeo champion played by Steve McQueen; Lupino and Preston, two pros, no longer young but each with a lifetime of show-biz experience, enact his separated parents and reveal in brief form the story of their marriage. Just before Preston leaves for Australia ("This time I'm really going"), he and Lupino have their final argument/love scene. "That's all you are," she says, "just dreams and sweet talk." After he asks her if she remembers the sweet dreams he used to give her, she slaps him . . . hard. He ruefully admits he had it coming. After a long pause, she says that if he's going, it'll be their last time together, and then, after stroking his reddened cheek, she leads him upstairs. The scene represents the inexplicable nature of what happens between a man and a woman, why they can't stay together, why they have to stay together, and why they don't stay together. In a subtle tour de force of acting power, Lupino and Preston convey what's underneath their relationship, the years of fighting, disappointing each other, and disagreeing with one another, yet still loving each other and caring about the children they've raised.

The vignette is often the best "marriage film," because it can contain both love and hate, success and failure, and move on without any need for detailed explanation. The dark shadow of a bad marriage hangs in the background of *The Wings of Eagles* (1957), a movie that tries to ignore—or even deny—its disappointment. *Eagles* is an exuberant tale based on the life of screenwriter Spig Wead, a World War I aviation ace. (After an accident left him partially paralyzed, Wead became a writer.) John Wayne plays Wead, and his longtime co-star Maureen O'Hara is his wife. As the movie unfolds, moving from a hijinks military comedy into a darker tale of a man who loses direction, their marriage also moves into troubled times. In the background to the story of the military, war, rehab, and Hollywood lies the Weads' courtship, early years, and family life. Bad things lurk in the marriage beneath the surface. Their jolly times are too drunken. Her protests about his neglect of his family are too angry. His fun away from her is too liberated. Their ultimate separation comes as no surprise, even though what caused it is never fully delineated and isn't the main thrust of the story.

Sometimes much information about a marriage is presented in something even smaller than a vignette. There are moments of an almost sublime visual eloquence about marital frustration in simple gestures. One of John Ford's best Cavalry films, *Rio Grande* (1950), stars Wayne and O'Hara as an estranged couple. Their relationship collapsed in the Civil War when he, a Union officer, was ordered to burn her family's southern plantation. Years have passed, but now their son has flunked out of West Point and turned up in his cavalry troop out west. O'Hara, highborn, with a view toward privilege and rank, has come to buy the boy out of service. Wayne, hard-core military and duty bound, says his son enlisted to serve and serve he will. (It's a variation of the Civil War drama idea of brother against brother: wife against husband.)

From the moment O'Hara arrives in camp, the physical pull between the couple hovers in the air. As they eat dinner by candlelight, listening to the howls of wolves, it's palpable, almost tactile. But the perfect gesture of marital frustration comes when they are not together—when Wayne and his men are on patrol beside the Rio Grande. As the light wanes, and the frame slowly darkens, Wayne walks alone down by the river. His regimental troops, sitting around a campfire, begin to sing: "My gal is purple . . . I know deep inside me she's the fairest of the fair . . . Tears get in my eyes when the purple shadows die." The odd lyrics, their poetic quality that conjures an image of a woman lost, left behind as purple darkness falls, cause the lonely Wayne to strike his cavalry hat against his thigh—one simple gesture that says it all. He loves her. He wants her. She loves him. She wants him. They both care about their son. Why can't it work out for them? Why are things so difficult? It's "What happened to us, Johnny?"—but this time with no words, only the frustrated slap of a cavalry hat.

The marriage on film—vignette or feature-length—visually focused on the same components. Because the audience knew all about the subject, these were simple and basic. Only three story elements were necessary: the couple, their problems, and their situation.

The Couple

Playing the Czarina Alexandra in *Rasputin and the Empress* (1932), Ethel Barrymore lovingly pats the hand of her mate, Czar Nicholas, and says, "I know you love me, Nicky, and that's all any empress could want." Nicholas and Alexandra are married, so hand patting and comforting words are appropriate. Whether it's rubies or rhinestones, palaces or apartments, married couples in the movies share a bottom line: they are the two main characters who validate the wedded state: a husband and a wife. The presentation of a believable *couple* was crucial to the marriage movie. Even if they're a czar and a czarina, they are expected to behave a certain way. Thus, after Alexandra and "Nicky" attend a spectacular religious ceremony blessing their son, replete with choral music, candles, incense, cavernous cathedral, and enraptured courtiers, Alexandra will enter their private quarters, sigh deeply, pull off her elaborate and heavy tiara, plop down on an embroidered sofa, and instruct Nicholas to sit beside her. She will pat his hand and reassure him, because she's more than a czarina: she's half of a couple, a movie wife. What's the difference between a czar and czarina returning from a state event and Blondie and Dagwood coming home after a dinner party at the boss's house? Nothing. They're married. Both have had to get dressed up to fulfill an obligation, and it is a duty directly related to the fact that they're married. A wife has had to accompany the husband in the duties of his job. That's *her* duty. A couple share their obligations, which weary them—but never mind, it's all any empress could want. She and the czar are married. Husbands and wives who behave in expected ways are the first required element in making a marriage movie.

The basic, most familiar idea that a married couple presents—at least initially, before the plot troubles arrive—is that of a comfortable union, one in which two people can work together smoothly because they know each other's rhythms. Significantly, the married couple is in contrast to the romantic couple. They dance to different tunes. The American romantic couple are locked in combat, battling each other until the inevitable occurs and they fall in love. (American movies traditionally tell audiences that if you meet an individual you absolutely cannot stand—someone you truly hope never to see again as long as you live—you've just met your life's partner.) The married couple, on the other hand, are low-key, probably bored, and if they have anything much to say to each other, it'll be offhand and irrelevant. In some variations, they'll be supremely simpatico, but that's not going to last. And in other variations, they are totally at odds, but that's not going to last, either. Marriage is an untenable plot position. What is true is that the movies present courtship as a battlefield and marriage as a field of dead bodies after the war is won.

Onscreen, "attracted" and "in love" are to be read as tension—something moving and dangerous. "Married" is to be read as something settled, preferably in a chair covered in chintz—that is, until the marriage has to become unglued and start moving somewhere. Married couples cannot easily maintain a status quo. The surface reason is easy: there has to be something happening in the plot. Underneath the surface is the implication that the couple are representing the battle of the sexes, and the way they behave toward each other will connect directly to any audience's sense of what a couple is supposed to be, actually is, and might ideally be turned into. "Couples" taught romance, marital behavior, and cultural standards. They were teachers in the classroom of marriage.

Romantic hostility—married or unmarried—was smart screenwriting. It created two things: a plot problem to be resolved and an antagonism that could represent sexual chemistry. It was a way to bring tangible energy to a romance that was being viewed in a flat, two-dimensional format. Audiences could hear, see, and understand the energetic war between a couple, and understand that what was going on between them was more than an argument. Arguing made an abstract concept (sexual attraction) concrete. The challenge to generate a tangible love between two people who were wed (and also for those just falling in love) was solved with two main devices: screenwriting and casting. Screenwriting constituted dialogue between two members of a romantic couple as clever banter; the married couple's variation was bickering. Casting was used carefully to select two stars who seemed to be sympathetically *wed*.

Bickering was an American Olympic sport for married people in the movies. How to write these arguments without losing audience sympathy for one or both characters was a challenge. Bickering is one thing in a romantic comedy. It provides a frisson, the censor's prudent presentation of sexual attraction. It can be made charming, witty, and alive with sexual possibilities. Bickering in marriage has no charm, no sex, no fun to it, because it has no place to go. It can't be translated into anything new, into anything the couple hasn't already experienced. When a couple are trying to get *into* love and marriage, bickering works. When they are already in it, bickering is a trap. Writers had to find a way to make it work.

In Joseph Mankiewicz's classic film about three marriages with problems, *A Letter to Three Wives* (1949), the excellent screenplay uses different types and levels of bickering that provide variety, further define the characters, and keep the audience from hating the situations. There are three distinctly different couples, with different economic situations, different backgrounds, and different levels of love and camaraderie, but they have one thing in common: they bicker. Jeanne Crain and Jeffrey Lynn are lowest on the bicker scale, playing two young people who married during World War II without having met each other's families. Back home, out of uniform and badly dressed, Crain feels uncomfortable among Lynn's fashionable friends. She and Lynn bicker gently, creating a low rumble beneath their song of love. Low, but definite—especially when his chic former love arrives back in town. Their bickering is inept, insincere; it has no verbal bite. They are amateurs who love each other so much they can't figure out how to really insult each other.

Linda Darnell and Paul Douglas—an inspired pairing—are wealthy. She used to live in a railroad shack, and he's the self-made owner of a big department store. Now that she's bagged him and is safely ensconced in his mansion, he feels used and she feels neglected. They bicker cruelly in a manner that suits their essentially lower-class ability to fight for survival, no holds barred. They're mean and desperate, throwing daggers at each other. Bickering—and its resolution—becomes the definition of both their love and their anger.

Kirk Douglas and Ann Sothern are a sophisticated, well-educated couple, parents of twins. He's a professor and she's a successful writer of radio soap operas, but her career is interfering with their home life. They bicker at a very high level, dueling quipsters armed with words to kill. Their fight has an edge to it, and it's out on the surface, but it's the verbiage of people who use words effectively to make their living. It's not as much emotion as it is one-upmanship.

"Bicker" was a language all Americans spoke. Any movie married people who did not bicker had limited screen time as a couple. One of them was going to die very, very soon, or be shoved aside while the other invented something useful . . . or a catastrophe was going to hit them both hard, like World War II, a spaceship, or another woman. The nonbickering couple was going to lose its status of bliss. Either that or they were, in the first place, a secondary unit of character actors, such as Judge Hardy and his wife. (And the Hardys actually bicker a bit: just a little bit, but a bit.)

The marriage movie is an arena of conflict. The compatibility of most couples is temporary. Couples who remain compatible are usually those who work together successfully, or ones in which the wife takes a secondary position in support of the man. Happily wed couples who do not have a problem with each

Married couples always
have to bicker: Jeffrey Lynn
and Jeanne Crain over
cocktails . . .

. . . Linda Darnell and Paul
Douglas by the piano . . .

. . . and Kirk
Douglas and Ann
Sothern in their
cozy living room—
all facing the issue
of *A Letter to Three
Wives*. Someone
ran off with one
of their husbands.
Who's the loser?

other usually turn up in movies not focused on marriage, and they turn up in unlikely places. Tarzan's jungle, for instance.* Tarzan and Jane are happily, harmoniously living together, and they are a picture of domestic bliss whether swinging through the forest on vines, romping with Boy and some cuddly lion cubs, or swimming naked in their pool. They don't argue or bicker, because each knows his own territory, each respects the other's skills, and they don't get in each other's way. Tarzan is king of the jungle; Jane is queen of their tree hut. Tarzan knows the laws of survival in a world of beasts; Jane knows the laws of survival in the world of humans. They pool their experience and add up to a perfect union. Tarzan and Jane have a perfect marriage—but, of course, they're not really married, are they? And certainly the *Tarzan* series is not a group of marriage movies.

In thinking about the couple as one of the three primary components of the marriage movie, the simple definition of a married couple is that they *are* husband and wife. For the movies, though, they also need to be something more metaphoric or emblematic. They needed to suggest union, and they need to represent an embodiment—possibly perfect—of their concepts: the Perfect Wife, the Perfect Husband. And they might also be instructional, representing what one should correctly *want* in a mate. If they could be *more* than just the sum of their parts, they could transcend their story and give it purpose as well as entertainment value. They also would not necessarily have to be *only* a husband and wife. Movies could suggest "coupling" to audiences in ways that implied union/marriage without the two characters being the simple definition of Mr. and Mrs. Two people in sync could be a couple and thus a marriage of sorts. Audiences could read "marriage" into unions whenever they saw or felt something they recognized as real.

Perhaps the most lifelike movie example of a real married couple's relationship is . . . surprise! Laurel and Hardy. They bicker, they disagree, they snipe, they challenge, and they yell, but if any outside threat arrives in their world, they instantly pull together. In their hearts they each know they've found the perfect other. The subtext of Laurel and Hardy is that of "married couple," not homoerotic lovers. They are in sync, and they share common attitudes. They can come together in unified action to achieve a goal without any debate. They communicate with each other directly, specifically, in that manner all married couples have: "Let's get out of here, I'm bored to death" is a little raised eyebrow. "Let's go home and watch TV" is a nod toward the doorway, "Let's

---

* Another outside-the-four-walls-of-conventionality marriage is one that appears in *Apache*, a 1954 western starring Burt Lancaster as a wild Native American who is domesticated by a willing squaw played by Jean Peters.

The happy jungle family: Tarzan, Jane, and Boy (Johnny Sheffield, Johnny Weissmuller, and Maureen O'Sullivan), their table set for lunch . . .

pretend we think this roast beef isn't shoe leather," the subtle placement of the knife on the dinner plate. In the case of Laurel and Hardy, the communication is simple: a nonverbal stare means "Let's destroy." And destroy they do, in a quiet ballet of mutual focus and rhythm. They can wreck the hall and go home happy. A little dance they amble into in *Way Out West* (1937) shows how perfectly wed they are. Arriving in town, dirty and dusty, their burro loaded with junk, Laurel and Hardy walk up to the porch of a saloon/hotel. A group of laid-back cowboys are casually singing and playing their instruments, giving off a tuneful and rhythmic little number, all about "take your partner and hold her . . . Commence a-dancin'. Commence a-prancin' . . . " It's catchy, and it catches Laurel and Hardy. They give it their attention, standing for a moment, listening. They then launch into an impromptu dance routine that's a true gem. At first, they move slowly, just bending their knees a bit, each tappin' a foot, Hardy tipping his hat forward at a jaunty angle. Then they begin to groove a bit more, daintily stepping, flapping their jackets, all in perfect unison and perfect time to the music. Then, confident of each other, they "commence a-prancin'." They get down, escalating the intricacy of their steps, finally grasping hands and really letting go. They know each other's moves, and barely make eye contact. In complete sync, Laurel and Hardy execute a little dance improv that shows a perfectly unified couple.

Laurel and Hardy *are* a married couple, without the marriage. The popular male comedy duos found in movies, in fact, are definitely an example of

... and the Tarzans at home: Mr. and Mrs., Junior, and the inestimable Cheetah, family retainer

pseudo-married couples. Like Laurel and Hardy, Bing Crosby and Bob Hope are always grousing at each other but can exchange a look and turn themselves instantly into a perfectly coordinated team to escape and destroy. They are the opposite of Abbott and Costello, who clearly do not like each other and who are never unified. Much of Costello's comedy takes place when he's alone or with someone other than Abbott, and their famous routines such as "Who's on First?" are grounded in frustration and anger that are never released into affection or unity. It's a form of atomic bickering. "Who's on First?" is hilarious—a classic—but it's also about a *failure* to communicate, showing a different kind of marital template. Abbott and Costello represent a bad marriage in which neither will let go of the other no matter how disgruntled they are. Yet they are still wed—unlike Dean Martin and Jerry Lewis, who are a couple on the brink of divorce. And, of course, famously they finally *did* get divorced. The couple they represent is lopsided: Lewis madly loves Martin, but Martin is cool, indifferent to Lewis's ardor. As the years go by in their work together, it's clear Lewis becomes more and more manic in order to attract love and attention, while Martin gets more and more detached. In the end, Lewis turns to others (the audience) and goes crazy, while Martin suddenly realizes he's being upstaged and looks really angry. Their partnership is the comic visualization of divorce.

It may seem odd to discuss these nonromantic, asexual male comedy teams as married couples, but all filmed couples were constructs. Two male comedians playing in a story in which they live together, work together, face problems

The picture of married bliss: Stan Laurel and Oliver Hardy . . .

. . . coping with a fashion malfunction . . .

. . . happy around the house, relaxing with the dogs . . .

. . . and smiling en famille (from *Their First Mistake*) . . . all portraits that could grace any marriage movie

together, quarrel and make up are as much a married construct as anything else. In fact, male comedians aren't the only nonsexual couples to show audiences marital compatibility without sex. *Anna and the King of Siam* (1946) and its musical variation, *The King and I* (1956), both depict a man and woman who grow together over time in a productive and mutually beneficial relationship. She educates his children toward the future, and he helps her learn patience and tolerance. Anna (an English schoolteacher) and the King were real people. There could be no suggestion of sex in such a movie "marriage": first of all, the material was biographical; and secondly, he was a king.* A marriage of purpose and mutual respect between a man and a woman—who never fall in love and never have sex—is also illustrated by the teacher/pupil relationship of Bette Davis and John Dall in *The Corn Is Green* (1945) and by the wartime survival story *Heaven Knows, Mr. Allison* (1957). In *Corn*, Davis guides Dall to the successful passing of an exam that will get him out of the coal mines, and in *Heaven Knows*, Robert Mitchum (as a U.S. Marine) and Deborah Kerr (as a nun) become stranded together on a Japanese-held island during World War II. These movies demonstrate a man and a woman in a committed relationship without sex, but the relationships *are* marital in the sense that they reflect an ultimately harmonious and respectful pairing.

A movie had to *build* a couple for the audience, and two actors had to be cast to create an illusion or enact a story. This inevitably meant the star system. If marriage movies were stories about couples, and couples were played by actors, then actors in movies meant stars. (Stardom, and the making and selling of movie stars, was the bread and butter of the movie business.) It was axiomatic that marriage movies would involve movie stars—a couple of them, a man and a woman—who would play married. Movie stars married to each other! On the other hand, did they have to be married, or could they just form a union of sorts that could *seem* like marriage?

Reflecting what Thomas Schatz calls "the genius of the system," Hollywood studios created a form of pseudo-marriage that the public embraced wholeheartedly: star pairings. It was simple and doable: cast and recast a leading actor and a leading actress to create a sense that this couple belonged together and were "married" as performers.† Wed them onscreen—in plot or not in plot, but

* Movies, of course, weren't always careful with biographical truth: they created romances wherever they felt they were needed. But the idea of Anna becoming the Queen of Siam would have stretched all credibility.
† This concept doesn't really apply to couples who were cast together only after they actually had gotten married, and the casting was designed to cash in on their publicity. Such couples include Tony Curtis and Janet Leigh, Debbie Reynolds and Eddie Fisher, Bobby

certainly in sickness and in health, for richer or poorer (preferably richer), and, with any luck at all, for better and better and more and more money at the box office. "Together Again!," "Your Favorite Couple Is Back!," "Always Loving, Always Laughing, Always Together!" were advertising tag lines associated with movie-star pairings, a subliminal link to the concept of a man and a woman who were not husband and wife but show-business mates.

Moviemakers could understand this kind of star marriage—it was fake. And moviegoers liked it. What the public joined together, let no movie mogul put asunder. The audience performed the ceremony in their heads, and Hollywood validated what they imagined. Successful pairings between movie stars were about acting chemistry, roles, and plots, but they were also about intangibles: size, coloring, vocal timbre, star personae, fashion, dialogue, and an inexplicable something that was behind the acceptance of what was onscreen. This quality—whatever it was—represented a kind of onscreen marriage that carried over offscreen for audiences. The business kept a successful pair together, as if they *were* married, by casting them again and again and again. And here was the real genius of the system: they dubbed these star pairings "love teams."*

"Love teams": it sounded ever so much more fun than "married couple." Hollywood found box-office success (as well as its own comfort zone) with these star pairings.† It was their best, most enduring form of making a marriage couple

---

Darin and Sandra Dee, and others. Bogart and Bacall first fell in love in front of audiences in 1944's *To Have and Have Not*, when they were not yet wed. They continued to be a fabulous team even after they were Mr. and Mrs., however. Their chemistry never died in films such as *The Big Sleep* (1946) and *Dark Passage* (1947). They were still excellent in 1948's *Key Largo*. Married offscreen, they're unmarried in the plot; yet they have a comfort in each other's presence, and a mutual timing, a real-life married rhythm. Like Bogart and Bacall, Elizabeth Taylor and Richard Burton notoriously fell in love while making a film—*Cleopatra*, in 1963—but they generated little heat on film. The movies they made together after their marriage (*The VIPs* [1963], *The Sandpiper* [1965], etc.) show no real sexual spark between them. Perhaps images really can reveal onscreen marital compatibility. Bogart and Bacall spent the rest of their lives together; Taylor and Burton did not.

* These offscreen ceremonies that took place in the heads of moviegoers sometimes went beyond reason. Fans wanted to believe in star "marriage" so badly that they wrote in, begging them to actually *get married right now*. Sometimes fans even began to believe the couple *were* married—it happened to Greer Garson and Walter Pidgeon, and later, as the result of an advertising campaign for Polaroid, to James Garner and Mariette Hartley.

† The two actors could be men, as in the "buddy" movies of Spencer Tracy and Clark Gable (*Test Pilot, Boom Town, San Francisco*), Paul Newman and Robert Redford (*Butch Cassidy and the Sundance Kid, The Sting*) or Michael Caine and Sean Connery (*The Man Who Would Be King*). Women buddies were less common, although the beautiful Thelma Todd made seventeen comedy shorts paired with Zasu Pitts and twenty-one with Patsy Kelly in the early 1930s. Marie Dressler and Polly Moran made features such as *Prosperity* (1932). One cannot forget, also, the spectacular twosome of Jane Russell and Marilyn Monroe in *Gentlemen Prefer Blondes* (1953). Talk about buddies!

Fred Astaire and Ginger Rogers seldom played married,
but when they did, as in *The Story of Vernon and Irene
Castle*, a real-life couple . . .

in the movies, and it confirms how important "the couple" was, not only in
marriage films but in *all* films.

"Love teams" shed light on what the public bought as an authentic "married" rhythm between two people. What was it audiences saw or felt between
two actors that made them believe they were a couple? What did the audience
think married couples looked like or sounded like—or what did they want to
dream they looked like and sounded like? What read "married" to an audience?

Fred Astaire and Ginger Rogers appeared together in ten movies, and in
only two of them were they married (*The Story of Vernon and Irene Castle*, the
last of their original RKO pairings in 1939, and *The Barkleys of Broadway*, their
decade-later reunion and final film as a dance couple).* Moviegoers had no

* Similarly, Nelson Eddy and Jeanette MacDonald, the singing version of Astaire and Rogers, made eight movies together and were married in only two, *Sweethearts* (1938) and
Bitter Sweet (1940). In *I Married an Angel* (1942) the marriage takes place inside Eddy's
dream, and in *Maytime* (1937), Eddy is shot before they can enjoy their life together. Eddy

. . . or in *The Barkleys of Broadway*, an imaginary one, it was still dancing that defined the relationship.

need to see them play an *actual* married couple because they wed one another so beautifully through dance. Astaire and Rogers were the living metaphor of a perfect union, and they didn't have to play married to show it. Their swooning, yearning, swaying-like-two-chic-cobras romantic numbers spoke to audiences about desire, but also about a spectacularly balanced, perfectly beautiful physicality. Theirs was a marriage set to music, and their dance-floor coupling was real and romantic. (Fred and Ginger seldom kiss in their films. There's no need for it. Their sex life takes place when they have on their dancing shoes.)

When they're not dancing, Fred and Ginger have an adversarial relationship. He's eager and in pursuit; she's disdainful, and holds out.* This strain between their characters' personalities pays off because it has a purpose: to resolve a potential imbalance. Fred has to earn Ginger in the plot because Ginger will have to earn Fred on the dance floor.

---

and MacDonald were wedded through song in the way Astaire and Rogers were through dance.

* As is almost always true in movie history, there's an exception in which Ginger pursues Fred: *Carefree*, with Astaire oddly cast as a psychiatrist who, of course, dances.

The movies in which Astaire and Rogers play a married couple are two of their least enjoyable: the tension of the pursuit is lost. The biopic (*The Story of Vernon and Irene Castle*) was made under pressure from their offscreen advisor, Irene Castle, who was still alive and demanded input as to how she and her husband would be presented. The onscreen Castles are harmonious but all business. Their marriage, which occurs early in the plot, is dedicated to their success, the dances they invent, and Mrs. Castle's fashion influence. The resulting film is the only RKO Astaire/Rogers film that's never in any way magical.* (In *Barkleys*, in which they play a successful Broadway team, the original pattern of Astaire's pursuit is maintained, because the couple quarrel and separate early in the story. The quarreling is heavy-handed and charmless.)

Greer Garson and Walter Pidgeon had an entirely different "married" chemistry. They gave off an aura of a calm, dedicated love that could stand the test of time. They were perfectly cast as a married couple in all but one of their eight films together, *Julia Misbehaves* (1948). (In *That Forsyte Woman* [1949], after spending most of the movie apart, they finally end up married.)† Garson and Pidgeon were at the height of their popularity as a love team during the years of World War II. The audience not only *wanted* to believe in marriage in those years; they *needed* to believe in it. Onscreen, Garson and Pidgeon answered that need, presenting a reassuringly mature relationship, a steadfast love for the duration, that was nevertheless just a tad spicy, a little saucy. They made marriage fun, but also comfortable and—most of all in a time of uncertainty—*reliable*. In their most famous movie, *Mrs. Miniver* (1942), they were youthful and stunning to look at, but still believable as a middle-aged couple with a son old enough to serve in the war. In the famous scene in which they are in their bomb shelter with their younger children and the Germans attack by air, they work in perfect harmony to comfort their children. They easily enact the silent telecommunication that grows between two people who've been married for a long time. Reflecting years of mutual agreement and habit, he reaches for the boy and she embraces the little girl. They don't look at each other but focus on their children while they withstand the assault.

Olivia de Havilland and Errol Flynn, another famous love team, were carefully cast as a couple, but seldom a married couple. They were the embodi-

---

* People often say that Astaire and Rogers are mismatched because she's very down-to-earth and American, and he's more sophisticated and European. Rogers was from Texas, and Astaire was from Nebraska. His onscreen personality is as jaunty, flip, and brash as hers.

† In *Julia Misbehaves* they're a divorced couple who act as if they're still married—and inevitably reunite at the end.

Greer Garson and Walter Pidgeon were one of America's favorite married couples onscreen, with Garson, the bigger star, always looking up to Pidgeon, because that's what wives were supposed to do. They were perfect as a brave British duo facing the challenges of World War II in *Mrs. Miniver* . . .

. . . or as a childless couple in *Blossoms in the Dust* . . .

. . . or as the real-life Nobel Prize winners Marie and Pierre Curie in *Madame Curie.*

ment of the romantic tradition of the swashbuckling film. They both have a touch of British class, look good in color as well as black-and-white, and wear period costumes well. Flynn is an outlaw type . . . but a gentleman. De Havilland's a dignified lady . . . but with spirit. (One of de Havilland's great accomplishments as an actress was her ability to bring the standard leading-lady role of such films to life.) He's on one side, she's on the other, and they must cross a chasm between tradition and rebellion to come together—a significant form of change and growth. As they do, his charm keeps her sweetness from becoming too cloying, and her intelligence gives his derring-do some gravitas. In the plots of their films, de Havilland and Flynn move toward each other from fixed positions, yet there's a unity of purpose required from them in their movies, and that unity seemed to audiences to be a marriage of sorts.

How perfectly "wed" they seemed to be is verified by *They Died with Their Boots On* (1941), the one film in which they were actually married for a significant portion of plot time. In their portrait of Mr. and Mrs. George Armstrong Custer, de Havilland and Flynn enact one of the most touchingly honest married scenes in the movies. As Mrs. Custer, de Havilland packs her husband's things in preparation for the Battle of the Little Bighorn, putting together what he will need in the field. Thinking she cannot see, he deliberately breaks his watch chain, and notes that, alas, now he will have to leave this cherished war memento behind. De Havilland *has* seen, and she knows what it means—he will leave it behind to become her most cherished memento of their married life together. (Also surreptitiously, he's placed in his jacket pocket a miniature portrait of her.) De Havilland, portraying a daughter of the military, knows her role: do not weep, do not show fear. They speak jocularly to one another of their future years, in which they will grow fat and happy together, but they both know it's a future they'll never have. He lies to her, and she accepts his lie. It's the agreement of a lifetime in a successful military marriage: each must play his or her role properly and not let down the other side. As the sound of bugles is heard from outside, Flynn embraces her, but not casually. He makes it important, final, a real goodbye, for that is what it will be. His last words are, "Walking through life with you, ma'am, has been a very gracious thing." After he leaves, she leans against the wall and the camera pulls back from her. She slumps, and falls to the floor in a faint. Outside, he mounts, yells "Forward, ho!" to his men, and the cavalry moves out to the traditional sound of fifes and drums. He's off to the Little Bighorn, because even a married man's gotta do what a man's gotta do. A married woman, of course, has gotta do what she's gotta do. She remains behind. (Audiences of the era were reported to weep at this scene. They *believed* in it. The "marriage" of de Havilland and Flynn was star pairing that conveyed conjugal truth.)

Olivia de Havilland and Errol Flynn portrayed General and Mrs.
George Armstrong Custer in *They Died with Their Boots On*, and
enacted a credible marital farewell scene.

Even when a happily-ever-after marriage was not necessarily the endgame
of a star pairing, the concept of "union" lay underneath. One of the greatest pairs in movie history was the young Judy Garland and Mickey Rooney.
Rooney and Garland brought to each other a gift no one else could give:
an astonishing talent that could do anything, and the shared misery and joy
of being a show-business tot. They were troupers, faux teens who were older
than old, show-biz pro to show-biz pro, talent to talent. They interacted like
a friendly Godzilla and Mothra (even though both were tiny: he stood 5′5″ to
her 4′11″). Because of their youth, marriage was not the goal of their onscreen
pairing, but their professionalism gave off the aura of a real-life merger in
which the participants honored each other and would troop onward together
no matter what.

Today the most written-about movie team is probably Spencer Tracy and
Katharine Hepburn.* The two made nine movies together, and from the first
one onward they were also a couple offscreen. In their most successful mov-

---

* It's interesting to note that when I first began asking people to name marriage movies they
remembered, only *one* person mentioned Hepburn and Tracy—and she couldn't think of
a single film they were in. (Later, she thought of *Pat and Mike* (1952), in which they *aren't*
married.) As I talked to people about marriage in the movies, I realized that Hepburn and
Tracy were famously thought of as *not* married. That was their triumph: as a high-profile,
cohabiting *unmarried* couple.

ies (*Woman of the Year* [1942], *Adam's Rib* [1949]), they were the epitome of modern man and woman, striving to cram their independent, tough-minded natures into a fair-sided male/female union. Some of their films (*Desk Set*, *Pat and Mike*) presented them as a cantankerous unwed couple who sparred instead of wooed, but in a way the audience clearly understood meant they were a simply perfect match. Without each other, it was implied, there was only the lonely life, because each was a unique individual.

Hepburn and Tracy are married in six of their nine movies. In *Woman of the Year*, *The Sea of Grass* (1947) *State of the Union* (1948), *Without Love* (1945), and *Adam's Rib*—five of those six—the marriages are troubled. In the sixth and perfectly harmonious one, *Guess Who's Coming to Dinner* (1967), their relationship is neither honest nor particularly credible. If Tracy and Hepburn weren't playing the roles, the couple would seem even phonier than they already do. Since audiences know that Tracy and Hepburn remained together for years in real life, they can accept the onscreen union; otherwise, the couple would be a ramped-up Judge and Mrs. Hardy in a very ritzy-looking house, with an Andy Hardy–ish perfect daughter who shows up with a social issue that had just become Hollywood-chic.

Woman of the Year, Tracy and Hepburn's first onscreen pairing, is a movie in which they meet, woo, and wed in one half, then try to make a marriage out of their essentially opposite lives in the other.* Thus they first appeared onscreen as an incompatible married couple who had to learn to compromise—something audiences knew was a real-life "couple" issue.

In *The Sea of Grass*, a dreary soap opera directed by Elia Kazan (who complained of the assignment for years afterward), Hepburn and Tracy are mismatched and never really solve their problems, despite a final reconciliation. After Hepburn commits adultery with Melvyn Douglas, Tracy exiles her and forbids her to ever see their children—and that's the story of that marriage. When *State of the Union* opens, the stars are separated and Tracy has taken up with the highly political and sophisticated Angela Lansbury. Hepburn must pretend their marriage is okay because Tracy's running for political office. In the end, they reunite—but only after he's forced to step down from his candidacy.

One of the most popular of the Hepburn/Tracy marriage films is *Adam's Rib*, which sparkles with rock-hard wit. She's a lawyer; he's a prosecuting attorney.† They're put forward as an idealized successful married couple. Today, we

---

* It's one of those fortuitous moments in film history when, as with Bogart and Bacall in *To Have and Have Not*, a couple fated to be together come together, right in front of our eyes. It's magic.
† The film makes an interesting comparison to *Without Love* (see pages 67–68), which is

could call them yuppies: no kids, plenty of money, both happily self-focused, very high-living and sophisticated. They're the people we'd be if only we had better brains, better clothes, and a better apartment. But in *Adam's Rib*, Hepburn and Tracy compete hideously; they try to humiliate each other publicly— and if the movie weren't so funny, it would break your heart. Professional couples, says Hollywood (in a position to know), seldom have any real chance at happiness or marital longevity.

At some level, this sense of intense competition that hovered between Hepburn and Tracy was what made them seem so right and true to audiences. Moviegoers knew that equality was hard. It wasn't really the romance between these relatively cold and unusual two people that drew audiences to them. It was the sense that here indeed was a real-life married competition and thus a real-life married couple. The Hepburn/Tracy movie "marriage" felt real to audiences because they were a couple who generated a sense of incompatibility, competition, class difference, and underlying tension.

The union of Hepburn and Tracy is often oversimplified—nearly everyone says it's a class thing, with her all upper-crusty and him all down-to-earthish.* Yet one only has to imagine *The African Queen* (1951) with Tracy instead of Bogart to realize that Tracy is pretty uppity himself. Where Tracy with Hepburn exudes a sense of honor and superiority, Bogart truly embraced the commonness of Charlie Allnut. He played it low, obedient, even dumb. He wasn't afraid to be less than Hepburn. Tracy's snobbery is often veiled, presented as a religious conviction, scientific knowledge, a moral code, or a peasant's intuition. It's self-righteousness all the same, but it helps Tracy in comparison seem more human, more understanding and tolerant, than Hepburn. He's an American kind of man, one to bring Hepburn (representing those traits we drummed out of ourselves when we sailed on the *Mayflower*) down to where she belongs. Tracy and Hepburn act out an intellectual's version of *The Taming of the Shrew*, in which Tracy masters Hepburn (not vice versa, as some people think). Hepburn has to learn her lesson, but what makes this palatable for most people is that Tracy, again by comparison, seems ordinary. If he took on a New England accent and played a rich guy who went to Harvard, audiences could see more easily why he and Hepburn were such a well-matched pair.

Adam's Rib without the sex, but also without a nasty undertone of competitive rivalry and distrust. *Without Love* shows Hepburn and Tracy working together successfully, in great harmony and without competition—until, of course, they fall in love and things fall apart. In *Adam's Rib*, in which they are allegedly happily wed and have plenty of love and sex, another story runs underneath the screen.

* It was said of Astaire and Rogers that she gave him sex appeal and he gave her class. Hepburn and Tracy reverse the idea: he gives her sex appeal and she gives him class.

Perhaps the most famous today of all the "love teams" paired in multiple movies are Katharine Hepburn and Spencer Tracy, who could play domestic and happy as they rustle up a late-night snack in *Adam's Rib* . . .

Tracy as an actor was always grounded, but Hepburn seldom was. (If, as Hepburn said of Tracy, he was a baked potato, she was his very sour cream.) He was in the earth, of the earth (onscreen), and she was always in some kind of nearly hysterical flight, a hummingbird. She's hoity-toity; he's homespun. She's idealistic; he's practical. He took the edge off her, even as she became spontaneous when working opposite him. Except for Tracy, Hepburn never really made an honest pairing with another actor, not even Cary Grant. Tracy, on the other hand, could be teamed up literally with anyone, including Lana Turner, Myrna Loy, Joan Crawford, Jean Harlow—and let's not forget Mickey Rooney, Jack Oakie, and Clark Gable.

Whenever they worked, star pairings were successful in creating a strong sense of a "married" couple—useful both in marriage movies and elsewhere. Nevertheless, they did present Hollywood with a financial challenge: the need to spend two dollars instead of one—that is, to cast *two* stars. In many Hollywood films, a big-name star, male or female, was used to introduce a younger one the business hoped to develop upward—an economical pairing. The marriage movie made it difficult for this system to work without throwing the balance of the "married couple" out of whack. (An audience's sympathy would gravitate

. . . or angry and estranged as they try to solve their sleeping arrangements in *State of the Union.*

to the "name.") Hollywood solved this issue for marriage movies by creating low-budget acting couples who could be repeated from film to film, ensuring business because of the characters, not the stars.

Series films, such as the Blondie and Dagwood and *Ma and Pa Kettle* movies or the imitation *Thin Man* plots,* were developed around low-budget performers who were actually cast as married couples. (There were also ongoing

---

* As soon as a movie like *The Thin Man* became an enormous hit, Hollywood not only went on making more *Thin Man* movies but also created imitations. There was the successful "Joel and Garda Sloane" series about two rare-book dealers who solve crimes—three movies, each with a different set of stars to play the married couple: *Fast Company* (1938) with Melvyn Douglas and Florence Rice; *Fast and Loose* (1939) with Robert Montgomery and Rosalind Russell; and *Fast and Furious* (also 1939) with Franchot Tone and Ann Sothern. Gracie Allen (without George Burns) paired with William Post in *Mr. and Mrs. North* (1941), a movie version of a popular radio series with married sleuths. Loretta Young and Brian Aherne played a mystery writer and his wife caught up in murder in *A Night to Remember* (1943), and Joan Blondell and Melvyn Douglas played married private eyes in *There's Always a Woman* (1938). An odd two-film series (also about a mystery writer and his wife who solve real crimes) paired Allyn Joslyn and Evelyn Keyes: *Dangerous Blondes* in 1943 and *Strange Affair* in 1944. The two films presented the characters as completely different couples: Jane and Barry Craig in the first, Bill and Jacqueline Harrison in the second.

portraits of marriage in "family" films such as the *Andy Hardy* series, the *Jones Family* and *Henry Aldrich* movies, even though the younger, unmarried characters were the primary focus.) One of the most typical—and successful—of these low-budget movies was the Blondie and Dagwood series. Blondie and Dagwood didn't need movie stars, because they came presold. The audience knew the Bumsteads offscreen.

Mr. and Mrs. Dagwood Bumstead were married on February 17, 1933, after a fairly long courtship.* They had first met on September 8, 1930, in the debut of a comic strip drawn by Chic Young. Dagwood, the bumbling playboy son of a billionaire railroad tycoon (J. Bolling Bumstead), was the kind of guy whose polo pony would pull up short during a chukker to nibble a bit of grass. Blondie, his girlfriend, was a typical 1920s flapper, with a great many suitors flocking around her. The Depression was already under way when the strip debuted, so when Dagwood decided to marry Blondie, J. Bolling conveniently disinherited him, turning the couple into two people who, like their readership, now had to worry about money. Their 1933 "wedding ceremony" features a guest who says, "They'll never be happy, mark my words." Dagwood, however, makes a definitive statement to his new wife: "I don't mind giving up everything for you. You're worth it. I'll get a job." Blondie serenely replies, mouthing words that would often be used in the movies in future years, "We'll live on love." ("What a pity," said Dagwood's still unsympathetic dad.) Blondie and Dagwood, however, defy the odds. They do live on love, and still do today, eight decades later.

The movies based on this enormously popular comic strip are unique. First, there were an unusually high number made (twenty-eight, starting in 1938 and ending in 1950), and second, they were all produced by Columbia Pictures and all starred the same two leading actors, Penny Singleton and Arthur Lake. It was formula filmmaking at its simplest, most economical and efficient, and also a rare example of a totally successful movie format that endured.

Singleton and Lake were a miraculous pairing, a perfect onscreen Blondie and Dagwood. They both had the physical definition required, and the solid presence to fill their roles. Both had talent, but neither had overwhelming star quality and neither was a name, either before or after the series. They were not second-rate, but they were not too big for their jobs. They were very much like the actors who become television stars today. Just as Barbara Billingsley became famous because she played June Cleaver, the Beav's mother, but

---

* Their son, Alexander (originally known as "Baby Dumpling"), would be born in 1934, and their daughter, Cookie (all of America participated in the contest to name her), in 1941.

Blondie and Dagwood were so much a part of American popular culture that they, cartoon figures, could be used to endorse products and promote advertising contests, as in this layout from the Johns-Manville roofing, siding, insulation, and ceiling materials company.

famous *only* as June Cleaver, Singleton and Lake became famous as Blondie and Dagwood. They *were* Blondie and Dagwood—and nothing else—for the rest of their performing lives.*

Lake seemed immediately to be the perfect Dagwood, but Singleton was

---

* Singleton and Lake were in the right place at the right time. Lake was born into show business, the son of circus acrobats. He played in his first film in the silent era, and also starred in *Harold Teen* (1928), another movie about a comic-strip character—a sort of underage Dagwood Bumstead. Lake can famously be seen in the Cary Grant/Constance Bennett success *Topper* (1937) and several other movies of the era. He worked steadily as a freelance actor, and in 1942 wed Patricia Van Cleeve, Marion Davies's young niece, who was rumored to actually be her daughter with William Randolph Hearst. Singleton originally had appeared on Broadway and in movies under her birth name, Dorothy McNulty, until she married Dr. Lawrence Singleton in 1937 and changed her name to Penny Singleton. As McNulty, she appeared in, among other films, *After the Thin Man* (1936), in which she sang and danced.

Blondie and Dagwood (Penny Singleton and Arthur Lake) pose
with their son Alexander (Larry Simms) and their family dog,
Daisy, a perfect family portrait . . .

cast as Blondie only after the original choice, an actress named Shirley Deane,
was let go because she seemed too harsh when she nagged Dagwood. Singleton had a softer, sweeter quality. (She *did* have to dye her dark hair blond.)
She takes the edge off the Bumsteads' bickering, making it more palatable, a
significant factor in what made the films popular for so many years. Blondie
and Dagwood relieved marital pressure for the audience by reconstituting their
ordinary problems into easily resolvable comedy. There's a comforting quality
to them: they never change, they never fail. In what Preston Sturges called
"this cockeyed caravan of life," they could be counted on.

The titles of the *Blondie* movies indicate the simple, recognizable events the
movies present, events that any audience understands: *Blondie and the Boss,
Blondie on a Budget, Blondie Brings Up Baby, Blondie Has Servant Trouble,
Blondie Takes a Vacation,* etc. Each movie maintains a simple plot structure:
Dagwood screws everything up, and Blondie sorts everything out. Thus, the
series defined a comic premise designed to empower the wife: Blondie was
smarter than Dagwood, and without her he would bumble his way into tragedy. *With* her, he merely bumbles into disaster, and she can save him from that.
Blondie Bumstead (née Boopadoop) was always unflappable unless she imagines Dagwood has gone off with another woman. Nothing but infidelity—not
even the sight of her husband eating dog food—can deter her from her daily

. . . and they share their morning toast, bacon, and eggs the way the average family is supposed to do. Alexander was known as Baby Dumpling until, as is shown here, he got too big for "Baby."

rounds of cleaning up after him in mistake after mistake, misunderstanding after misunderstanding, mess after mess.

The earliest *Blondie* movies were sweet, low-key, and very natural, featuring simple problems an audience would recognize: broken vacuum cleaners, budget shortages, old girlfriends, and the neighbors' smart-ass little boy (Alvin), who calls Dagwood a dumbbell. Later entries in the series became somewhat more complicated in their story lines, involving haunted houses and wartime shortages.

Every Blondie and Dagwood movie featured the couple enacting familiar events. Just as Judge Hardy and his son Andy were sure to go into the judge's library for a "man-to-man" talk, Dagwood was sure to leave his home late for the office. He would dash out the door just as the mailman was coming up the walk, and no matter how many ways that beleaguered civil servant tried to avoid the crash, Dagwood would knock him down and scatter the mail. At some point, Dagwood was sure to emit his traditional beleaguered scream for help: "BLOOOOOOOOOONNNNNNNDIE!" It was simultaneously his Tarzan yell, his SOS, and his mating call. Blondie always responded.

The series cleverly maintained a cartoonish universe. Blondie and Dagwood became flesh and blood onscreen, but they remained the cartoon figures that Americans loved. Their physical world was lightly etched, never fully filled in, and never made heavily realistic. Blondie and Dagwood lived in a kind of domestic drawing, not in a real-life domesticity. There were only two main settings, both continually repeated: the Bumstead home, indoors and out-, upstairs and down-; and the office of the J. W. Dithers Construction Co., where Dagwood worked for his always irritated boss, Mr. Dithers. Very little was needed onscreen because the definition of the married couple, Blondie and Dagwood, validated the marital storyline.

Because of the success of the *Blondie* movies, Hollywood was alert for any possible similar series, and they found one inside *The Egg and I* (1947). When fan mail for *The Egg and I* referred over and over to the secondary characters Ma and Pa Kettle, Universal Pictures set up the Kettle series by first rereleasing *The Egg and I* with an advertising trailer that said, "We're bringing it back because you asked for it. If you saw it once, you'll want to see it again." Then they immediately followed with *Ma and Pa Kettle*, starring the original players, Marjorie Main and Percy Kilbride, who were featured in their own low-budget series of seven films. As was true for Blondie and Dagwood, the same actors always played the Kettles, and the same sets and the same comic routines (such as Ma's hilarious way of setting up mealtime for her brood) were repeated endlessly. Audiences loved the Kettles, who had fifteen kids, all sorts of animals, and a real mess of a house. There was something about their don't-give-a-darn attitude about keeping up with the Joneses—or with anyone—that gave subversive pleasure to American audiences. Ma's philosophy of housekeeping was a comfort to one and all. When she first married, she says, she tried to be neat and clean, but simply couldn't make her family work with her on it. "I can't make Pa change and be neat," she says, "so I might as well change and be dirty. There's been peace in this house ever since." The fundamental thing about the Kettles is that they are a happy couple: they leave each other alone.

The *Kettle* series, which was highly successful, was less about an actual marriage than was the *Blondie* series. The *Kettle* movies took on issues such as postwar housing for returning GIs, advertising contests, newfangled labor-saving devices, etc. They confirmed something about audiences that Hollywood was soon enough to learn from television: they liked familiar characters in repeated situations, and it was just fine if those characters were married. Series stars, series situations, and low-budget filmmaking with no-name stars would become more and more familiar in the media during the 1960s and 1970s.

The success of series movie couples like the Kettles and the Bumsteads was directly related to the presentation of a recognizable married couple. Their marital woes were ordinary, solvable, and funny, never grounded in any *real*

A real American happy marriage: the Kettles of *Ma and Pa Kettle* and
The Egg and I: Marjorie Main and Percy Kilbride.

threat. This type of comic reference to marriage issues was a sort of plotted
stand-up comedy routine.*

Even the shorts that accompanied features often undertook a jokester look
at common marriage complaints from couples. For instance, a 1950 Pete Smith
Specialty was titled *A Wife's Life*, which presents the beleagured woman wring-
ing her hands as she copes throughout her day with dirty dishes, bad plumb-
ing, naughty children, a leaky icebox . . . and a sleeping husband, blissfully
unaware and unconcerned. In 1946, Pete Smith presented *I Love My Husband,
But!* The star of the Smith short subjects was Dave O'Brien, who in this episode plays a husband designed to demonstrate what's wrong with the species.
The short begins by announcing that its goal is to "present some husbands and
wives, with emphasis on some annoying habits of husbands." These are: the
husband who leaves home looking natty and well groomed, leaving a sloppy
bathroom mess behind him; the breakfast grouch (his wife pushes a grapefruit
in his face, thus avenging her sex against Jimmy Cagney for all movie eternity);
the guy who can't fix anything around the house ("Chances are there's a guy

* It was also an updating of the old "make fun of marriage" situation from the silent era,
a newer version of Mabel and Fatty. The public also seemed able to believe in marriages that were clearly cartoonish—and that clearly did not try to bend a big-name-star's
persona down into the plot. "Star pairings" required a star's level of plot, fashion, and
furniture.

like him sitting next to you"); the man who constantly loses everything and can't find it even though it's right in front of him (one of those would be sitting right next to me); the one who doesn't notice his wife's new hat until the good-looking blonde next door comes over and tries it on; the bridge monster, who criticizes his wife's game; and finally, the problem "waker-upper," a type who comes in several variations. First there's the nice guy who gets up on his own, never disturbing his wife, tippy-toeing around quietly—until he hits the kitchen and drops and breaks everything. Then there's "Slumbering Sam," who can't be gotten up even when his wife slaps him silly; and the valiant one who tries to save his wife from hearing the alarm, but pokes her in the nose while trying.

Naturally there was a companion piece for *I Love My Husband, But!*—the opposite list of complaints. *I Love My Wife, But!* (1947), another Pete Smith Specialty, wasted no time listing the things that annoy men about their wives. Waiting for a woman to finish dressing when they are going out makes a man "unhappier than a glass blower with the hiccups." Men hate listening to their wives' endless gabbing, waiting while they can't make up their minds when shopping for a hat, and having them say "uh-uh" (meaning "no, no") to smoking in the house. Then there are the slave drivers who make their husbands do chores on the weekend—Mrs. Simon Legrees, they're called. The pièce de résistance for the finale is the wife who thinks she can back the car out of the driveway all by herself—a maneuver no wife, it seems, is even capable of accomplishing without knocking down trees and wrecking the car.

Audiences loved these shorts, which addressed them through a narrator who talks directly to them about what they know all too well to be often true.* Movies such as the *Blondie* series did something similar, but without the voice-over pal describing what they could see onscreen and recognize as the experience of their own lives. "Might as well laugh about it" was the effective strategy for these presentations, in which they reached audiences directly through the identification figures of a married couple.

Shorts like the Pete Smith Specialties reveal another issue Hollywood considered in relation to married couples: what did the audience want in a mate— what was a good wife or a good husband? Couples, as they were designed in marriage movies, were partly created to suggest the definition of an ideal mate. Audiences embraced one set of star "love teams" so thoroughly that the actress was labeled "the perfect wife," even though in real life she was married

---

* There were many about marriage: *Wedding Bills* (1940), *How to Hold Your Husband— Back* (1941), *I Love My Mother-in-Law, But!* (1948), *I Love Children, But!* (1952), etc.

unsuccessfully four times. Myrna Loy was effectively paired as a wife with many actors, but it all began with William Powell. Their first film together was *Manhattan Melodrama* (1934), but the one that "wedded" them for all time was *The Thin Man* (also 1934), in which they played the glamorous screwball couple Nick and Nora Charles. Their pairing as the Charleses was so effective that they went on to star together in five more *Thin Man* movies.

At first glance, the sophisticated Loy might seem to be the least appropriate candidate for the title of "perfect wife"—why not June Allyson, or Ruth Hussey? No one ever fully defines exactly why this super-elegant and cool female was found to represent the aproned masses better than any other Hollywood actress, but most likely it *was* all because of her casting as William Powell's wife in *The Thin Man*. As Nora Charles, Loy was the epitome of married equality and fun. In the early films, Nora is rich and sheltered and chic, but she gamely enters Nick's world of guys and dolls, hoods and hoodlums, showing no class judgment or fear.*

The marriage of Nick and Nora Charles was the one most moviegoers coveted. The one with the cocktails, the furs, the noisy parties, the fun, the excitement—and all the money. *The Thin Man* told audiences that, instead of dull arguments about who was going to take the kids to school . . . instead of yet another meat loaf on the table . . . instead of in-laws and bills and dull routines . . . a married couple could be out on the town trading clever remarks with each other, solving crimes, and throwing back martinis. Loy and Powell are an alternative to Hepburn and Tracy's yuppie-competition marriage. Hepburn and Tracy have material advantages and freedom from dull routine, but the best they can think to do with it all is try to one-up each other. Loy and Powell know how to have fun with their assets. And how to cooperate without losing individuality. They're Fred and Ginger *off* the dance floor. The Nick and Nora routine is still, almost eighty years after the first *Thin Man* movie, the marriage everyone thinks is perfect. Of *course* it's perfect—it's not a marriage, it's a relationship. Nick and Nora (at least in the early films) don't live a conventional married life. Neither has a job, and they rove from New York to San Francisco, from case to case. Even after they become parents to Nick Jr., the issues of their daily life have more to do with whodunit than with what-are-we-going-to-do-about-it. Nothing interferes between them other than Nick's cases. Loy's chore is to dress up and find a way to insert herself into

---

* In later *Thin Man* movies, Nora becomes more domesticated. She becomes a mother, accompanies Nick on a visit home to his parents, and even dons an apron, but the movies are always Nick's.

William Powell and Myrna Loy found marital fame as Nick and
Nora Charles in the celebrated *Thin Man* movies: the Charleses
"at home" in a gambling den, looking sleek and sophisticated in
tuxedo and long gloves *(Song of the Thin Man)* . . .

Nick's sleuthing, and his is to pretend to walk the dog when he's really going
off to chase a murderer . . . or visit his bookie. The dog, Asta, is more a child
to them than their child. (Asta, by the way, is impeccably played by the inestimable Skippy. All over America, people name their dogs Asta, thinking they
are naming them after a real dog. They are, but the dog's name was Skippy.)*

Loy's ability to be resigned in the face of utter stupidity made her the perfect wife onscreen because all too often that's how the wife's role was depicted.
Stand by. Watch horror happen. Stand by, and accept that you have no control
other than subterfuge, and the ultimate weapon: the mate's love. Loy could
stand by, all right, but with a look of disdain and an ever-so-slightly raised
eyebrow. She could lay down a trench of implied disapproval, disgust, or contained impatience. She was American womanhood—Blondie for the smart set.

As "the perfect wife," Loy had another asset. She could pair well with any
actor. She was comfortably married to William Powell, Cary Grant, Fredric
March, Clark Gable, Ronald Colman, Spencer Tracy, Robert Taylor, and Clifton Webb. She adjusted accordingly. For Powell, she was cheeky and sharp, but

---

* Skippy appeared in many movies, including a star turn with bowler hats in *The Awful
Truth*. Skippy later changed his name to Asta to simplify the problems he had with fans
over the issue. On April 10, 2010, he was the clue in a *New York Times* crossword puzzle:
"Skippy's most famous role." Answer? "Asta."

... or "at home" with gangsters and murder invading their domesticity (with Edward Brophy from the original *Thin Man*).

for Grant, sophisticated and real. With Gable she was sexy, and with Clifton Webb, a suitably desexed life partner. She knew to get in her co-star's groove, and be the yin to her partner's yang. If her own screen personality had been more dominant and less laid-back, she could perhaps not have found her stardom. (She underwent a long apprenticeship, often originally cast as an Asian.) She was born to be the other half, but without losing her own presence in the frame. If her half of the married couple was the lesser role, she was never diminished by it. She could establish equality with very little.

A demonstration of why Loy could continue to be thought of as "the perfect wife" beyond Nora Charles is revealed in a scene in the 1948 *Mr. Blandings Builds His Dream House*, in which Loy is "married" to Cary Grant. Her ability to play inside a couple, both with and off a male actor, is on full display. When Grant and Loy wake up in the morning in their overcrowded Manhattan apartment, and set about preparing for the day, balancing their needs with those of two young children, it's clear that someone, somewhere, understood the pressures of daily marital life and knew that Loy could play them effortlessly. (*Mr. Blandings* was based on an autobiographical book by Eric Hodgins.) When the couple wake up, it's 7:30 a.m., and the image is focused on a ringing alarm clock. From frame right comes an obviously masculine arm and hand that grope sleepily around until the buzzer is found and shut off. This is immediately followed by an obviously female arm that emerges from frame left to turn it back on . . . back and forth, back and forth. A relationship has been established. The man wants to avoid the inevitable, and the woman won't let him. Grant and Loy: Mr. and Mrs. Blandings.*

As this urban couple arise, they enact an honest early-morning ritual for a couple who've been together a long time. Grant and Loy barely speak. He gets up and blindly begins to drag himself through what he has to do—shave, shower, dress, and juggle his timing for the use of the single bathroom to avoid its monopoly by his two young daughters. Loy does not get out of bed . . . she just sits up and stares blindly ahead. Then she drops her head and, still sitting, goes back to sleep. He brings a cup of coffee and hands it to her. She responds by murmuring an automatic and impersonal thank you to him. They never look at each other, acknowledge each other, or register each other's presence. Each knows what the other needs, wants, feels, and will do. She knew he'd turn the alarm off and that it was her job to turn it back on to force him up. He knew she'd not be able to get out of bed without her coffee. When they finally begin to communicate, the issue is where are his socks? "Jim, dear, I do wish you'd try to make a little effort," she murmurs, barely aware of what he's asking. "I'll try, dear," is his own detached, meaningless reply. He might as well be promising to find a cure for cancer. (Grant and Loy are dancing their version of Laurel and Hardy's "commence a-prancin'.")

Throughout *Mr. Blandings*, Loy nags at Grant when she has to, and he nags back. ("Bicker, bicker, bicker," observe their daughters.) Most of the time, however, she accepts her fate, knowing that nothing is ever really going to change between them. They're a committed couple. Whatever happens with the bum deal they make in buying a house—they pay double what it's worth, then learn they have to tear it down and rebuild—they'll just go on: they'll argue, lose faith, get jealous and resentful, but they'll stick it out. In short, they're married. ("It isn't a house we're building, it's a home.") Audiences read the Blandings as a real couple because the movie doesn't just stress their domestic situation (something of a disaster); it also gives it hope through the building of a new home, a newer, better domesticity.

Loy lasted longer as a top star than many other actresses of her generation. (Perhaps that was because she aged so gracefully, so negligibly. Always beautiful and youthful, she had no need to hide her maturity.) Unlike other great female

---

* *Mr. Blandings Builds His Dream House* created an ad that depicted its stars, Cary Grant and Myrna Loy, standing on a bed, kissing each other, while two cartoon figures watch. "What are they doin'?" asks one, and the other answers, "Playin' house, you square, the Blandings way."

Myrna Loy continued to play the perfect wife throughout her career, here with "husband" Cary Grant, giving him architectural instructions in *Mr. Blandings Builds His Dream House.*

stars who began their careers in the late 1920s or early 1930s—Joan Crawford and Ginger Rogers are two good examples—Loy never became frozen-faced or hardened. She always remained relaxed, natural. Where another contemporary, Katharine Hepburn, embraced the signs of aging as an asset, letting her hair grow gray and showing herself to be an unusually spry, agile, and energetic older woman, Loy just seemed to stay the same. In other words, she *accepted* age; she neither used it nor had anything to fear from it. In this same way, onscreen she *accepted* marriage, her husband's idiocies, and whatever tiresome chore came her way. She was long-suffering, but in the most delicious, languid way possible, a way that said: "Well, I will put up with this, but believe me, it's not because I have to." She clearly indicated what nonsense it all was, but she *accepted*. As a result, she endured. There was an honesty to her, and a subtext that put her quietly in charge of everything.

If Loy was "the perfect wife," was there a movie "perfect husband"? This issue reveals how differently Hollywood defined the roles for a married man and a married woman. If Loy is the perfect wife because of her patient forbearance, then the perfect husband is . . . W. C. Fields. He forbears! Right in your face. Nobody forbears the way Fields forbears. Trooping along, muttering under his breath, a phony smile pasted on his puss, Fields can weasel his way out of any tight spot, or at the very least, bear up under its weight. Fields is no real parallel to Loy: he's the Imperfect Husband, and as such represents the male aggrieved rather than the male as an object of female desire. Where Loy is onscreen to demonstrate to men what a perfect wife is all about (a companion to play with, a beauty to love and possess, an equal in wit and sense of fun) and to show women what an ideal life could be (as well as to remind them to put up with things on their own terms), Fields is there to endorse a male idea that it is women who wear the pants in marriage and that men should best avoid the situation if they want any peace out of life. For men, he was a comic relief from an oppressive married status; for women, he was a nightmare husband.

Fields does not always play a married man—but when he does, look out. He's a really mean version of Dagwood. Fields makes a triumph out of his loser status, ramping it up into our American favorite: the underdog. He makes kvetching an art form, a noble cry for recognition and recompense. Oddly enough, he is, although perfectly harassed, a perfectly believable husband. The movie business always claimed that female filmgoers didn't like Fields—only men did. (I'm one female who disputes this claim—I find him hilarious.) Fields represented a man trapped in a horrible situation, and genuinely angry about it. He struck back in whatever little ways he could (such as getting drunk in the basement). Fields is never really half of a couple even when he plays a married man.

Three of his movies illustrate Fields as the husband's favorite husband: *My Little Chickadee* (1940), *It's a Gift* (1934), and *The Bank Dick* (1940). Each provides a slight variation on the role. In *Chickadee* he's a newlywed. In *Gift*, he's satisfactorily settled down, and in *Bank Dick* he's trapped in a marriage that's as horrible as it gets, because when W. C. Fields is a married man, he is a miserable man, a beleaguered man. *It's a Gift* weds him to a wife (Kathleen Howard) who just never quits. Fields is the classic male victim of a shrew. "Of all the driveling idiots!" is her standard evaluation of her mate, and she follows with a never-ending set of instructions for him ("Don't smoke at the table," "Don't throw matches on the floor"), a continuous list of complaints ("I haven't a stitch to my name," "I have no maid, you know, and probably never shall"), and a real lineup of warnings ("If any money comes into this family, *I'm* going to handle it!" "*I* am the master of this household!"), always at top volume, never letting up ("Are you listening to me? . . . I just have to SHOUT, SHOUT, SHOUT!"). Her admonition when he trips on a roller skate and falls down the stairs is, "Don't be kicking Norman's skates all around the house. I just got them fixed." ("Do it again, Pop," says his ruthless kid.) As he finally falls asleep one night, she yells, "Wake up and go to sleep!" He suffers a domestic hell of rotten children, collapsing porch swings, wrong telephone numbers, noisy milkmen, and falling coconuts (don't ask). Each morning, trying to shave and shoved away from the mirror by everyone, he dances a domestic ballet of disregard, forced to use first a small mirror and then the reflection off the bottom of a can. His world shows both the small, routine ways an ordinary man must suffer at home and the bizarre, unexpected ones (those coconuts). Finally frustrated, Fields winds up to take a swing at one of his nasty children, who has complained that Fields doesn't love him. "Don't you strike that child!" warns his wife. "Well, he's not going to tell me I don't love him!" is Fields's only defense. There is no good news in his married world, but Fields forbears.*

In comparing Loy's "perfect wife" to Fields, the cultural attitude to male and female roles in marriage is clear. Loy's duty is to put up with her husband, but she's allowed a little attractively covert attitude about it. Fields gets to damn women with misogynistic fervor, expressing criticism all over the frame.

Sometimes Hollywood spent a great deal of time in the movies talking about what men and women wanted in a mate—what should the other half of their coupling be for maximum happiness? Again, they had no answers. In *Valley of the Sun* (1942), a character speaks the truth when an older man tells a young one, "There are only two things in life a woman wants . . . and nobody knows what they are." What the movies will admit is that male and female goals regarding marriage are different. In *Men in White* (1934) Clark Gable plays a driven doctor, Myrna Loy his wealthy, pampered fiance. She feels he should be spending more time with her after they marry; he disagrees because his career is so important to him. She explains to him that she, too, is "trying to have a career: you!" Gable, patiently talking to her as if she's a child, explains that his work and his success will make their life together *important*. If that doesn't happen, she will lose faith in her own "career." The movie presents this opinion as not necessarily the male outlook, or even a woman's outlook, but as society's preferred plan for a man and a woman. The man is supposed to drive himself to be successful while the woman stands behind him, receiving her reward indirectly. *The Fountainhead* (1949), on the other hand, a filmed version of Ayn Rand's novel, presents a more specifically male/female disagreement. When the willful heroine (Patricia Neal) confronts the purist architect she loves (Gary Cooper), each articulates a male/female polarity regarding marriage. "Take a meaningless job," she advises him, even begs him, "and we'll live only for each other." In response to her passionate plea, he has a simple and direct answer: "No." This *is* the man's view versus the

---

* The plots of women's films indicate that women thought a perfect husband was a kind of daddy figure. He was rich, he gave you everything, he solved all your problems—and then he died and got out of your way so you could marry a really hot guy.

Maureen O'Hara managed to find two versions of the same
husband in *The Forbidden Street*: Dana Andrews as a bad one,
bearded and unreliable . . .

woman's. She says live for love so I can be happy, and he says that won't work
for me: *I'm* an architect.

Marriage movies often used a couple this way to define what men and
women wanted from each other. They suggested that men wanted something
noble in a wife, something fine and beautiful and pure. (This meant he wanted
sex.) What a woman wanted was never that simple. If she was a bad person, she
wanted a meal ticket, and if she was a good one, she wanted love; but . . . indications are that what she *really* wanted was just to get out of town, to escape, to
become free and/or empowered. And yet, when movies addressed the *responsibility* of what an audience member should want in a mate, what a man should
want in a wife seemed easier to define. Working with the idea that a man
should want something good and reliable, it was easy to make a movie in which
a man made a bad choice. Movies warned men that if they didn't look out,
they'd settle for physical beauty (which meant sex), and if they didn't keep a
grip on their egos, they'd fall for someone who just pretended to admire them.
Over and over again in the movies, men marry the wrong woman because she
is beautiful (sexy) or because she flatters him into it. Women also marry for
the wrong reasons, but they have higher stakes. They marry for money or for
adventure or because they have to (again, sex). Their errors are more spectacular, but also more fun.

There is a somewhat melancholy aspect to certain films that indirectly pre-

. . . and also as a good one, clean-shaven and watching out for his little woman (with Sybil Thorndike).

sent an audience of women with what they want in husbands. *The Forbidden Street*, a 1949 film starring Maureen O'Hara and Dana Andrews, illustrates the idea. Based on the best-selling novel *Britannia Mews* by Margery Sharp, the film is covert but clear in suggesting that most women want a more successful, cleaner, more supportive and loving version of the man they actually married. O'Hara plays a reasonably wealthy young lady whose big family home overlooks an alley: the Britannia Mews. O'Hara is drawn there by her sense of life, adventure, freedom, and, of course, sex. As a young adult, she defies her parents and runs away to wed her drawing teacher, a bearded Dana Andrews whose voice is dubbed. The marriage goes sour over his inability to make a living, his drunkenness, and his admission that he never really loved her. After shocking her with this cruel statement, Andrews conveniently falls down the stairs and dies. O'Hara, having been disowned by her family, is left alone in the slum world. Quite soon, however, a slightly tipsy ne'er-do-well comes along: another Dana Andrews, this time without his beard and speaking in his own voice.

The new Dana Andrews moves in downstairs from O'Hara. With her help, he sobers up, becomes a famous theatrical puppeteer, rids her of an odious blackmailer, dresses neatly, cuts off his beard, and always addresses her as "my darling." The two live "without love," but everyone assumes they're married.

O'Hara begins calling him "Mr. Lambert," her former husband's name. In the end, she is reunited with her family and living happily and now comfortably wed to Andrews. The Mews is no longer a slum but thoroughly respectable, a metaphor for her married life.

The Forbidden Street indicates that marriage is a woman's escape route from her family and from conformity. It is also her only legitimate ticket for sexual experience. The movie endorses "art over commerce" in husbands: they are ever so much more fun if they aren't bankers, but you do have to take charge of them regarding money. (O'Hara has a convenient small inheritance.) The film's most interesting aspect is the one that reaches out to female moviegoers who might be disappointed—or even abused—by their husbands. It presents a dream of the *other* husband: the same one you married only better, the one you originally imagined he would be. To suggest this idea, the same actor plays two different men. O'Hara is given the gift of her original dream man, her exciting lover who swept her away, returned to her after the original model got all broken and died on her. This new one is much better. Gone is the messy beard. Gone is the drunkenness, the laziness, the cruelty. A movie such as The Forbidden Street suggests that marriages are undone by many things in real life, but on the screen they are undone by plot. The Forbidden Street is happy to reverse the concept: it suggests marriages can be restored by plot. It speaks in a secret language of women that the men in the audience can't hear: we want better men, better husbands.

In selecting a mate, movie coupledom laid out three possible choices: what you wanted, what you got, and what society thought you should have. In other words: Tyrone Power, Eddie Bracken, and Lewis Stone—or Lana Turner, Joan Davis, and Ethel Barrymore. Movies about married couples played across these variations, always juggling desire, reality, and appropriateness. Movies presented perfection in a husband and wife through physical beauty and/or noble actions, made comedy about the foibles and failures of mates, and suggested (even dictated from time to time) what careful behavior might designate the perfect spouse. They played with married couples, using them in many different ways, addressing the idea of what one ought to do on the surface and hinting at what one felt like doing in the subtext. (In Hollywood movies, there is always a subtext.)

Kiss and Make-Up (1935), starring Cary Grant, is an unusual film that confirms the subtext of other films, directly discussing how bad an idea marrying for physical beauty can be. Grant, strangely cast as "Dr. Lamar, the high priest" of cosmetic surgery at the Temple de Beauté in Paris, is a bachelor whose mantra is "Ugliness is a disease, and I'm curing it." His medical methods are shown via tracking camera: mudpacks, manicures, massages, and workers plucking eyebrows to the tune of "The Song of the Volga Boatmen." When Dr. Lamar broadcasts about beauty, his listeners are any woman and every woman: a wealthy dame in a boudoir, a maid with a broom, an Eskimo outside her igloo, an African tribeswoman, and an Osa Johnson–like desert explorer sitting in a tent with her camel parked outside. Grant's character is clear about what advice to give women ("Bandage your ankles," etc.) as well as his philosophy: "To deprive a woman of love is to deprive her of life itself." To this highfalutin notion he adds a touch of practicality: "But men are selfish brutes . . . and they demand beauty . . . beauty at any price."

The movie's plot, such as there is one, is a story of how one wife (Genevieve Tobin) has devoted all her energy to Dr. Lamar's theories, remaking herself completely to please her husband (Edward Everett Horton),* who is not pleased: "You've lured her with lotions," Horton complains to Grant, adding that all this advice has added "a couple of dimples to my wife's knees" and "made them look gaga." Horton divorces his wife, and Grant, a sucker for his own handiwork, marries her, ending up having to face firsthand what he has done. To maintain her perfection, his new wife can't go swimming and can't be touched. She needs hours and hours to get ready to go out, and greases herself up head to toe at bedtime. Thoroughly chastened, Grant gives up his beauty business and opens an experimental science lab, settling down with his very natural, nicely freckled secretary (Helen Mack). A man has learned that marrying for beauty may end up meaning no sex!

The celebrated British movie *The Private Life of Henry VIII* (1933; directed by Alexander Korda) turns a historical character and his life into a rather ribald and sly discussion of the marriage couple. As history requires, the movie gives us wives being beheaded, but inside that drama is a lot of comedy. In an Academy Award–winning performance, Charles Laughton plays Henry VIII as a man who really just wants to be left alone. Poor Henry: he's greatly put upon by these wives! He's a-roisterin' and only wants to enjoy life, biting lustily into a woman's back as if she's little more than a plump chicken leg. He just wants to be half of a functioning couple—but, oh, how these women bedevil him! When he's busy at work, discussing the future of England with his advisors, his little wifey Jane Seymour bursts in to ask his advice on which headdress she should wear. ("Softly, sweetheart," he admonishes, "we have affairs of state

---

* When Grant unwraps Tobin's bandages, she comes out of her surgery in full makeup, with mascara, lipstick, and eyeliner. Grant purrs, "When you first came to me, you were merely pretty, and you've become my most beautiful creature."

In *The Captain's Paradise*, Alec Guinness found the solution to every man's problem: two different wives. With Yvonne De Carlo, out on the town for a hot rhumba, he was able to have his cake . . .

here!") Henry sums up his marital adventures with cold appraisals ("My first wife was clever . . . my second ambitious . . . ") and advises Thomas Culpeper (Robert Donat) that if he wants to be happy, "marry a stupid woman." He tells his courtiers that marriage is "the victory of optimism over experience." This motif is further carried out by Henry's servants, slaving away in his kitchens and offering running commentaries on marriage as a dangerous venture ("You never know what you're getting," "Marriage is like pastry—you've got to be born to it"). The cook sums up Henry's track record: he "got in the soup" with his first wife, found "stinking fish" with the second, "cooked the goose" of his third (who died after childbirth), and gave "the cold shoulder" to the one he sent packing (Anne of Cleves). One of the female servants tells the cook that a man "needs regular meals," and the cook replies, "But not the same joint every night." At the end of the movie, Henry VIII is an old man gnawing on a haunch, bleary-eyed and burpy, while his final "good woman" of a wife nags him ("If I let you out of my sight for one minute, you're up to some mischief!"). She snatches the food out of his greedy paws, barking, "You *know* you can't digest it!" After he pretends to be asleep, she leaves the room. He jumps up, grabs more food, and continues chowing down. Looking directly into the camera, and thus directly at the movie audience, Charles Laughton as the much-married Henry VIII

. . . and eat it, too, at a cozy little luncheon at home with his reliable wife, Celia Johnson.

delivers his final evaluation: "Six wives . . . and the best of them's the worst." King he may be, but when it comes to marriage, Henry appears to be a husband who just wants to be left alone with his roast beef.

What a movie man wants in a movie woman can easily be summed up: everything. This fundamental desire (and its attendant unlikelihood) is hilariously represented in the 1953 comedy *The Captain's Paradise*, starring Alec Guinness as the captain of a passenger ferry that crosses the Mediterranean from Gibraltar to North Africa. Guinness, it seems, has spent his life in search of Paradise, and has actually found a way to have it. On the Gibraltar side of his journey, he has a perfect little wife, a placid and loving homemaker who keeps his life in order and provides him with a restful and comforting haven. Well played by Celia Johnson, Maud is the dream wife of a certain kind of middle-class man: his mother, only younger and more obedient. Over in North Africa, Guinness has man's other need: a sexy and glamorous spitfire of a wife who loves to go out dancing all night and who makes him the envy of every other man they encounter. Nita is played by the youthful Yvonne De Carlo (née Peggy Middleton) at the point in her career where movies were discovering that she might be able to do more than wear harem pants.

Guinness sails back and forth: his Paradise a hot life a few nights a week followed by a reassuring recuperation. Alas, as everyone but Guinness apparently knows, Paradise can only be lost. When he accidentally mixes up some gifts he's bought for his women, everything crashes to earth. By mistake, De Carlo is given an apron intended for Johnson, and Johnson gets a sexy outfit designed for De Carlo, triggering hidden longings in the two wives, who clearly have their own ideas about Paradise. De Carlo suddenly wants to stay home and cook the captain's dinner, and Johnson wants him to take her out on the town to rumba the night away. To make the story short, Guinness ends up facing a firing squad—and so much for the idea of the Captain's Paradise. While it lasted, of course, it met the basic needs of the movie man.

What women want on their side of the married couple is less clearly presented in films. On the surface, women want love and reliability and a chance to kill themselves taking care of a man and a bunch of kids. However, what a woman is *supposed* to want and what she *might* want and what she *gets* are all muddled up, and there's no one answer. There's the simple level (a home), the noble level (to care for her man), the romantic level (love), and the venal (a fur coat). It is clear, however, that one of the major purposes of the marriage film as far as women were concerned is the empowerment they were lacking offscreen.*

Empowerment for women sometimes comes in a socially acceptable format: not as what a woman *wants* but as what she *needs*—or, more bluntly, what she *ought* to need to be considered a good woman. She *needs* a good learning experience. Thus, the marriage story is often presented as an emotional and educational journey for a woman, in which the emotional learning process becomes geographical. After she becomes half of a couple, the bride-is-taken-to-her-new-world-by-her-groom story is a fundamental strategy of the marriage movie, and the "new world" comes in many forms. In *Never a Dull Moment* (1950), a smart-talking Park Avenue songwriter (Irene Dunne) marries a cowboy (Fred MacMurray) and goes out to Wyoming to learn to be a ranch wife. In *Mrs. Mike* (1949), bride Evelyn Keyes is taken away from her urban life out to the Canadian wilderness by her Mountie husband (Dick Powell). In *I'd Climb the Highest Mountain* (1951), Susan Hayward is carted off to a rural mountain retreat where she must learn to cook and sew and support

---

* This need for power is carried to an extreme in movies in which the woman, knowing she is about to die, fails to mention it to her husband and micromanages what his life will be after she's gone. In *Sentimental Journey* (1946), Maureen O'Hara tricks her husband into adopting a child to "carry on her spirit" after she's dead. (In 1958 the film was remade as *The Gift of Love* with Lauren Bacall.) In *No Sad Songs for Me* (1950), Margaret Sullavan uses the last six months of her life to set her husband and daughter up with a new woman, Viveca Lindfors (in the "I am an Ingrid Bergman look-alike" phase of her career). Sullavan's plan is unnecessary, because her husband has already pretty much selected Lindfors on his own. Sullavan endorses their affair, because Lindfors is a draftsman who will be useful in her husband's architectural business. In the end, Sullavan and her clueless husband (played by Wendell Corey, an actor born to play clueless) enjoy a hot night of reconciliation, followed by their dream trip to Mexico, where she dies offscreen.

her circuit-riding preacher husband (William Lundigan). In *Drums Along the Mohawk* (1939), the wealthy Claudette Colbert is taken to the frontier by Henry Fonda, and in *The Howards of Virginia* (1940), the very, very aristocratic and wealthy Martha Scott is relocated to the cruder, earthier wilderness world of her pioneering husband, Cary Grant. (This common marriage ploy also appears in two Elizabeth Taylor films, *Giant* [1956] and *Elephant Walk* [1954].)

The bride-on-a-journey story carries an obvious metaphor. By removing the leading female character from wealth and ease, the subtextual issues are turned into concrete challenges: marauding Indians, bears, wolves, hostile other women, weather, loneliness, et al. Most of these brides can't cook, can't sew, can't do the basic tasks required to survive in their new situation. They must *learn*. They must *change*. Furthermore, they must accept their position as wife and understand that their role is to support. These films aren't meant to suggest this is really what women want; rather, it's what society agrees is good for them to learn.*

The ability to tell the movie story in a way that could be read from different points of view and still come out in the same place was a phenomenon of the Hollywood product. Men could watch a bride's journey and see it as exactly what he would expect from a woman he married. She could learn what she needed to be able to do in order to carry out his needs and accept the role assigned to her. A wife, or an unmarried woman, could read the same information as an example of her getting away from the restrictions of her unwed life (and her virginity) and becoming free to cope and to manage things, to take control and learn how much she can do on her own. This ultimate strategy of the marriage film followed the sly-boots tricks of all Hollywood movies, with their crime-doesn't-pay (but isn't it fun?) and sin-isn't-good (but let's have a look at some) approach.

The bride-on-a-journey movie always shows the first moment the bride sees her horrendous new home: an isolated shack with no amenities. Her face is a study in shock and disappointment, creating a strong alliance with any woman in the audience who's been let down by her own expectations of dwelling space, not to mention romance and excitement. A neat variation on this moment of revelation occurs in the screen adaptation of *Rebecca* (1940). Joan Fontaine,

---

* The stories also gently suggest the husband's need to learn to be sensitive, because these marriage films were really women's pictures. The idea was modernized in 1981 with a role reversal in *Continental Divide* (1981). A romance grows up between a naturalist living in the Colorado Rockies so she can observe the activities of eagles (Blair Brown) and a tough-living, hard-driving Chicago newspaperman (John Belushi). When he comes out to the mountains to live with her, he has to learn to cope, city boy that he is.

the shy little bride, intones, "Last night I dreamt I went to Manderley" on the soundtrack in a dream that opens the film. Later she is shown really arriving at that mansion. As she anxiously peers out the window, the car rounds the corner to reveal: yikes! There sits Manderley in all its gigantic, overwhelming, aristocratic glory, showing her at once that she doesn't belong. As she enters its hallowed halls for the first time, the servants have lined up to greet her. They are not hostile Indians or wolves or bears, but they might as well be as far as she's concerned.

One of the most successful bride-on-a-journey movies was the film that introduced the characters of Ma and Pa Kettle, 1947's *The Egg and I*, starring Claudette Colbert and Fred MacMurray. Based on a best-selling book by Betty MacDonald, *The Egg and I* was among the year's top-ten hit films. Everyone loved the story of the sophisticated and witty young woman who learned on her wedding night that her husband had quit his office job and, unbeknownst to her, bought a little chicken farm out in the boonies. Betty MacDonald became a household name, a popular speaker at women's clubs. Her charming story told how a couple bonded together in hardship, split up over a minor misunderstanding, and reunited when their baby daughter was born. (Offscreen, MacDonald divorced the dope who sprang a chicken farm on her. The movie worked even if the marriage didn't.)

The Egg and I presents a woman who's the center of the story. When she first hears about the chickens, she says, "Whatever my husband chooses to do is all right with me." What she says is one thing—how she looks when she says it is another. They set out in his car, and as they drive farther and farther up into the thickly wooded hills on their way to their new home, the goat they are bringing with them eats her new hat. (Every woman in the audience immediately knows that this hat thing is a terrible omen.) When the "house" is revealed, he's delighted, she's stunned. "Hasn't it got a lot of character?" he booms out. What he sees and what she sees are clearly delineated to the audience as not the same thing. "None of that streamlined stuff," he exults, as he shows her the pigpen, the chicken coop, and the stove from hell. When he attempts to carry her over the threshold, he can't get the front door open. He has to set her down and force the door, knocking it off its hinges as she walks in behind him (another awful omen). She breaks a window, he falls through the porch, the roof leaks, and that's their first night at the old chicken ranch.

Colbert, always a good sport, digs in. After she falls off the roof into the rain barrel and over into the muck of the pigsty, Ma Kettle says out loud what everyone can clearly see about the elegant actress: "You don't look like a farmer to me." Ma, happily if messily wed, gives Colbert some marriage advice: do it the guy's way and it will work. Colbert actually complies. She gardens, she cooks, she sews, she repairs, she builds, she reaps and plants. She wears jeans and overalls and little dirndls. And, of course, she gathers eggs and hatches chicks. Lest we should all wonder why this woman even remotely considers staying out in the wilderness with a guy who pays no attention to her, we are allowed to see them have a romantic evening in which they dress up in their wedding clothes, consume a romantic dinner, dance lovingly together, and he actually *does* carry her over the threshold.

Living within proximity of Colbert and MacMurray is a glamorous and wealthy woman whose own farm is a thriving business (Louise Allbritton). She has money, a station wagon, and connections. When the other women at the square-dance party are in little blouses and skirts, she arrives in a fur stole, a cocktail suit, and a hat with a giant white feather on it.* Allbritton's wardrobe (and her interest in MacMurray) ultimately causes Colbert to pack up and leave. (One might wonder why she didn't flee when she saw the pigpen.) Colbert goes home to Mother, has the baby she forgot to tell her husband about, and finally returns to him, happy to learn he's bought Allbritton's farm to give his wife a better life. All ends well.

The film was full of oddball characters, good spirits, and refreshing humor. Seen today, it's hard to believe it was such a huge box-office draw, but what it says about couples and marriage is significant. First, it reaffirms the institution very strongly, definitely endorsing the idea that a man and his wife must work together to create a home for themselves, no matter what difficulties they face. Second, it says women must learn to accept whatever circumstances their husbands provide; and third, it suggests couples should make friends and turn to the community for help both as a couple and as individuals. It even endorses female friendship, as Ma Kettle and Colbert's Betty help and support each other. It also warns a woman to watch out for the "other" woman, the one who's after your husband for the wrong reasons. (With her *own* ranch, she doesn't need him the way you do.) *The Egg and I* instructs women: they're supposed to want what they're supposed to have. Back in her mother's expensive apartment, with its uniformed maid and an obviously luxurious lifestyle, Colbert takes her baby daughter in her arms for the first time and tells her mother that this places everything in the right perspective. "This is what really counts. I'm going back to Bob."

The Egg and I is an example of how a movie marriage could work the

---

* Since this was the sort of outfit that Colbert usually wore in movies, there's a subtle message here. Allbritton has shown up in Colbert's duds! It's possible to think of her outfit as an anti-marriage suggestion: "This is how you *could* dress, if only you hadn't married a chicken farmer." Hollywood always believed in clothes, which were clearly, by its standards, more important than a happy marriage.

The Egg and I tells the story of a marriage: bride Claudette Colbert carried over the threshold by groom Fred MacMurray . . .

. . . bride Colbert coping with groom MacMurray's pigs . . .

. . . and bride Colbert getting it across just how she feels about it.

double standard for an audience. On the surface, the husband is a nice guy. We aren't supposed to hate him, but we are allowed to think of him as *wrong*, especially because we are allowed to see the subtle reaction to everything he does from Claudette Colbert, who could *imply* like no other actress could imply. It is possible to watch this movie and have pure fun, a happy experience (especially since it's going to turn out all right), or watch it in a horrified state as it speaks out loud of problems women might know and feel ("He never asks me what I want to do," "I'm killing myself with work," "We have nothing," etc.).

Ambivalence—show both escape and an underlying truth—is built into the marriage movie's pattern of affirm, destroy, and reaffirm. *The Egg and I*, a bride-on-a-journey film, shows everyone how hard it is to make marriage work; but in the tradition of the format, it suggests that if a woman keeps at it and follows the rules, it will endure. Once again, a movie suggests to viewers that marriage is all most couples will ever have: it will be children, a home, and each other. Make the best of it and, as MacMurray says in *The Egg and I*, "believe in each other."

On the other hand, a great many small, forgotten movies clearly spell out marital disappointment. *Under Eighteen* (1932) presents a disastrous marriage as a lesson to be learned for a young girl who is "under eighteen." (Presumably, there is time for her to learn.) The very pretty and almost totally unknown Marian Marsh plays the girl, who watches her older sister (Anita Page) enter into marriage through a glorious ceremony with orchids, bridesmaids, and starry-eyed optimism. "There are lots of reasons for marriage," says their mother. "Convenience . . . money . . . infatuation . . . but the only ones that last are those based on love." The teenager believes it.

Within no time, however, the father of the family (who was going to help the young couple financially) is dead and the Depression is on. Marsh and her mom are living in a slum ("I'm sick of everything," she says) and she's refusing to marry the boy she loves (Regis Toomey) because he's only a trucker and hasn't got enough money. As if to reinforce her determination, Marsh is confronted daily with the sight of sister Page and her worthless husband, who are sponging off Mom and Sis. Hubby has no real job—he's a part-time pool hustler. There's a kid, they argue night and day, and their marriage is an ugly picture.

There's an opposite lesson for Marsh, who works as a seamstress in a fashion house. The models aren't married, and they have spending money, fur coats, and flowers from their "boyfriends." ("They like to make believe they're happy," the store matron warns Marsh.) Her unhappy sister tells Marsh that "marriage is a great game for guys—using girls like us, the saps that we are," but Sis needs no warnings. "If I hand myself to a man for life," she says, "it's cash on delivery . . . Marriage is the bunk, at least it is for poor people."*

Ambivalence was built into stories about the choices women make in marriage. What sort of couple would they become part of? Who was a good "better half"? Three women could choose three different husbands (and thus three different lifestyles) and suffer the consequences of each. (The answer to what women wanted, on Hollywood terms, was clearly: everything—or whatever worked at the box office.) Movies that offered choices most commonly presented three unmarried young women, alone in life but trying to make their way forward. Marriage was one of three end goals: one would want money (and thus was doomed to die); one would want a career (and end up lonely and miserable); and one would want to find true love and get married (the cop-out role model, often played by the least stellar of the group). There could be variations on this format: the money grubber could end up in the gutter, and the career woman might die (prostitution and alcoholism hovered over both), but the idea was that the three choices available for women were love and marriage, money, and career. Films such as *Three Blind Mice*; *Sally, Irene and Mary*; and *Our Modern Maidens* were about what young women *should* want, but showed what they secretly *did* want. There was a subversive subtext.

The "three choices" format was still going strong in the 1950s as the studio system began to wheeze its way out: *Three Coins in the Fountain* (1953), for example, and *The Best of Everything* (1959). The story of three working girls was perked up with wide-screen location shooting in Rome for *Three Coins* and in New York City for *The Best of Everything*. Romance—but really marriage—was pursued in *Three Coins* by three females who each represented a different age group. Dorothy McGuire played a fully mature secretary to an (as always) acerbic Clifton Webb; Jean Peters was a nubile, ready-for-life young woman who nearly goes wrong with an Italian, Rossano Brazzi (because we all know Europeans want sex, unlike us Americans); and Maggie McNamara played a late-teenage virgin who wins the heart of rich Lothario, Louis Jourdan.

In *The Best of Everything*, based on a best seller by Rona Jaffe, Suzy Parker, Hope Lange, and Diane Baker were updated into modern Manhattan career girls. A glossy presentation with high fashion, glamorous settings, and more than enough plot, *The Best of Everything* suggests that marriage is still the proper goal for such young women, but that in the meantime, it's not careers

---

* *Under Eighteen* does have some relief from the Depression and its financial woes. When Marsh, modeling a chinchilla coat, encounters the rich womanizer Warren William, he invites her to a party at his penthouse. All the girls are wearing bathing suits and diving into his swimming pool to recover jewels they can then keep.

they need—it's sex. At least, sex is the bottom line for each of their story lines: one has an affair with a stage producer; one gets pregnant while unwed; and one is offered what is politely termed "an arrangement" instead of a traditional wedding. *The Best of Everything* provides an imaginary depiction of the book-publishing world as a hotbed of sexual intrigue in which an occasional book gets published. Its best fun is found in the small but meaty role played by Joan Crawford, already in her legendary era. All by herself she's a cautionary tale. She's a frankly older but highly successful career woman who has clung to a longtime affair with a married man. The part isn't much, but Crawford sets it on fire, fueling it with repressed rage to depict her trapped status as the "other woman" who finally realizes she's wasted her life. (*Variety* said a good subtitle for *The Best of Everything* might be "Except for Men—Who Are Beasts.")

When marriage is the subject of the "threesome" picture, all three women get married, and each of the resulting couples represents a level of marital success or failure. A perfect example of this format is *The Sisters* (1938), starring Bette Davis, Anita Louise, and Jane Bryan. These actresses play daughters of a turn-of-the-century pharmacist in Silver Bow, Montana. All three have as their goal becoming part of a married couple, but their sense of what they want from a partner is very different. Davis begins the film engaged to a solidly reliable man, but she romps off in the dark of night with Errol Flynn after the two of them spot each other during a do-si-do at a local dance. Flynn is in town for only one night, but when he and Davis lock eyeballs, that's it. He marries her before the train pulls out, and takes her to his life as a sportswriter in San Francisco. Davis didn't want a dull and secure marriage; she wanted *love*, and a very exciting version of it, too. The second daughter, Louise, is coolly calculating. She wants to get out of Silver Bow and have "things." She opts to marry the older, widowed (and very wealthy) father of a disapproving school friend, and she makes this choice because he (Alan Hale) promises to give her everything and expect nothing in return. (She has told him frankly she doesn't love him and never will.) The third daughter, Bryan, is a cheerful, tomboyish type with no particular goal other than the safe marriage Davis rejected. Young and inexperienced, she happily scoops up Davis's abandoned fiancé. The two of them have a friendly relationship which she interprets as love. They wed, settle down to a comfortable life in Silver Bow, and babies arrive around the calendar.

Ironically, all their marriages are disastrous. Flynn turns out to be an alcoholic who can't accept the day-to-day grind of marriage. He loves Davis, but feels guilty when she loses their baby because of their impoverished circumstances—and then even worse when he gets fired from his job, can't finish his novel, and keeps on drinking. When Davis finally gets a job (at which she excels, heading toward a career),* Flynn is devastated and hops a freighter out of town. Davis is left behind to suffer through the San Francisco earthquake all by herself—so the lesson for women is that if you want to keep out of earth-quakes, marry the boy back home. Make a safe coupling.

The Sisters doesn't have a lot of plot time for the other sisters. Louise, whose story was more fully developed in the best-selling novel of 1937, falls in love with a young nobleman on a trip to Europe. When Hale has a convenient heart attack and she becomes a widow, she marries outside her class. This marriage doesn't work, either. (She is on her third one when she arrives home in Silver Bow toward the end of the film.) Bryan has to face the fact that her husband is not only ignoring her and his kids, but is also having an affair. (Davis and Louise arrive home to fix this. They threaten the other men who have dallied with the very same local hussy: unless they run her out of town, the sisters will tattle to their wives.)

Although all three marriages are failures, the plot focus endorses the Davis/Flynn arrangement. These two, after all, are stars, and thus entitled, but they also are *in love,* and thus *really* entitled. Although it makes no sense, an unshaven, still-alcoholic Flynn returns to Silver Bow to once again claim Davis during a do-si-do. One might say their love has come full circle, and one would be right. It has gone around in a circle and is apparently headed the same way again. The film endorses Davis and Flynn because they represent the choice of *love.* Louise married for money, and Bryan didn't know what love really was—she just wanted to be married.† The film says that the sisters knew what they wanted, but they were wrong about it. Only Davis has the right goal: love. She will suffer, but it's worth it because she loves her husband and he loves her. They are an appropriate romantic couple, even if their marriage stinks. Although Louise has money and travel and "things," and Bryan has comfort, safety, and children, Davis has what they *don't* have—she has love. *The Sisters* thus becomes a romantic melodrama about married couples, designed to both reassure women in the audience with failed marriages and still provide them with a visual endorsement of their misery.

Star pairings, definitions of what men and women wanted from each other,

---

* Davis goes to work in a department store, a female territory, and the owner naturally falls in love with her and gives her everything. They are super-compatible, and he stands around waiting to marry her in case she should ever be of that mind. She never is.

† These three daughters are parented by Beulah Bondi and Henry Travers, a constantly kvetching pair who have nonetheless obviously made a solid marriage with each other and a good home life for their girls over the years. Why can't the daughters make good marriages?

how "union" could be defined and/or seen, the standards for perfection in a wife or husband, reflections of audience behavior, suggestions about what to look for in a mate: all these things were the purpose of the presentation of "the couple" in the marriage film. The couple was the first element in a marriage movie. Their problems were the second.

Their Problems

Audiences knew a marriage movie would always be about a couple, but such movies had to search beyond two recurring characters (a husband and a wife) to be interesting. They needed recognizable events, settings, problems, and audience goals. In movie marriages, as in real life, wedding bells ring, brides come down the aisle, cakes are cut, babies are born. Meals are cooked and shirts get ironed. Paychecks are brought home. Jobs are won and lost. Quarrels and disagreements erupt, and misunderstandings lead to walkouts. Couples live in homes with bedrooms and kitchens. People sit around dinner tables, celebrate birthdays, anniversaries, and holidays. Unlike the events of a horror movie or a western or a musical, the events of a marriage movie were the events of day-to-day life, and these events and settings were so familiar that they were difficult to think of as interesting story material. Even when the generic setting suggested danger, marriage could dull things down: in *Son of Franken-stein* (1939), the baron and his missus have to juggle servants, mealtime, the needs of their little son, and redecorating the Transylvanian mansion as well as monsters and angry villagers. What happened in marriage that could be made exciting, fun, tear-jerking, explanatory, and meaningful?

The movies found a set of problems that actually plagued real marriages and that could be used to identify story type, connect to audience experience, and still provide drama. Just as in a horror movie an audience knows not to shower alone or go down to the basement or up to the attic to check out those strange noises . . . just as in a western they know to get out of the dusty street before the final shootout . . . they came to know what the problems were going to be in any movie marriage. The difference is that in a movie about marriage, the audience made the rules. The problems were theirs to give, and the movies were receivers, not definers. The audience was living the marriage definition, or had lived it, or was watching someone else live it. This shifted everything. Although there *was* generic definition onscreen, nobody needed to identify it or label it as such. Hollywood didn't always avoid the truth; it just reshaped where it was headed. Audiences responded in kind. They knew truth, and they knew fantasy. (That's often forgotten today.) The audiences of the past knew when they were escaping, and they knew what they were escaping from. They could accept a link between the two. When it came to day-to-day living, and the ins and outs of marriage, audiences were not confused, and the movies played with that knowledge. In Paris, Peoria, or Patagonia, no matter how tarted up with typhoons, revolutions, musical numbers, and lumberjacks, no matter how many distracting decorative touches such as rose gardens and fringed lampshades, the same seven problems were the repeated reasons, excuses, plot points—the whatevers—of conflict in marriage movies. Audiences recognized them, understood them, believed in them. According to the movies, the issues that threaten marital bliss are:

1. *Money.* Money kills love. And whereas you probably *can* buy love with money, you can't buy money with love.

2. *Infidelity and/or adultery.* Someone will get the itch, and it probably won't take seven years. Benign or deadly, true love or brief dalliance, outside the domestic window the grass is always greener.

3. *In-laws and children*—the baggage of marriage—are supposed to be blessings, but, alas, they are humans. Families interfere. The movies clearly teach that the ideal mate would be an orphan.

4. *Incompatibility.* Couples rush to the movie altar without noticing fundamental differences: he says "either" and she says "eye-ther." He eats a potato, and she eats a po-tah-to. Movies suggest that incompatibility—with the attendant issues of competition, control, and communication—can't be understood until *after* the words "I do" are spoken.

5. *Class.* Americans claim to have no class distinctions, but the movies say otherwise. If the wife wears a dress with too many ruffles, she's dead at the party up at the big house on the hill. For Hollywood, the ruffle is like the British cockney accent—a dead giveaway that your background is not up to snuff. Unless you're Audrey Hepburn, and it's a single emerald-green satin ruffle starting at the tip of your toes and winding around your skinny-mini body up to your swanlike neck so you can peer over it with your doe eyes, you'd better not show up in ruffles. (Such snobbery is a two-way street: if you can't dunk a donut at a local

diner, you're not only no fun at all, but drop-dead stupid.) No matter how strong your love, class differences will surface . . . and bite you in the ass—or in the ruffle.

6. *Addiction.* Addiction kills everything—love, the economic balance, the marriage, the family, the career, the reputation. An addicted partner must reform, or die.

7. *Murder.* When you marry a murderer, your marriage is in trouble.

One or more of these seven problems appears in all marriage movies. Each one can be evaluated in terms of realism, with the most realistic being money problems, followed closely by the temptation of infidelity and problems with in-laws and children. These three—money, infidelity, and family issues—exist on the scale toward the side of truth for the audience. Somewhere mid-center lie the complicated issues of compatibility (competition, control, etc.) and various forms of class differences, often redefined by Hollywood as "education" or "money," so that the difference was specifically social, encompassing manners, fashion, behavior, or a difference in lifestyle goals. Moving toward the "unrealistic" were stories in which marriage was marred by addiction of some sort; and finally there was the truly bizarro issue, murder. Murder was on the crazy side—and yet, who has not said to a loved one, "I'm going to kill you if you . . . "? Audiences loved movies in which one mate tried to murder another. One does not need to speculate why.

Each of the seven issues had flexibility. Each had its own appeal, its own credibility, its own "fun" quota, and its own goals of audience identification. Each could be presented as comic or tragic, positively or negatively. For instance, lack of money could destroy love, but the need for it could unite a couple in their goals. A poor couple might struggle along, fighting their way forward, and despite their hardship learn that true love is the very best currency there is (audience identification strong), or a rich couple, with all their good stuff on display—including the usual mansion, chauffeured car, furs, jewels, and kitchen the size of Phoenix—could learn that losing their money would make them better people and certainly a better couple (audience identification skeptical, but happy with the shopping tour). Similarly, stories of infidelity could be sexy fun, or they could be dramatically tragic. In-laws could be hilarious comedy relief or a bunch of lying spongers. "Class" differences offered audiences the delicious opportunity to experience plots in which someone like them broke free of the restrictions of their backgrounds and became rich . . . and that could turn out well (giving hope) or turn out badly (sending them home reassured about their own situation). Incompatibility was ever reliable, offering screenwriters the chance to write all sorts of witty male/female bickering in different moods and tones. (Some of the very best writing about marriage in the movies is linked to stories about competition, control, and lack of communication. Since these movies were almost always about *resolving* the problem of incompatibility, this "problem" was popular.)

Obviously the most limited of these seven issues were the two that carried the strongest negativity: addiction and murder. These offered great drama and performance opportunities, but they were the least flexible, the hardest to inspire empathy in the audience. Addiction was no fun at all, and filmmakers quickly learned that this was a topic with limited appeal. In general, movies about addiction in marriage did little to cheer audiences up. To make it work, the addict had better be a really great movie star—preferably a singer tackling a serious role—or there was going to be trouble at the box office.* It did, however, have two strengths: it was believable, and curing it gave audiences hope. And it provided the opportunity for a great box-office hit starring a potential Oscar winner. (Sometimes movies would have a drunk scene in a marriage, but this didn't make the movie about addiction. In *The Male Animal* [1942], Henry Fonda, husband of Olivia de Havilland, gets roaringly and hilariously drunk when her old boyfriend, an unlikely Jack Carson, turns up.) As for murder as a marital sin, it blew the rules out the door; but on the other hand, it loosed the hounds of hell onto marriage, thereby visually satisfying many audience members who were never going to avenge their disappointments any other way. And it *could* be made funny, as in the wonderful Preston Sturges comedy *Unfaithfully Yours* (1948), in which orchestra conductor Rex Harrison creatively imagines murdering his wife (Linda Darnell) in three different ways, each one reflecting the mood of the music he's conducting.†

MONEY

In the movies, there are two amounts of money available to married couples: too much and too little. Neither works. When it comes to money, there are no

---

* Frank Sinatra was a heroin addict in *The Man with the Golden Arm* (1955), and Bing Crosby an alcoholic in *The Country Girl* (1954). Both men received Oscar nominations for Best Actor. Susan Hayward played an alcoholic in *Smash-Up: The Story of a Woman* (1947) and in *I'll Cry Tomorrow* (1955), and was Oscar-nominated for both performances.
† *Unfaithfully Yours* was less successfully remade in 1984 with Dudley Moore.

solutions, only platitudes. Money, always money: the subliminal message Hollywood sent audiences was: "Just shut up about it. We're giving you a way to escape that you can afford."

Money was not only a marriage issue—it was an American cultural issue. It was the root of all. Movies had from the beginning tapped into the public's desire to see what they didn't have, to take visual ownership of luxury if they couldn't get it any other way. Movies, no matter how serious or deep-dish, usually were a shopping trip. Beauty, love and sex, travel, clothes, cars, jewelry . . . and, naturally, good furniture. Moviegoers *came* to shop, and they didn't go home empty-headed, just empty-handed. They "bought" in a form of mental rental, and they always came back another day to see their goods, those fabulous things they had selected but left up there on the screen when the lights came up and they had to go home.

Movies acknowledged—but never endorsed—the audience's greed. In *But the Flesh Is Weak* (1932), starring C. Aubrey Smith and Robert Montgomery as a father-and-son gold-digging team, the father advises his son, "Love dies. Money lasts." And in *Merrily We Go to Hell* (also 1932), a cynical male reporter muses, "When we're young, we want to marry for love . . . and when we're a little bit older, we want to marry for a Rolls-Royce."* These coldhearted, even cruel observations are presented with conviction, and yet the final fade-out of both movies finds love and romance triumphant. (Movies are amazingly two-faced, but they get away with it.)

When a marriage movie presents a couple who are struggling financially, the sympathy is always with the struggle; but when a marriage goes wrong because of too *much* money, there's blame to be assigned. Hollywood cheerfully endorsed poverty, one of the most hypocritical aspects of the moviemaking business. Over and over again, not just during the Depression, audiences were told that having no money was not only okay, it was probably better than having too much. If you're poor, you can make up for it by singing around the piano, popping corn (assuming you had any—not to mention a piano), and really caring for each other. If you had money, you'd have none of this good fun. You'd be going out to lavish dinners, shopping for furs, and tolerating your servants, and who could possibly want any of that? The lesson to be learned was a simple one: do not make money your goal in marriage. The pursuit of money, or even falling into it accidentally (discovering oil or inheriting millions) can unsettle your relationship. Poverty was treated as a form of pseudo-security for the average moviegoer: you have no money, therefore your marriage is safe.

---

* Marriage movies dare to say out loud what people in the audience might be thinking, but might never say.

Money as a topic provided reassurance for moviegoers by telling them over and over again three things:

1. Marrying for money is always wrong, and will never work out.

2. Money is a problem for everyone: it makes both rich and poor suffer.

3. When money comes into your life, it will bring changes you may not like—possibly even danger. You're probably better off as you are.

Almost all marriage movies deal in some way with money issues. (Even Blondie had to go on a budget.) One of the most familiar formats is one in which a young couple rise from poverty to wealth—and lose everything that counts along the way. (Their love, and their children, die.) These rags-to-riches plots are very American, as they address the immigrant experience. In this case, the "journey" is not from a foreign country over to America, but from the "other country" of poverty to the one of wealth. It is about the dream of luxury and success that the mythology of America always promised. Since most citizens didn't find it, the format reassured them. A rags-to-riches movie has all *three* of the above-stated goals: warning, suffering, and change.

The rags-to-riches rise of a couple is beautifully exemplified by a movie that should be better known: *The Power and the Glory* (1933), starring Spencer Tracy and Colleen Moore, directed by William K. Howard, and written by a young Preston Sturges. The script (a forerunner of *Citizen Kane*) tells an overlapping, out-of-sequence tale of a man and his wife who journey from the railroad tracks to the top of the financial mountain—and who, in gaining everything, lose everything.

A story that's told not just in flashback but out of chronological sequence offers the opportunity for an audience to view all events, even happy ones, with melancholy.* When we see what a couple become (old and miserable) before we see what they once were (young and optimistic), their story takes on an inescapable sadness. The optimism of love and devotion in marriage is seriously, deliberately undermined. (*The Power and the Glory*, like so many portraits of misery in marriage, was not a huge success at the box office.) It begins with

---

* Fox Film, the company that made the movie, proudly labeled this technique "narratage" and put up a plaque in a New York theater commemorating "the first motion picture in which narratage was used as a method of telling a dramatic story." The ad campaign said narratage "embodies the action of the silent picture, the reality of voice, and the searching penetration of the novel."

the lavish and laudatory funeral of the railroad tycoon hero, Spencer Tracy, who has actually committed suicide. The film is "narrated" by Tracy's faithful lifetime friend Ralph Morgan, who at the same time also has an ongoing conversation with his own wife about Tracy's character. In a series of transitional scenes, these two give an audience both the male and the female view of Tracy's marriage. Their words become almost the equivalent of an audience debate, although the actual voice-over narration is always a single voice—Morgan's. His explanation for what happened to Tracy is simple: "He fell in love, that's all . . . he couldn't help it."

This "falling in love" is not the event in which Tracy met and wooed his wife, Colleen Moore. After "He fell in love" is heard, the audience is shown Tracy's rural childhood, his lack of formal education, and the deep bonding between the two boys, Morgan and Tracy. The film then moves forward to them as old men; Tracy is president of a railroad and Morgan is his secretary. They work side by side high up in a huge and expensive urban office. Tracy is shown browbeating his board of directors, overruling them about a transaction to buy a faltering rail line, the Santa Clara. He is calm, confident, and cruel. He is also articulate, well dressed, and sophisticated. The movie then returns to another point in his past: when he was twenty, illiterate, and a low-level track walker on the rail line. In this sequence, he first meets Colleen Moore, a schoolteacher who will teach him to read and write and do arithmetic, during which they become close and decide to marry. ("And they stayed happy for a good long time," says the narrator.)

The story then returns to the two older men, and a scene in which the president of the Santa Clara brings his daughter to meet Tracy. Tracy's son also arrives, bringing the news he's just been kicked out of Yale. The son is a spoiled young jerk, whose mother (Moore) has allowed him to grow up to be a useless, irresponsible wastrel. At home that evening, Moore and Tracy quarrel angrily over the boy because Tracy has said he's had enough of the kid's nonsense— he's putting him to work as a low-level, poorly paid bookkeeper. ("I won't have him treated this way," cries Moore.)

The strength of the movie's structure becomes apparent when the film immediately returns to the past, with Tracy and Moore as loving newlyweds. In this scene, Moore expresses her ambitions for their future. She dreams of clothes, a better house, a horse-and-buggy. She wants Tracy to "try to be somebody." She volunteers to walk track for him while he goes to school, supporting him while he becomes educated. The narrator says that walking the track at night in harsh weather turned her hands permanently red and raw, and that's why she always wears gloves. It is after this scene of marital unity and sacrifice,

Money, especially the rise to enormous wealth, is always trouble
for a couple who marry in poverty, and then everything changes.
The Power and the Glory shows Spencer Tracy and Colleen Moore
loving and happy in their railroad shack . . .

of shared purpose and vision, that the film returns to the place in time in which
Tracy has fallen in love with Helen Vinson and is forced to tell Moore the
dreadful words: "A terrible thing has happened. I'm in love."

At his office, Tracy explains to Moore that he has "fallen in love" with
Vinson. Moore then leaves, appearing at street level, wearing her fur jacket,
her long gloves, and her diamond pin. The narrator tells viewers, while they
watch, that she went to where "her big, beautiful car" was waiting, dismissed
her chauffeur, and threw herself under a streetcar, a modern Anna Karenina.
Moore's car, her fur, her diamonds—even her gloves—haven't made her happy
or saved her marriage. Wealth has been useless when it really counted. Since
Tracy's idea of "love" is thus defined as infidelity, the audience begins to see
everything ahead in a negative way: Tracy's character, the narrating friend's
judgment, the Tracy/Moore marriage, and the birth of their son. Infidelity
intrudes and will lead to not one, but two suicides, both Tracy's and Moore's.
The problem at the root of the marriage turns out not to be Tracy's infidelity,
it's his money. Infidelity is the by-product of his having made too much money.

The scene that follows Moore's death shocks an audience, because they
are taken directly back to the sight of Moore and Tracy as a young couple,
blissfully happy—and poor. Moore tells Tracy she's pregnant. "They'll never
stop me now!" he says, and after his son is born he goes to his wife in awe and
gratitude. "You . . . you gave me a son." The couple are again seen as united in

. . . and estranged and miserable in boardrooms and furs.

devoted parenthood. The cut that follows this scene takes the audience forward for another glimpse of that worthless son. Tracy, preparing to have his own fun by marrying Vinson, advises the young man to have fun in life because "you only live once . . . I guess I can earn as much money as you can spend." Unfortunately, the young man takes his father's advice to heart.

The inevitable trouble comes when Tracy marries the beautiful Vinson, who only wants his money. Vinson plays what was known as a "socialite," a term once in wide use but seldom heard today.* In some films, the socialite is venal, but that is not a necessary characteristic of the type. The socialite *must* become a society matron to survive—and that means marriage. Vinson's father is a successful businessman who needs a large infusion of cash for their way of life to continue. His beautiful daughter—a young but sexually experienced divorcee—is the perfect pawn for him to use in his game of finance. The pawn herself is eager to keep up appearances, as it were, and will be happy to scoop up Tracy . . . and his money. Tracy, with his poor-man background, is unable to see past Vinson's veneer. When she gives him a second son, he is once again

---

* A "socialite" was someone who did not necessarily have money herself, but had been raised in the arena of money and knew how to behave—which fork to use and how to write a proper thank-you note. (Lee Radziwill might be the Last of the Socialites.) The term was associated with all the graces, but also with the sense that it was absolutely necessary for such a woman to marry for money. In fact, the occupation of the socialite (and her family, especially the mother) was to find a rich husband to marry before the bills piled too high. The socialite is the high-toned gold digger. Where the gold digger wants only money, and doesn't know how to act around it, the socialite fits in and is doing the work her family has trained her to do.

thrilled. Unbeknownst to him, however, the son is not his, but the son of his son, who is having an affair with his stepmom (another infidelity powered by money). When Tracy discovers this, he shoots himself. *The Power and the Glory* shows what happens to marriages when there is too much money. All values are lost, all hope is lost, all reason is lost. All is lost. Tracy and Moore were happiest when they had nothing.

It's no surprise that the 1930s presented many different kinds of pictures that featured a couple who were strapped for cash. Sometimes the most minor film lays out the barest truths, as in *Love on a Budget* (1937 or early '38), one of a series of movies about the Jones family.* The Joneses were a bargain-basement version of the Hardys. Where the Hardy papa was a judge, the Jones patriarch (Jed Prouty) was a small-town mayor. Where the Hardy series developed Mickey Rooney into a star, the Jones family made do with Bonnie, the mayor's oldest daughter, played by Shirley Deane, who never became a name and is forgotten today.

Love on a Budget opens up just as Bonnie returns from her honeymoon. She and her husband (Russell Gleason) have taken up residence "in their beautiful new cottage." All seems idyllic. Bonnie sings in the kitchen and her husband shaves. Unfortunately, there's no hot water, the icebox isn't working, the toast burns, and she scalds her hands, crying out, "Why can't we have things like other people? I want a new stove and a dining-room set and dishes and . . . " Bonnie sings the blues that women in movies always sing: *I want things.* The entire movie turns out to be a warning about buying on credit. ("This foolish extravagance is the cause of most marriages going on the rocks," says her dad, who steps forward to advocate a balanced budget.) But Bonnie must have things, and when the couple buys a full set of household furnishings on the installment plan, disaster occurs.

It's remarkable how often a youthful marriage goes to pieces over furniture and appliances. "Keeping up with the Joneses" is not a mythical concept in American culture. The Joneses, in this case, are driven by their own desires, particularly those of the wife, who just wants everything in her home to be perfect—and to be perfect *right now.* The sense that young women were looking at magazine and newspaper ads and movie sets and feeling that all this stuff they saw—this chic couch, that toaster—should belong to them is palpable in the movies. Things. A consumer-driven society that went to the movies learned what they *should* have, yet also learned that having it might ruin their mar-

* The Jones family figured in both a popular film series and a successful radio show. *Love on a Budget* was the eighth film of the series. In 2009, a bad movie called *The Joneses* told of a group of individuals hired to live in the suburbs, pretend to be a real family, and stimulate product sales by inspiring consumer jealousy among the neighbors.

riages and plunge them into debt. What, really, did anyone think was going on with these obvious contradictions? *Variety* didn't seem to care, praising the movie as "a box office asset" and pointing out that the series was building a "consistent audience following." (When it's all over and settled nicely, the mom of the Jones family, Spring Byington, offers her own marriage wisdom: "The first hundred years are the hardest.")

Sometimes a movie about a poverty-stricken family was distanced (and thus softened) by setting the movie in another country. Frank Borzage's beautiful drama *Little Man, What Now?* (1934), starring the forgotten Douglass Montgomery and the luminous Margaret Sullavan, is an example. This film arrived on American screens with a very lofty purpose, as stated by the head of Universal Studios, Carl Laemmle: "In presenting *Little Man, What Now?* to the screen, I strove to render a social service. The story of *Little Man* is the story of Every Man, and the question of *What Now?* is the WORLD'S DAILY PROBLEM, a problem that men can only hope to overcome by a courage born of great faith in the hearts of women. Against the tide of time and chance, *all* men are little, but in the eyes of a woman in love, a man can become bigger than the whole world."

In other words, you are poor and miserable, your marriage is a shambles because you haven't got enough money; but love and the little woman will see you through. Love, not marriage, is established as a goal. (Love was always Hollywood's alternative to marriage.) The realistic side of the film pulls no punches. Montgomery and Sullavan travel out of town to visit a gynecologist. The music for "Here Comes the Bride" is heard only *after* they receive the news about a baby and learn they cannot obtain an abortion. "We met, we loved, we married, and we're gonna have a child . . . that's paying the full price for the privilege of living," says Montgomery. When their son is born, he says, "Poor little fellow, what now?" She is stronger. "We created life, so why should we be afraid of it?"

Little Man, What Now? is a tender and touching film, beautifully directed and played, but it walks the line between showing audiences what they had (not enough money) and what they didn't have (riches) and ends up with everything sorted out for them through a hollow miracle. (A former friend of Montgomery's who moved to Amsterdam suddenly comes back to Berlin and hires him.)

The ability of Hollywood to update a Depression story and resolve it positively for a postwar audience shows how the marriage movie could adapt the money problem from decade to decade. A mature person in a movie theater in 1946 had been through both the Depression and World War II and was now facing rehabilitation and return to life in a postwar economy. *From This Day*

Forward, starring Mark Stevens and Joan Fontaine, keeps its drama small, tied directly to the marriage of an average couple. Identified in the American Film Institute's catalog as a "domestic drama," the movie was based on a 1936 novel by Thomas Bell entitled *All Brides Are Beautiful.* RKO bought the rights to the novel in 1940, planning to make it into what would have been a typical Depression story of a marriage undergoing financial pressures. The war delayed production, so when the film was finally made (in 1946), the story was updated to include World War II service by its hero (played by newcomer Stevens, who was introduced to audiences in the role). The movie begins in an employment office after Stevens has been discharged from the army. Overwhelmed by the job hunt, he remembers the story of his marriage in flashbacks. Stevens and Fontaine were a young couple who, despite warnings from Fontaine's older, married sister, went ahead and wed on slim prospects. They were ecstatically happy in their early days, but then Stevens is laid off from his factory job and can't find another. Although Fontaine works in a bookstore to cover their basic expenses, Stevens feels humiliated, and things begin to go downhill not only *for* the couple but *between* them. Ultimately, they move into a tenement, and the early promise of their love and devotion begins to shatter. World War II bails them out. The film ends with a return to the employment office for a happy hiring by sympathetic postwar employers. No matter whether America was in financial famine (the Depression) or financial boom (the war) or financial adjustment (postwar), money was always a viable marital-story problem. Even as late as 1993, in an easy-credit economy, *Indecent Proposal* floated an unlikely story of a super-rich gambler (Robert Redford) offering a cashless husband (Woody Harrelson) a million dollars for a one-night sleepover with his wife (Demi Moore). Harrelson's acceptance destroys the marriage—until the final scene.

The Breaking Point (1950) is an example of reused Depression issues, including John Garfield's 1930s star persona of the guy that society "pushes down." The film is a tense story about a husband so desperate for money that he's willing to smuggle illegal immigrants on his boat. *The Breaking Point* is based on Hemingway's novel *To Have and Have Not,* and unlike the earlier film of that title starring Bogart and Bacall, this version sticks close to the original material.* Garfield plays the husband and Phyllis Thaxter the wife. The movie opens up with Garfield's sad and melancholy voice-over saying, "You come ashore and it starts . . . you're up to your ears in trouble and you don't know when it

---

* The story was told a third time as *The Gun Runners* in 1958. Directed by Don Siegel, this version starred Audie Murphy, Eddie Albert, and Patricia Owens. This time, the skipper was smuggling guns into Cuba.

Poverty crushes Phyllis Thaxter and John Garfield in *The Breaking Point*, based on Hemingway's *To Have and Have Not*, but their marriage endures the hardship.

began." When he arrives home, his wife is still in her bathrobe and is washing dishes in the sink. Her news? "I can think about you anytime and get excited." His news? "Everybody in town is squeezing me for money . . . No sooner do I get my head above water than someone pushes me down again." Money is dominating his sex drive. He's briefly tempted by a good-time girl (Patricia Neal at her hottest), giving as his excuse the ages-old male logic: "A man can be in love with his wife and still want something exciting to happen." Even then, however, the pressure of his money worries drive him away.

The Breaking Point was shot on location, and the little house occupied by Garfield and Thaxter (with their two daughters) *is* a little house. His boat is small. His world is small. There is an authentic sense of a couple truly trapped in limited financial straits. There is honesty and real anger in Garfield's tension. When casually asked, "What's the good word?" he snarls, "Crud. That's a good word." When he and Thaxter quarrel, it's ugly and raw. Their household is a grim little world, but Garfield loves his kids and his wife. He has to get his hands on some money . . . so he agrees to take eight illegal Chinese aliens into the country.*

---

* The tradition of the beleaguered spouse who has to risk importing aliens was brilliantly varied and updated in 2008's *Frozen River*, in which Melissa Leo, a financially pressured single mom, smuggles illegals across the frozen wilderness of Canada and into the United States.

The Breaking Point presents an onscreen image of marriage that's not prettied up, not romanticized. Although it says these two people love each other and will gut it out, it's clear that not having enough money will continue to chip away at their love and their self-worth. Although, like most movies that show marriage too grimly, with no resolution, *The Breaking Point* didn't make money, it's well remembered and respected by those who have seen it.

An example of how married conventions can be varied is illustrated by comparing *The Breaking Point*, black-and-white and noirish, to a Technicolor musical, *Has Anybody Seen My Gal?** directed by Douglas Sirk in 1952. *The Breaking Point* is about an average couple who are being destroyed by having no money. *Has Anybody Seen My Gal?* tells a tale about a happy, ordinary family of the 1920s who unexpectedly inherit a fortune, and the money ruins them. Luckily, the stock-market crash bails them out and sends them back to normal.†

The familiarity of money as a primary marriage problem is validated by how quickly its story can be told. In a taut ten minutes, *That's Why I Left You* (a 1943 short from the famous *Passing Parade* series) clearly outlines how money can ruin a marriage. A young couple meet, marry with great joy and optimism, and settle into their life. They have very little, but are happy to "live on love," the traditional Hollywood form of sustenance. As time goes by, however, the husband (James Warren) feels burdened by the pressures of money, and one day the wife (Jacqueline White) sees a white envelope shoved under her door. It's a letter from her husband that explains "why I left you," an action that's taken place between cuts, as it were. As the husband's voice-over is heard on the sound track, he explains clearly how he longed to get away from the financial pressure and have the adventures he'd always dreamed of. Audiences see the sailboat he worked on as he traveled to the South Seas, photographed in gorgeous moonlight on Tahitian waters. The glory of escape, exotic travel, and total freedom is explained, but then the voice says it was wrong of him to feel this way, and "that's why the writer of this letter is waiting now outside the door for your forgiveness." The young wife laughs and runs to the door, where she finds her husband—who has merely gone out to buy a bottle of milk—sitting and waiting. As they tease and embrace, the audience is told that he'd never *really* leave her . . . he's sorry for even having the dream.

---

* *Has Anybody Seen My Gal?* is a charming little film with Charles Coburn, Lynn Bari, Piper Laurie, and Rock Hudson, but its main claim today is its fleeting glimpse of a young James Dean.

† Similarly, Judge Hardy and his family are nearly undone when they inherit an estate and become wrapped up in false values (*The Hardys Ride High*, 1939). In the movies, too much or too little, money just chews away at marital happiness.

That's Why I Left You locates a *problem* that causes marriage to fail—money—and builds the marital story around it swiftly and economically. The audience could fill in details—from other movies *and* from real-life experience. Happiness turns to restriction and to financial problems and failed dreams. Escape is enjoyed visually, but not really endorsed, and order is restored. This pattern deviously affords audiences nothing new. It's the usual one employed for the women's film, the crime film, the gangster film—a formula well defined for the marriage film in the silent era: let the audience enjoy what it doesn't have and is never going to have, a form of the Roman Saturnalia, in which for a few days at the end of the year, the slaves became the masters before being sent back to the scullery.

Money problems that beset young couples who find themselves in over their heads often lead audiences to a sentimental affirmation of love as currency. "You have love, therefore you are rich." An odd offshoot of this concept is its corrollary: "You are poor, but you have love, so you're rich." Movies that concern themselves with couples who live in poverty, or outside normal social circles, are generally about the entire family structure: *Tobacco Road, The Yearling, The Sundowners,* and *The Southerner,* for example. *Tobacco Road* (1941) is the filmed version of the long-running stage play by Jack Kirkland, which was based on the best seller by Erskine Caldwell. It's a quirky comedy about folksy backwoods Georgia. Not really a marriage movie, it has at its center a couple, Charley Grapewin (as Jeeter Lester) and his wife, Elizabeth Patterson. They accept poverty because Jeeter doesn't want to embrace work, and, after all, they have each other.

The Yearling (1946) is based on Marjorie Kinnan Rawlings's celebrated novel about a young boy and his pet deer, but central to the story is the marriage of his backwoods parents, played by Gregory Peck and Jane Wyman. Beautifully shot on location in Florida, *The Yearling* shows poor people to be wise, even noble, and the marriage to be steady as a rock despite disagreements. *The Sundowners* (1960) is the story of a family of sheepherders in Australia, with Deborah Kerr and Robert Mitchum as a couple whose goals are different. She would like to settle down, have a home; he loves the nomadic life of herding. Their passion for each other, and their commitment to their marriage, is again seen as having a nobility and truth to it that might not be found in richer, steadier homes. Perhaps the best film about a couple struggling to make a living in an outback arena is *The Southerner* (1945), directed by Jean Renoir, starring Zachary Scott and Betty Field. Scott and Field face hardships every step of the way to make their farmland support their family, and the film has an honesty and a sensitivity that is especially real in the marriage of Scott and Field, who are presented working side by side, accepting their fate, and fighting hard for their kinfolk and children. All these movies have marriage as a secondary issue, but the presentation of couples who are not distracted by trivia and who really *must* work together for survival and who as a result find little pleasure except in each other, are films that cannot be ignored when considering issues of "money" in marriage movies.

INFIDELITY

In 2010, state legislators in New Hampshire attempted to repeal the state's two-hundred-year-old adultery laws. The original punishment included standing on the gallows for an hour with a noose around the neck. Over time, the penalty had been softened to paying a $1,200 fine. What was personal and physical had become financial. Adultery had become a misdemeanor with a fine and no jail time, and was rarely, if ever, enforced by criminal laws. New Hampshire State Representative Timothy Horrigan (a Democrat) stated firmly, "We shouldn't be regulating people's sex lives and their love lives."

This could be bad news for Hollywood, which has been regulating them for quite a while and charging money for the privilege. The Production Code that was adopted by the motion-picture industry on June 13, 1934, and put into action at that time was specifically vague—or vaguely specific—about infidelity in the way only the canny movie business could be. One of its three general principles stated that "no picture shall be produced which will lower the moral standards of those who see it . . . Hence the sympathy of the audience should never be thrown to the side of crime, wrong-doing, evil or sin." Under the category of "Sex," along with instructions about "scenes of passion" and "seduction or rape," the Code stated: "The sanctity of the institution of marriage and the home shall be upheld. Pictures shall not infer that low forms of sex relationship are the accepted or common thing. Adultery, sometimes necessary plot material, must not be explicitly treated, or justified, or presented attractively." After paying lip service to good taste, morality, etc., etc., the Code concluded with a section entitled "Reasons Underlying the General Principles." This section had a few significant reminders, such as: "Note: Sympathy with a person who sins is not the same as sympathy with the sin or crime of which he is guilty . . . The presentation of evil is often essential for art or fiction or drama. This in itself is not wrong . . . Sin and evil enter into the story of human beings and hence in themselves are valid material . . . such subjects are occasionally necessary for the plot . . . ," etc. In other words, "sin and evil" would be open to interpretation if "done in good taste" because the movies just might be reluctantly forced into presenting them for the purpose of plot. It would be, of course, only in everyone's best interest.

Infidelity—and its legal judgment, adultery—was from the very beginning of movies a favorite topic for a story about marriage. Infidelity involved love, however misguided, but its physical action was sex, always the real glamour of Hollywood's "love" scam. The myriad variations that could be found (good man sleeps with bad woman, good woman takes on bad man, two good people justified, two good people not justified, two bad people, and so on) were solid box-office business.

The infidelity movie was potentially the really fun version of the marriage film. It brought viewers excitement—a little dash of naughtiness at the local movie theater. Everybody could get dressed up in tuxedos and furs, flirt around all bare-shouldered in the moonlight, misunderstand each other, stomp off with a rival to a luxury spa or a ski lodge or a foreign city to swill champagne on a hotel terrace, and then make it all right again with kisses and hugs.* The marriage story about infidelity could easily embrace the exotic, and provide sensuous settings, clothing, and design. As the years went by, the subject always remained on the screen, sometimes as comic bedroom romp (*Up in Mabel's Room*, 1944), sometimes as an emotional disaster (*Strangers When We Meet*, 1960), sometimes as a sly and witty suggestion (*Captain's Paradise*, 1953), and sometimes as a cautionary tale (*Unfaithful*, 2002).

The popularity of the infidelity movie was established in the silent era with movies like *The Cheat*. The goals were always contradictory but clear. Movies rode a fine line between censoring (as required) and liberating (as desired). Infidelity provided an opportunity for filmmakers to use visual imagination, because it had to be implied, not specifically shown. Some of the movies' most beautiful and memorable scenes involve infidelity. The discordant goals of caution, love, exotic escape, disaster, and sexual excitement could also be modulated to reflect changing morality over the decades.

Infidelity was everywhere onscreen, which is really fascinating, since, because of censorship, technically it couldn't be anywhere at all (unless someone was going to die and pay for it). It is absolutely appropriate that one of the most honest and touching movies ever made about adultery is a movie in which it is denied: *Brief Encounter* (1945). How ironic is that?† The point of the movie is to depict the emotions that might generate adultery, not enact

---

* Most of these movies are screwball comedies, and not necessarily about marriage.
† People disagree on whether or not the couple actually ever make love. It's clear they don't have sex in his friend's apartment, but what happened when they were alone in the boathouse?

it. The concerns of the film are the loneliness of marriage, the dullness of its daily comforts. *Brief Encounter*, starring Celia Johnson and Trevor Howard, is all the more devastating—and honest—as a result, and it doesn't matter whether they actually have sex or not. The two leading characters are not looking for adventure or cheap excitement. They are not fooled or hoodwinked by each other. They meet accidentally, are drawn together, and are as confused by their feelings as they are excited by them. They are excellent audience surrogates.

Brief Encounter presents a story that could happen to any two people. Johnson is a housewife, and a good one. She is cheerful, humorous, and loyal to her husband and family. Her husband is a good provider, and is always kind to her and appreciative of her efforts. They reside in a cozy little cottage with a fireplace and plenty of rose-patterned chintz chairs and good hot cups of tea. They have settled into comfortably ignoring each other most of the time. The audience never sees Howard's home or his wife. It's implied that he's less happily situated, but he's not a philanderer. Neither of these two people is actively looking for an affair, and yet one day in the railroad station, between trains, they have a brief encounter.

The story that unspools tells of an unfulfilled love between two middle-aged married people, based on a famous one-act play by Noël Coward. Expanded into a full-length motion picture, it has filled in the gaps without losing the original sadness. A voice-over (Johnson) has been added that helps repress any censorship issues and that also creates a deep sympathy for the wife. "There will come a time in the future when I can look back . . . and it will all be in perspective," she says. As she knits, her husband works his crossword puzzle. They listen to Rachmaninoff. Her voice-over says, "We're a happily married couple . . . This is my home . . . I'm an ordinary woman." An audience can hear the very large "but" hanging in the silence. "I have fallen in love."

A great deal of explanation and justification lies in the sound track of the film. Johnson admits to being "like a romantic schoolgirl" and that she "imagined [Howard] holding me in his arms" and "all kinds of glamorous circumstances . . . It was one of those absurd fantasies just like one has when one is a girl—being wooed and married by the ideal of one's dreams." Johnson says she pictures herself and Howard when they were both young—at a box in the opera, in Venice on a gondola, traveling to "all the places I've always wanted to go." (So where does she actually go? To the movies.)

The unfulfilled desires of Johnson and Howard represent the dreams that will never come true for the audience, and the realization (and final acceptance) of that fact is the genius of the movie. When both characters realize

A *Brief Encounter* between two lonely married people (Celia Johnson and Trevor Howard) leads to a return to their spouses, who will never know what happened.

how hopeless things are, he takes a job in Johannesburg (that's far enough), and tells her, "Let's prepare ourselves." After they say goodbye, she runs out toward the tracks just as the express is roaring through, but "I was not brave enough" to be an Anna Karenina. When she returns home, her husband gently tells her, "Wherever you've been . . . a long way . . . thank you for coming back to me."

Brief Encounter was, and is, a beloved and highly respected film, an international hit. Its tender and low-key tale (British manners cover all trauma) touched a chord in adults. It is a story about longing, yearning, and knowing it's too late to really be able to do anything about it that could possibly work. It may be the finest adultery movie ever made.

Brief Encounter is as British as it gets, but there's a Hollywood movie about middle-aged married people who are lonely and yearning for something more in their lives, who also learn they must keep a grip on reality. Its rhythms, attitudes, and events are purely American, and a useful contrast to the British version. *The Facts of Life* (1960) stars Lucille Ball and Bob Hope. It, too, is an "almost adultery" story about settled people who accidentally, against all expectations and intentions, end up falling in love with each other. Since Ball and Hope are primarily known for comedy, an audience might expect to find nothing much but a silly slapstick affair. While it is true that the story does ultimately disintegrate into physical comedy, the movie opens up honestly and moves forward with a touchingly sad portrait of marital isolation and disappointment. A precredit sequence shows the arrival of an airplane, happily anticipated by an ordinary-looking Bob Hope. A lovely Lucille Ball disembarks, and he embraces her—"Hello, dear"—and goes to get her luggage. As far as any audience can see, they are a happily married couple, because that's what they look like and that's what they act like. (They don't know any other way to behave.) And that, as it turns out, will be what the movie is all about. No matter what illicit love they desire, they really only know how to be married people.

As she sits waiting for Hope to return, Ball's voice-over reveals the truth. "Am I really doing this? Me? Kitty Weaver? Pasadena housewife? Secretary of the PTA, den mother of the Cub Scouts? Have I really come to Monterey to spend the weekend with my best friend's husband?" On comes the jaunty credit sequence, but the answer to the question "Am I really an adulteress?" will be the usual "Yes, but not *really.*" As the flashback story of "how she got that way" unfolds, an audience sees a portrait of marriage that is indigenous to the coming decade of the 1960s. The film is set in the typical world of highly successful couples who interact through the country club, community events, weekly card games, and various parties they give and attend in order to keep a social life going. Hope is married to Ruth Hussey, who runs his house with military efficiency and wryly tolerates him. She's a kind of super-detached version of Myrna Loy, without the humor. Ball is married to hard-driving, hard-drinking salesman Don DeFore, who's more interested in playing the horses than he is in spending time with her. At home, Hope is surrounded by his wife, their kids, and his maid. Ball's problem is the opposite. She is almost always pictured playing solitaire or sitting around all dressed up with no place to go. Neither is happy with his marital situation. Hope is never alone, and Ball is deeply lonely.

When the movie begins, it's made clear that Ball and Hope don't particularly like each other. They're in the American tradition of a romantic couple who are at first antagonistic. Since they are part of the same social set, they must pretend to get along. When a group from their country club decides to vacation together in Acapulco, plot events will end up throwing them together. (There's a sick child, food poisoning, etc.) Their "courtship" is not unlike what unfolds in *Brief Encounter,* but it's very American—all about jokes, high-school memories, and sing-alongs.

The movement from dislike and disapproval on both sides to appreciation and enjoyment is accomplished effectively through only one scene—the two of them fishing off the back of a boat. This scene is superbly acted by two old pros—it's one of the best courtship scenes in any marriage film. (Ball and Hope had appeared together earlier in *Sorrowful Jones* [1949], *Fancy Pants* [1950], and on TV, and they work together like a well-oiled machine.) They're frankly not young, but as they play their lines, acting out a blossoming friendship, they suddenly seem like kids falling in love for the first time. As they talk of high school, they become more relaxed, looser, and happier. They burst out laughing, and tension disappears. There's none of Hope's false smarminess, and none of Ball's cartoonish antics. They look and act like what they are: two no-longer-young people who are lonely and a bit sad, and who begin to find another human who's interested in what they have to say, who will pay attention to them, who'll appreciate their special qualities.

As Ball and Hope try to find time together back at home, the film begins to fall apart. It's made clear that they never find a time or a place—or the determination—to actually commit adultery. The movie loses its honesty, except in one excellent and highly revealing scene. Having finally decided they *will* go away together for an assignation, no matter what, they become trapped in an open convertible during a drenching downpour. Trying to cope with directions, the rain, and their nerves, they begin to quarrel. Up to this point, there's been nothing but concern and tenderness between them. Suddenly, they are at it, and when it comes to quarreling, these two people are pros. Married for years—just not to each other—they leap right in with all the experience of a lifetime. They don't need incentive. They don't need facts. They don't need evidence. They can just take the high road and *quarrel.* They know the drill. They are not so much quarreling over the situation they're stuck in as quarreling with their own spouses on behalf of married people everywhere. It's authentic. After this, the film goes into wacky comedy (they fall out the back door of the house they're trying to have an assignation in), ultimately resolving itself with a no-harm-done coda.

The appeal for any audience of *The Facts of Life* is the sight of two frankly middle-aged people yearning for young love, and almost finding it, but recovering their sanity before any real disaster occurs. Infidelity movies are best loved by audiences when they are reassuring and only about a flirtation, nothing that could actually hurt anyone. Audiences liked infidelity stories that came close, but didn't deliver.

A wonderful way for the movies to flirt with adultery was a story in which a beloved mate has been lost at sea, only to turn up alive later on. (This plot is used by Hollywood in drama, comedy, and musical versions, and is a take on the Enoch Arden theme, from the Alfred Lord Tennyson poem that also

Married (but not to each other), Lucille Ball and Bob
Hope are happy when they first begin to eyeball each
other in *The Facts of Life* . . .

inspired movies in the silent era.) The way the theme worked is illustrated by
two movies released in 1940: *My Favorite Wife*, starring Irene Dunne and Cary
Grant, and *Too Many Husbands*, with Jean Arthur, Melvyn Douglas, and Fred
MacMurray. (It's significant that two films with the same basic plot could come
out in the same year and no one really noticed or even cared. There were so
many movies out there—and all the audience wanted was some fun. Audiences
were willing to have the same old elements repeated in new ways.) *My Favorite
Wife*, by far the superior effort, had Dunne as the disappearing mate, while *Too
Many Husbands* had MacMurray. Grant was the husband in *Wife*, while Jean
Arthur was the wife in *Husbands*.

Too Many Husbands, based on a play (*Home and Beauty*) by Somerset
Maugham, lays it on the line: while MacMurray was presumed dead, Arthur
married his best friend and business partner, Melvyn Douglas. And a year has
passed. There's no ambiguity about sex. She's slept with both of them, albeit
legally and, as it were, innocently. And it's the men who have to deal with her
"infidelity." In *My Favorite Wife*, Dunne arrives home just as Grant marries

. . . but when their actual moment for infidelity
arrives, they become rain-soaked and apprehensive.

Gail Patrick, which allows for a blocked-wedding-night farce that keeps things okay by censorship standards. (Grant hasn't yet bedded Patrick.) Since Grant and Dunne have children, which Arthur and MacMurray do not, the sanctity of motherhood is respected. Why should Dunne, a mommy, have to return home and confront infidelity? Dunne's focus is on winning back the father of her children, and Grant's is on learning that his children need their mother, not Gail Patrick. "Love" is also parenthood. It's chaste. At the same time, however, there's a saucy undertone to *My Favorite Wife*, which, having established its basic decency, is free to hint at things in a way that *Too Many Husbands* won't go near: Dunne was marooned on an island with another guy—and he looks just like Randolph Scott! (In fact, he *is* Randolph Scott.)

Too Many Husbands uses the story to present a woman directly with a sexier problem: which husband should she choose? It's quite a problem, since she likes both. (Complaining about the issue, Arthur intones, "These things always happen when I eat veal.") Suddenly, she realizes she has a good deal—these men are going to fight over her, and in so doing will pay attention to her. "I've been a very lonely wife . . . *twice*," she says, thinking she deserves their discom-

Movie posters celebrated the delicious possibilities in *Too Many Husbands*, but only in advertising.

It was always the woman who got to make the choice in the "too many husbands" marriage movie. In *My Favorite Wife*, Irene Dunne was married to Cary Grant but stranded on a desert island with Randolph Scott.

fort and their attempts to woo her. They decide to draw lots for her—"like I was a free trip to Niagara Falls," she complains.

If the person stranded is a woman, these movies say, the husband must remain faithful, particularly if they have children (a key issue). If, on the other hand, the stranded person is a man, the woman is free to sleep around, because that's probably what those gross men would do. Besides, it is stated, "Any woman would be thrilled if her husband fell in love with her all over again." And *two* husbands . . . ? Well. The "infidelity" is a safe form of fantasy for women in the audience, the available soft-core porn of the era. In the end, both films go for saucy resolutions, but true to itself, *My Favorite Wife* stays within safe boundaries, made deliciously titillating only by the skill of Dunne and Grant.*

Movies about infidelity could shape audience sympathy toward either the male or the female point of view. Was it a henpecked man, desperate for the love he deserved, committing the sin? Or was it the woman who was not properly loved by a cold husband, finding at last the love all women dream of? Whose fault was it? Was it justified? Was it noble or was it cheap? And who had to pay? Because someone for sure was going to have to pay. The very same night Mildred Pierce sleeps with her landlord (and she was actually separated and getting a divorce), her daughter dies of pneumonia. There are direct causal relationships in the movies when infidelity enters the scene. And the location of sympathy for the wronger or the wrongee must be spelled out clearly.

When it came to deciding where an audience should put its sympathies regarding adultery, most Hollywood movies of the decades 1930–1960 were more sympathetic to women than to men. Marriage was deemed to be a woman's career, not a man's. Since marriage stories often starred the iconic female actresses of the studio system, plots were shaped around them and their sufferings; these movies were women's pictures. For a woman, adultery was thought to be a serious decision, while for a man it might be casual. (If the woman adulterer is an unsympathetic sinner, the movie is built as a cautionary tale.)

---

* The popularity of the story held true: *Too Many Husbands* was remade as a musical in 1955 called *Three for the Show*, starring Betty Grable, and *My Favorite Wife* was remade in 1963 as *Move Over, Darling*. It was originally meant to be called *Something's Gotta Give* and to star Marilyn Monroe, but illness required her to be replaced by Doris Day. *Three for the Show* updates the dreary *Too Many Husbands* very cleverly. There's more comedy, and less talk about the problem. Grable figures things out more quickly than Jean Arthur: "I've got what every woman wants—a husband *and* a love—and they're both legal." She imagines herself as an exotic woman with a fully stocked male harem. All the men are in cages with labels as to their particular day of the week, and she feeds them lovingly as she sings, "Down, Boy!"

Thus, the more dynamic plot could be worked up over a woman's straying, although there were always exceptions. (*Carrie*, for instance, the 1952 movie made from the Theodore Dreiser novel *Sister Carrie*, starring Laurence Olivier and Jennifer Jones, remains true to the original, in which a man is destroyed by his adultery. Similarly, *Nora Prentiss* [1947], starring Ann Sheridan and Kent Smith, tells a story of a man's downhill slide after he falls in love and becomes unfaithful.)

Most movies about infidelity created sympathy for women as a link to female viewers. Two infidelity films offer examples: *The Sea of Grass* (1947), starring Hepburn and Tracy, and *East Side, West Side* (1949), with Barbara Stanwyck and James Mason. The wife is the adulterer in *Sea of Grass*, and the husband is the sinner in *East Side, West Side*.

Sea of Grass shows viewers clearly that Katharine Hepburn is a lonely and unappreciated wife. Her husband (Tracy) ignores her for his cattle business and has no sympathy for her eastern ways—her interest in little things like art and beauty and conversation. When a man appears who *does* like all that, and even more, in the form of Melvyn Douglas, she resists and resists, as is appropriate, but finally gives in as the plot requires. While she is giving birth—in a demure and censorially appropriate place offscreen—she apparently blurts out the truth about the newborn son. He's Douglas's, not Tracy's. (Audiences can infer this by the disgruntled look on Tracy's face when he exits the birthing room. Viewers have been asked to await the news out in the hallway.) Since the film was made in 1947, no details about the infidelity are ever fully clarified, and yet, as is typical for movies of the time, it is still made abundantly clear. Hepburn is "suitably" punished, separated from both her baby son and her little daughter, and sent into exile. Years later, after much tragedy (too much) has ensued, Hepburn is allowed to return for a formal reunion with Tracy, and the film completes its circle of sin and punishment for its leading lady. The presentation has never once strayed from its position of sympathy for her—*not* for her sin, the actual adultery, but for her emotional needs, which generated an understandable action. Movies did not condone adultery, but they explained it and thus, by extension, justified it as escapist need.

East Side, West Side is a marriage film that is somewhat confused. It's a marriage story but also a murder mystery—who killed Ava Gardner? (As it turns out, a minor character did it, leaving the audience in one of those "Huh?" positions.) Primarily, however, it *is* the story of the marriage between the very wealthy Stanwyck and the ne'er-do-well Mason. He has been spectacularly unfaithful with Gardner, but has gained his wife's forgiveness and returned to the fold—a very rich fold—largely because Gardner left town. Alas, she returns, and everything between them starts over. The details are not very interesting, but the final speeches between Stanwyck and Mason are significant. Stanwyck, usually a fiery presence who burns disobedient men with her cigarette lighter, has in this movie effectively played the role of the genteel and long-suffering wife. After Gardner is dead, Mason tries to return to Stanwyck yet again, working his charms to recover status. First, he goes to Stanwyck's mother (well played by Gale Sondergaard), begging her to intercede because, as he puts it, "your happiness and peace of mind" mean so much. He calls Sondergaard "Mother." "Mother" tells Mason she cannot help him, because "you're vain and self-centered and worthless . . . I no longer have to make you welcome in this house." Mason is stunned, but warns his mother-in-law he is confident he can worm his way back into Stanwyck's graces. In that case, says "Mother," who doesn't believe it, "it will be dinner as usual next Thursday night."

In his attempt to persuade Stanwyck not to leave him (she's all packed), Mason gives an interesting speech that a viewer has heard many times in movies, a speech designed to remind audiences that it's important to stick things out, to go the distance. (No matter how badly old Hollywood depicted marriage, it never endorsed divorce.) Mason says he has no real defense, but "I just want you to look at this marriage of ours coldly and objectively. Make a balance sheet of it, the good and the bad, the assets and liabilities, before you throw it away, before you throw away both our lives. We started with as much excitement and hope and love for each other as two people ever had. We started a good marriage, Jess. It grew better as it went along. We came to terms with it . . . We said a hundred times a week, 'How did we live before we met?' We planned exactly how we'd be when we were old. I made you promise not to die before me. You remember?" (He counts on it.) During this speech, which would fit into almost any marriage movie about adultery, Stanwyck has stood listening, her eyes like little slits. She tells him, "Yes, I remember." However, in a surprise move, she leaves anyway. In the doorway she turns and says, before exiting, "I thought my love for you would never end and if it did the whole world would end . . . But I was wrong."

This is clear punishment for the male adulterer, and strongly, boldly sympathetic to the wronged wife. Stanwyck is not leaving him for someone else (although there may be a future love with a character played by Van Heflin). She does not forgive him. There are no children to influence her, no parents to persuade her. The sanctity of marriage is not held up as a standard to be respected and maintained. She just goes, leaving him standing there. The idea of the wife sacrificing for marriage, for her man, for her family and her class, is off the books, out the window. And Mason has mounted the main movie argument: LOVE! We must respect and honor our love, he says, but she doesn't buy it. Stanwyck packs and leaves in the kind of movie that previously would have had her melting into Mason's arms and saying, "You're right, let's start all over again." Instead, she's outta there. When a female moviegoer put her money down, she got sympathy (even empowerment) when the sin was Ava Gardner.

The 1960s were kicked off by many stories of suburban couples who were facing issues of adultery and divorce. One that maintained the female viewpoint, and created sympathy for an unfaithful wife, is *Strangers When We Meet* (1960), starring Kim Novak and Kirk Douglas. Based on a novel by Evan Hunter (and with gowns by Jean Louis), the film presents again the suburban world in which active social life is maintained: dinner, picnics, barbecues, and dances; the women dress up to go grocery shopping, wearing high heels as they push their carts down the aisle, keeping busy while the husbands work. Nobody is happily married. Douglas's wife (Barbara Rush) interferes in his business, and Novak's husband is cold and unloving, rejecting her advances at bedtime (and Novak's in a negligee!). Douglas and Novak have a torrid affair, but in the end, Douglas's wife takes him back ("I want us to be the way we used to be") and Novak is left with her loneliness and her cold bedroom. Although there is the implication that her future will be more affairs with other good-looking men, Novak is seen sympathetically throughout the film.

Sympathy for male adulterers was possible, but only under carefully constructed circumstances. Cary Grant, Carole Lombard, and Kay Francis star in a marital triangle that shows how it could be done without the censors clamping down. *In Name Only* (1939), based on a novel called *Memory of Love* by Bessie Breuer, sets up a careful situation. Lombard is a commercial artist, supporting herself and her five-year-old daughter. Her husband died four years previously, and she has moved to the country with her divorced sister, Flora. Grant, an extremely rich man, lives nearby with his very social, very evil wife, Kay Francis.

Lombard is established as innocent, in that she's not looking for either a husband or a lover, and she works hard for her living. She's a good mother. And when she first meets him, she doesn't know that Grant is married. (He forgets to mention it.) Flora is conveniently set up in the film as the voice of anti-love, which in movies is always wrong. A disillusioned divorcee, she tells Lombard that "your husband died while you still had faith in him . . . You don't know how men are . . . Underneath, you're still romantic and as full of illusions as any schoolgirl." Flora's speech delineates the film's tensions. Flora is right,

The eternal movie triangle: husband, noble lover . . . and bitchy wife, as portrayed by Cary Grant, Carole Lombard, and Kay Francis, and as defined by such movies as *In Name Only.*

but Flora is wrong. Lombard is right to believe in love, although she will be hurt, deeply hurt, but still end up rich and with Cary Grant. (Even Flora will reconcile with her husband.)

In Name Only can justify its position about sympathy for a male adulterer because of Lombard's widowhood and motherhood, and because she is on the side of true love. Grant can be excused because the adultery is not really presented as such (it's *love*), and because he is miserably married to the horrific Francis. Francis is the key figure in absolutely decreeing where the audience's sympathy should be. She lies, she manipulates, and she doesn't give a tinker's damn for Grant. She just wants his money and the social position he buys her. In movie terms, the fact that she doesn't love him means she shouldn't have him. He's got to nearly die first, and Lombard has got to trust him again (as well as nurse him back to health), but the law of the marriage movie is simple: Lombard gets him because she *loves* him, and he's sympathetic for the same reason.

Stories of infidelity on film are clearly influenced by social changes. The shifting attitudes toward adultery, and how movies could manipulate source material to accommodate them, are illustrated by three versions of the Somerset Maugham novel *The Painted Veil*. The book, first published in 1925, was made into movies in 1934 (starring Greta Garbo, Herbert Marshall, and George Brent), 1957 (called *The Seventh Sin* and starring Eleanor Parker, Bill

Travers, and Jean-Pierre Aumont), and in 2006 (starring Naomi Watts, Edward Norton, and Liev Schreiber). The story is fundamentally the same in all three versions: A young woman marries a doctor who takes her to an Asian country to live. Bored and lonely, she falls under the spell of a sophisticated man and has an adulterous affair. When her husband finds out, he is enraged, and her lover lets her down because his career would be ruined by the scandal. Her husband then punishes her by carting her off to "the interior," where he puts his medical skills toward making the lives of peasants better. Her surroundings are alien and difficult, but she grows, learning to look outside herself.

Each of the three films shades the basic tale to appeal to audiences of its era. In the 1934 version, all advertising was simply about Greta Garbo. GARBO, said the posters; and GARBO, said the ads. Some posters had only her name with the film's title in small letters underneath. Others carried large portraits of Garbo, with her supporting cast and the film title underneath. The casual eye sees only the real draw: the name GARBO—not even GRETA GARBO, just GARBO. Even the credits just say GARBO (all caps). And her name never disappears off the screen: as the other credits roll, her name remains in black letters behind the new information. Nobody was going to be allowed to forget what the main draw was. The 1934 *Painted Veil* was a star vehicle. The novel was put in service to the Hollywood star system, and, as was the standard policy, no mention of marriage appears in the advertising.

Garbo's *Painted Veil* (directed by Richard Boleslawski) begins with a wedding in the rain—her sister's. (One of the most astonishing things about the film is that it casts Cecilia Parker, a pudding-faced blonde, as Garbo's sister.) Thus, the concept of marriage is immediately introduced. At the ceremony, Garbo is thrown together with Herbert Marshall, a scientist who once was her father's pupil. Garbo envies Marshall his sense of purpose in life, saying it must be wonderful "to be able to have something to absorb oneself." Marshall is sincere, decent looking, but not very exciting. (When her mother tells her to find a "good husband," Garbo asks ironically, "*Must* he be good, Mother? It's not very exciting to be good.") Marshall, who is returning to China ("like all the places I haven't been," Garbo muses), blurts out a proposal while she's brewing him a cup of tea. He has been in love with Garbo ever since he first saw her when she was only twelve years old. With nothing else on her horizon, Garbo accepts. Thus begins her adventure toward adultery.

Significantly, the audience is never shown Garbo actually accepting Marshall's proposal. After he babbles about loving her, and the tea kettle boils over, she asks for time to think about it. (He says he'd like to change his request for a cup of tea to a scotch and soda. This seems to influence her, as she smiles.) The

The STAR *whose flame*
fires the world!

A Metro-
Goldwyn-
Mayer
PICTURE

THE

GARBO

in

Painted Veil

with HERBERT MARSHALL
and GEORGE BRENT

Poster, lobby cards, previews, credits—everything related to presenting
the first version of *The Painted Veil* sold Garbo, Garbo, Garbo. No
mention of marriage or even love. Just Garbo.

movie then cuts to Garbo and Marshall in a boat, arriving in China, and married. Cuts like this are efficient, and eliminate boring plot developments the
audience already knows are going to happen, but they are also very effective in
letting the audience know something important to the story of this marriage:
there is no courtship, no falling in love—basically, no kisses. Thus, it's made
clear that Garbo has accepted Marshall, but not because of romance. With
nothing else on her horizon, and with her thirst for travel and excitement, she
has said yes. The cut, in its own way, explains her adultery.

In China, Garbo meets George Brent, a married attaché at the British
embassy. He is not presented as a cheap philanderer, merely as a charming and
experienced man with a keen eye for beauty. Since Garbo clearly does not fit
into the bridge-playing set at the club, and wants to see the real China, and
since Marshall is awfully, awfully busy with his formulae, Brent begins to show
Garbo about. An audience *is* shown this romance, this courtship, and certainly
those kisses. Brent says, "It's fun showing you things you haven't seen before,"
by which he means her excitement thrills him and he wants to have sex with
her. Since she is a married woman, he feels no guilt. When he first kisses her,
she's shocked and says, "How could you?" "I could," is his cheerful reply. He
finally asks Garbo the question about her husband that the audience needs

In *The Painted Veil*, Garbo found herself at home with a rubber plant, a teapot, and a starchy husband, Herbert Marshall . . .

answered. "If you are in love with him, why?" When Garbo turns the question back on him about his own wife, he replies simply, guiltlessly, "Not and never have been."

This *Painted Veil* sets up its adultery very carefully, turning it into love, at least on Garbo's part. All the footage of the film that would normally be given over to showing a couple falling in love goes to the adulterers. Ultimately, it finds a perfect setting for their physical union: "the festival." "The festival" is an unnamed Chinese holiday, and it's a very *big* festival. Having been kissed and aroused in the afternoon, but running home instead of succumbing, Garbo finds herself yet again sitting at her dinner table, spooning up her soup all alone. Hearing the "festival" outside, she decides she must experience it. She puts on an Asian-style turban, the visual metaphor for the lure of adultery. She then steps out into a dark and velvety night, lit up by moonlight, fireworks, sparklers, and smoke bombs. There are blossoms on the trees, a silvery-gold Chinese fire dragon, gongs, masks, glitter, dancing, twangy music, a sun god with a naked chest, long fingernails, plenty of hokum—and, of course, George Brent. All are out there waiting.

Garbo's outfit, pure white, is a fine example of high-Adrian structure and cut. All she wants to do is wear it and learn about the natives and what makes them restless. When she bumps into Brent, it's not her fault; it's her geography. (And her turban.) This was how adultery was presented to audiences in the early 1930s: inside a tale of erotic, exotic escapism. If it took Somerset

. . . but with the opportunity to go out in the
moonlight with an eager lover (George Brent), a
turban, and the mysteries of the Orient.

Maugham to do it, so be it. *The Painted Veil* lays out an adultery any filmgoer
might like to have—one with all the trimmings. It is also presented safely: not
in *their* neighborhood. It's an adultery happening only on the screen, and it's
happening over there in China. It's also happening to Garbo, a one-named
unreal presence. Everyone knows there's no one like her around town.

Brent takes Garbo into a darkened temple, and she has her fortune told.
"Radiant happiness follows trouble profound . . . impatient hands that reach
for great love . . . beside you a great love, consuming as a great fire . . . but eyes
cannot see close, love is too close to see . . . powerful as an avalanche." (Any
one of these things might have been enough.) When Brent laughs at the statue
of the god of fate, Garbo laughs too.* She and Brent passionately embrace,
or as she says, "Things happen." (He has suggested they could be "unhappy
together.") In case anyone in the audience is sleeping, there is a strategic cut to
fireworks exploding.

---

* So much for *Ninotchka*'s 1939 tagline, which advertised "Garbo Laughs!" as if it were happening onscreen for the first time.

After Marshall finds out, Garbo delivers a speech that is important for her character's right to sympathy. "I fell in love, blindly, madly. I reached for the happiness I could get, and like a fool I stole it . . . There was nothing cheap about it . . . No apology. I don't love you. I never did." ("Are you speaking for him, too?" asks the dubious Marshall.) When Brent lets her down ("My career . . . your reputation . . . if you're willing to sacrifice everything, so am I, of course"), an appalled Garbo is taken to the interior, where cholera is raging.

MGM obviously felt the audience for this movie would largely be made up of women, and that sympathy for Garbo needed to be maintained. The movie gives her three excuses: (1) Marshall neglected her. (2) She truly loves Brent. (3) Brent is not a *bad* man—her judgment shouldn't be that wrong—just a man who has a different social standard than she does; he *will* do the right thing if she insists, but he feels it's unnecessary (his "unhappy together" policy). The 1934 *Painted Veil* stays true to itself all the way to its finale. After "all this death and destruction" the couple experience in the interior, an exhausted Marshall realizes how "small" Garbo's adultery really was. He plans to send her back to Hong Kong, but instead they become friends again. Marshall is stabbed by an unhappy peasant whose home is being burned because of the cholera epidemic, so Garbo does not leave, staying behind in the convent to help. Meanwhile, Brent makes his way to them, having changed his mind. "Once I waited for a word from you," says Garbo, but "I was selfish . . . we thought only of ourselves." She sends him packing, because "that's why I lost Walter . . . thinking of myself . . . But his life, his work, everything he does is love." Brent leaves, Marshall promises to recover, and the marriage is restored. "Don't leave me," says Garbo. "I won't," says Marshall, and "I love you," says Garbo. These are the final words of the movie.*

The 1934 *Painted Veil* says marriage is love, and if it isn't, it won't work. Garbo didn't understand what love was until she faced "death and destruction" and saw the nobility in her husband. He, too, had to get his priorities straight. ("I went blind in Hong Kong.") Hollywood, specifically MGM, turned *The Painted Veil* into a star vehicle that would maintain its fundamental sales pitch for audiences: love. And glamour. And wardrobe. With just a little safe sex thrown in. It's designed to be an imaginary adultery for lonely women. The wonderful mixture that DeMille had understood—give 'em what they want, then take it back and say it's naughty, but you can come again tomorrow for a little more—was safely in place.

The 1957 version has a different focus, but still maintains a primary goal. It

---

* Brent, in leaving, remains a good sport: "All the best," he says.

opens with a title card that firmly locates the audience in reality: "Hong Kong 1949." There'll be no goofing around with temple gongs and smoke bombs here. Viewers are immediately taken into a close-up view of erotic objects via a camera movement around a lady's boudoir. There's a dressing table with cosmetics, brushes and combs, perfume bottles and jewelry, and as the camera tracks across the carpeted floor—like a dog sniffing a trail—there's even more. High-heeled slippers, obviously kicked off in haste. A pair of silk stockings, abandoned. A man's jacket, with his bulky wallet alongside. Cigarettes in an ashtray. It's clearly an assignation scene, suddenly interrupted by an insistent twisting of the handle on the door into the room. The heroine, this time played by Eleanor Parker, sits up from the bottom of the frame à la Gilda when she hears the sound and says in a hoarse whisper, "What's that?" so the husband, an unexpected early arrival home, gives up and leaves. Parker, in her dressing gown, consults with her paramour (Jean-Pierre Aumont) about the strange sound. He's in his shirt with his tie loosened, but smoking the telltale postcoital cigarette. He doesn't know what it is, but as long as her bedroom door is locked, he's sure he doesn't need to know. In case the audience doesn't know, either, the story of *The Painted Veil* has been retitled *The Seventh Sin*.

It's an adultery movie, all right, and it wastes no time in establishing that fact. Gone is the meeting of the central couple, their courtship and marriage, their arrival in Hong Kong, her increasing boredom, his immersion in his work, her experiencing the lure of the exotic. Eleanor Parker will not need to put on a turban. "I love being with you, Paul," she tells her lover. "I never really got very acquainted with my husband." In fact, she doesn't even know his telephone number at the medical school where he works while she makes love with Aumont. By beginning *The Seventh Sin* in flagrante delicto (and giving it a new title), the 1957 version of the story announces itself as a cautionary tale. However, since the heyday of the type has passed, it's a sort of semicautionary tale, and is willing to pull its punches as necessary. The adultery of Parker is never presented with any suggestion that the audience should care about it, or that it's a love match. Parker plays a sophisticated woman rather than a country girl yearning for travel. She's an American—from Baltimore—and she has already adopted an Asian style of dress (an imaginary turban). All her clothes have frog closures, mandarin collars, and silken fabrics. She decorates her hair with Asian hair ornaments, at least until she has to live among the nuns in the cholera territory.*

Garbo yearned (like her viewers) for true love, travel, and adventure, and was

---

* This Asian style of dress was popular in the late 1950s among young American women.

thus entitled to sympathy. Besides, her adultery was with a handsome movie star associated with leading-man roles, George Brent. Eleanor Parker, the lead of *The Seventh Sin*, is a bored and selfish American woman wed to a stalwart British bacteriologist (Bill Travers). Her affair—and it *is* just an affair—is with a married man who's a weakling with a history of preying on married women. And he has children! This is naughty. On top of all that, he's played by a Frenchman, and he's a man who is mostly immersed in running the successful shipping business he acquired through marriage. Aumont tells Parker he has great regard for his wife and could never consider living without his children. The affair reflects no sense of love (although he claims he loves her), only sexual dalliance. Travers as her husband is clearly mismatched with Parker's cool elegance. (Herbert Marshall, a fine actor, was an excellent foil for Garbo's star power, and could hold his own.) Travers is a likable film personality, but he doesn't fit well into a world of Asian sexual frustration. He does, however, seem boring; an audience can find sympathy for Parker on that level. His miscasting does much to impair the story's basic triangular structure. In the original movie (and the novel), the husband is a central force, a key figure in the wife's learning experience. Travers's role is to help an audience understand the level of Parker's frivolous behavior. He provides, through his angry confrontations, the back story of Parker's character. In this film, unlike both other versions, she is explained as a former belle from Baltimore who refused offers of marriage until her "ugly younger sister" suddenly got married, making her look bad. Travers says, "You were desperate to get a husband." She was motivated to escape her embarrassment by marrying, and he, a sort of catch because he was British and a doctor, came along and liberated her. When he confronts her with her infidelity, he tells her: "I knew you were shallow and frivolous and vain . . . but I loved you." She fires back that she's repulsed by him, and always used "the headache gag" on him because if she had not met Aumont, she would never have known "what love is," adding, "I wonder how many women wouldn't." This statement is at the heart of the primary audience connection the movie hopes to establish: a link to frustrated women, disappointed in their sex lives, using the "headache gag" and wondering if there really was anything romantic out there for them. *The Seventh Sin*, of course, plans to work the DeMille ploy on them: yes, there is, but it won't work.

After Travers drags Parker off to the interior, they argue about everything, even about whether to eat their lettuce or not (the cholera epidemic from the earlier film is still raging). He forces himself on her in an angry attack—it's fundamentally a rape scene, with her saying, "Walter, don't . . . don't" repeatedly—throwing some much-needed sympathy her way, but basically throwing everything out of whack regarding any noble finale for him. When

In the first remake of *The Painted Veil*, retitled *The Seventh Sin*, Eleanor Parker found herself struggling to hold off the unwanted advances of her husband, Bill Travers.

she becomes pregnant, he dies. The movie ends before the baby is born, and Parker, no longer a cynical wife, sets out to find full redemption. Needless to say, there's no positive resolution with Aumont, who disappears after the couple leave Hong Kong, with no more screen time, his purpose achieved.

Unlike the Garbo film, *The Seventh Sin* is not selling a star (although Parker was a big name and a fine actress). It is definitely not selling love. It is reminding audiences that infidelity is a bad idea—a *sin*—that will bring no good news to anyone. As a result, this *Painted Veil* diminishes the exotic lure of the Orient. Times have changed, and the East is no longer the world of beaded curtains to be proffered as an excuse for adultery. The audience of the late 1950s won't buy the kind of escapist hokum presented so effectively, so visually, so gloriously (so crazily) by Metro in the 1930s. Advertising for the movie put the final stamp on the new approach: "*The Seventh Sin*," said the ads, "A Woman's Mistake."

By the time *The Painted Veil* was resurrected for a 2006 audience, adultery had become passé, no longer a big box-office lure. Thus, the politics of the story were expanded to a more current issue (American involvement in a foreign land), and the exotic is represented by a franker look at the act of sex. When the film opens up, the couple are already in China and already married. Location shooting replaced the studio-designed sets. The movie has the elaborate time shifts back and forth that tart up many contemporary movies, because just having an affair is no longer a big deal. Cinematic tricks are needed. (The story of how the couple met is presented through flashbacks.)

The modern *Painted Veil* is a period piece set in China in 1925, whereas both the Garbo and Parker versions were in a "current" time frame. This China is one of heat and dirt, with no air conditioning but plenty of sweat and political unrest, not the former filmed world of exotica. The location work makes China very gritty, very tactile, and very real.

Once the couple (Edward Norton and Naomi Watts) go into the interior (after her romp with Liev Schreiber is revealed), Norton never looks her in the eye. The husband's role is now once again equal to the wife's.* There is no longer a star caste system with GARBO, or even Eleanor Parker. If anything, it is *his* story. He's a man of science, trying to make China healthier, safer, better. When the couple come together again, it's after a drunken night. It *is* purely sexual and equally desired on both sides, and she becomes pregnant. After Norton's death from cholera, Watts returns to England with her little son and by chance meets Schreiber on the street. He opens the door to something more, but she moves on. When her son asks who the man was, she replies, "No one important, darling." This is an entirely different view of adultery than either of the two earlier films presented. Morality has changed. The movie shifts sympathy toward the man's perspective; the woman does not need to be overtly redeemed for society, only to find herself and her own sense of self-worth; it doesn't matter who fathered the child; neither love nor sin is the focus. Infidelity isn't the main purpose; it's just one of the elements in a marriage story, as the couple learn to respect each other and find common purpose before one of them dies.

In particular, the concept of motherhood illustrates the differences in the three films. The Garbo version is about love: romantic, exotic, passionate, escapist love. What would motherhood have to do with that, especially if the mother is supposed to be Garbo in a turban? She does not become pregnant, but Marshall lives. The Parker version is about a woman doing the wrong thing—becoming a bad wife, committing a sin, and having to atone for it. Her baby is never born onscreen, and her husband dies. The modern version easily *uses* motherhood. It adds drama by raising unanswered questions: How far along is she? And who is the father? (Norton even asks her aloud, "Am I the

---

* This couple also fights over whether to eat their salads because of the cholera epidemic. Their quarrel is a tour de force by Norton and Watts, who make it a power struggle over tomatoes—a brilliant metaphor for married disagreement. Ordinary edible objects become the weapons of destruction. *Both* eat defiantly. "You'll dare to kill yourself? I dare to kill myself even better!"

In the 2006 version of *The Painted Veil*, Edward Norton and Naomi Watts lead separate and unconnected lives under umbrellas on location in the very real Asia.

father?") Norton dies, but it's no longer a problem for a woman to raise a child alone. She and her son are seen years later, happy together in the streets of London. Modern social attitudes have been projected onto the filmed "past."

Besides the main trio in each of the three different versions of *The Painted Veil*, there are two other main characters from the novel. When the couple go out to the "interior" to face death and the problems of their marriage, they encounter two people: a nun and the British district commissioner. The nun is eliminated as a major character in the 1934 *Painted Veil*, and the other two versions of her (Françoise Rosay and Diana Rigg, respectively) don't differ much. A nun is a nun; they're out there to cluck, and act as a sounding board for Parker and Watts. Waddington, the commissioner taking up his life away from England, does reflect a difference that helps define the changes in each film. In the 1934 version, the character is played by a minor actor, Forrester Harvey. He's a friendly comic relief, and his role is very small. He has no personal life developed, no Asian wife or paramour. With Garbo as the film's central focus, his only job is to interact briefly with her. In *The Seventh Sin*, George Sanders undertakes the role and becomes a supportive friend to Parker; he's as cynical as she is. (When asked about his love life, he tells Parker that "there was a girl in Hong Kong I gave a hot plate.") Sanders plays an important role in helping

Parker fill her time. He will guide her toward working at the convent to help the nuns with their orphans. (The nuns won't take her unless her husband okays it, so Parker begs Travers, asking his forgiveness for her "silly woman's infidelity.") Sanders is also frank with Parker about Aumont, whom he's known for years, telling her that "some men need a lot of women . . . He never lets these little romances interfere with his marriage." Because George Sanders was at the time a bigger star name to American audiences than Bill Travers, he gets more screen time and almost becomes the leading man. He's also the source of the second major difference between this version of *The Painted Veil* and the other two (the first being the shift to emphasize the concept of "sin"). Sanders, after knowing Parker long enough to find he likes her, tells her he'll take her to tea "at my place." "My place" turns out to be a lavish and exotic home, well run by an Asian wife whom Parker didn't know he had. Sanders's wife speaks no English, obeys his orders, spoils him totally, waits on him hand and foot. She wanted to commit suicide when he tried to leave her and, as he tells Parker, is a person that "no Western woman could ever understand." His wife is happy to be his wife and nothing more, and the movie suggests that, as a result, he himself is happy. "You are too liberated, too American," Sanders tells Parker. Made in 1957 and set in 1949, this marriage movie is intended to reinforce women in their roles as wives and mothers, and to help them see that straying from these tasks will bring only misery. The Asian woman is set up as a kind of model, the perfect doll wife. (When she gives Parker a gift of a pair of her own slippers, Parker's feet are too big.)*

In the final version, the Waddington character is portrayed by the successful character actor Toby Jones. Jones presents Waddington as strange, alienlike, and enjoying life with a young Asian mistress. He provides a deeper level of meaning regarding a Westerner's acceptance of Asian culture, and a wiser, more sympathetic companion to the heroine. These three versions of the characters shift from insider to outsider-by-choice to outsider-by-type, and their acceptance of the Asian world goes from not at all, to respectable, to total (so much so that it ceases to be a main point). They reflect the changes in the films: the first version a typical romance of its time, with exotic overtones, the second a story that reaffirms mainstream society's values (you must be faithful in marriage), and the last trying to tell the original book's story, since today there are no censorship restrictions and no need to reshape events for a mass audience that might be offended by certain elements. The 1934 *Painted Veil*

---

* This "Asian doll" motif is present in other films of the era: *Japanese War Bride* (1952), *Sayonara* (1957), and others.

is about love, not infidelity. *The Seventh Sin* is about infidelity, not love. The 2006 *Painted Veil*, an independent film, is about faithful literary adaptation. Connecting to a large mass audience is no longer a prominent goal for a marriage movie's use of adultery. With different shadings about the importance of love, the need for sex, the issues of motherhood, obedience, couples working together, reputations ruined by affairs, *The Painted Veil* offers options to each generation, and each era can make the *Painted Veil* it needs.

Two great literary models of female adultery inspired Hollywood movies: Tolstoy's *Anna Karenina* and Flaubert's *Madame Bovary*. The first was filmed several times, most notably in 1935 (starring Garbo) and in 1948 (a British film with Vivien Leigh).* *Madame Bovary* was filmed in 1932 as *Unholy Love*, then in France twice—in 1934, directed by Jean Renoir, and in 1991, directed by Claude Chabrol. The most celebrated (and lavishly produced) version was made in Hollywood in 1949, directed by Vincente Minnelli, starring Jennifer Jones, Van Heflin as her husband, and Louis Jourdan as the wealthy lover, with a script by Robert Ardrey.

The two celebrated film versions of *Anna Karenina* both present her adultery with sympathy. There are three reasons why this works: she is played by a beautiful and well-loved star (Garbo or Leigh); her husband is coldhearted and domineering (Basil Rathbone or Ralph Richardson); and she is a loving mother to her little son (played by the shameless scene stealer Freddie Bartholomew for Garbo and by the lesser light Patrick Skipwith for Leigh). *Anna Karenina*—with its restrictive society, loveless marriage, and endorsement of a relentless passion that just can't be controlled—was ready-made for Hollywood.

Madame Bovary, however, presented a problem.

When men and women needed love, Hollywood was right there with them, in plots as well as in ads. Love always meant money at the box office. And when men and women wanted to have (or at least *see*) beautiful things, Hollywood was right there with them once again—but not for the same reason. In Hollywood movies, wanting stuff could always tip the moral scales to the negative. "I want you to have beautiful things," Mildred Pierce tells her daughter, and she supplies them so bountifully that the daughter becomes a murderess.

Madame Bovary is also a woman who wants beautiful things . . . *and*

* A television movie was made in 1985 with Jacqueline Bisset, Christopher Reeve, and Paul Scofield, and in 1997 a film called *Leo Tolstoy's Anna Karenina* (in case we thought it was someone else's), starring Sophie Marceau, was released. The latter was the first English version to be actually filmed in Russia. There are also other *Karenina* films, such as *Love* (1927), a silent with Garbo and John Gilbert.

Greta Garbo brings to life one of literature's most tragic adulteresses, Anna Karenina. Anna has everything: a wealthy and successful husband (Basil Rathbone), a lavish home, and a little son, but she throws it all away for love.

love . . . *and* excitement . . . but the novel lets everyone know that this is because as a young girl she was too heavily influenced by romance novels and false images that only a naïve girl could believe in. Hold on! Could those "romance novels" be just a little bit like Hollywood movies? (No wonder the 1932 version was titled *Unholy Love*, not *Madame Bovary*.) When the studio system finally made its high-budget *Madame Bovary* in 1949, the project was given to Vincente Minnelli, partly because he was one of the industry's best directors but also because he was on the side of the audience's need for beauty. He saw the love of beautiful things as poignant rather than greedy. His Emma Bovary is more than sympathetic; she's also emblematic of women in the audience, although the 1949 *Madame Bovary* does not shirk Flaubert's intentions. The movie begins with a framing device (much hated at the time) in which James Mason portrays the author on trial for censorship in France. Flaubert/ Mason pleads for understanding for the young girl and her naïveté, telling "society" to see her sympathetically and understand where the responsibility for her errors really lies. After taking care of that, and locating the problem over there in France and back there in time, the movie that follows lets audiences sit in the dark, become Madame Bovary, and understand how right she really was in wanting to escape her restrictions and find love. When Jennifer Jones asks pathetically on her deathbed, "There's not something wrong with things being beautiful, is there?.," the movie is practically begging for the audience to shout out "No!" (And then come back next week and see something else with really good clothes and furniture.)* One of the best moments in any costume film is the great ball scene, in which Jones, spectacularly gowned in white with black-feathered trim, swirls and swirls and swirls around the floor, the camera following and following and following until she calls for air and servants smash open the ballroom windows. Minnelli brilliantly found a cinematic equivalent for her passion, which was coupled with a hunger for society, fashion, the affirmation of beauty, and a whirling, passionate physicality that ends in physical wreckage.

Madame Bovary ends tragically, of course, and reminds everyone how wrong the poor wretch and her downhill adulteries were. But, oh, that ball sequence, those clothes, and that haunting question: Is it wrong to want beauty . . . things? Is it wrong to go to the movies? The ability of the marriage movie to serve two different masters is well on display.

Madames Karenina and Bovary, of course, were great literary heroines, to be respected. Hollywood knuckled down and got serious with a lesser figure. Morals would and could be stretched for two great women of literature, but the cheap antics of Bette Davis in *Beyond the Forest* (1949) were not meant to be as easily accepted. Davis's Rosa Moline is a kind of modern American "Anna Bovary," a half-and-half version of the two women who wanted love and who ended up dead by their own decision to go there. Rosa Moline, however, doesn't have the literary pedigree required for a totally sympathetic adultery, whereas Anna Karenina and Emma Bovary carried the endorsement of being characters from two great novels of understanding about the restrictive roles of women in society (both written by men).

Davis is married to a small-town doctor in *Forest*, not unlike Madame Bovary. This character, played by Joseph Cotten, is not coldhearted, but he's very busy all the time and seems passionless. Davis wants to "go to Chicago"— that's all, just have a trip to Chicago. When a wealthy cad (David Brian) shows up, she finds the excitement she's looking for in an adulterous affair that she hopes will turn into marriage, or at least a ticket to the Windy City. This adultery is never condoned by the movie, and neither is Davis's behavior. (Some women find sympathy for her anyway. She's heroic in her raging boredom.)

---

* Earlier in the movie, trapped in a seedy hotel room with a would-be lover, Jones has wept and also asked directly: "Is it a crime to want things to be beautiful?" It's a strong theme of the film.

Davis's adulteress cannot be condoned for two basic reasons: she shoots her lover and tries to abort her child. Censorship at the time could not okay either of these acts, much less both. (Davis dies just short of the railroad tracks, keeling over as she tries to board the midnight express.) Seen today, Davis can be an understandable figure of female desperation. She wants freedom, respect, her own identity, and, at the very least, something to do with herself. Today she's like an angry Valkyrie demanding liberation, even if it's only a train ride to Chicago. At the time, however, she was a villainess, although the ads told the truth: "Nobody's as good as Bette when she's bad."

American moviegoers were always caught between a warning—"Don't want too many things"—and a consumerist cornucopia of good stuff all over the screen. They were sold the idea that only the things they saw onscreen—the ones they could not touch or possess—were their portion in life. Just being able to *see* was a good enough form of ownership. One of the most successful goals of movie stories about marriage was this ability to give and to take away, to show generously but to warn against. For those trapped in unhappy marriages, or even those just stuck in the rut of an ordinary one, the movie marriage provided alternatives. To show the other and restore the usual—nowhere was this better accomplished than in the marriage movie about adultery.

IN-LAWS AND KIDS

There was one thing every moviegoer had in common with any marriage movie and all moviemakers: a family. Even orphans had a family—a non-family. No matter how awful some movie relatives behaved, an audience was willing to believe it: when it came to monstrous in-laws, the audience was out in front and ahead of the game. They would believe anything. Just tell them Fay Bainter, Joan Crawford's sister-in-law in *The Shining Hour* (1938), burned the honeymoon house down over poor Joan's head, and it seemed not only credible but probable. When it came to portraying hideous family behavior, Hollywood had a free ticket.

And they used it. All over stories about marriages are relatives who lie, cheat, steal, murder, connive, and at the very least interfere. It might even be said that to interfere was so much a relative's purpose that movie in-laws came to represent fate. As such, they had rock-solid credibility with audiences, well able to appear as the unexpected thing you didn't look out for that rises up, catches you unprepared, and unhinges you. Joan Leslie in *Born to Be Bad* (1950) happily welcomes a visit from her cousin Joan Fontaine. Leslie is preparing to marry a very, very rich man (Zachary Scott), and she's just so busy with the caterer and the color of her napkins that she doesn't notice Fontaine has married him out from under her. In *A Stolen Life* (1946), Bette Davis's naughty twin sister (*two* Davises for the price of one!) steals her fiancé just by flouncing around at a square dance. *The Secret Heart* (1946) has June Allyson (of all people) as a girl so obsessed by memories of her dead father that she tries to destroy any future life or happiness for her stepmother (Claudette Colbert).

The marriage movie with in-law problems—as well as problems with children—has very little to offer that isn't obvious. Simply because it *was* so common, so well understood, the concept never seemed to find much that was really original. This type of problem was very close to the audience's real life, but it also offered very little imaginative variation (unless it moved toward the murder scale). Once in a while there was a kindly old aunt (usually played by Edna May Oliver) who could help figure out marital woes. And sometimes a husband's snooty family, such as the Brits in *The White Cliffs of Dover* (1944), learn to appreciate their very American daughter-in-law (Irene Dunne), especially after the United States enters World War I on their side. And sometimes they learn to accept a daughter-in-law from another culture, as in 1952's *Japanese War Bride*. But for the most part, movie in-laws are just a very plain old disaster . . . and predictable.* That very predictability was what made the in-law "problem" so popular in movies. And besides, it was the "problem" for which viewers felt no responsibility, no guilt.

In-laws were often used as plot devices to drive a happy couple apart, to destroy marital love and trust. Presumably because they had known one of the partners forever, they could tell the mate "the awful truth." A sensitive marriage film (both comic and tragic) that illustrates how a family can destroy happiness is the 1940 *Primrose Path*, directed by Gregory LaCava, starring Ginger Rogers, Joel McCrea, and Marjorie Rambeau in an Oscar-nominated role as Rogers's prostitute mother. Based on a novel called *February Hill* by Victoria Lincoln, the movie needed deodorizing to get past the censorship office, so it opens with a printed quotation designed to excuse any bad behavior: "We live not as we wish to, but as we can—Menander, 300 B.C."

Primrose Path is not really a movie about the in-law issue, nor is it even

---

* For instance, giving in-laws any type of control in the lives of a young couple was always a mistake. In *This Time for Keeps* (1942), newlyweds Ann Rutherford and Robert Sterling find their marriage going to pieces because Sterling has to work for Rutherford's father (Guy Kibbee). Old Dad won't let his son-in-law do anything on his own, and the young wife is caught between them.

specifically a marriage movie. Yet it builds its story of romantic love turned to believably married life on one large problem: the bride's family and what it represents seriously derails her marriage until the prerequisite happy ending. *Primrose Path* presents two marriages in subtle contrast. The first is that of Rambeau and her drunken husband, once a Greek scholar and now an unemployed bum (Miles Mander). Rambeau is forced to provide for the family, which consists of two daughters, Ellie May (Rogers) and Honeybell (Joan Carroll) and a perfectly cynical and odious grandmother (Queenie Vassar). The family lives in a shantytown ("Primrose Hill") in sad and near-desperate conditions. Whenever it becomes necessary, Rambeau disappears with her "good friend Thelma" (Vivienne Osborne) "to go to the fair and have some fun." When Mom returns, always in a prepaid taxi, she's usually sporting some new glamour (like a fur piece), and she's loaded with groceries and presents for everyone. Nobody, even little Honeybell, is very confused about these disappearances; but Rogers feels it necessary to put a good face on it: "Ma just likes to have a good time."

The marriage between Rambeau and Mander sits on the screen as what it is, with no real explanation, no long apology—or reformation. Rambeau even comes home with a present for her worthless mate: money for booze. "Take it," she says, "and have a good time." She has accepted her life for what it is, which for her means her marriage as it has turned out to be. What can she do? She has to support her family; her only skill is the one she uses with as much dignity as she can. She tries to be cheerful, even when her husband threatens to someday kill himself. When he flops onto their bed, she sits down beside him, rubbing his head gently and murmuring, "Poor boy . . . poor boy."

The second marriage in the movie is the one Ginger Rogers makes for herself with the handsome young Joel McCrea, who operates a hamburger shop at the beach. Until she meets him, Rogers has kept her hair in pigtails and hidden her body inside lumpy clothes, preferring to look like a kid so she won't attract men. Her view of men and marriage is grim, but she respects her dad's former scholarship ("He went to college") and listens to his advice ("Keep your dreams, Ellie May"), because if she lets those dreams get away from her, they won't come back, and she'll "have to invent new ones and they're never as good." Rogers is a suspicious and angry young woman, well aware that Granny's plan is to replace the meal-ticket mom with herself and later with the younger Honeybell. The in-laws that will be on offer from Rogers as a dowry are a Dogtown variation of the Gigi dynasty.

Everything changes, however, after Rogers meets McCrea. For the first time in her life, she dresses up: hat, purse, silk stockings, makeup. The couple act out a movie courtship that contains the recognizable anger of sexual attraction: their language of love is the trading of insults. Yet Ellie May knows she's hooked, and sets out to leave her family and get her man. Understanding what has happened, Rambeau speaks privately to her daughter about love: "It just happens. We can't help it. Pa's weak, drinks too much, but I made my bargain and I gotta stick by it. Somebody's gotta take care of the family. I've done the best I can." She reassures her daughter, "Your ma's with ya." But after Rogers leaves, pushing off on her female destiny, Rambeau sits down at her miserable table and weeps. "Poor little Ellie May," she cries. "Poor little Ellie May."

After Rogers and McCrea wed, there emerges onscreen a second—and very different—marriage: one between equals, with honest fun and a genuine sexual component. Rogers works alongside McCrea in the hamburger shop, and their former trading of insults becomes an amusing patter that delights their customers. They turn their banter into a little vaudeville routine that everyone can see is happiness with an electric sexual current crackling underneath. When they take time to snuggle under an overturned boat on the beach, laughing and tickling, teasing and kissing, an audience sees a real relationship, a real marriage. All is well—except that offscreen await the in-laws. (The innocent McCrea thinks Rogers has a strict family who threw her out because she went for a man like him, one without money.)

In-laws waiting in the wings: the believable force of marital destruction that marriage movies could call up as needed. When McCrea finds out Rogers is really from Primrose Hill, he tells her, "I don't like lyin'," but finally, because he loves her, says they must go to visit because "they're your folks, ain't they?"

The disaster that occurs is an emotional roller coaster, half hilarious and half heartbreaking. Granny openly insults McCrea. Honeybell recites her "piece" for him, a ribald poem entitled "Don't Swat Your Mother, Boys." Mom tries hard, but when Dad reels in drunker than a skunk, he mistakes McCrea for Mom's usual customer, Mr. Hawkins. As quarrels, shouts, and misery erupt all around, Pa defines McCrea's in-laws for him: "Outcasts! All of us! Outcasts!" McCrea is suitably appalled, but Granny snarls at him, "What kind of a family did you expect to meet?" It's the question he finally has to ask himself, and slowly, slowly, he zeroes in on the key issue: "Who works in this family?" he asks. Granny coldly replies, "Well, we ain't on relief." McCrea, nobody's fool, replies, "I think I begin to get the idea."

The happy marriage is ruined. The in-laws have killed it. Rogers tried to keep herself and her new life as separate from the taint of her family as possible, but in the end, her family could not be denied. When McCrea cruelly dumps her, Rogers softly murmurs, "Please don't do this to me," but her fam-

When you take your new husband home to meet his in-laws, no matter how nice everyone tries to dress up the situation there's likely to be trouble ahead. Husband Joel McCrea meets wife Ginger Rogers's nasty little sister (Joan Carroll) and even nastier grandma (Queenie Vassar).

ily has defined her. Since this is a popular movie with two big stars, love will be restored but not without plenty of in-law complications first: Mom is shot by drunken Dad; the crime is covered up; Mom dies; Granny lies to McCrea when he changes his mind and comes to find Rogers; Granny makes McCrea believe Rogers has become a prostitute; etc., etc., etc. When *Primrose Path* ends, McCrea has returned, sucked it up, and put Granny in her place. He takes charge of Rambeau's legacy, a family who'll clearly be nothing but trouble all his life. The young marriage has survived, but what lies ahead? What is the bargain that McCrea has made for loving Rogers? Although *Primrose Path* has set its story inside a shantytown, a distance from the average viewer's world, the lessons it offers are those they could relate to—particularly in the basic one about interfering, dependent, and destructive in-laws.

Movies with interfering in-laws and kids are often presented as comic, the ridicule bringing welcome relief to beleaguered married folks suffering off-screen at the hands of relatives. In-laws tended to be treated like punch lines in a stand-up comedy routine. To sit in a theater and see annoying in-laws ridiculed (or destroyed) was reassuring. A movie like that lifted burdens off weary shoulders. Even if the film only fulfilled an audience's secret opinions by presenting these freeloading, interfering bums the way they were, it was

comforting. Yes, that's just how they are! Yes, let's laugh at them! Let's punish them! Let's move away from them! Let's kill them! This is good fun. The
movies were always more careful with children, but even so, movies that could
show the burden of little ones, good or bad, were a covert relief for some people
who went to the movies to escape. Movies endorsed unwanted ideas by putting
them into story form and resolving them up there on the screen. The goal was,
as always, identification, but also *relief.*

The marriage movie is different from the family story, however. Movies
about family, or a dominant parent—*I Remember Mama, Life with Father*—are
about life from the point of view of one of the children. The dynamics are
shifted away from the couple and onto the larger unit, and the stories define
the concept of marriage only tangentially. In *I Remember Mama* (1948), the
marriage is definitely a secondary substory. *Life with Father* (1947) is about how
Mother (Irene Dunne) can cleverly manipulate Father (William Powell) in all
directions for the benefit of individual goals inside the family unit. The joke is
that she's the boss; he only imagines he is. The true marriage movie involving
in-laws and children is a story about how marriage is directly affected by *external* characters who impact the central relationship in various ways.

The most popular in-law problem in marriage stories lies in the shenanigans
of domineering mothers-in-law. It's an old joke, but a reliable one.* The ghastly
mother-in-law is well represented by a little comedy film of 1952: *No Room for
the Groom,* directed by Douglas Sirk, the fine German director more famous
for his melodramas that humanely criticize American morals and values. *No
Room for the Groom* is a nightmare disguised as a comedy. Tony Curtis plays
a sweet army private who marries a cute Piper Laurie. Curtis loves her uncon-
ditionally, and the only other thing he cares about is his family's vineyard and
the old house that stands on it. His fondest hope is that when he leaves the
service, he can activate the family vineyard and live peacefully on the land for
the rest of his life—with his little bride, of course. So it is perfectly natural that
to save money for their future, he urges Laurie to move into the house and stay
there while he is away. In she comes, followed by her mother . . . followed by
her uncles and her cousins and her aunts. All freeloaders. And if that weren't
enough—and it is—Curtis and Laurie have their wedding night interrupted by
his coming down with a case of chicken pox. Before he ships out, they have
only a day and a half to marry, so they go to Las Vegas to locate a swift justice of

---

* Mothers-in-law were most commonly used in comedies, but not always. For instance,
1933's *The Silver Cord* presented Laura Hope Crews as a narcissistic mother who dominates the lives of all her sons. When one of them (Joel McCrea) marries a strong-minded
career woman (Irene Dunne), the clash is very serious.

the peace. They choose a man whose shingle says "Marriage Without Delay." Laurie has said they should choose the cheapest, but Curtis says the fastest would be better—he's in a hurry. ("You know how it is," Curtis says to the judge, who responds, "I did.") The pox strikes right after "I do!," and Curtis is taken immediately to a hospital. Laurie returns home, he's shipped out, and by the time the war is over, her entire family has taken over his home. There are sixteen of them, but none matter except for Mama, played by Spring Byington in a cheerful Madame de Farge kind of style, if Madame de Farge had been a master of French farce—and someone's mother-in-law.

When Curtis is discharged and arrives home, Mama tells the family they have one week to break up the marriage so she can sell Curtis's land to Laurie's former boss, Herman Strouple, the Cement King (Don DeFore). All they have to do is never allow the couple to sleep together—since they never have.* This is a peculiarly American kind of weird comedy—an entire family of sixteen people doing everything they can to achieve coitus interruptus. It's up one stair-case and down another, indoors and out, tears and shouts and, above all, vigilance. The couple never get a minute alone; Mama herself insists that her daughter needs to sleep with *her* because she's not well ("my heart!")— although she smokes and keeps her bookie on the phone most of her spare time. What is stunning about this movie is that the complications add up to only one thing: interfering in-laws who have their own designs on what the couple can do for them. There's a sadness underneath the surface, and an ugly honesty about greed and family relationships that literally eats the comedy and spits it out.

Movies with interfering in-laws suggest that if they don't watch out, couples can easily be influenced against each other by family members. Collectively, such stories seem to be simple warnings to married people not to live with relatives or let relatives live with them. Better yet, move away—far, far away.

If other relatives, especially mothers-in-law, were movie punch lines, children in movies became little more than plot developers. Children were sacred cows, and thus a challenge in the movies. In a serious film about marital stress, an audience still wanted respect for parenting. In comedies, naughty children

---

* These mothers-in-law are still around today: see Jane Fonda in *Monster-in-Law* (2005) and Doris Roberts in TV's *Everybody Loves Raymond* series. A 2010 survey by the iVillage Web site showed Americans would prefer to do a great many awful things rather than visit their mothers-in-law: stay home and clean (51 percent); visit the gynecologist (36 percent); figure income tax (28 percent); or have a root canal (28 percent). In-law problems apparently never lose their movie appeal. In 2003, Ashton Kutcher and Brittany Murphy (in *Just Married*) spend their European honeymoon coping with in-laws (and her former boyfriend).

Mothers-in-law always know how to poke their noses in: Spring Byington hovers over her daughter (Piper Laurie) and brand new son-in-law (Tony Curtis) to no good end in Douglas Sirk's comedy, *No Room for the Groom*.

were good for rueful laughs of recognition, and in a world populated only by children, such as the *Our Gang* comedies, anything could happen. But in a marriage movie, the world of the adult in the audience, some caution had to be exercised. A little dickens of a kid might be funny (Jane Withers in Shirley Temple movies), but a truly evil child was offensive.* Movies usually opted to present undisciplined youngsters who interfered in their parents' lives in comedies or musicals, such as *And So They Were Married* (1936) with Mary Astor, *Three Smart Girls* (1936) with Deanna Durbin, *Listen, Darling* (1938) with Judy Garland, or *Three Daring Daughters* (1948) with Jane Powell. Three versions (one British, two American) were made of *The Parent Trap*, in which twin girls seek to break up their father's plans for remarriage, steering him instead to remarry their mother. The child as marriage counselor was a useful plot that could go either way: reunite a couple or wreck one.†

* Evil children had to wait for the horror movies of the late 1970s and onward to take hold, which is why so many people fondly remember Patty McCormack in *The Bad Seed* (1956, not really a marriage movie). She was an oasis of really hideous behavior in the world of movie children.
† Douglas Sirk made another low-budget "comedy" besides *No Room for the Groom* that illustrates the point. In *Week-End with Father* (1951), widowed Patricia Neal and Van Heflin fall in love and decide to wed; but before they do, they feel they must reconcile

Children were often used with a kind of fiendish humor as excuses for keeping married couples from having sex. It was a perverse retaliation for all the romantic comedies in which the censors kept an unmarried couple apart. In *Family Honeymoon* (1948), the popular romantic team of Claudette Colbert and Fred MacMurray (seven films together) are wed at the film's beginning. Colbert has been a widow for nearly five years, and she has three small children (Gigi Perreau, Jimmy Hunt, and Peter Miles). ("The bride-to-be is what you might call a crowd," says Colbert's rival, Rita Johnson, who hasn't given up yet.) MacMurray's a bachelor professor, and has no parenting experience. (The children refer to him as "that man.") As the wedding ceremony gets under way, Colbert's sister (Lillian Bronson), who's going to babysit the kids during the honeymoon, falls down the stairs and breaks her leg. Result? A family honeymoon. It's a clever twist on the romantic comedy, but a dreary portrait of three dreadfully behaved children who provide a series of complications (aided by Johnson) that ultimately drive the honeymooners apart. Of course, they reconcile in the last reel, but the sight of the ghastly children interfering between an obviously loving couple is hardly entertaining, even though Colbert and MacMurray handle everything with their typical grace and style.

Movies do admit that children really *can* cause marriage trouble. They die out from under you; but even when they don't, they cause disasters. If you are widowed, they'll break up any new romance. If you become wealthy, they'll turn into lazy louts who scorn you for your work ethic. If you educate them or take them to Europe, they'll develop a set of personal habits that are nothing but trouble, and will essentially remain ignorant despite your efforts. Once in a while you'll see a little dream tot in the movies, but it's usually Shirley Temple, and in that case all the married adults have failed *her*. It's just a difficult thing having children on film—or as Carol Burnett said in her parody of *Mildred Pierce*, after she learns that her daughter is a murderer: "Kids. They sure keep ya hoppin'!"

Why would movies present the child/parent relationship in such negative terms? Obviously for the same reasons they always had to present the ordinary in negative terms: to create a dramatic arc, to get something—anything—to happen in the plot. (In this regard, Hollywood was not so different from theater and literature; it just turned out more product, and its product was consumed by a mass audience.) The marriage film also presented frustrations in marriage

---

their children to their union. The kids do everything they can to break them up. Technically not a marriage movie but a stunted courtship story, *Week-End with Father* is really depressing. There are also serious dramas about children trying to destroy a parent's new marriage, like *The Secret Heart* (1946) and *A Woman Obsessed* (1959).

that were caused by children to connect to any similar disappointments that audiences might have.

Movies found their best use for children in marriage movies as facilitators of the entire list of seven basic marital problems. You needed money to feed and clothe children and pay their doctor bills. Mothers and daddies who committed adultery, neglecting their little ones, could be lured back into the fold full of remorse when they focused on the kids, etc. Thus many marriage movies featured small children, or perhaps teenaged children.*

Hollywood understood that bad children changed the equation in marriages. It was hard to do much with good children—except kill them off in some sentimental bid for sympathy. Mean ones were more interesting, with all their evil little tricks that could end in opportunities for redemption. But introducing children into the marriage plot inevitably locked the parents down, tied them to the homestead. Movies found the best way to use children effectively was to keep them under the radar, indirectly linking the success of the marriage to the parenting issue. Children could be kept offscreen as much as possible† and still have a full impact on marriage. *Penny Serenade* (1941), starring Irene Dunne and Cary Grant, is a perfect example of how a story that appears to be about romance, compatibility, money problems, and even earthquakes was really all about children.

It's the story of an impending separation and divorce, typically told through flashbacks inspired by a record album entitled *The Story of a Happy Marriage*. It opens with a portrait of Grant and Dunne in a silver frame, followed by the

---

* One excellent movie presented a portrait of how grown-up children could fail their parents. *Make Way for Tomorrow* (1937), directed by Leo McCarey and starring Victor Moore and Beulah Bondi as an elderly couple, is not technically a marriage movie, but it is one of the saddest, most touching films ever made—a heartbreaking combination of humor, pathos, and brutal honesty about what to do when parents become too old to care for themselves. The two old people have to be separated "temporarily" while a solution is found. Bondi will live in New York City with their oldest son, and Moore will live three hundred miles away with a daughter. Moore comments that parents living with their kids has never worked out before, and he wonders why it should work out now. He's right, of course: the movie finds no happy ending. Ultimately, the old couple face the fact that after decades of marriage, they'll never be together again. They share a day in the city in which a group of strangers they bump into are all nicer to them than their own kids have been. Alone at the train station, they say their final goodbye ("In case I don't see you again . . . it's been lovely, the whole fifty years"). It's an unusual story, and a very honest one.

† Child actors were often unreliable. For one thing, they grew bigger right in front of your eyes. And they had to go to school on set, cutting down the hours they could work. The business often had problems with them, and many adult actors really fought working with children. (Everyone remembers W. C. Fields's famous warning not to "work with dogs or children.")

credits. Dunne is leaving Grant. The couple's best friend (Applejack, played by Edgar Buchanan) reminds her solemnly, "You and Roger have been married a long time." She responds by saying, "We don't need each other anymore. When that happens . . . there's nothing left."*

The audience is set up for the usual form of marriage story (love, failed love, and rejuvenated love) featuring two of Hollywood's best, most compatible co-stars. *Penny Serenade* turns out to be something different: a carefully modulated tale about parenting, in which having a child or not having a child is the key to success in marriage. When the couple meet and fall in love, an important issue is whether or not Grant, a carefree spirit, can grow up and settle down. Can he be a husband, and thus a parent, if he remains a child? This issue is solved when he accepts a fine new job as a foreign correspondent. They wed and go to Japan, where they live beyond their means (lots of good Japanese furniture), and she worries about it, but all is bliss when she becomes pregnant. This up is followed by a down: she loses the baby in an earthquake. This is followed by another up when he gets a job back in America, and they start their own little newspaper . . . followed by the down of financial failure . . . followed by the up of adopting a baby girl . . . followed by a down when the state threatens to take the child away because Grant's work isn't steady . . . followed by an up when they get her back . . . a down when she dies. The film has begun just after this last devastating down; a coda will provide an eternal up when the kindly adoption agent (Beulah Bondi) who found their first baby finds them a little son. *Penny Serenade* makes clear that success in marriage is linked to children, producing them, raising them, keeping them alive. The happiness of the couple rockets up and down according to the childometer.

Penny Serenade was a big box-office hit, and received five Oscar nominations. Grant is wonderful in his atypical, unfamiliar role. He has all the careless charm to make the unreliable part of his character attractive, but when the time comes for him to plead with authorities to let them keep their daughter despite his having no income, he is magnificent. Cary Grant begging, promising he'll do anything, is a scene that can tear anyone's heart out.

Although the movie presents Grant's unreliability about money as the main surface issue of the marriage, what an audience sees onscreen is a link to their

---

* Each "memory" (or flashback scene) is triggered by Dunne's playing one of their recordings, the first one being "You Were Meant for Me." The records are a perfect motif, as the couple first meet-cute in a record store. She's a saleslady, so Grant stays all day and buys a giant pile of records. (Only later will she discover that he has no phonograph on which to play them.)

The baby makes the marriage, says *Penny Serenade*, with Cary Grant,
who's happy because his wife, Irene Dunne, is happy. Baby makes three.

own roles as parents. Without a child, this marriage cannot endure. With one,
poverty is bearable. What the filmmakers understood was that here was an honest look at what really keeps a great many marriages together: children. *Penny
Serenade* doesn't present itself that way, though: it's got recordings of "My Blue
Heaven," "Happy Birthday," and "Together"; it's got Grant and Dunne; it's got
Japan and an earthquake and a great cast of character actors. But it links itself
to viewers by saying that the purpose of marriage is children. A family will hold
you together and get you through the tough times. And that was a message that
paid off at the box office.

Bad parenting was never endorsed. The need to be an unselfish parent was
often stressed. Since divorce was socially unacceptable, sympathy for the children of divorce was often a movie plot point. In such cases, however, the movie
is not about marriage but about the effect of divorce on a child—two different
issues. The focus becomes less what goes wrong in marriage and more how
children suffer from what was perceived at the time to be the selfishness of
their parents. Such a movie is the 1934 *Wednesday's Child*, starring Frankie
Thomas as an eleven-year-old whose parents (Karen Morley and Edward
Arnold) get a divorce. Morley portrays a bored housewife who falls in love
with a man who brings her excitement and wealth, while Arnold portrays the
typical businessman who pays no attention to what's going on at home until
it's too late. Thomas is tormented by his friends, who know of his mother's

affairs, and is ultimately shipped off to military boarding school when his dad needs time with a new woman. In the end, both Morley and Arnold overhear a tragic conversation between their son and another child of divorce. While both realize how selfish they've been, Morley goes back to her new husband (wearing fur), but Arnold gives up his new woman, accepting what the film is clearly endorsing: the burden of parenthood, which, it's made clear, is his job. There's a "someone's gotta do it" quality to the story. *Wednesday's Child* focuses on the child's view of how children suffer from a failed marriage, but under the surface it's a warning of how they can prevent remarriage and make parents rue a divorce.

Children and in-laws were workhorses in marriage movies. They were recognizable and reliable, but seldom did anything unpredictable. They usually appear in the least interesting of the marriage stories, perhaps because they are the inevitable results of almost all marriages.

CLASS DIFFERENCES

Class is not supposed to be an American thing . . . and yet we can't leave it alone. The marriage film was its natural habitat. A marriage meant stepping out of your place (your own family) and hooking up elsewhere, the perfect metaphor for class. Movies could define the concept in many different but clearly understood ways. It might be actual "class"—that is, a commoner marrying a nobleman—or it might be "class" as defined by economics, rich or poor. It might also be an educational gap, a social background, an age difference, nationality and ethnicity, or even a political background or ranking. Used in a marriage movie, it had a single, dominant, and very clear message to send viewers: you'll be happier if you stay where you are. Marry your own kind and stick with what you understand. The "class" idea, however it was defined, was presented to affirm an essentially American idea: class stinks, and it should not exist. The movies endorsed our national superiority: we are better because we are a classless society.

And yet—"and yet" being one of the most important aspects of mass moviemaking's ambivalence—and yet you might want to give it a try, because *you*, the individual in your seat, are special and might against all odds make it work. You can marry up, or down, because you are you. The class story of the marriage film represents the very strongest example of how movies simultaneously affirmed and denied things for moviegoers, and how their wish-fulfillment system worked. On the positive side, the marriage story presented one half of the couple as challenged by a fundamental difference, or lack, or need. The result was the presentation of an *urge*, the desire to achieve, to grow, to move, to change—a basic American motivation. Up that ladder! Across that ocean! The story of a marriage was an excellent way to fulfill the goal of discussing class without discussing class, and to tell an audience that they were upwardly mobile. You *could* cross those tracks. On the other hand, those tracks were very, very visible, and laid down with a heavy hand. Characters were very definitely either from the right side or the wrong side, and the fact that such sides existed was a plot staple in all kinds of movies. As Ann Sothern laments about the family of her beau in *Panama Hattie:* "They're from the other side of the tracks, and I don't wanna have to get over crossin' 'em."

Marriage movies always reminded audiences that marrying uptown brought trouble. The downtowners were the better guys. As stated earlier regarding "money" marriages, movies tend to say that the rich have bad values (that's how they got rich) and the poor are noble (that's their lot in life). Naughty rich, noble poor—it's practically our national anthem. One example of this mentality is *The Valley of Decision* (1945), in which Greer Garson is a poor Irish housemaid who loves—and is loved by—the noble son of the house, Gregory Peck. But Greer is noble herself, and knows it wouldn't be fittin' for the two of them to marry, so she goes away and he takes a mean-spirited bride in the form of Jessica Tandy. Greer suffers, Greg suffers, and there are labor troubles everywhere; but in the end, the family's matriarch (Gladys Cooper) dies and leaves all her money to Greer, automatically upgrading her to first class. *The Valley of Decision* doesn't say much about marriage, but it says a lot about class.

That Forsyte Woman (1949) is a veritable cornucopia of class-conflicted marriage issues. Based on a novel by Nobel Prize–winning author John Galsworthy, who will marry whom, and why, across what class lines, and whether it will work or not, is the foundation of the story. The lavish MGM production was Merchant Ivory before there was Merchant Ivory, full of period clothes and furniture, "significant" attitudes toward women's roles, and plenty of la-di-da acting of a high-minded nature. In fact, the MGM stock company of Greer Garson, Janet Leigh, Robert Young, Walter Pidgeon, and others handle themselves well as they steer their bustles and waistcoats around Victorian couches and tables. They are joined by Errol Flynn, more familiar to audiences for his dashing roles in Warner Bros. westerns and swashbucklers. Flynn is cast against type as the cold, money-obsessed Soames Forsyte (and he gives an excellent performance). At the core of the love affairs and the misunderstandings, the ruminations on the mores and social restrictions of the Victorian era, and the suggestion that artists are the only people who know how to live, lies a marriage movie with a full list of marital problems: adultery, money, class, competition, family, and in-laws. There is even talk of murder, a threatened suicide, and an ultimate death as a horse-and-carriage drive over a hapless would-be lover in a thick London fog. The biggest conflict, however, is class.

That Forsyte Woman shows the audience something outside their daily world—lavish sets, period costumes and attitudes—but grounded in what they understood: marital trouble that grows out of marrying outside your tribe. Old Jolyon Forsyte (Harry Davenport) ostracized his son, Young Jolyon (Walter Pidgeon), an artist, because he ran off with the nursery governess less than a year after his wife died. A chip off the old block, Pidgeon's now-grown daughter (Janet Leigh) seeks Old Jolyon's permission to marry an architect (Robert Young), another unreliable artist type outside her class. Old Jolyon has previously, against all family wishes, contradicted his own instincts by approving the marriage of his nephew Soames (Flynn) to the genteel but poverty-stricken Irene (Greer Garson). Garson has to take in music students to pay for her lodgings, but not, apparently, for her wardrobe, which is spectacular. She doesn't really want to marry Soames; but, being a man who gets what he wants ("value for his money"), Soames keeps after her until she relents. There is a Greek chorus of three elderly aunts, one unwed (and thus a failure in society) and two who represent society's attitude toward the proper roles of marriage. (Naturally, they hate Garson.)

The Way We Were (1973) is another example. It's a believable story about an unlikely marriage that cannot last, even though it's based on true love between two people (Robert Redford and Barbra Streisand) from different backgrounds. In this case, the "class" clash is fundamentally politics, the left versus the right, or at least Democrat versus Republican.* It's the American version of the British class system. When interviewed about what drew him to play this role, Redford found lofty purpose: "The questionable nature of free speech was a provocative notion and I attached to that." Nevertheless, it's fundamentally a marriage story about class.

The Way We Were tracks ruthlessly forward, delineating all the social issues of America from the mid-1930s into the late 1950s. To do so, it uses the marriage between two perfectly mismatched types: a frizzy-haired leftist (Streisand) and a handsome WASP (Redford).† As the film opens, they are college

---

* Another example of politics as class dooming a marriage is *The Searching Wind* (1946), based on a Lillian Hellman play that basically condemns the American diplomatic corps that let Hitler rise to power in Europe. The story features Robert Young as a U.S. ambassador who weds a woman from his own class (Ann Richards), but whose true love is a leftish American newspaperwoman (Sylvia Sidney). The political issues—which are also "class" in terms of wealth versus work—are framed most clearly by the love story itself.

† Movies were good at verifying what audiences learned the hard way: love is blind. Picking the wrong person is a cottage industry in movies.

students. Redford is a football hero, part of the in social crowd, and Streisand is a scholarship student working several jobs to pay her tuition. She wants his Fitzgeraldean perfection and status, and he wants her feisty ability to question and break out of conformity. Since an audience brings in the credible knowledge that people often marry someone who is their ideal other self, or their high-school/college dream catch, this film taps perfectly into the viewers' sense of the world. It was a big, big hit, and one of Hollywood's best-remembered marriage movies, although by grounding itself in trendy political issues, it avoids ordinary day-to-day marital problems. Its bottom line is, however, marry your own kind.

Having an American marry someone British can stimulate the class issue and still maintain a pro-Yankee twist. The idea of Europeans seeking out the wealth of vulgar Americans wasn't owned exclusively by Henry James. In *Our Betters* (1933)—which carries the hilarious credit of "Technical Advisor—Elsa Maxwell"*—what happens to such Americans is swiftly laid out at the very beginning of the movie. HARDWARE HEIRESS TO WED PEER, screams a headline, followed by a well-dressed couple exiting a church under crossed swords, surrounded by top hats and pealing bells. The bride (Constance Bennett) tells her groom, "I'm going to make you a good wife, darling." She feels very humble and proud to be part of his long family heritage, and he sniffs and says *she* can afford to be proud, catching himself just in time to add swiftly, "You're the best looking of the whole crew." After they kiss, the movie cuts ruthlessly to a scene in which she walks in on him with the woman he really loves but couldn't afford to marry. The movie then cuts to two more headlines: IS AMERICAN LADY GRAYSTON RUTHLESS AS LONDON'S SOCIAL DICTATOR? and BRITAIN'S FADS AND FASHION NOW FOLLOW THE COMMAND OF LORD GRAYSTON'S DARING WIFE.

Our Betters goes on to demonstrate the agreed-upon rules of upper-class marriage between money and title. (Violet Kemble-Cooper as an aging aristocrat with a gigolo in tow says: "Marriage is so middle-class. It takes away all the romance of love.") It's a cruel and trivial world, superficially brittle, witty in a Wildean manner, but with real pain and disappointment underneath. Bennett has accepted her fate: "Think of the people you know who've married for love," she tells a friend. "After five years, do they care for one another any more than those who've married for money?" She says you can't remember how love feels when it's over. However, it's made clear to the viewing audience that this is not

---

* Elsa Maxwell was a self-appointed social advisor to party-throwers and movie stars, a hefty old broad whose claim to class was a hoot. If they'd made a movie about her, Marie Dressler would have been perfect casting. (Maxwell, of course, would have insisted on playing herself.)

the proper way to think or behave, and that Bennett is suffering from the wrong done her. She's got American pluck, though, and has sucked it up: "I've made myself the fashion . . . I've got power, I've got influence . . . I've bought it." The true marriage/class lesson emerges when Bennett's little sister decides to wed a penniless marquis instead of the decent and honest young American man who voices what the audience is supposed to endorse: that the world Bennett is living in makes no sense, and neither does her approach to marriage. *Our Betters* plays out in the usual ambivalent tradition: marriage is a bore and we all know it, but marriage is the only thing that matters, and it must be done for love.

A charming comedy, *The Mating Season* (1951), illustrates a successful example of how to reconcile the class issue. A handsome young couple, John Lund and Gene Tierney, meet cute and immediately marry.* He's an up-and-coming businessman, and she's the daughter of a sophisticated woman who's managed to bring her up in wealth through a series of strategic marriages and divorces. Lund and Tierney don't know each other very well, and one thing Tierney doesn't know is that Lund's mom is a hash-house waitress, brilliantly played, as always, by Thelma Ritter. (Tierney's own mom is the waspish—but very well dressed—Miriam Hopkins.) As the inconsequential plot plays out (all about Lund's rise to success, his boss's lumbago, and country-club snobbery), an out-of-work Ritter becomes Tierney's maid without Tierney knowing she's really her mother-in-law. When Hopkins comes to town to join everyone in the newlyweds' small apartment, a perfect battlefield across class lines is laid out. Lund's mother represents democracy in the flesh, and Tierney's mom is a real upper-crust bitch. The clever twist to provide balance is that Tierney is democratic—it's Lund who's a snob. The half-and-half situation signals to the audience that all will end well, because both Tierney and Lund have a touch of democracy somewhere—Tierney in her soul, and Lund in his blood. Everyone could be comfortable with the story, which took no real sides, especially when, in the end, Ritter marries Lund's boss and solves the problem. The marriage is used as a lesson in democracy, with love as a leveling force.

The novels of Sinclair Lewis were very popular sources for American movies. His tales of small-town life, fraught with unhappy, uncommunicative marriages, had great appeal for both moviemakers and audiences. *Dodsworth, Arrowsmith, Main Street, Babbitt*—all were made into movies.† One of Lewis's

---

* Tierney is sitting in a convertible that hangs halfway out over a cliff. Every time she moves, the car rocks, threatening to plunge her to her death. Lund drives up and rescues her, pulling her out just as the car crashes over. Holding her in his arms, he buries his nose in her hair and asks, "Where'd you get this hair . . . off a lilac bush?"

† *Main Street* was retitled *I Married a Doctor* (1936). *Babbitt* was filmed twice, once in 1924

strengths as a writer was his ability to describe a specific milieu accurately, both physically and psychologically, so Hollywood art directors and writers found adaptation of his work easy to do. Lewis also had the ability to satirize his world, to point up its limitations and absurdities, as well as to create characters that were both sympathetic and immediately recognizable as American types.

By 1945, when he published *Cass Timberlane*, Lewis was regarded as an aging enfant terrible and was being devalued as a literary figure. For Hollywood, however, his status as a reliable commodity had been established, so it embraced *Cass Timberlane*, even though the book was not appreciated by critics, who thought of it as a middlebrow offering. Perhaps it was inevitable—and somehow perfect—that the middlebrow studio Metro-Goldwyn-Mayer turned it into a hit movie for the middle class. The book had sold well as a hardcover, was serialized in *Cosmopolitan*, and was selected by the Book-of-the-Month Club. That was all MGM had to know—the studio purchased the movie rights as a vehicle for the oddball romantic teaming of Spencer Tracy (as Cass) and Lana Turner as the young woman he weds.

The novel *Cass Timberlane* is *Main Street* revisited, set in an imaginary Minnesota town called Grand Republic. It tells the story of the respected and reliable judge Cass Timberlane, who sits comfortably on the bench and equally comfortably (perhaps even smugly) amid the town's established social elite. He is not so much *with* this crowd as he is *of* them by birth, profession, and schooling. The judge has survived a painful divorce from a socially ambitious wife who left him for a more glamorous existence, a Carol Kennicott who got away. (This marriage, summarized in an excellent section of the book, is *Main Street* boiled down and revisited from a more modern point of view.) The novel is the story of how the judge is shaken out of his comfort level when he meets a slightly Bohemian young girl, Jinny Marshland. Their romance is that of an established professional man in his forties with an attractive young girl in her early twenties.

How the movies defined class in marriage is well delineated by the changes made to the novel in order to turn it into an MGM movie. The first and most significant step lies in redefining Cass and Jinny by the onscreen personae of the superstars Spencer Tracy and Lana Turner. This, in fact, means they are seriously rewritten. Tracy had come to represent goodness, honesty, and reliability in men, and Turner a warmhearted sexuality in women. The original Cass and Jinny don't have a chance. Gone is Cass's smugness, his vacillation,

---

as a silent film and again in 1934 with Guy Kibbee in the title role. The character was reshaped to fit Kibbee's blowhard persona, and the film is not completely true to the spirit of the novel.

When you marry outside your tribe, your age group, or your own social
level, you're going to find it hard going. "Judge" Spencer Tracy learns his
lesson in *Cass Timberlane*. He should have stayed behind his desk in his
safe, upper-class world . . .

his blindness to the faults of his world. In their place stands Spencer Tracy,
who, by way of his screen personality, presents the viewer with a man of instant
decency, dependability, and excellent judgment. Tracy Timberlane will not
make a wrong judgment—his side *will* be the right side. The film version opens
with Tracy on the bench in front of a couple seeking a divorce—he is telling
them that marriage is sacred, and he doesn't grant the decree. Jinny, turned
into Lana Turner, inevitably becomes a sex symbol, a young woman who is
confident around men. The heroine of the novel is coy and flirtatious, but
she holds out on Cass, often teasing him to incite his jealousy. Turner doesn't
bother—why would Lana Turner have to do that? The novel's Jinny is from a
happy and respectable family, but Lana's Jinny is from the wrong side of the
tracks, to make her more appealing and democratic for the audience, and to
sharpen the issue of class. In the novel, the relationship between Cass and
Jinny is tense, tedious, and desperate. They are wrong for each other and the
reader knows it. In the movie, the love story is warmer, kinder, more relaxed
and happy. The reason Tracy and Turner's marriage nearly fails has nothing
to do with them or how they feel—it has only to do with the issue of whether
Tracy's lifelong friends will allow Turner into their circle. She's from the wrong
side of the tracks—a class issue.

Another major difference between the book and the film lies in the balance

... but instead he strayed over the tracks and found a ballplaying tomboy in the person of Lana Turner.

of power between Cass and Jinny. In the book, Jinny walks out on Cass, and thus she is the controlling force in their relationship. He sits home and waits, unable to do anything to alter the situation until an illness makes her weak and helpless. In the movie, Cass walks out on Jinny because of an imagined adultery. A male in the person of Tracy, who sits on the bench as judge and who works for Metro-Goldwyn-Mayer, is going to be the one who calls the shots in a mass-market motion picture. Lana Turner is abandoned, left alone and frightened, except for some money Tracy gives her. It's a clear statement that women are dependent on men in marriage, a distinct departure from the emasculation theme of the novel, but no doubt one designed to have more mass-market box-office appeal. It's also reflective of the typical marriage-movie view of infidelity: women who do it are wrong, but they need love and are driven to sin by a man's coldness or indifference. In the end, they will still be losers, because society will vote against them. (Men do it because—well, they're men, and they'll usually end up all right.)

The novel ends ambiguously. Cass submits to Jinny for the sake of their marriage. "Cass gave up his vested right to be tragic, gave up pride and triumph and all the luxury of submerged resentment, and smiled at her with the simplicity of a baby." (In *Main Street*, Carol Kennicott gave in to her husband's wishes and returned to him on his terms. Cass is forced to accept Jinny's.) In the movie, there is no ambiguity to the resolutions. Cass takes Jinny back and is lucky to have her: after all, she's Lana Turner. And she didn't *really* sleep with Zachary Scott. It was Cass's snotty "classy" friends who caused all the trouble, by just *thinking* she did. The ending is happy. Their marriage prevails.

Reading the novel and viewing the film made from it reveal a shifting tone. The movie is moral, familial, romantic, made more agreeable for a mass audience. It endorses both Lana Turner's wrong-side-of-the-tracks warmth and Tracy's libertarian urge to wed her. Its world is folksy and, except for Cass's social set, full of honest conviviality. Its approach to its audience can only be described as friendly—as opposed to Lewis's often cynical relationship with readers. The movie script changes things in ways that soften the characters and make them more middle-of-the-road, less controversial or questionable. For instance, Cass Timberlane is a divorcé in the novel. In the movie he's a widower, whose wife died early in their first year of marriage, leaving him practically a virgin and thus acceptable as both a court judge and a mate for Turner. The book's Cass is a semi-prude. Tracy has a charming Lincolnesque sense of humor, and he's stoic, gentle in the face of loneliness. (Tracy follows the MGM template for all movie judges: Judge Hardy, Andy's dad.)

One of the great lessons of the "class" marriage movie is for mothers in the audience: don't send your sons to New York to bring home a straying sibling. It's like war—you can end up losing *all* your boys. In *Vivacious Lady* (1938), James Stewart, a mild-mannered professor, is sent by his parents to retrieve his brother (James Ellison), who has become a nightclub habitué. Getting him onto the 4 a.m. train is all that's required of Stewart as "nursemaid." Unfortunately, making the rounds of nightclubs, Stewart casts his small-town eyes on Ginger Rogers, all shimmery and sparkly and slim, singing "You'll Be Reminded of Me" in a white-hot spotlight. (Stewart tells her later that seeing her for the first time was just like the time his dad ran him over when he was a kid.) Within minutes, Stewart and Rogers are eating corn on the cob, riding a double-decker bus, and walking the wet streets of Manhattan at dawn. Before one full day has passed, they're married and riding the train home together—and ominously listening to an older couple quarreling: "I know what I'm married to" and "I'll pin your ears back" and "You can't fool me."

When Stewart and Rogers arrive home in the boondocks, a form of class conflict emerges. Rogers learns Stewart's father is the president of the local university, and begins to worry a bit. "What's a professor's wife have to do?" she asks, but that's not her most immediate problem. Stewart is actually engaged to "a thoroughbred" and hasn't had the guts to tell anyone, including his parents, about his marriage. ("Darling," says Rogers, "would I be too much of a bore if

I suggested you break off your engagement to that girl?") As the events unfold, mixing in-law issues with class issues, a basic story of background differences emerges: nightclub girl, small-town professor—two different worlds, and she's not welcome in his. The movie also presents a parallel portrait of marriage, that of Stewart's parents. His father (Charles Coburn) is the primary locus of success, position, snobbery, and the movie's definition of "class." He dominates everyone—his staff, his university, his son, and his wife (Beulah Bondi). He is the force that must be overcome in order for the marriage between Stewart and Rogers to survive. As "class," he is the problem, and the American definition of the wrong thing to be. Bondi, on the other hand, represents something subversive. On the surface, she is obedient, suitably middle-aged, and proper, the perfect wife for a successful university president in 1940; she has survived a lifetime of oppressive marriage by pretending to have heart trouble, her possible death being the only leverage she has in her union with Coburn. ("I've spent the best years of my life in bed with heart trouble," she confesses to Rogers. Again, a mother uses "my heart!" as a secret weapon of marriage war.) Her public behavior is always proper, but secretly she smokes. Her maid, Hattie McDaniel, says, "If I had a husband that wouldn't let me smoke, I'd get a new husband." (Rogers, ever the wise girl, points out that it "depends on what you enjoy the most.")

Vivacious Lady juxtaposes these two marriages. It definitely endorses the younger one, and definitely criticizes the older one. It's an example of a movie comedy in which the richer, better-educated, snobbier characters have to learn they are *wrong*, and must learn not only to accept the hardworking, commoner, more down-to-earth characters, but also to know that people who are "without" are better than they are. Since marriage movies existed to reassure audiences, they pretend that class differences can be overcome by love, but what they actually demonstrate is that characters use manipulation and lying to get the job done. The older marriage is successful only because the wife is a trickster; the younger one between two unsuited people from different backgrounds, with different goals, is resolved through chicanery and comedy. (If it's funny enough, any marriage problem can be overcome.) Casting Ginger Rogers as the uneducated wife who hoofs it in a nightclub helps solve a large part of the class problem. Rogers has a phenomenal wardrobe, and the audience, like Jimmy Stewart, first sees her bathed in a white-hot spotlight of glamour, presented as desirable, as a star. By opting in favor of the unmoneyed, lesser-educated class (the have-nots), as represented by a radiant Ginger Rogers, Hollywood didn't lose its audience. Everyone would be willing to step down to Rogers—the men to bed her and the women to look like her.

When Jimmy Stewart goes to New York City, he finds a fabulous bride
(Ginger Rogers, in a nightclub), but bringing her back to his college
classroom isn't as easy as he thought it would be. With Phyllis Kennedy
and Grady Sutton.

Jimmy Stewart wasn't the only small-town brother asked to retrieve an err-
ing sibling from the clutches of a big-city gal. In *The Shining Hour*, Robert
Young travels from the family dairy farm (a pretty palatial place) to New York
to knock some sense into Melvyn Douglas before it's too late. Actually, it *is*
too late: he's already proposed to the famous nightclub dancer played by Joan
Crawford, who has herself warned him it's not going to work. "The difference
between the Wisconsin Lincolns and the Tenth Avenue Rileys is *more* than just
a thousand miles," she's told him in one of her many class-motivated refusals
to his proposals. Just before Young arrives, Crawford finally gives in. Not only
does Young himself end up madly in love with Crawford's character, "Olivia"
(real name Maggie), but the third sibling, a very irate Fay Bainter, burns their
honeymoon house down. Unfortunately, all that does is trap Young's own wife,
the patient and forgiving Margaret Sullavan. Crawford has to run into the con-
flagration and rescue her while the men stand around.

Movies such as *Vivacious Lady* and *The Shining Hour*, the first a comedy
and the second a drama, illustrate the same fundamental lesson about class
in marriage. If you marry outside your tribe, something is likely to destroy
you, your home, your career, and certainly your ill-considered marriage. These
movie lessons *are* tribal—they remind audiences of the basics the elders want
enforced. Your own ways are the best, the safest, and the most reliable. One of

the great achievements of the Hollywood movie was its ability to reinforce the tribe's rules while offering a glamorous glimpse of the other: the bride from the nightclubs of New York City. Overall, there's a fundamental endorsement of the American concept of democracy in such stories. The bride, despite her adoring audiences, her furs and gowns, her tiny feet that fly over the parquet dance floor, is at heart someone who wants what Wisconsin (or the audience) has: a home, a family, and love.

If one is going to marry outside one's class, the direction to go is for the most part downward. To be happy, a rich man or woman should marry someone from the lower classes, an energetic opposite, full of life and good old American know-how. For instance, in *One More Tomorrow* (1946), rich boy Dennis Morgan tries to marry working girl Ann Sheridan, but she initially spurns him. The conniving Alexis Smith catches him on the rebound and marries him solely for his money, although promising faithfully to be a happy homebody and have lots of children. (Earlier, a friend tells Smith that "there's more to marriage than a shopping trip," and she cynically replies, "Like what, for instance?") Smith turns Morgan's life into a false hell of socializing, political correctness, and lack of love (and children). The lesson is obvious: working girl Sheridan was the right one for him. She would have given his life purpose, working alongside him and having kids, too.*

For Americans, one of the simplest ways to delineate a sense of "class" or any hierarchical difference was just plain sex. Male vs. female: two different worlds, two different levels of mobility, two different, albeit oversimplified and sexist, attitudes toward life. In *Woman of the Year* (1942), Hepburn and Tracy marry across "class" lines that are essentially male and female. He's a sportswriter (male) and she's a high-class political columnist (female for the times—the brink of World War II, when Eleanor Roosevelt was setting a pace for women). He's ballpark and pub, she's the corridors of Washington and cocktail parties, yet they fall in love, marry, and have to sort it out.

Woman of the Year, a delightful film, gets its strength from the fact that its co-stars, playing two oddly matched individualists who fall in love, were in fact, offscreen, two individualists who fell in love. And it shows. The movie

---

* Hollywood made a lot of movies, and there are exceptions to every plot form. When rich John Boles married Barbara Stanwyck's Stella Dallas in the 1937 film, he learned class barriers could not easily be crossed. He later gets a socially appropriate wife (a good person), and Stella has to suffer, giving up their child to her more socially correct replacement. Stella's goal is always the welfare of her daughter, so she makes the sacrifice. Thus Stella is proved to be both low class and high class. She lacks social grace and good clothes, but she has humanity and grace in her soul. (*Stella Dallas* is more of a motherhood movie than a marriage movie.)

Joan Crawford, another import from the nightclub scene, tries to be a
good wife to Melvyn Douglas, but disapproving in-laws Fay Bainter,
Robert Young, and Margaret Sullavan hover in the background in *The
Shining Hour.*

story charmingly reverses male-female marriage ideas. She's too busy for him,
forgets to come home for dinner, neglects an adopted war refugee, and doesn't
notice his new hat—all things associated with husbandly behavior. When he
finally leaves her, she chases him down to make breakfast and prove her love.
Much has been made by feminists over the clever political analyst's inability
to work a waffle iron, but the point of the movie, as stated clearly by Tracy, is
that anyone can make breakfast; he just wants *her*, as herself, to be with him
as his companion. By reversing the traditional marital roles—Tracy becomes a
sort of wife, Hepburn a powerful husband—the movie suggests that it's wise to
know where you fit and marry accordingly. The concept was simultaneously
strengthened and diminished by its remake, the stylish *Designing Woman* of
1957. Gregory Peck plays the Tracy role, and he's still a successful sportswriter.
Lauren Bacall takes over the Hepburn part, but she's not a powerhouse political figure—she's a fashion designer. She *is* highly successful, independent, and
wealthy, but her role is feminized by the standards of the time. He's sports,
and she's fashion. They really *are* in two different worlds. (Tracy and Hepburn
were working for the same newspaper, just in separate departments.) On the
one hand, Peck and Bacall finally understand each other and come together in
Designing Woman, which says something honest about compromise. On the

It's love at first sight between Hepburn and Tracy in *Woman of the Year*, both on and off the set. She's a globe-trotting columnist and he's a sportswriter, but they wed anyway.

other hand, it also suggests men and women don't like the same things and can never live together, being, as they are, fundamentally different. It's the class issue sexualized, polarized, even trivialized.

Difference, for the movies, was difference. Making marriage work was an unlikely task in which you needed everything on your side. Movies could call it "class," but what it meant was an unmistakable attitude toward matrimony that the audience understood: marriage was hard to make work, so, once again, you'd better marry within your own kind.

INCOMPATIBILITY
(COMPETITION, CONTROL, COMMUNICATION)

Incompatibility movies had multiple goals and different shadings and different tones of comedy or tragedy, but they all boiled down to one thing: they were about the marital mistake. They were all about not getting along with your mate, about the reasons your mate is wrong, about relieving your disappointment (through laughter or empathy). These movies speak loudly to people who don't like being married, or at least have decided they don't much like the person they're married to. Of course, in the great tradition of the history of motion pictures, they are also charmingly designed for people who *do* like their mates, or are glad they got married, etc., etc. These are the heart of the "I do" and "I don't" versions of married life. Incompatibility is clever, and easily varied, but it also carries a melancholy subtext. Movies that depict competition between men and women, the day-to-day fight for control, or a lack of any real communication all carry a sadness running underneath the surface. They speak to loneliness, the desire for a true companion, for balance and for comfort. They are a desperate subliminal cry for love and an even more desperate cry for what was promised by the romantic comedy. *Those* couples all started out disliking each other and then found harmony and joy. *They* reconciled all of their little issues—so why can't *we*? Incompatibility seems trivial, solvable, but it's the murky category into which all the bad stuff gets dumped. These films say to audiences: "Laugh if you can at the well-written version of the marriage movie that is, in fact, usually trying to pretend it's a romantic comedy, but in your heart you know the truth." The subliminal message was that marriage isn't like the movies, and not like you thought it was going to be. That was the point of the "incompatibility" marriage: it was used to illustrate conflict, control issues, competition, and lack of communication between a man and a woman, with or without the laughs.

"Incompatibility" was a subject well understood by Hollywood. In fact, grounds for divorce in that world were almost always "incompatibility," so much so that it became a familiar comedian's schtick for jokes about movie stars. (It was also called "irreconcilable differences" in Hollywood divorce cases.) A classic example of how easily the concept could be defined is the opening scene of *The Bride Wore Boots* (1946), starring Barbara Stanwyck and Robert Cummings.* A couple are horseback riding along a trail in an idyllic setting. The very first words heard on the sound track present what is obviously a very old quarrel between Stanwyck and Cummings, who have already been wed seven years. As she is reminding him how much she really, really loves horses, he is seen behind her falling off his. As she sits her mount perfectly, ignoring his dilemma, she nags about how he *said* he loved horses before they wed. ("On a boat," he reminds her.) He says he actually hates horses: "First thing I remember hating was my hobby horse . . . I hate merry-go-rounds . . . I hate *Black Beauty* . . . I've wanted to tell you this for seven long years." She

---

* *The Bride Wore Boots* uses several screen minutes to tell us what *The Bride of Frankenstein* (1935) tells us in a matter of seconds. Brought to life by the good doctor, Elsa Lanchester takes one look at her intended and lets out a blood-curdling shriek.

listens, and asks him the thing all marriage movies ask: "What's happened to us, Jeff, what's the matter?" He responds bitterly, "You mean, besides horses?" This movie opens directly into incompatibility, fully defined, using horses as the metaphor. As is always the case in these two-faced movies about marriage, it will end there, too. To win Stanwyck back, Cummings is forced to ride a bad horse in an amateur riding contest, getting thrown and nearly breaking his neck. This illustrates the Evel Knievel Theory of Marriage: no matter how unlikely you are to succeed at your task, just keep getting up and trying to do it again. "My hero!" she cries over his bandaged body. They kiss. All's well. According to *The Bride Wore Boots*, a perfect marital relationship would have a man trying and trying by falling down, getting up, falling down, getting up, and finally nearly killing himself so his bride can claim him as her hero. It's a story of incompatibility, but incompatibility made allegedly compatible by a comedy overlay with sinister undertones.

Hollywood was skilled at depicting incompatibility. In 1941's *Appointment for Love*, starring Charles Boyer and Margaret Sullavan, almost everything on the screen screams, "No, no, no, a marriage between these two will never work." The first thing an audience sees is a couple standing in front of a bed, locked in a passionate kiss. But then a stage curtain comes down, revealing the scene as part of a play, a false marital happiness. One could leave right there and have had the only moment of real entertainment the film has to offer. Onscreen, however, events plow onward. In the audience sits Sullavan, a very bored theatregoer, barely able to stay awake. She grabs her wrap and tries to flee, but before she can get up, the cry of "author, author" is heard, and she's trapped when from out of the wings comes *that* author, a very pleased Charles Boyer. As he begins to address the crowd (on his own behalf), Sullavan sits back down and promptly dozes off, her head rolling forward. Boyer notices, and armed with the ironclad ego of a theatrical writer/director, he assumes she's fainted—how could he possibly be boring her? Boyer calls out the line one hears only in the movies: IS THERE A DOCTOR IN THE HOUSE? Sullavan snaps awake at once, ready to go, because—and here's our big witty reveal—she's a doctor!

Appointment for Love has opened up grounded in a fake reality (the stage scene), a grotesque misunderstanding, a display of egoism, a lack of mutual appreciation, and a disconnected professionalism. In short, it has established all too well its theme of incompatibility. In their first meaningful conversation, Boyer tells Sullavan that "love is illogical and unreasonable," and she explains to him that, no, "love is logical, a chemical reaction." Naturally, within minutes they are wed.

Dr. Margaret Sullavan checks out playwright husband Charles Boyer with her stethoscope. Is he up to a nightly *Appointment for Love*? Or will their separate schedules, hers by day and his by night, render him incapacitated and her appointment schedule out-of-date?

The film then devotes itself to the problems of their married world. Because he works all night and sleeps all day, and she gets up bright and early to have breakfast at 7 a.m. and walk to work, their "incompatibility" is defined as temporal. (When Sullavan suggests they have lunch, Boyer laments: "In the middle of the night?") When he wants her to meet him after his show, she can't because she never stays up late. (Of course, when we first saw her, she was out on the town alone, in an evening gown, attending a theatrical opening night.) Sullavan takes charge. "When we were married you knew that I was a doctor and that I was going on with my work. I have to be at the hospital at all hours, and you couldn't possibly fit your life into that kind of crazy routine." She organizes things accordingly. His apartment is on the seventeenth floor, so she rents one for herself on the twenty-second. That way, they won't disturb each other going in and out. (Boyer says, "I only know one thing. When a man marries a woman it's because he wants to be married to her.") Sullavan's solution is designed to be clever, our modern surprise twist on their love, but it's merely tedious. The movie is in no way a portrait of a real marriage. They never consummate their vows during the running time of the film, and they are denied all forms of domesticity except for a single breakfast together. (Eating lunch in a restaurant, which they do once, doesn't constitute "domesticity." Technically, this movie probably shouldn't even count as a marriage movie.) Boyer and Sullavan are a couple who spend no time together and don't even live in the same space. (Sullavan says the different apartments will keep their marriage "perfect.")

Appointment for Love lays out the very modern issue of the two-career family, but it never resolves the problem. It drops it with a kiss. Although they are both free to do their own work, Boyer and Sullavan are living in a fundamentally unworkable situation. She says the most important thing is for a marriage to last, and he says the most important thing is for it to begin. (Women want security; men want sex.) When Boyer takes his troubles to his producer, Eugene Palette, Palette lays out his answer as if it were a marriage movie plot: "Act I, wife won't play house. Act II, husband makes wife jealous. Act III, they wind up in each other's arms. Curtain falls." This, apparently, was the play Sullavan was watching when she fell asleep in the first place. (Boyer's no dummy. He evaluates the idea as "too old-fashioned.") The movie plays out with farcical elevator rides to the wrong floor, rival lovers, faked jealousies, and a confused elevator boy—all distractions grafted onto a basic story of incompatibility that was meant to be charming, witty, surprising, but that ends up just proving its own plot twist: Boyer and Sullavan *are* incompatible.

Unfortunately, seen today, many allegedly charming stories of male/female marital competition often do convey the opposite of what was originally intended. *The Moon's Our Home* (1936) is similar to *Appointment with Love* in this regard. Despite the charm of its leads, Henry Fonda and (again) Margaret Sullavan, the story undermines itself. Sullavan is a famous movie star (Cherry Chester) whose real name is Sarah Brown, and Fonda is Anthony Amberton, an equally famous writer of books with titles like *Astride the Himalayas*. His real name is John Smith. Her marital philosophy is that it should be "like a ski jump, a sudden swift recklessness, starting on the heights, leaping into the void, never knowing the end, never caring." His is more basic: "Give me a simple primitive woman with a small, high chest." The plot maneuvers them to Moonsocket, New Hampshire, known to each other as Brown and Smith. (It is carefully explained to the audience that he never goes to the movies so he has no idea who she really is, but there's no explanation for her not knowing who *he* is, since everyone else does. It just assumed that any moviegoer would realize a famous star would never read a book.) Marriage is treated as a game, and yet also offered up as the single most important goal that either could pursue. "I hate marriage," he says, "it's so unimportant." He then promptly proposes and she accepts. They fight their way onward to the expected finale that unites them. He's still arrogant and devoted to his career, and she's still spoiled and devoted to hers, but they're married, and marriage is the sacred goal of love. Never mind that he tricks her, puts her in a straitjacket, and then kisses her in the "romantic" conclusion. Like Sullavan and Boyer, Sullavan and Fonda are incompatible. The movie is so good at defining how inappropriate they are together, the lesson learned reverses the original purpose.

When one looks at the history of the American motion picture, one identifies a great many dominating female characters. Obviously, making a movie built around a great female movie star required that her character get out and do something to generate plot complications. Movies about marriages, if they were to feature two major Hollywood players, needed significant actions for both characters. Thus, "incompatibility" often meant a couple in competition with each other in some fashion: opposites in a law case in *Adam's Rib* (1949), a sheepherder and a rancher in *The Westerner* (1940); on different sides of a feud in *Roseanna McCoy* (1949); and many other variations.

Hollywood moguls really understood competition. They lived it daily. Thus, many movies about professional couples suggest that happiness and marital longevity are rare when both partners work outside the home. Whenever the movies present a couple who are working together, the result is usually going to be competition, resentment, and other people hovering around waiting to hop into bed with one of the leads.

Show business was a perfect setting in which to pair two stars in an "incompatibility" conflict that could stress the power dynamics between two professionals. Musicals were particularly useful, because they were an easy way to make the woman an equal to the man. Given the glamour-girl musical stars of the studio era—Betty Grable, Rita Hayworth, et al.—it was believable that the woman could even triumph over the man, outsucceed him, as it were.

Many films of marital competition and discord are set in a show-business format. The granddaddy of the form is *The Dance of Life* (1929), also known as *Burlesque* and starring Hal Skelly and Nancy Carroll. There's also *You're My Everything* (1949), as well as *Love Me or Leave Me* (1955), *A Star Is Born* (all three versions, 1937, 1954, and 1976), *April Showers* (1948), *When My Baby Smiles at Me* (1948), *Kiss Me, Kate* (1953), *Orchestra Wives* (1942), *I'll See You in My Dreams* (1951), *The Barkleys of Broadway* (1949), *Everything I Have Is Yours* (1952), and *Blue Skies* (1946), among others.* Musicals often put all the negative issues of marriage forward—competition, money, control, the struggle to get ahead, adultery—and then disguised them through musical numbers and the glamour of show business. The couple starts out poor and happy, unit-

---

* It is curious that the musical format, an allegedly lighthearted entertainment mode, became the locus of so much marital trouble. Perhaps moviemakers thought the song-and-dance would take the sting out of the bad news.

ing perfectly in song and dance. The big chance comes—but only one of them is called. The other must sacrifice. Fame goes to the head of the one who has it, or the mate's success destroys the one who doesn't. And walking around everywhere is temptation: unclad other women and rich sugar daddies, all of whom want the partner.*

The Barkleys of Broadway is about Josh and Dinah Barkley (Fred Astaire and Ginger Rogers). As always, when Astaire and Rogers dance, it's easy to see they are perfectly wed: rapturously interpreting "They Can't Take That Away From Me," they're in sync, the living embodiment of the concept of harmony. When they aren't dancing, however, they bicker. This, Hollywood tells us, is marriage: heaven and hell. The heaven can be real on the dance floor if you're Astaire and Rogers. Otherwise, you've just got to go out to the movies—yet again, the solution to be offered for a reasonable price.

Astaire is the dominant member of the Barkley team. As such, he is both mentor and parent figure to his wife in their working world. The problem is that he carries this superiority over into their private life. The question arises: could she ever have been a success without him as her Svengali? The issue hovers over their dance partnership and also over their marriage. To answer for herself, Rogers leaves Astaire and goes off with a pretentious French director to play Sarah Bernhardt in legitimate theater, where she allegedly has a great triumph.† It seems as if she *can* be a success without Astaire—but, the film shows the audience, not really. Behind the scenes, she cannot work with the French director, so Astaire hides in the theater to watch rehearsals, then imitates the Frenchie over the telephone, calling her at night and giving her instructions in secret. Astaire gives Rogers her success as a theater actress, just as he gave her a musical success. The job of the audience is to endorse the physical union of Astaire and Rogers as dancers and ask no further questions. (Sarah Bernhardt indeed. Could she tap-dance?)

A movie such as *The Barkleys of Broadway* is subliminally about the wife's role in a marriage. No matter how much music there is, or how many feathers Rogers puts on, the movie cannot disguise the fact that the plot suggests that a wife and a husband should not break up a working partnership. To accomplish this, the wife must understand her proper role. The subtext of such a movie was clear: to be compatible in marriage, a wife should not compete.

---

* Musicals also afforded plots that were ready-made because many real-life show-biz couples existed: Nora Bayes and Jack Norworth (*Shine On, Harvest Moon*, 1944), Vernon and Irene Castle, Flo Ziegfeld and both Billie Burke and Anna Held (*The Great Ziegfeld*, 1936), and others.
† In reality, Rogers is pretty awful as Bernhardt.

The changes in moviegoing audiences regarding charming musicals that easily reconcile a competitive incompatibility are illustrated by a latter-day example, Martin Scorsese's *New York, New York* (1977). The story reflects a different perspective on the female role. Liza Minnelli is not only free to compete, but also to *win* the competition with her husband, played by Robert De Niro, and also to become an international superstar, single mom, and independent force. To bolster the realism, De Niro is not left behind in the gutter—or dead in a convenient war or automobile accident. Good musician that he is, he becomes the owner of a successful nightclub and is well remembered for his one great hit record. He isn't poor, or a nobody, but he's not, let's face it, Liza Minnelli in her 1970s prime.

In *New York, New York*, De Niro represents all the reasons women could be frustrated with marriage. He's unfaithful, unreliable, angry, and abusive, jealous of his wife's success, and unable to make his own career work at her level. Furthermore, he's outrageously self-focused and uncaring. At his wife's bedside in the hospital just after she's given birth, he breaks down and cries over their impending separation. He wipes his eyes and blows his nose on her bedsheets, explaining that he can't use his pocket handkerchief because "it's the only one I have." (This scene might just be *the* one to illustrate why women divorce their husbands.) Writing in the *New York Times*, critic Stephanie Zacharek said the characters in *New York, New York* "know the real meaning of singin' in the rain."

The marriage presented in *New York, New York* ends in divorce and never retracts that status. The story is not told in flashbacks. It presents a couple with different agendas, levels of ability to succeed, and an inability to adjust to each other. In the end, although the opportunity to reconcile presents itself to them, both avoid the trap. A movie married couple has learned a lesson, and the era of the 1970s doesn't require reconciliation for a happy ending. De Niro and Minnelli are the new version of Josh and Dinah Barkley.

Musicals about married couples who struggle have one issue that separates them from other marriage movies: they're telling stories that are essentially excuses for musical numbers.* Because of the inherent joy and optimism usually attached to performance, most of these stories, unlike *New York, New York*,

---

* It goes without saying that the perfect male/female dialogue about competition should be musical. In *Annie Get Your Gun*, both Broadway musical and film adaptation (1950), the unmarried (until the end) sharpshooters Annie Oakley and Frank Butler square off with "Anything you can do, I can do better . . . I can do anything better than you," a musical variation of their shootouts with rifle and pistols, the final one of which she will fake losing.

can hit bottom but bounce back in time for a happy finale that erases all discord. Everyone can shuffle off to Buffalo. Most musicals end with a big wow number, often the performance of the title song, with both male and female leads involved. This concludes a story with a strong sense of union, or a simple erasure of conflict.

It was also possible for a musical number to be used for an ironic statement or subtle comment on marriage. In *The Great Ziegfeld*, for instance, Ziegfeld married the French chanteuse Anna Held (Luise Rainer, in an Oscar-winning role). On the date of their first anniversary, she is seen onstage, happily performing the song: "It's delightful to be married, to be-be-be-be married, / With a house, a man, a family, / When you laugh and play the livelong day, / That's the life for me." Radiant, at the top of her game, Held returns to her dressing room to find her anniversary gifts: a roomful of lavish floral displays, a loving note, a diamond necklace with matching bracelet. Holding her sparklers up to the light, she exults, "All the flowers in the world and the stars from the heavens, too!" She rushes upstairs to the chorus girls' dressing room to share her good fortune, but one of those girls is the beautiful blonde who will soon replace her and have her own flowers and diamonds. With the great efficiency of 1930s movies, within brief minutes a newspaper headline appears on screen: ANNA HELD LEAVES ZIEGFELD. The audience is then shown the title character (William Powell), alone in his lavish apartment, picking out a tune on his piano: "Oh, it's delightful to be married . . ." The former marital joy and affirmation is sadly undercut by the ironic use of the tune. Instead of being a celebration, the song becomes an ominous warning about the longevity of happiness in marriage. Another ironic juxtaposition, without a song, is the scene in which Rainer, with tears streaming down her face, congratulates Powell on the telephone about his new marriage. Assuring him that she herself is "so happy, so excited about my new play," she also pretends great happiness for him. After she hangs up, she breaks down and sobs, saying she only divorced him because she thought it would bring him back. Joy and misery over marriage are again played as the true picture of what happens.

There is a subcategory to the competition issue in marriage movies in which a couple work together and do *not* run into problems. It's a story in which one of the two partners, almost always the woman, consciously steps back out of the spotlight and becomes "the little woman behind the great man."* These films

---

* Or "the helpful man behind the great woman." In the latter category of films (a smaller one) are such titles as *Blossoms in the Dust* (1941) and *Madame Curie* (1943), both of which star the popular "love team" of Greer Garson and Walter Pidgeon. Garson was always the bigger star of the two, but her association with Pidgeon was such that it didn't

are almost always biographies, and the approach suggested this was the only way to achieve greatness if you're married: one of you has to serve the other one. The "little woman" movies include *The Story of Louis Pasteur* (1936), *The Life of Emile Zola* (1937), *Wilson* (1944), *Dr. Ehrlich's Magic Bullet* (1940), and *The Magnificent Yankee* (1950), among others. Significantly, the "little woman" is strong, intelligent, and wise, but always played by an actress who is not of the top tier of stardom: Ruth Gordon, Ann Harding, Ruth Hussey, etc. The actress embodies the concept: she is not a star.

There are also marriage movies in which real-life couples are depicted as equals, even though the man is far more famous. Such biopics about marriage include *The President's Lady* (1953, about Rachel and Andrew Jackson), *Eleanor and Franklin* (the 1976 TV movie about the Roosevelts), and *Cheaper by the Dozen* (1950, about Frank Gilbreth Sr., a famous time-management expert, and his engineer wife, Lillian). In these cases the casting announces the equality: Susan Hayward and Charlton Heston as the Jacksons, Jane Alexander and Edward Herrmann as the Roosevelts, and Clifton Webb and Myrna Loy as the Gilbreths. The "equality" on film regarding these marriages is tempered by clever plotting. *The President's Lady* is turned into a story of class, in which Heston must defend Hayward's honor again and again. In the case of the Gilbreths, Loy works alongside her husband but also runs their home and cares for their children. She steps up into the spotlight and out into the world only because she *must*, after he dies, to feed her family and to carry on his work. And the Roosevelts are now almost equally revered: Eleanor's lifelong service is known and respected by Americans, and she has become a person in her own right.

But for the most part, "great man" movies suggest that there was only room for one boss, one star, one leader, in every couple. Otherwise, there will be destructive incompatibility. This philosophy finds its most extreme expression in movies where the husband is a clergyman. In movies, a religious marriage is the complete opposite of a show-biz or legal-profession marriage. A movie centered on religion openly tells viewers there must be *no* competition in marriage. The couple's relationship is the background to a larger issue of affirmation of belief, and the marriage functions as proof that faith can keep them going. They are united toward a higher purpose, one that constantly asks them to deflect their own small and petty differences in service to a higher cause. These movies

seem inappropriate that she was stepping into the limelight without him. (In the case of the Curies, of course, Pierre Curie was also a Nobel Prize–winner, and hardly a lesser light. His early death by accident simply removes him from competition in the plot, as it did in life.)

A *Man Called Peter* told the story of the United States Senate chaplain Peter Marshall and his wife, Catherine, as depicted by Richard Todd and Jean Peters. A huge hit, the movie stressed the duties of a wife whose husband was a clergyman.

present audiences with role models that endorse sacrifice, lack of competition, and the acceptance of duty. For most audiences, this wasn't a very entertaining idea, yet two examples of religious marriages grounded in biography were hugely successful: *A Man Called Peter* (1955), about Peter Marshall, a Scotsman who became the United States Senate chaplain, and *One Foot in Heaven* (1941), the story of clergyman William Spence, based on a book written by one of his sons, Hartzell. Both films present marriage as a sacrifice for the woman who chooses a man of the cloth, because she agrees to accept his own, larger, more purposeful sacrifice. She agrees not to compete. These are movies that clearly say there must be *no competition* between a man and a woman in marriage. In the book *A Man Called Peter*, Catherine Marshall wrote the story of her life as the wife of Peter Marshall, and it became a best seller. Her goal was to glorify her dead husband, but she ironically also gained glory for herself by stepping up to tell his story. By "standing by her man" after his death—that is, actually, *seeming* to stand behind her man, but really standing out in front of him—Mrs. Marshall became famous. Translated into a film, *A Man Called Peter* became a top box-office draw. Although Mrs. Marshall suffers a mysterious malaise and takes to her bed while her husband thrives, the marriage was not defined as a problematic one; the Marshalls' story doesn't have a fully developed negative subtext. It does, however, suggest that success came to Mrs. Marshall because she did not compete and because her goal was service to him after he was gone.

In *One Foot in Heaven*,* the character of Mrs. Spence, played by Martha Scott, is seen throughout the film but never in a scene in which there are decisions made. When her husband (Fredric March) visits members of his congregation, he goes alone. When he hustles business at the marriage-license bureau, he goes alone. When he meets with prospective builders for his new church, investigates why his son has been expelled from school, accuses gossips of ruining his son's young life, argues with a doctor about the definition of a soul—when anything resembling a give-and-take happens—Mrs. Spence is left out of the frame. When there's a crisis for the oldest son, he admonishes the boy not to tell his mother. "It will only worry her." She isn't considered a partner but more of a servant or support system. There is no possibility of the wife being competitive. Thus we see a marriage that works, that endures, but in which the husband dominates.

The respective roles for the couple—boss and servant—are established immediately in the film's opening scene. Hope and William Spence are seen briefly before their marriage at the home of her parents in Stratford, Ontario. It is 1904, and the young couple plan to marry in the summer after he ("a brilliant student") finishes medical school. He arrives unexpectedly to let her and her family know that "last night" he went by a church and heard Bishop Hartzell (a Methodist minister) speak at a revival meeting, and suddenly decided to become a minister ("I got the call"). Her parents are appalled, but Hope, without a moment's hesitation, accepts his decision. When he asks, "Will you come with me?" she replies, " 'Whither thou goest . . .' "

Their arrival in the small town of Laketon, Iowa, is a classic example of the bride-taken-away-from-her-world subplot. Scott is wearing a beautifully cut, fur-trimmed ensemble with matching hat and muff, flowers on her hat, lace at her throat. As they ride in a wagon through muddy streets, they are asked by their driver how they like "our little town." Before she can speak, March answers for her: "Of course we like it, don't we, dear?" This will pretty much be how it is for her through the next twenty years. As they try to settle into the monstrous, broken-down parsonage, March teaches her two primary lessons for being a minister's wife. First, the parsonage belongs to the congregation;

* *One Foot in Heaven*, adapted from Hartzell Spence's book, had an illustrious technical advisor: Dr. Norman Vincent Peale. The film also had input from the Advisory Committee of Clergymen organized by the *Christian Herald*.

thus, their home will never really be theirs, and she must accept the ugly things with which they have decorated it. (As she puts it, "every ugliness in its place.") She also needs to understand there will be no using her lovely wedding gifts or they will think she's "stuck up," and that would not be good for *him*. Secondly, she shouldn't wear her pretty clothes, either, because it won't do for her to outshine the ladies of the congregation.

With these rules laid down, the story of his religious journey and ministry unfolds with the story of their marriage running a poor second—possibly even fifth. Mrs. Spence irons, cooks, cleans, scrimps, bears children, and follows the Methodist rule book, which says no fun and certainly no divorce. She grows gray and pale. When she wishes to name their third son William Spence Jr., the good reverend does not like juniors, and he wants the boy's name to be "William Frazer Spence, called Frazer." Because of this disagreement, the child is three months old before he is baptized. Mr. Spence finally promises his wife to accept the "junior," but in church, when she brings the baby up, he loudly names him "William Frazer Spence." There is a close-up of her stunned and obviously hurt face; but back at the parsonage, she says and does nothing. She merely calls the child "Frazer" and moves on. Mrs. Spence speaks out directly only once. After one of their parsonages burns down, she expresses hope the new one will be livable. "You don't know how it hurts me to bring up my children the way we've had to," she says, "always on the move, never really being able to settle down anywhere . . . They're entitled to a respectable, permanent home even if they are the minister's family." After her husband tells her, "Don't get your hopes up," the new place proves worse than ever.

For the most part, March ignores Scott. Only once in the film does he really seem to see her or address her. Upset by the fact that their new home leaks, he says, "I'm seeing you as you are, Hope. A parson's wife." He describes how she accepts all hardship with serenity, and never has anything she herself wants. He determines he will build a new church, and thus get a new parsonage. The fact that this is only incidentally something for her and largely something for his own ego seems to escape him. Examined years after the film was released, the character of William Spence seems autocratic, ego-driven, and self-serving, highly manipulative and very demanding. (There's one line with an ominous subtext. After struggling with a very selfish rich congregation, March musingly delivers a strange line: "Hope says I let it out at home later on her and the kids.")

One Foot in Heaven, a successful movie, is a grim picture, which suits its theme of sacrifice for religious standards. As the portrait of a marriage, it's a frightening time capsule in which a once-sparkling young woman, full of life

Married couple Fredric March and Martha Scott look at the planned church that will fulfill March's career as a clergyman, a goal that he has worked for and she has made enormous sacrifices to help him achieve. With Grant Mitchell and Gene Lockhart in *One Foot in Heaven*.

and love and hope (her name), leaves her comfortable home and her adoring parents to enter not just a life of poverty, sacrifice, and crushingly hard work—that would be bad enough—but also one in which she has no say in her fate, no real respect, and no equality in her marriage. Competition is not just inappropriate for her, it would be a sin; but the denial of her right to compete at least on an everyday marital level crushes her spirit.

Sometimes incompatibility could be very simple: the couple just want different things in life. *Blue Skies* (1946), an easygoing musical, has at its base a plot in which Bing Crosby woos Joan Caulfield away from Fred Astaire and marries her. As their union unfolds, she wants stability, and he wants change. He constantly opens and closes a series of restaurants with different motifs, and never really makes any of them work. Caulfield can't take the uncertainty. The idea that the woman needed security and the man wanted change is woven into many marital plots that have already been mentioned: *Chicken Every Sunday, Penny Serenade,* and others.

Competition in marriage movies is often about control. It's not just "Who's in charge?" or "Do not compete," but who *really* has the upper hand. In *Father Takes a Wife,* the female point of view is: "Men are like children. Always let them think they're getting their own way. Never let them suspect you're really getting yours." The male attitude is equally smug: "Don't let her get the upper hand. I trained Leslie from the very beginning." Movie women who are ignored by their husbands always begin covert operations to gain control in order to get the attention they need. *My Life with Caroline* (1941) is a dreary portrait of a silly marriage (and a dreary film except for the ever-reliable Ronald Colman). It's the story of a neglected wife (Anna Lee) who carries out elaborate schemes to make her husband believe she's in love with someone else. She believes she controls him, but he's just humoring her. He controls her by letting her imagine she's in control. (The movie presents an insufferably male point of view, but cleverly designed to appeal to women, as the husband asks himself questions wives want their husbands to ask: "Do I really understand? Do I really know all her hopes and dreams, or am I just selfish?")

In *You Belong to Me* (1941) the neglected-wife issue is cleverly reversed for a variation on who's in control. Henry Fonda plays a super-wealthy man with nothing to do all day. He marries Barbara Stanwyck (a successful doctor) in a whirlwind courtship, and then has to sit home all day while she's out seeing her patients, some of whom are men. He becomes wildly jealous. Fonda behaves badly, interfering in Stanwyck's work, embarrassing her, and trying to get her to give up her career through a series of schemes to gain mastery of her work life. Their problem is solved only when he finds something useful to do with himself (and his money): build her a hospital. He buys himself a partial control that's useful.

Columbia Pictures' 1933 *Ann Carver's Profession* clearly demonstrates a Depression-era issue: disparity between men's and women's opportunities to find work, and the resulting tension if it's the woman who gains financial control in the marriage. Although the fundamental Depression problem—men were out of work and women had to take in boarders, take up laundry or sewing, or become domestic workers—is glamorized into "Ann Carver's Profession" (she's a headline-getting trial lawyer), the issue touched a familiar chord with viewers.

Ann Carver's Profession stars Fay Wray and Gene Raymond. The script was written by Robert Riskin, based on a story called "Rules for Wives." The dialogue is sharp, witty, and the story moves swiftly. Step by step, *Ann Carver's Profession* lays out for an audience what goes wrong when there's an imbalance in a couple's earning power.

The movie defines its "Should the female work or not work?" issue quickly. The opening image is of a newspaper headline: GIRLS VOTE FOOTBALL PLAYER MOST POPULAR IN COLLEGE. The opening line of dialogue is: "I want to make it clear right now—the woman I marry has got to know how to make flapjacks. Not those comical things . . . good old-fashioned flapjacks!" This dubious philosophy is spoken by the actor who plays the football hero—Gene Raymond, confidently posed in front of his pals, impeccably dressed in a form-fitting tuxedo. *Ann Carver's Profession* has staked its claim for the male point of view, and within seconds it adds its female attitude. Ann Carver (Wray) works in a diner as waitress and cook ("I'm just that poor Ann Carver who has to work for a living"). She tells Raymond (after a steamy kiss) that "I've got a profession, why not use it?" She's just finished law school, putting herself through, and he's gotten his Bachelor of Architecture and they are getting married. "Okay," he tells her, although he adds that she won't have to work because he's going to make a "million dollars."

The movie spends under five minutes setting up this potential conflict, which is actually all we learn of their courtship. They immediately marry, and the film turns into a fight for the upper hand—with a vengeance. They move to the city, he takes a job, and she keeps house. It's immediately established with the same economical swiftness of the opening that he's getting nowhere, and she's bored silly. When he does agree to let her work, their happy marriage begins to malfunction. As Wray climbs the ladder of success, Raymond falls lower and lower, and loses more and more confidence. ("Bill, Bill," she says, "you're not getting jealous of my success, are you?") He has to appear at dinner parties that advance her career. While she's off on business trips, he starts drinking and hanging out in nightclubs. She's too busy to pay any attention to him, which is made clear when she pours him a cup of coffee and has forgotten he doesn't take sugar. They argue over decisions, and she points out that since she's the one who pays the bills, she's entitled to be the decision maker. After he gets nowhere as an architect, he takes a job as a nightclub singer (Raymond was more a singer than an actor), which puts him in the limelight and earns him more money. However, this embarrasses Wray in front of her friends. ("A crooner! . . . The thought of it makes me sick!") Inexplicably, Wray and Raymond reconcile in the end. The restoration of compatibility between them is a fade-out in a little cottage with him once again an architect (in control) and her once again at home (not in control).

Ann Carver's Profession addresses the question of the woman's right to *earn*, as well as her ability not only to do so but to do so at a higher level than her husband. This issue arises often in marriage movies from the silent era into the 1950s. The wife thinks that working outside the home will be an excellent solution to money woes, but the husband always disagrees. ("No wife of mine should have to work!") The fact that she apparently *needs* to do so is undermined by the traditional view of a married man and a woman as breadwinner and homemaker.*

* There's an interesting dichotomy between black women and white women on film regarding this issue. For instance, in *The Bride Walks Out*, groom Gene Raymond insists he and

Ann Carver's Profession is lawyer. Her husband's profession is failed-architect-turned-nightclub-singer. Fay Wray and Gene Raymond have to sort the inequities out to make their marriage work.

One of the most bizarre variations on the who's-in-control? marriage movie is 1934's *Journal of a Crime,* starring Ruth Chatterton, Adolphe Menjou, and Claire Dodd. At its base, it's the old story of infidelity: playwright Menjou's hot affair with his glamorous star, Dodd, which wife Chatterton discovers. Chatterton deals with her pain and humiliation by shooting and killing Dodd; presumably that's the end of the affair. Yet it's only the beginning of the plot. The murder becomes the motivation for a struggle between husband and wife over her punishment. Menjou, the clever writer, has no trouble deducing the fact that his wife is the murderer. (The police, however, are much dimmer and blame a bank thief who just happened to be escaping through the theater at the same moment.) Menjou confronts his wife as she's calmly powdering her nose, sitting in her boudoir in front of her lavish makeup table. "What kind of

---

his wife (Barbara Stanwyck) live in the small apartment he can afford on his salary, but they have money problems she could solve by working. "I'm tired of playing nursemaid to three rooms and a canary," she tells her maid, Hattie McDaniel. McDaniel's reply describes a husband with a different attitude: "I can't see why white men don't want their wives to work . . . My husband retired the day we signed the marriage certificate." Stanwyck had a career and gave it up to please her man. McDaniel started working the day she got married, with no end in sight, to please hers.

woman are you?" he demands, and then answers his own question. "You're a murderess." Making no attempt to deny it, she quietly replies, "I'm your wife." She powders on, then calmly presides at their previously planned dinner party, charmingly chatting up guests and ringing her little bell to summon her butler.

Menjou and Chatterton begin an elaborate cat-and-mouse waiting game. "You'll die of it," he tells her, warning that she will lose in the end. She feels she's already won: "I wanted to keep you. I've kept you." Months pass. He waits. She doesn't crack. It's only when the bank thief is executed for her crime that she's overwhelmed. She passes out, even though she visited him in prison and received his blessing. ("The joke's on them," he says, admitting he had killed others.) Finally, Menjou wins the competition when she decides she must turn herself in. After all his hatred of her, his ugly remarks, his writing in his diary how he wanted to be rid of her, he does the inexplicable marriage thing and decides to accompany her to the police. "Whatever happens, I'll be with you," he remarks, advancing the plot to the place many marriage films go—that is, to remind audiences that no one really understands marriage. Conveniently for Menjou (and perhaps for Chatterton), she's run over on the way to confess and suffers amnesia. She's returned to the status of "newborn child" with no memory of the murder. The movie ends with them blissfully happy. He's spoonfeeding her lunch out on a terrace, and she knows nothing. In other words, he has regained control.*

Lack of communication between a married couple is another dimension of incompatibility in marriage movies. James Mason, playing a guardian angel for Lucille Ball in *Forever, Darling* (1956), looks right into the camera—and thus directly at the audience—and lays it on the line. "There are some people who go through all their lives without ever knowing the companionship of another soul. You've seen them. Married people." Mason goes on to add that such couples are "going through all the gestures and the acts of love, but each is living his life alone, each on an island apart from the other." Not listening, not paying attention, not communicating—audiences not only recognized this form of incompatibility, they did more than respond to it: they loved it.

Paul Newman and Joanne Woodward, famously and successfully wed in real life, played married couples in three movies that illustrate lack of marital communication in three different ways. They starred as a suburban couple in the 1958 comedy *Rally 'Round the Flag, Boys*; as an example of the John O'Hara

---

* As Menjou has learned, having a mate who doesn't know much isn't always a problem. Tarzan's mate, Jane, points out: "I love saying things to a man who doesn't understand."

universe of misguided Americans in *From the Terrace* (1960); and as an aged couple bewildered by how their lives turned out in *Mr. and Mrs. Bridge* (1990). When it came to portraying couples who never directly connected, the Newmans were the Olympic gold champions. For two people who were apparently happy together, they played marital isolation with astonishing credibility. Their ability to be side by side in the frame, each radiating outward to the audience, projecting an individual character, and still maintaining an inside-the-frame breakdown of communication, defies description. They could play married, both happy and unhappy, like no other acting couple have ever played married. They're the Lunts of the American marriage movie.

In *Rally 'Round the Flag*, the couple simply doesn't listen. They represent a modern (for 1958) suburban couple. He goes to work in the city early every morning, and she busies herself all day with various committees and causes. When he comes home tired, she's got plans—they must go to a meeting for one of her projects. There's no time to talk. Based on an amusing book by Max Shulman, the dreary movie illustrates an allegedly funny premise: two married people who are leading separate lives, with the husband desperately trying to get his wife alone only so they can have sex. What a joke! The movie reached audiences who were actually beginning to live similar married lives, separated by the train and the car and the distance between a work life and a home life, with wives who had so many appliances that they didn't need to stay home all day to cook and clean.

From the Terrace is not a comedy but a serious film based on an O'Hara novel about a disastrous marriage between an ambitious young lawyer and a well-to-do society belle. The movie shows how the concept of marriage is defined for individuals by both society (with its rules of class and proper behavior) and family. Newman is the product of a marriage destroyed by his mother's infidelity. His father (Leon Ames) is bitter, and his mother (Myrna Loy) is an alcoholic. Newman has no model for a successful marriage. Woodward is the product of a wealthy, socially structured marriage in which everything is correct on the surface and nothing else matters. For Newman, winning a girl like Woodward is about climbing the ladder of success; and for the spoiled Woodward, it's about getting what she wants and defying convention. They're off to a bad start.

As their story unfolds, the couple never communicate their true feelings to each other. Woodward is sly and manipulative, and there's a hint that she's a nymphomaniac. She's married Newman for sex, but he doesn't realize it. (She has, true to her upper-crust background, also checked out some basics first. "Are you going to be somebody?" she asks him, because that is of great importance. He assures her that he is, because it's equally important to him.) Woodward's background has taught her what is expected from a husband (he must succeed) and from a wife (she must entertain, look good, and keep any affairs secret). Since Newman is the product of a marriage in which the wife's affairs destroyed everything, they clearly are not communicating anything about their expectations, backgrounds, or needs. They are, and always were, hopelessly incompatible. He has made the marriage he felt society expected of him if he wanted to be successful and upwardly mobile. She has made the marriage her status of rich princess made possible. She gets what she wants.

As Newman claws his way upward, becoming more and more successful, Woodward becomes more and more bored. (They have no children.) Ultimately, she slips into having affairs and drinking, while he's increasingly out of town on business for extended time periods. Newman finally finds true love with a straightforward young woman whose own parents are devoted to each other, and he walks out on his job and his wife. *From the Terrace* is a male weepie: we're asked to place our sympathies with Newman, and understand his point of view. He is honorable, just working his butt off while Woodward becomes an adulteress and therefore a bad person. Earlier in the film, we are asked to see his mother's adultery sympathetically, so there's a fundamental confusion, although the rules of incompatibility in the marriage movie are intact. Communication should be kept open; wives must stand by their men; husbands must not neglect their wives; and children ought to be born.

For obvious reasons, very few films exist about middle-aged or older married couples. Where's the interest, where's the glamour? Where's the optimism or hope for the future? Excellent films do exist on the subject, however, and one is a pure marriage movie in which Newman and Woodward make it work. *Mr. and Mrs. Bridge* exists to tell moviegoers that the marriage of their parents— especially if they were those tragic dogsbodies, Midwesterners—were fogbound. The film depicts a steady relationship that has no real communication between its couple.

Mr. and Mrs. Bridge presents a mid-century American couple in Kansas, taking them from their prewar lives, through World War II, and over onto the brink of the social changes that followed the war. The initial thing of note is the title of the film: *Mr. and Mrs. Bridge*. In it, the couple are united, although onscreen they seem to exist in separate universes even while living in the same house. Significantly, the film is based on, not one, but two books written by Evan O'Connell, the first entitled *Mr. Bridge* and the second, *Mrs. Bridge*. O'Connell originally presented them as living the same events from totally different emotional perspectives and responses. United inside a movie frame, the disconnect between them is inevitably more visible and unmistakable, yet

A mid-century Midwestern married couple: Mr. Bridge (Paul Newman) with his newspaper . . .

. . . Mrs. Bridge (Joanne Woodward) with her music and her embroidery . . .

. . . and *Mr. and Mrs. Bridge*, out in public, where they appear to have each other the way married couples are supposed to have each other.

somehow less troubling. In film, action is character, and seeing Mr. Bridge buy a painting Mrs. Bridge had admired on their trip to Paris so he can surprise her with it at a sidewalk café, softens him, humanizes her, and romanticizes their relationship in ways that allow audiences to see them as better suited for each other than the original author may have intended.

Newman, a real-life midwesterner, understood the man he was playing. Mr. Bridge is rigid and controlling, but not unsympathetic. He's a prude, but not sexless. He *can* listen and he *can* change and he *can* care, as when he has to bail his black maid out of jail. (Earlier in the movie, he walks into his house and takes a glass of lemonade right out of her hand, just after she's poured it for herself. On another occasion, he walks right by her without looking as she sits at the kitchen table, throwing his order for a drink at her with no acknowledgment of her physical presence.) For the most part, however, he is insensitive because there seems to be (to him) no need for sensitivity. He is the master of his domain. He has no time for his wife's suicidal friend (Blythe Danner) and has ignored his faithful secretary of twenty years, not even remembering the twentieth anniversary of her coming to work for him. He has his little lustful secrets—seeing his nubile young daughter sunbathing outside his bedroom window prompts him to jump his wife's bones in midday when she walks into the room. Most of all, he has his acts of kindness and his small observances of his wife's pains and disappointments. When their son is the only boy in the Eagle Scout ceremony not to turn and kiss his mother when prompted, Mr. Bridge notices, feels it, and offers loving kisses and embraces to his wife later. Equally, when her problems are small and petty, he makes her sit in his lap so he can pet her, as if she were a child. He is, in short, presented to the audience, not as a bad man, but as the man you don't want to be—and the man you no longer *have* to be, because we're all freer, smarter, hipper, and wiser. He's not a villain, just a repressed and unfashionable man who never directly communicates—even though he's Paul Newman.

Joanne Woodward's Mrs. Bridge is one of the best performances ever given on film of a middle-aged woman. Woodward presents herself as an authentic example of a fortyish woman of that era: plump and frumpy, despite being still pretty and very well dressed and coiffed. It's the look that the mothers of my own youth had—looking good, actually, but also dressed as if they were twenty years older than they were. When she goes out, Woodward always wears her hat, her pearls, and her gloves. She is sweet, sometimes befuddled—a character living life the way she was taught to live it, sometimes wondering, sometimes sad, and sometimes breaking into little moments of joy. She busies herself playing cards with her friends, attending country-club events, decorating her Christmas tree, and taking appropriate "lessons" such as a drawing class. She loves her children, always reaching out to them and offering them the platitudes she believes are real nuggets of truth. She adores her best friend, the Danner character, but as Danner sinks into alcoholism and confusion, ultimately killing herself, Woodward can't understand why. She doesn't question things; she just goes along. She does what's expected of her, and she knows what those expectations are. When her husband refuses to take shelter in the country-club basement when a tornado strikes, she stays upstairs with him even though she's terrified. When the lights go out, and he orders her to get up and search around for some butter for his bread, she does it. She's passive, because anything else would be inappropriate. Woodward's subtle performance never makes Mrs. Bridge look like a fool, but never undercuts the meaning of the role. She ends up trapped in her car on a snowy day, unable to back out of the garage, unable to open the car doors, and with no one to hear her cries for help. (It's the maid's day off, and Mr. Bridge is where he usually is and where indeed the American husband resides: at the office.) Her problem is that she doesn't know how to communicate, and doesn't even understand she has the right to express herself.

Mr. and Mrs. Bridge live on parallel tracks but are moving in reverse directions. Their total lack of any real communication locks into place. Mr. Bridge grows more rigid and interior, and Mrs. Bridge grows more vulnerable and melancholy. He grows more and more fused into the world as he believes it exists, and she grows more and more out of it, detached and alone. The characters are presented to the audience as a cautionary tale, and a sympathetic justification for change in the roles to be played by men and women, not only in marriage but in life in general. *Mr. and Mrs. Bridge* was made outside the studio-system era, but it nevertheless reveals moviemaking strategy at work on the subject of marriage. Showing a union in which two people never really connect or communicate, it suggests to viewers, "But that's not you—it's your parents."*

Another superb movie about a mature marriage grounded in a fundamental lack of communication is *Dodsworth*, based on the Sinclair Lewis novel. *Dodsworth* is a great movie by any standard. It's more than just a "marriage movie," but its marriage nevertheless illustrates incompatibility. Fran and Sam Dodsworth are not young. They're a middle-aged couple in a midwestern city. Their daughter is grown, and as the movie opens, Mr. Dodsworth has just sold his extremely successful automobile factory. He's a bit sad, having left behind "twenty years" of his life, but his wife's perspective is that "after twenty

---

* The film was a commercial failure. This type of plain reality regarding marriage was not reassuring to audiences, even though it was made after the Sexual Revolution.

years of doing what was expected of us, we're free." She clearly states: "I want a new life—all over from the very beginning, a glorious and perfectly free, adventurous life. It's coming to us, Sammy. We've done our job. We've brought up Emily and seen her married . . ." For Mrs. Dodsworth, life has not ended; it's just begun. For Mr. Dodsworth, his job *was* his adventure. For her, the job was her obligation, her half of a marital agreement. When he chides her a little for being so down on their hometown (ironically named Zenith), she is once again very clear: "Have you ever thought what Zenith means to me? You go down to the plant and deal in millions, have a perfectly marvelous time. I go down to the kitchen and order dinner." She reminds him that while he was enjoying becoming a tycoon, she was dealing with "ladies' luncheons, always the same ladies, and bridge . . . boring dinner parties with the same people . . . children, the garden club . . . I want all the things I'm entitled to. I'm begging for life . . . No, I'm not. I'm *demanding* it." After twenty years, Mrs. Dodsworth is finally communicating what she thinks—it's "my turn"—but Mr. Dodsworth hears without truly understanding that what she really wants will dismantle their marriage, which was successful because it was defined by duty, society's expectations, small-city responsibilities, and obligation. What unfolds is a tragedy that liberates only one of the Dodsworths into a freer, happier marriage—Mr. Dodsworth, brilliantly played by Walter Huston (who had also played the role onstage).

Few movies depict the collapse of a happy, successful marriage of twenty years, and those that do present it as a temporary crisis met and overcome, with a return to the status quo. *Dodsworth* is the story of the death of a marriage in which the couple, when they begin to really spend time together without tasks to fulfill, discover they are incompatible. They talk to each other, but never really hear each other. Throughout the film, both of them at various times refer to their twenty years, and to how much they meant, and to their love. Chatterton, the weaker of the two, tells her husband, "Sam, you've got to take care of me. I don't trust myself," and he says, "I've got to take care of her. A man's habits get pretty strong in twenty years." Neither one of them knows what else to say, but the truth is, she wants out from under his management, and he tires of her "free" behavior.

And that is who the Dodsworths are: a couple who have acted out a happy marriage by the rule book that society provided them. He worked hard to become a success, and she worked hard to become a successful man's wife. He managed his office and she managed their home and daughter. As their twenty years passed by, they were cohabiting, but really living apart in different worlds. She didn't see how tough he really could be and how down-to-earth and unpre-

Dodsworth, one of the best marriage movies ever made, tells the story of a wife who becomes dissatisfied (Ruth Chatterton) with her husband (Walter Huston) . . .

tentious he was. He didn't see her potential to become vain and fussy, or that she was afraid of aging, wanting some thrills, wanting to be admired. On their trip to Europe, he's amused by her lying about her age, and tolerant of her flirtations, but as she sinks deeper into the world of superficial Europeans, he decides they should go home. She begs to stay. "Let me have my fling now . . . because you're simply rushing at old age, Sam, and I'm not ready for that."

It's the decision that will ultimately destroy them. Sam Dodsworth returns home without her, and she stays behind to begin an affair with a European played by Paul Lukas. When Huston finally journeys back to bring Chatterton home, she has dyed her hair blond and he has checked up on Lukas. When Huston brings the adulterous couple together in a hotel room, Dodsworth the hard-nosed businessman and Dodsworth the determined husband merge as one. "I wanted to see you two together . . . I wouldn't have gotten where I am in life if I didn't have it in me to be a bit ruthless . . . I'm sure you've given her things she needed and wanted, and never got from me. But I'm interested in what *I* need and want, and that happens to be peace of mind." Lukas tries to play the sophisticate, jocularly reminding Huston that "in Shakespeare's *Othello*, things end badly for the hero." "Yes, well, I'm not Othello," snaps back Huston, the confident man who became a self-made millionaire. When he asks point-blank if they wish to marry, Lukas suddenly fades out the door, leav-

. . . but when she tries to find herself a younger, more sophisticated
mate, she runs afoul of her potential mother-in-law (the formidable
Maria Ouspenskaya).

ing Chatterton to say, "I'm so sorry, Sam, so terribly sorry." He says, "I'm willing
to wipe the slate clean if you are."

The hotel-room scene is the point where most marriage movies of this type
would end. They would return home and be buoyed up and in each other's
arms again as their grandson is born in Zenith in December. ("Zenith . . . in
December . . . ," murmurs Chatterton when she hears the news about the
baby.) But *Dodsworth* tells the truth. Chatterton has changed, and she *does*
want what Huston can't give her. The Dodsworths stay on in Europe to finish out their trip, and when a chance to wed an impoverished young Austrian
count arrives, Chatterton grabs it, telling Huston, "You've never known me."
He asks her only to put off the divorce for two or three months, just to feel sure
of her young count. When they say goodbye at the train station, he stands on
the steps as the train pulls out, saying what he automatically said to her while
they were wed: "Did I remember to tell you today that I adore you?" She says,
in an attempt to be perky, "Try not to be too lonely." As the train moves slowly
out, and they look at each other, it's the inexplicable ending to a marriage,
the sort of thing that no one can ever figure out. Neither articulates it, but the
traditional words of the marriage movie—"What happened to us?"—are felt all
over the scene.

The movie moves to a conclusion in which Chatterton *does* lose her count.

His mom, played by the formidable Maria Ouspenskaya, shows up to flat-out announce that, as a divorced woman, Chatterton will be unacceptable as a wife for her son—and if that's not enough, she's too old to have children, a must for his lineage. When Chatterton gamely tries to counter that she has money, and the count's family may be noble but they are also poor, Mom isn't having any. "Can you think," she says calmly, "how little happiness there can be for the old wife of a young husband?" Devastated, Chatterton calls Huston to take her home, and he comes, even though he has found his own new energy and happiness with the beautiful young Mary Astor in Naples.

The Dodsworths do not survive. Mr. leaves Mrs. before the boat back to America departs. She challenges him with "What's going to happen to me? Do you think you can ever get me out of your blood?"—and he responds with the famous movie line "Maybe not, but love's got to stop some place short of suicide." Was this the film's message? In 1936, when *Dodsworth* became a hit, earning seven Oscar nominations, was its appeal that finally someone was saying that when a marriage doesn't work, get out of it? Was it a message to women—to accept aging, or not to tie themselves down to home and kids while they were young, or . . . exactly what? The great success of *Dodsworth* is that it eloquently says marriage is mysterious. You can go through it without thinking, carrying out its ritual, and then suddenly wake up and find you don't know your mate.* In *Dodsworth* can be seen on the surface many thoughts and ideas that were lying doggo under the surface of most other movies about marriage. It speaks about things people couldn't articulate easily: lack of communication, marital boredom, a couple in which one is content to be a simple American and one aspires to European "glamour"; about how life goes by, just goes by, without anyone really understanding what a mate might really want or who a mate might really be.

A variation of the noncommunication problem between a couple is often creatively developed: deliberate deception. According to movies, married couples lie to one another. Constantly. About small things (how much a new hat cost) and big things (sleeping with a sister) and the most outré (the mate is an ex-Nazi or an alien from outer space). Deception is a convenient plot strategy for a marriage movie, but it was so commonly used that it's almost presented as a life strategy. Why do movie couples always lie to each other? Apparently so events can move on to some entertainment involving big problems. Yet couldn't there be more *honest* ways to do that, or even some more honest prob-

---

* It also carries the double standard of the day: a man has a better chance of survival than a woman in the aging process.

lems to cope with? The movies use deception as if it were part of the wedding vows: "I promise to lie to you about anything that might hurt your feelings, cause me inconvenience, stop me from having what I want, or get in the way of our daily role playing with each other." The movies create a sense that two people cannot really live together on a day-to-day basis and be totally honest about things. Honesty is an unworkable concept. Even if it's only a simple "Do I look fat in this dress?" played for comedy, if a husband tells the truth it's over for him. Movies don't address the suggestion of "don't ask the question," and the conclusion is simply that movie marriages are built on lies and therefore real ones are, too.

Two movies that illustrate "deception"—bad communication over noncommunication—and its consequential incompatibility represent the tragic and comic sides to the issue, *Deception* (1946) and *My Wife's Best Friend* (1952). *Deception* (Bette Davis, Claude Rains, and Paul Henreid) shows what can go seriously wrong once a bride starts lying to her husband. Davis and Henreid were young lovers when World War II broke out in Europe. Davis was able to flee, leaving Henreid behind. Told he was dead, Davis has pursued a life in New York in the upper-crust music world, becoming the mistress of a famous conductor (Rains). Henreid, a cellist, turns up suddenly, the way men who are supposed to be dead always do in movies starring women. When Davis finds him, she is rapturously motivated to marry him instantly, while Rains is out of town.

The return of Rains, who arrives uninvited at the wedding celebration, motivates Davis to start lying in all directions. She has never told Rains about Henreid, and she's certainly never told Henreid about Rains. Rains is furious and humiliated in front of their elegant and sophisticated friends. Henreid is confused about how Davis is able to live in a posh loft apartment with a fridge stocked with pâté and champagne. (She says she gives music lessons.) In the end, Davis is forced to shoot and kill Rains because she fears he'll ruin Henreid's cello debut by making him too nervous to play well, just the way he did when he took the couple to dinner before Henreid's audition. (Rains kept changing his mind about what to order for dinner, deliberately delaying things to increase tension at the table. In an acting tour de force, he thoughtfully toys with his menu, and it's ". . . ah, the pheasant, but hold the cream sauce . . . no wait, let's have the woodcock . . .") Davis, remembering that woodcock, shoots Rains on the stairway before he can get out to conduct her husband's debut.

Deception, a serious movie, has no truth, only consequences. The comic variation, *My Wife's Best Friend* (Anne Baxter and Macdonald Carey), has no serious consequences, but one dangerous moment of truth. Baxter and Carey have been happily married for eight years, with happiness defined by Carey

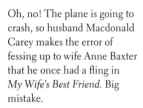

Oh, no! The plane is going to crash, so husband Macdonald Carey makes the error of fessing up to wife Anne Baxter that he once had a fling in *My Wife's Best Friend*. Big mistake.

being a highly successful businessman and Baxter a spoiled wife with a beautiful home, furs, and jewels. It is a movie in which all the women—Baxter, her mother, and her sister-in-law—seriously nag their husbands. The portrait of marriage is both offensive and depressing. Carey and Baxter, off on a vacation, are on board an airplane when its starboard engine catches fire. Believing they are going to crash and die, they turn to each other for a soupçon of honesty. "Let's not lie to each other," says Baxter, admitting, "I've been a rotten wife. I've been selfish. I've nagged you." To make her feel better, he reciprocates, telling her that when she went to New York three years earlier, he became involved with her best friend. ("I paid for it. I've been sick over it.") She forgives him—that is, until they land safely. ("You poor slob," their lawyer says when he hears about it.) The movie chugs forward through their ugly divorce, which is supposed to be lightened with little jokes such as her imagining herself as Joan of Arc or the wife of a desert sheik or Cleopatra, none of which are even remotely amusing (the martyr, the slave, and the adulterer being her available roles). Baxter and Carey are presented as the 1950s version of the 1930s screwball couple, an el cheapo *Awful Truth*. Apparently truth doesn't just go a long way in marriage—it goes too far.

ADDICTION

Incompatibility in all its varied forms was a guaranteed audience connection, but why did marriage movies about addiction have any appeal? And what was their logical entertainment goal? For a married member of an audience, addiction was at bottom a statement about marital misery in which the person you wed made you unhappy by bad behavior. Underneath the surface was something that moviegoers and moviemakers both understood: marriage partners can fail you. (Or as the Countess in *The Women* intones, "*L'amour, l'amour,* how it does let you down!") Addiction had metaphoric resonance, and an unhappy wife or husband could watch a story about addiction and identify with it outside its own parameters. (An unmarried audience member could see a cautionary tale.) It was a link that might be sad, frightening, or only loosely connected, but it nevertheless was a link. The character that is an addict is the character (or marital partner) who is out of control and who demands too much. The addict wants *more*—more things that are *bad*, but also, by implication, more than his or her share. Selfishness in marriage was something audiences could recognize and understand.

There were two basic forms of movie married addicts: the ordinary human one and the celebrity.* Of these two forms, audiences much preferred the celebrity. Biopics such as *I'll Cry Tomorrow* (1955, Lillian Roth), *The Joker Is Wild* (1957, Joe E. Lewis), *The Outsider* (1961, Ira Hamilton Hayes), and *The Gene Krupa Story* (1959, drummer Krupa) linked stories of addiction to music, to gangsters, and to war heroics. Such films were appealing to people who had not become successful or heroic. The message was that the people who *had* weren't perfect, so regular people had no need to feel inadequate beside them. When these movies ended in confession, possibly even rehabilitation, they provided satisfying escapism in their own way. Movies about fictional addicts were less popular, because they suggested more of a this-could-happen-to-you frame of reference.

---

* Perhaps the most celebrated movie about addiction is *The Lost Weekend* (1945), for which Ray Milland received the Oscar for his portrayal of an alcoholic writer. His character isn't married, but the movie nevertheless illustrates how alcoholism (or any addiction) destroys all kinds of relationships. Milland has a patient and supportive brother, who finally gives up on him, and a lovely young girlfriend (Jane Wyman in one of her first serious roles) who does everything she can to help. In the end, however, Milland is on his own, a self-destructive personality who can't really make relationships with other people work.

Movies in which one of the partners becomes addicted—alcohol, drugs, gambling—have little new to say about marriage. The bottom line is simple enough: this isn't going to work. Addicts spend all the family's money and savings, lose their jobs, bring dangers into the household, and become cruel and unloving. Some addiction films ask who's at fault, and assign blame to a *bad* character conveniently set up for that purpose. In *The Man with the Golden Arm* (1955), Frank Sinatra (a heroin addict) is wed to a woman (Eleanor Parker) who keeps him tied to her by pretending she's crippled as a result of his carelessness. When he's not home, she jumps up out of her wheelchair and trots around the apartment. (Sinatra is in love with Kim Novak, and their love is thwarted by his marriage to Parker.) Barbara Stanwyck in *The Lady Gambles* (1949) falls from happy wife to dyed-blond streetwalker because of her gambling addiction, but her problem is really her sister, who has convinced Stanwyck that she killed their mother because the woman died in childbirth when Stanwyck was born. In both cases, family members set the stage for addictive behavior by allowing the movie plot to locate guilt outside the addict.

The issues of addiction in movies are often external to marriage dynamics, and little domestic life is observed. (The drama lies in the mesmerizing portrait of the addiction itself.) *The Lady Gambles* opens up in Las Vegas, where Stanwyck is drawn into gambling while her husband (Robert Preston), a newspaperman, is working on his story about the Boulder Dam. There's a brief domestic sequence when they try to get away from her problem by moving to Mexico and renting a small place by the ocean. Preston is working on his book ("about the Colorado River") and they are reunited in love. When he goes off to San Diego to do research ("in the library"), Stanwyck falls in with gamblers again. While trying to fight her temptation, she irons like a madwoman, burning holes in things and then folding them with a frenzied determination. This brief scene is the only time Stanwyck is observed as a typical wife, and her actions are demented, showing clearly that domesticity is not the issue of this movie.

One film that does portray married life destroyed by addiction is the harrowing *Days of Wine and Roses* (1962), an unrelentingly tragic tale of a young couple (Jack Lemmon and Lee Remick) who sink into alcoholism. *Days of Wine and Roses* is a deeply depressing film. Unlike most stories of addiction in marriage, in which one partner is addicted and the other one suffers, this movie is about a couple who are both alcoholics. (Double your misery.) Well directed, with two terrific performances from Lemmon and Remick, it tries to say how problems like this are not easily solved. It ends in sadness. As a portrait of marriage, *Days* illustrates how two young people who are right for each other can be right for each other for the wrong reasons. Neither can escape the pain of childhood.

It's a world of shadows, distrust, and degradation when alcoholism hits both halves of a married couple. Jack Lemmon and Lee Remick in the tragic *Days of Wine and Roses*.

Scene by scene, the movie shows a marriage literally hitting the skids. Each episode moves the couple forward over time—first as two people who hate each other when they first meet, only to fall rapturously in love; then, married and successful, with a new baby; then suddenly both drinking too much, he on the job, she sitting around alone at home with the baby.

The film is structured like a binge—it starts happy, goes out of control, and loses detail and coherence (deliberately) as events career forward. The couple grow out of sync. When she is willing to give up drinking, he lures her back. After he's institutionalized with DTs and wants to stay sober, she entices him. In the end, he is sober, living alone with their daughter in a modest apartment, and steadily employed. He wants her back, but she can't stay sober. There is no hope for this marriage, and there is no happy ending. Addiction is the marriage "sin" in which, unless it's a musical, there is no optimism about the ability of the couple to turn things around. It was Hollywood's ultimate marital warning sign.

One of the most successful stories about an alcoholic is a woman's film, *Smash-Up: The Story of a Woman* (1947)—a striking film because it clearly and absolutely presents marriage as *the* problem that causes Susan Hayward to become a drinker. It is covertly a feminist film. Hayward is young and beautiful and on her way to a successful career as a singer when she meets and falls in love with a man who sings but isn't really going anywhere. (The movie is told in flashback form, as Hayward lies in a hospital bed with burned hands. She remembers how she met her husband, etc.) She and Lee Bowman marry, and Hayward gives up her own career to manage his. When he becomes an enormous success (a sort of Bing Crosby),* there is suddenly no room for her in his life. Since they are wealthy and have servants, and since he hires new people to manage him, she has no purpose, no role to play, nothing to do all day. So she drinks.

Smash-Up carries a subliminal message for women. It allegedly shows what can happen to a woman (alcoholism, burned hands) if she doesn't accept her life as it is. It also, however, accomplishes an opposite goal. It asks: What is the point of your life? Are you sitting at home with nothing to do? You could have had a career of your own. *Smash-Up* is an excellent example of the dual appeal that stories of marriage could exert for women in the audience.

Bigger Than Life (1956) is a highly effective addiction movie. Its hero (a superb James Mason) is not a war veteran under pressure from his memories of combat, nor is he a jazz drummer tempted by a world of easy drugs and nomadic lifestyle. He's a high-school teacher. Furthermore, he's happily married to an intelligent woman (Barbara Rush) and the father of an adoring young son (Christopher Olsen). He's not rich, and for once a movie home doesn't give the lie to that by being lavish. The husband (even though he *is* the elegant James Mason) presents an audience with an ordinary man in an ordinary house in an ordinary town. Mason and Rush have a believable marriage. They're in tune with each other, loving and supportive, but they're not waving the flag of idealized perfection. They have a partnership, one honed by years of loving, fighting, sharing, agreeing, and disagreeing. Mason works hard to support his family, and has taken a second job to make ends meet. Rush keeps herself and her house neat and clean, and supports her husband's career by entertaining his co-workers. The possibility of a general movie audience understanding such a couple is maximum—yet, inevitably, since they are at the movies, they must watch something go wrong. What goes wrong, true to the base of the film, is not something wildly out of whack with a high-school teacher's world. Mason doesn't begin hanging around gambling casinos. He doesn't suddenly invest in Florida oil wells. He doesn't become enamored of a teenage beauty queen who works at his local coffee shop. No. He develops bad headaches, and his doctor prescribes the miracle drug of the day, cortisone.

---

* Crosby's first wife, Dixie Lee, was a onetime star who became an alcoholic after she gave up her career.

Addiction isn't always alcohol and drugs. Everyman James
Mason is happy and healthy with his family (Christopher
Olson and Barbara Rush) . . .

He's told to be careful of his dosage and not take too much . . . but soon he's
gobbling the little pills, and soon enough after that, he's become "bigger than
life." In his own mind, that is.

Bigger Than Life is a monster movie in which the monster is a very nice husband. It's a mad-doctor movie in which the mad doctor administers to himself,
and a Frankenstein movie in which the good doctor turns himself into his own
crazed creation. Above all, it's a look-out-for-science movie, but it's also a marriage movie. As Mason changes, so does the daily life of a married couple, and
so, accordingly, does Rush. As Mason grows "bigger than life," Rush becomes
smaller than reality. Initially a woman with her own distinct personality, she
fades and becomes fearful. What the movie accomplishes is the demonstration
of a couple who lose their original identities, making their marriage go out
of balance. The lesson of sharing, taking turns, working together is shattered
by an external force—medication—that was not only not their fault, but even
prescribed for them by society's trustworthy guides, doctors.

. . . until he starts taking his doctor-prescribed cortisone and begins to believe he's *Bigger Than Life.*

Mason and Rush are destroyed. Mason changes in his behavior toward his wife. He begins to lie to her and treat her as a doormat. Audiences see this happen at first through little things, small disrespectful actions on his part. Sitting in his bath, he barks out an order to her to carry another kettle of hot water for him up from the kitchen. ("Get it yourself!" she yells, and slams the medicine-cabinet door so hard it shatters.) He takes her shopping and buys her a bright orange dress that they can't afford. He's rude and boorish to the sales staff. Rush tries to tell Mason she has no place to wear such a dress, so he forces her to wear it to church. Sitting in the pew, she sticks out like a forest fire amid the other, somberly dressed women. In fact, she appears to almost *be* on fire, a great visual metaphor for her situation. These small things—the kettle of water, the new dress in church—are in keeping with a true-life marital world.

As *Bigger Than Life* demonstrates what can go wrong in marriage, it turns into a subtle criticism of 1950s America. Rush is a character who is considered smart by their friends, and she often openly questions her husband. She always says what she really thinks, and the movie also makes clear that before she married, she had a job—and that she could return to it should it ever be necessary. (Mason, true to the times, prefers she not work, and takes a second job himself instead. The pressures of this second job are what drive him to the doctor in the first place.) Mason has made a mistake, and his mistake is destroying his marriage. But *Bigger Than Life* is about a couple sharing a life, so Rush also makes a mistake. To survive their crisis, she relies on two prevalent attitudes of American 1950s life as touted in movies, television, and magazine ads: she follows the current "rules" on how to be a good wife—that is, obey—and remembers society's dictum that it's very important to consider what other people think of you (and thus hide your secrets, deny your problems). The first keeps her from overruling her husband until he has gone too far downhill, and the second holds her prisoner after she begins to understand fully that something really terrible is happening in her home. She ends up standing by her man so long that she nearly goes down herself, taking everything with her. Mason crosses a final line into complete madness, attempting to kill their son.

Bigger Than Life, like the majority of marriage movies, tells the audience that if they'll just "face" things, everything will end up all right. The movie ends with the loving family reunited, and Mason superficially healed. He pleasantly agrees to take his cortisone more carefully, and the doctor tells Rush she really must supervise him more closely. *Bigger Than Life* is an excellent movie, with a great sense of color, wide screen, lighting, decor, and an outstanding performance from Mason, but its ending is neither convincing nor reassuring. Addiction has destroyed the norm, thrown the routine off balance, and made ordinary domesticity unworkable. The purpose of such a marital-problem movie was undoubtedly the usual one for a marriage film: reassurance. Audiences apparently found catharsis in seeing that while *their* lives were pretty awful sometimes, things could be a whole lot worse.

MURDER

When it comes to movie marriages, women are always making the Big Mistake. What melancholy impulse is it that prompts a woman to marry a man who wants to kill her? The movies don't know, and they don't care. They just like the idea. It works for them. Movies about marriage often set themselves up like Buster Keaton sitting in his rowboat, infuriated by his idiot girlfriend. He reaches out to strangle her, but stops himself and kisses her instead. In a marriage movie about murder, Keaton would kiss the girl and *then* strangle her. Audiences liked both versions of the action; one was as satisfying as the other.

It's significant that movie women are so easily swayed toward marital mistakes, because the idea was designed to make a direct connection to unhappy women in the audience.* Men don't *marry* as much in movie plots. They take

---

* Even the most glamorous female stars fall prey to bad men in movies. In *Gilda* (1946), Rita Hayworth piteously observes: "You wouldn't think one woman could marry two insane men in one lifetime, now would you?"

up with gun molls and fall prey to blond murderesses (*The Lady from Shanghai*, *Double Indemnity*, et al.), but they know not to *marry* those babes. (Even the dumbest man knows wedding dresses don't come with slit skirts and fishnet hose.) However, movies don't suggest that men can't also be marital idiots. They, too, can be flattered to the altar, and be easy marks for gold diggers, liars, and connivers. Over and over again, as in *Bad for Each Other* (1953), *Chance at Heaven* (1933), *China Sky* (1945), and more, they give up a lovely little woman who would bake pies for them for something sexier, edgier, and more alluring. But men seldom marry women who are trying to kill them. It's a plot form that seems out of balance.* Women just don't see it coming.

Although it may seem that very few real people marry in order to murder their mate, it was a popular marriage-story form. (And today, according to the tabloids, it may be becoming more common than we think.) But if one thinks of "murder" as a stand-in for abuse, then the credibility of such a story—as well as its ability to appeal to women in an audience—becomes greater. Furthermore, murder plots focused on a woman uphold a gothic tradition of storytelling in which women are in jeopardy.

Of course, to be really successful, murder movies needed to have appeal to both men and women. Some films about women who marry unwisely were cleverly pitched toward both. In Orson Welles's *The Stranger* (1946), Loretta Young's new husband (Welles himself) turns out to be an ex-Nazi, conveniently hiding in the small academic town in which she lives. In Hitchcock's *Sabotage* (1936), Sylvia Sidney's husband turns out to be a spy, even though he's working alongside her in a small movie theater. In *Conspirator* (1949), the young and innocent Elizabeth Taylor marries a dashing soldier who is secretly a Communist agent (Robert Taylor). In all cases, the wives are endangered by their cruel and ruthless husbands, who have assumed false identities. Such stories appealed to men, who took them as cracking good spy yarns, chock full of danger and intrigue. A woman was free to think about the melancholy subtext: Young and Sidney and Taylor married men they couldn't trust. (Men may let you down; they may not be who you thought they were when you married them.) Similarly, in a film inappropriately titled *Christmas Holiday* (1944), musical stars Deanna Durbin and Gene Kelly played a naïve girl and a murderer who marry. Realizing the title and the stars would make the audience think the movie was light holiday entertainment, the ads for once decided to

---

* Two films in which husbands are murdered by their wives are *The Strange Woman* (1946), in which Hedy Lamarr offs Gene Lockhart (and anyone else who gets in her way), and *My Cousin Rachel* (1952), although it is never exactly clear whether Olivia de Havilland is really a murderess. That's Richard Burton's problem. He suspects her . . . but will never know for sure, since she dies before he can figure it out.

warn them honestly, screaming: "Marriage, Murder, and Mayhem!" Ironically, people still went believing the film would be a musical, and many demanded their money back. *Christmas Holiday* was a failure; neither men nor women wanted to see Kelly turn ugly on Durbin.*

In *Cause for Alarm!* (1951), Loretta Young plays the long-suffering wife of the crippled Barry Sullivan. She works like a dog all day taking care of him, trying to please him, keeping house, cooking, just hoping he'll be happy. She has accepted her fate. (Her opening narration over the image of their little house with a white picket fence says: "This is where I live. I'm a housewife.") Her husband's "ill" in some mysterious way, but mysterious only to her. To an audience it's perfectly clear: he's nuts! A psychopath, he writes a letter to the police, telling them she's trying to kill him. He innocently asks her to mail it for him, and she does. Then he tells her what it contains, and says he plans to kill himself and thus ruin her life. The remaining movie is minute after minute of hysteria and tension, as Young tries to retrieve the letter and save herself.

Cause for Alarm! is an extreme example of how a married woman found her love returned with hatred. As the ad for *Undercurrent* (1946) starring Katharine Hepburn as the wife and Robert Taylor as the husband who tries to kill her, put it, "Beneath the surface of an overpowering love may surge an undercurrent of vicious hate! She was deeply in love with him . . . yet coming between them was a fear, a strange jealousy on his part that she could not explain!" It's sad but true that some women in an audience might be tied to men who dominate them and keep them cooped up at home in a restricted relationship. They might find solace in movies in which Loretta Young and Katharine Hepburn shared their misery. And the rest of the audience might just enjoy the tension, and not even think of the movie as being about marriage.

And yet of all the misguided and melancholy reasons that might inspire someone to marry, what can possibly inspire a woman to marry a man whose plan is to kill her? "What did she see in him?" doesn't cover it. In the opening scene of *Julie* (1956), a marriage-from-hell movie, Doris Day is driving a convertible along a treacherous coastal road. Her husband, played by Louis Jourdan, rides beside her. They have just left a country club, where, she tells

---

* Another form of man-victimizes-woman marriage movie, which apparently didn't have as much appeal, was the story of bigamy. It's possible to posit bigamy as a form of disguised murder—that is, a tale in which a woman is shattered (if the crime is discovered) by her man. There are very few bigamy movies—it's a strangely unbelievable idea that a man could get away with it, even though they do—but at least two examples exist. There's a tragic one, *The Bigamist* (1953), starring Edmund O'Brien, and a comic one, *The Remarkable Mr. Pennypacker* (1959), with Clifton Webb.

him as the conversation begins, he has humiliated her "in front of all those people." She makes a definitive statement on their relationship: "Well, if this is what married life is going to be, then we have nothing—absolutely nothing." And this is *before* he tries to kill her. Immediately after Day makes her little speech, Jourdan tromps down on the gas pedal, his foot covering hers, and the car takes off on the dangerous winding roads, out of her control. Jourdan just doesn't care, and Day has to cope. Ultimately, she has to run away from him, and it's one darned thing after another. Day is even forced to land an airplane on her own (she's a stewardess) after Jourdan shoots the pilot.

Julie is a marriage nightmare. Jourdan not only decides to murder Day, he announces his intention to her. Furthermore, he admits to killing her first husband so she'd be available. ("He admitted to killing my husband," she laments. "He admits that he wants to kill me, and nobody can help me do anything!") The police, useless in her dilemma because she's legally wed, casually inform her that if they "called in every guy who threatened his wife, we'd need a jail the size of the Pentagon."

At least one movie tries to explain why husbands murder their wives. In *Conflict*, Humphrey Bogart murders Rose Hobart so he can, he hopes, marry her younger and prettier sister, Alexis Smith. (Bogart has tried elsewhere to trade up through murder. In *The Two Mrs. Carrolls* [1947] he murders his wife so he can marry Barbara Stanwyck and then tries to murder Stanwyck when Alexis Smith appears.) Sydney Greenstreet, playing a psychologist, pontificates at a dinner party celebrating Bogart and Hobart's fifth wedding anniversary: "A happy marriage is indeed a rare achievement. Marriage is a very tricky business. People have impulses, compulsions, drives, that are set toward escape, an escape from loneliness. They seek that escape in the companionship of someone else, and just when they think they've achieved it, they find they've put on their own handcuffs." (Later, Greenstreet helps put some real handcuffs on Bogart.) Greenstreet's explanation of how men want to escape the trap of marriage isn't much of an excuse for murder, but at least it's a try. Mostly, however, film history just asks audiences to accept it. It's like those years when all the women in film are walking around with strange things on their heads. They call them hats, but what we see are teapots, arrows, wastebaskets, flower gardens, and bowls of Jell-O. We just have to accept it. Similarly, we can only speculate as to what the appeal of the murdering spouse really was to audiences. Perhaps there's no depth to it at all—people just liked murder mysteries, or just wanted to imagine getting rid of their own obligations in some fanciful manner. It was a safe plot, because the movies almost always put things back to right in the end. Yet the idea that a couple would "strangle each other's identity" was

All stewardess Doris Day can do in *Julie* is hang on to her coffee tray when her crazy husband (Louis Jourdan) pulls a gun on her passengers. Later, she'll have to land the plane by herself, but for now, the coffee tray is challenge enough.

something movies could make tangible, real, and powerful. Movies didn't shy away from talking about how marriage could smother someone's chances in life. In *No Marriage Ties* (1933), Richard Dix asks point-blank, "Why is it two people take a beautiful emotion like love and do everything they can to kill it? They walk up to an altar and say, 'I love you . . . I'll honor and obey you,' and then it's gimme, gimme, gimme. Work for me, you're mine. Live for me. Think for me. Live for me. Die for me. They strangle each other's identity."

The aspect of the murder marriage that develops the traditional woman-in-jeopardy format is akin to the horror film or the detective plot. As stated earlier, this "marriage problem" is the farthest away from the normal life of a traditional couple. (Perhaps it requires a leap into an escapist fantasy that might be appealing only to base instincts.) Such movies have always had great popularity, with their shadowy worlds, murky motives, and spiral staircases. In fact, there are a considerable number of murder-the-wife marriage movies. Many of the great female movie stars faced jeopardy in movie marriages. Ray Milland hires an old friend to strangle Grace Kelly while he's building his convenient alibi by attending a formal banquet in *Dial M for Murder* (1954). Hedy Lamarr, exquisite in ribbons and furs, is held captive by bad husband Paul Lukas in *Experiment Perilous*, but manages to escape with the help of George Brent. In

Midnight Lace (1960), Doris Day, yet again, is victimized by telephone calls from a man threatening to murder her—who turns out to be her husband, Rex Harrison. Claudette Colbert adores her handsome husband, Don Ameche, in *Sleep, My Love* (1948). She doesn't realize he's keeping a chippie (Hazel Brooks) on the side or that he's drugging her with the hot chocolate he lovingly brings her every night. Marriage is a perilous condition for women, because they're locked into it. And if they have money, and their husband doesn't have his own, well . . . it's a hard-knocks world.

Rich women—or women who own things—are vulnerable to marrying cads. In fact, it's usually a rich woman who's in jeopardy. Very rich men . . . or very mean men . . . are sometimes the victim of a desperate mate, but usually it's the wife.* There's something "okay" about a super-rich woman being victimized. The plots usually tell us that, after all, she didn't do anything to get that money—no worthwhile enterprise or effort or hard work that would justify her having it. She got it from her daddy—maybe from a former husband, maybe from her mother, but mostly she got it from Daddy. This entitles someone to try and take it away from her. An exception to this is the character played by Joan Crawford in *Sudden Fear* (1952). Crawford is a very wealthy playwright who made it herself. She worked hard for it, and continues to work hard for it. Her faithless spouse and his hard-boiled mistress (Jack Palance and Gloria Grahame) are clearly villainous and have no right to take Crawford's hard-earned dollars. And besides, we know that in former movie selves, Crawford had to bake pies or work in a factory or take in washing to make a go of it. This poor kid—fifty years old in *Sudden Fear*—just doesn't deserve this! Crawford is the center of the film, and the audience's story identification is through her. (And she triumphs. Palance and Grahame think up an elaborate plot to kill her, but once she finds out, she outplots them and kills them instead. She's a professional plotter, after all—a playwright.)

Wealthy wives whose husbands have designs on their riches are not always murdered—that is, strangled, stabbed, poisoned, or pushed off a roof. Sometimes movies show a process that is more subtle, more ominous: the husband drives the wife mad so she will dispatch *herself*, or at least be suitable for carting off to an asylum. (A movie husband can kill without weapons.) Both *Midnight Lace* and *Sleep, My Love* are variations on this theme, but the best-known

---

* Sometimes she's shrewish (*The Suspect*, 1944), unattractive (*The Two Mrs. Carrolls*), or stingy (*Greed*, 1924). A woman murders her mate because he's abusive or because she wants a better husband (*The Strange Woman*), but the most common motivation for either males or females to murder their spouse is that other major marriage problem: money.

A portrait of a marriage gone wrong: Jack Palance
hides in the shadows so he can move on wife Joan
Crawford before she knows he's there . . .

example is *Gaslight*, starring Charles Boyer and Ingrid Bergman (who won
the Oscar for her role).* Boyer impeccably portrays a suave European man of
the sort a young and impressionable girl (Bergman) would see as her romantic dream. He is handsome, attentive, deeply caring, and adjusts to her every
whim and need—before they're married. After they wed and he is ensconced
in her London home, where he hopes to find hidden jewels, his attentiveness,
so charming at first, suddenly turns smarmy—and then menacing. He con-
fuses her about little things: a forgotten social event, a lost piece of jewelry.
She begins to doubt herself, and he slowly drives her mad. The spectacle of
Bergman, a beautiful, healthy, intelligent woman, crumbling into doubt, confusion, and fear is tragic. The metaphor of how a husband can control his wife,
their household, her comings and goings, and her entire definition of herself,
is a powerful statement about marriage.

* *Gaslight* (1944) was based on a successful Broadway play, *Angel Street*. The play was
filmed earlier in Great Britain in 1940, starring Anton Walbrook and Diana Wynyard also
under the title *Gaslight*. When it was first released for television in the United States, it
was retitled *Angel Street* to avoid confusion with the later American version. It now plays
on Turner Classic Movies under its original title.

. . . but Crawford's already drawn a bead on him. It's a film noir marriage in *Sudden Fear*, a cat-and-mouse game of marital murder.

Movies tell us that when men marry for money, they aren't content just to live a wealthy life; they want control of the funds, so they plan to murder the wife and inherit. Women, on the other hand, have no master plan. When they marry for money, they're content just to go shopping. As a character in *Paris Model* (1953) explains it, wives want "jewels and motor cars and costly raiment." Men, however, want financial control. It's sexism buried in plot. Women can be bought off with knickknacks and trinkets, but men, being men, understand high finance. Occasionally, movies present a man who lives off a woman, such as William Holden's character in *Sunset Boulevard* (1950). But this is clearly a no-no, and it isn't connected to marriage. Besides, Holden ends up floating dead in a swimming pool. There's always the sense that a man who takes money from a woman is a gigolo, married or not, whereas a woman who marries for money may be merely a gold digger, or perhaps a very clever little minx. This is not the same level of bad behavior as the man's. The man who weds for money is weak, while the woman who weds for money is strong. She may be naughty, even evil, and certainly without suitable values, but it is indirectly implied that this is one of the few avenues women have to gain wealth. If a man marries for money, he lacks manly definition and would therefore have

Why do movie women marry movie men who want to hurt them? In *Gaslight*, the beautiful Ingrid Bergman pleads with her cruel husband, Charles Boyer, to give her proof she's not insane, but why would he do that since he's the one trying to drive her mad?

to be a secondary character. To elevate his status, he's made into a mastermind, a murderer who plots. There is a grim lesson in male/female status when one confronts old movies that tell us that men can be murderers because, after all, they're men and know business and planning, but women, poor souls, can only coax men to buy them stuff. (This suggests that equality means more women murdering husbands on film, as in the 1987 *Black Widow*, in which Theresa Russell murders several rich husbands until she's tripped up by another canny female, Debra Winger, or *Original Sin* [2001], in which Angelina Jolie ultimately spares Antonio Banderas.)

Marriage murder plots were often gothic in origin, presenting a beautiful heroine in crinolines and in peril from a dangerous husband. *Dragonwyck* (1946), starring Gene Tierney, is a variation on a *Jane Eyre* theme in which Tierney plays a naïve country girl yearning for excitement and luxury. She marries the drug-addicted Vincent Price after he murders his first wife (with an oleander plant, a neat trick) so he can have Tierney as his bride and future mother for healthy sons. (True to tradition, the ads for *Dragonwyck* ignored marriage—and even murder. "The romantic drama of a woman whose heart challenged her conscience," blared the posters and the film's trailer, claiming the film to be an "unusual impassioned drama [of] a woman's love.")

Sometimes women just *think* the men they married are trying to kill them. Such films reveal much about female psychology as imagined by Hollywood filmmakers, and they give insight into what audiences could or would respond to emotionally. They also suggest under the surface that married women may feel they're caught in a trap. Two excellent films, both directed by Alfred Hitchcock, superbly illustrate a plan to manipulate an audience's thinking, create a credible subtext, and weave story elements out of female doubt. *Rebecca* (1940) and *Suspicion* (1941) are stories that have a central character who is female, and they not only have the same director but also the same star, Joan Fontaine, whose co-stars are, respectively, Laurence Olivier and Cary Grant. These are both award-winning movies, critical successes as well as top box-office draws. *Rebecca* won a Best Picture Oscar, beating out stiff competition.* Fontaine was nominated for *Rebecca*, but lost to Ginger Rogers in *Kitty Foyle*—and the next year she won for *Suspicion*.

Although *Rebecca* is the visualization of a best-selling novel by Daphne Du Maurier, and *Suspicion* is based on *Before the Fact* (by Anthony Berkeley writing as Francis Iles) and both films are murder mysteries, it is nevertheless possible to see them as two classic examples of the marriage movie. Marriage is the foundation of the credibility of both stories. In both, the central character is a woman who unexpectedly marries a man who she (and the audience) can easily believe is the ultimate dream man (the young Olivier and the eternal Cary Grant). Both movies make clear to the audience that these two women are without any real assets. The heroine of *Rebecca* is naïve, inexperienced, unsophisticated, without social status, and poor. She works as a travel companion. For that matter, she doesn't even have a name: never once, in either novel or film, is the leading character of *Rebecca* ever called by a specific first name. (The novel was a first-person "memory.") This character is also something of a ninny by modern standards, although she is supposed to be seen as sweet, fresh, gentle, and easily cowed only because of her lack of experience, a situation that will change. In *Suspicion*, the character is also without experience or sophistication. She does, however, have some money and some social status, but not a great deal of either. It's also suggested that she's without sex appeal or beauty. Her clothes are dowdy, and she wears glasses—the movie equivalent of a wart on the nose.

In both movies, the audience is shown that, quite unexpectedly and quite rapidly, these two leading ladies without glamour, funds, or wit capture spectacular men. Olivier is even stinking rich, although Grant is not. (He just acts, and lives, as if he were.) The two movies both make it all extremely clear.

---

* The other nominees were *All This and Heaven Too, Foreign Correspondent, The Grapes of Wrath, The Great Dictator, Kitty Foyle, The Letter, The Long Voyage Home, Our Town,* and *The Philadelphia Story.*

In case we want to believe that Joan Fontaine in both roles is really, underneath it all, très chic and clever, we're told by other characters in the movie that we're just plain wrong. The gauche American woman Fontaine travels with in *Rebecca*, Florence Bates, says Fontaine is mousy and will never marry, and Fontaine's own father in *Suspicion* (Sir Cedric Hardwicke) describes her as "spinsterish." Both behavior and costuming confirm their opinions. The Fontaine of *Rebecca* wears little-girl dresses, sweaters, and flat shoes, and she knocks over the flowers in a restaurant and generally stumbles around. The "spinsterish" Fontaine of *Suspicion* wears severe suits, buttoned-up blouses, and the aforementioned glasses. She purses her lips and snaps her purse shut whenever Grant looks her over.

How does Fontaine capture Olivier and Grant? We might be as confused as Bates and Hardwicke, except that Hitchcock, after establishing how society sees her, gives us, the audience, a special private look at Fontaine's two women. We are allowed to see what society and family can't see but Grant and Olivier can. Olivier says clearly that he wants Fontaine because she is an unblemished "child." "What a pity you have to grow up," he says. She's not a threat to him. She's honest, and, as it will turn out, totally unlike what he knew before in his former wife, the dread *Rebecca* of the title. Grant, it's established through his point-of-view shot, is a shrewd observer of women. He glances up at a hunt to see Fontaine rear up on her spirited horse, taming him easily and loving the thrill. Grant glimpses the passionate and potentially sexy woman underneath the prude. She can be open and wild, and he later asks her, "How do you feel about me in comparison to your horse?" The audience can see what society doesn't see, and therefore is given a reason to accept the marriages as credible.

The most important event in both women's lives is marriage, a ritual that directly leads each to a confrontation with doubt (a psychological problem) and murder (a physical and legal problem). Both women start living in new houses that represent their states of mind: *Rebecca*'s heroine lives in a gigantic mansion (the famous Manderley) that is literally too big for her as she wanders around in it, finding all the physical markers of Rebecca—her things, her taste, and her giant monogram, the intimidating "R." The heroine of *Suspicion* lives in a new, more modern (but also large) home that is designed with a gigantic spiderweb window, a visual metaphor that speaks directly to her situation. In both movies, other characters tell the women that they were lucky to have these men, because no one believed they ever would, could, or should. And, finally, both women begin to misunderstand their husbands and their motivations. In other words, they begin to doubt that their husbands actually love them—to believe what society has believed: that they're unworthy of their husbands, so

The fish-out-of-water bride arrives at her new home. Joan Fontaine in *Rebecca* is accompanied by super-rich hubby Laurence Olivier as she first sees his mansion, Manderley. She faces an army of servants headed by the scary Judith Anderson.

why should their husbands love them? The audience is presented with a female subjectivity, so we agree with what the women are thinking and feeling. We live out their doubts and suspicions, and thus undergo two tales of marriages that start falling apart due to female misunderstanding. The appeal is to insecurity in women, and a sense of the dominant importance of men.

Rebecca and *Suspicion* are stories of marriage from a female point of view. In *Suspicion*, Fontaine "has," but feels it's these material goods that attracted Grant. In *Rebecca*, she "has not," and fears she won't be able to hold Olivier's love because of that. Fontaine illustrates the wife's marital role: to accept, to be grateful, but most of all to try to be worthy. She must give all if she "has" and give all if she "hasn't." What she gives can be either her physical goods or her physical self, but her job is *giving*. *Rebecca*'s Fontaine believes that her husband still loves his ex-wife, the mysterious figure who is never seen onscreen, Rebecca de Winter. The other Fontaine begins to believe her husband is plotting to kill her for her money. The marriages thus are based on misunderstanding, imbalance, blindness, and failure of perception. The female's point of view is reinforced by the fact that the two men also begin to misunderstand their wives. Olivier in *Rebecca*, as Maxim de Winter, doesn't recognize his wife's pain or insecurity at all. He doesn't seem to notice how lost and out of place she is, or that the really scary Mrs. Danvers (Judith Anderson) is bullying her; he just thinks her faltering insecurity is "charming." In *Suspicion*, a movie with an ending that many people find unacceptable, Cary Grant is presumably going to kill, not his wife, but himself—because he thinks she will be too ashamed of him when she finds out he stole some money. (*Suspicion* does such a good job of aligning audiences with Joan Fontaine's suspecting her husband is going to kill her that they're furious when he doesn't, and reject the film's final scenes.)

Beneath their murder stories, these movies are about marriage, and women responded to them as women's films during their original releases. Stories about women who feel unsure in their marriages found female acceptance, and with potential murder thrown in, the men could enjoy them too. (That both wives are willing to die for their husbands apparently seemed very entertaining to men as well as to women.)

What movies like *Rebecca* and *Suspicion* tell audiences is that women are more vulnerable in marriage than men are. They have more to lose. Women need marriage emotionally; men don't. A woman can't hire someone to love her and support her, but a man can get a good maid—and there's always his mother. As it all turns out, both Olivier and Grant really love Fontaine, but she's the one who had to worry. Olivier had an unfaithful wife (the adultery problem) who was dying of cancer, and Grant was badly short of hard cash (the money problem). These issues put the two husbands out of sorts and made them even a bit suicidal . . . but, again, it was Fontaine who had to do the worrying.

One truly great movie in which a husband tries to kill his wife perfectly captures the lure of the murderous variation of the marriage movie. *Sunrise* (1927) is unquestionably a visual masterpiece, but it tells a very simple story. A young farmer (George O'Brien) is lured into the bushes (literally) by an exotic "woman from the city" (Margaret Livingston) for a sexual encounter that sets him on fire and opens him to the excitement of sin. He decides to murder his sweet little wife (Janet Gaynor, in a luminous, Oscar-winning performance). This is all there is to it—he wants what he wants and his wife is in the way. She must go. But the creation of the events cinematically lifts the film upward into one of those mysterious explanations of the unexplainable—no one in the average movie audience would ever do such a thing, and yet everyone understands. Everyone gets every moment of it, from his excitement, his plan, his bungled attempt, his wife's horrified response, her subsequent fear of him, their slow journey back into themselves, his nearly losing her to drowning in a storm, and their return to normal, back at the farm, still alive, still man and wife. *Sunrise*

Is it murder or misunderstanding?—that old marriage bugaboo. Cary
Grant and Joan Fontaine are locked into a lack of awareness of each
other that lasts until the very end of Hitchcock's *Suspicion.*

is about the mystery of any one marriage, the inexplicable nature of a successful union. Everything movies have to offer—the beauty of an image, camera movement, set decoration, lighting, superb acting—combines to present a
haunting, mysterious evocation of the rigors of marriage, its ups and downs,
its need for escape, its need for a reliable unity, and its anger, disappointment,
and bizarre behavior. As is true of lesser films, *Sunrise* gives—here's sex outside
of marriage with a woman from the city—and then it takes back: a restoration
to normalcy that teaches the lesson that true love and marriage are the better
things to have. For once, however, the lesson is both art and entertainment. For
once, the marriage movie finds its true purpose: to evoke the unexplainable
nature of the union.

Were all these marriage problems unique to America? Three marriage movies
from differing cultures are the French *Bed and Board* (1970), directed by Fran-
çois Truffaut, the Swedish *Scenes from a Marriage* (1973), directed by Ingmar
Bergman, and *The Flavor of Green Tea over Rice* (1952), from the Japanese
master Yasujiro Ozu. Admittedly, these films are all personal cinema under
the guidance of recognized directors, but each in its own way reflects the culture and attitudes of its own country of origin while still reflecting the same
fundamentals as its American counterparts.

Sunrise depicts a married man's dilemma. George O'Brien has got himself a pretty, sunny little wife (Janet Gaynor), and she loves him . . .

Bed and Board is the fourth movie about Truffaut's famous character Antoine Doinel, played by Jean-Pierre Léaud. (Antoine is sort of a French Andy Hardy, a boy who grows up and finds love, adventure, knowledge, and a little maturity in a series of movies.) In *Bed and Board*, Antoine is in his late twenties and married to Christine (Claude Jade). They are a larky young couple clearly not ready for the responsibilities of married life. She gives music lessons, but forgets to charge her pupils. He works for a florist, dyeing white carnations red and ruining most of them. She buys a photo of her crush, Rudolf Nureyev, to hang above their bed, and he peeks into the top of her nightgown and dubs her breasts Laurel and Hardy. What are their problems? They don't make enough money. Her parents are ever present in their lives. Unexpectedly they have a baby, who becomes his rival for her attention. He becomes enchanted by a beautiful Japanese girl (Hiroko Berghauer) he meets at his new job and has an affair; Christine finds out and throws him out. Thus their problems are very American—money, in-laws, children, and infidelity. What is different is the charmingly Gallic view of married love and romance. The couple are chic; the Japanese other woman is *très exotique;* even the baby, Alphonse, is adorable. There is no sense that any of the problems cannot be overcome, or that any of it is a terrible tragedy. It's only marriage, after all.

Where *Bed and Board* is a soufflé, *Scenes from a Marriage* is a blood pud-

. . . but also out there in the reeds lurks temptation: the dark and sexy other woman "from the city" (Margaret Livingston) who can teach him a thing or two. What's a man to do?

ding.* It's intense. Shot in long takes and unrelenting close-ups, its goal is to probe and reveal and expose. Can a man and a woman actually keep marital love alive? *Scenes*'s couple (Liv Ullmann and Erland Josephson) are professionals. She's a divorce lawyer and he's a scientist (and failed poet). Everyone thinks of them as perfectly wed. In particular, Ullmann is presented as an example of an earth-mother wife, nurturing, parenting, obeying, and directing household tasks and family gatherings with great skill. Josephson seemingly appreciates all this. The story takes hold when Josephson abruptly leaves Ullmann for another woman. She—and everyone else—is forced to confront the truth about their marriage: it wasn't *really* working. As years go by, the couple divorce, take other lovers, marry others, and yet they cannot ever really break their bonds of intimacy and connection. They can read each other's minds, understand each other better than anyone else, and can never forget or lose the original desire that first united them. They share a passion that can emerge as both love and hate, but it's passion for and about each other. *Scenes* makes an audience suffer the ups and downs of their relationship, always suggesting that

---

* *Scenes* was originally created as a six-part miniseries for Swedish television; it was released in America in 1974 in a three-hour theatrical version. Bergman's original television version ran five hours.

Marriage is apparently a universal language. In the French film *Bed and Board*, Claude Jade (wife) and Jean-Pierre Léaud (husband) ignore each other in bed with their separate books . . .

these two people are deeply linked, whether or not we can understand why. In the end, however, despite their Scandinavian doom and gloom, their list of troubles are the familiar ones of American films: children, family, competition, and infidelity.

Ozu's *Flavor of Green Tea over Rice* is the story of a childless middle-aged couple living in an "uptown" mansion in Tokyo. Despite the luxury of their home, its spaces, which the camera often sits observing, are empty, soundless, and vibrating with a sense of loneliness. The husband (Shin Saburi) is an executive at an engineering company; the wife (Michiyo Kogure) is traditionally at home in charge of the household. He is a reliable, quiet, and rather taciturn man from the country. She's snobbish, bored, and believes her husband to be dull. In particular, she's irritated by his table manners: he's loud, eats like a peasant, and always pours green tea over his rice. They have, however, survived many years of marriage. In their story, nothing dramatic happens, but that's part of Ozu's directorial style, which uses the camera as a patient observer. *Green Tea over Rice* tells an audience as much about marriage as any movie, but it's information gleaned only by intensive watching. Minor crises *do* occur. The wife lies to her husband, pretending to be taking care of a niece while she really escapes to a spa with her friends. There's strife when the husband's family instructs the wife to arrange a marriage for that same niece, and the girl, a modern type who always wears Western dress, wants to make her own choice.

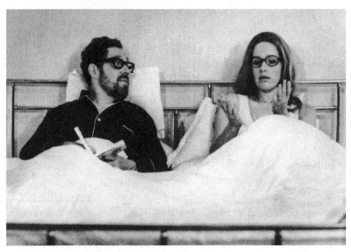

. . . and in Sweden, Erland Josephson (husband) and Liv Ullmann (wife) more or less do the same in *Scenes from a Marriage*.

The final crisis comes when the wife leaves Tokyo on a train trip, going away alone.

It's possible, despite their minimalist issues, to classify the couple as having the recognizable American movie problems about marriage: children (lack of), incompatibility (she's uptown, he's provincial), relatives (the niece and his family), etc. Although the movie was made sixty years ago in Japan, cultural differences fade. (As David Thomson wrote about Ozu: "The intensive viewing of Ozu—and such stylistic rigor encourages nothing less—makes questions of Japaneseness irrelevant . . . The intentness of the image, and its emotional resonance, is . . . as relevant to the West as to Japan.") Nowhere is this more clearly demonstrated than in the two final scenes of *Green Tea over Rice*, the first depicting the couple and the second indicating the beginning of the niece's potential marital relationship.

In the first scene, the husband returns home unexpectedly early from a business trip, having had plane trouble. It's late at night, and he and his wife go into the kitchen to prepare a simple meal. The wife is somewhat unfamiliar with where things are in the kitchen (they have servants), but the two work together, finding what they need. As they sit down to eat, she tells him she won't go away again without telling him. They begin their meal, and he pours green tea over his rice. She does the same. Nothing much more needs to be said. It's an act of marital acceptance. In the unscheduled shared experience of food preparation, their marriage, their reunion, and their future are defined. There is no other filmed or recorded explanation for why they will remain side by side for the rest of their lives. Tradition and habit prevail.

In the final scene of the film, the husband's young male friend and the feisty niece are seen walking along the sidewalk. Suddenly, they begin to engage in playful sparring. He tries to embrace her; she runs from him and hides inside a kiosk. He tries to enter; she pushes him out. This action is repeated several times, and then they run off together, away from the camera, away from audience scrutiny. Their conflict—a game of advance and reject—and its repetition unto familiarity and commitment indicate to a sharp observer that these two people have already embraced the basics of marriage.

All three of these foreign films share a bottom line of recognizable American marriage problems, suggesting that marriage films transcend cultural differences. They also suggest, as most Hollywood movies do, that there is no easy way to explain or understand marriage. Croissants, smorgasbords, or green tea, marriage is just marriage.

The universality of international movie marriages is brilliantly confirmed by the Iranian *A Separation* (2011). A film of depth and complexity, *A Separation* is not only about marriage; it's also about the clash between modern and traditional customs and attitudes in Iran, about the different ideologies and cultures the nation reflects, and about its political structure. Yet although what an American viewer sees onscreen about Iran may be a world we don't expect to see, what we see about marriage is what we know and recognize. Modern Iran is urban, traffic-plagued, and a melange of unfamiliar cultures and religious attitudes, but the two marriages depicted have familiar problems: money, incompatibility, in-laws, and children.

A Separation begins where we've been before: a married couple disagrees over something serious. The wife (Leila Hatami) wants to leave Iran and take their young daughter (Sarina Farhadi, the director's own daughter) with her, but her husband (Peyman Moadi) wants to remain so he can take care of his elderly father, who suffers from dementia. Since the couple cannot agree on what to do, Hatami moves out, going home to live with her parents. This decision triggers the arrival into their lives of a second married couple. The husband hires a young woman (Sareh Bayat) to care for his father while he goes to work, and allows her to bring her own young daughter to work with her. Moadi doesn't realize two things: (1) the woman is pregnant; and (2) she has not told her husband that she's working. Bayat's husband (Shahab Hosseini) is an unemployed shoemaker, and the couple are deeply in debt. The conjunction of the two marriages leads to disaster.

Movie marriages cross international borders once again, as in *A Separation* (from Iran). Married couple Leila Hatami and Peyman Moadi reflect the status of their marriage in body language and the space between their chairs.

Both marriages are disintegrating and, although at different levels of the social scale, suffer from similar problems: lack of communication, pressure from their families, and financial strictures. Both are at an impasse. Neither husband deals with his spouse honestly (and they are all living within a legal system that places its citizens in a similar position). Both couples quarrel. Neither are fully aware of the intense feelings of their daughters: their fears about the family, and their uncertainty about their own roles in their parents' problems. Both couples freeze one another out with deadly silences. Both must deal with government bureaucracy on a daily basis. The upper-social-strata wife is a doctor, and the lower is a housemaid; the doctor at first appears to be more liberated, but the maid finds her own ways of defying her husband's controls. The more educated husband is a bank employee, and in a position to cope with legal issues, and yet the shoemaker is able to bring him into court and get him in trouble. There's a feeling of unease during the viewing process, as if at any moment something totally unexpected—and awful—can erupt. There is a constant question as to what is true, who is correct, what is the right way to feel, and even what is actually happening. A viewer doesn't know where to locate sympathy and what to believe. And there lies the film's complexity: instead of a typical movie picture of marriage, there exists onscreen the mystery of two real marriages. We can easily recognize surface events, familiar from life and other movies, but, as is true of what we know about offscreen unions, we can't really understand either marriage, and it's not because the setting is Iran. Marriage in the movies, it seems, is Esperanto only in its problems, not at its core.

Their Situations

Viewing the marriage movie throughout the decades, I began to see the evolution of this mysterious entity that was never identified by its own name. I observed its birth in the silent era, with its bipolar goals of amusement and caution, and with its escapist additions of spectacle and erotic pleasure. In the sound era, I located the "pure" versions that faked an "honest" story line while still maintaining reassurance and escape, and I realized that the three main components of any marriage story were the couple, their problems, and their situations. At first, it seemed that "situations" would be simple to grasp. After two people married, preferably before the movie started or certainly in its earliest minutes, and well before they encountered their inevitable problems, they took up a life that would become their "situation." That is, they would live in a city or a small town, on a farm or in a mansion. They would have kids or not have kids, face troubled times or live peacefully. Their "situation" would be the setting, which would showcase the background selected for variety, familiarity, shock, comfort, or whatever. But the real situation the couple would be in was fundamentally marriage itself, so this other "situation," or context, wasn't really all that important. It was, after all, marriage. The problem or problems would be what made the movie tick. "Situations" would be the least of the three main elements.

As it turned out, however, one of the most difficult problems in tracing and defining the marriage film was that a large shift in marriage movies took place. During and after World War II, when a movie married couple faced a large, historical situation outside their control, such as the war (and later the Sexual Revolution), their problems were subjugated to the situation. The couple endured and the old problems still exerted themselves, but the situation the couple were living in and trying to resolve their problems in took over the definition of the film. "Situation" became a trump card in the movie-marriage deck. Nowhere was this more obvious than during the war itself, the "situation" that began the trend and solidified it for the future.

On December 7, 1941, the Japanese bombed Pearl Harbor, and America entered World War II overnight. During 1942, eleven million men left home to go to war. The result was a confluence of changes in the world, the home front, the audience, and the film business. It was a time of sudden and intense patriotism. People who worked in movies, like everyone else in the country, were citizens who cared about what was happening. A significant number of big-name leading men enlisted in the armed services: Tyrone Power, Jimmy Stewart, Douglas Fairbanks Jr., Robert Montgomery, Wayne Morris,* Clark Gable, and others. (The youngsters in the pipeline to replace the Powers and the Stewarts and the Gables had themselves also decamped: William Holden, Glenn Ford, Dan Dailey, et al.) This meant an immediate lack of leading men and a need to find new ones who would not be drafted.

The newly formed Office of War Information asked Hollywood to help Americans understand their new circumstances—understand *and* support the effort to win. As Hollywood assessed the government guidelines (articulated in the OWI's *Government Information Manual for the Motion Picture Industry*), the businessmen who ran the studios moved to cooperate fully. First of all, they would have to address the need for new male stars. They would also have to make better use of the men left behind: the exempted older stars with families, the teenagers too young to serve, and the foreign-accented émigrés arriving from Europe. The studios still had a strong set of established stars available: the fabulous lineup of females from the 1930s, the older, solidly established actresses in their prime (Olivia de Havilland, Barbara Stanwyck, Joan Crawford, Bette Davis, Myrna Loy, etc.). There was also emerging a sexy young set of up-and-coming beauties (Betty Grable, Rita Hayworth, Dorothy Lamour), and unlimited access to new female faces that could be developed. There were plenty of women to star in movies, and there were also plenty of women in the audiences to watch them. When the men marched off, these women had time on their hands and, once they started working in war plants, more money in their own pockets than they had ever had. With no men to date, and with husbands overseas, women were restricted in their social lives. (As the popular song put it, "Saturday night is the loneliest night of the week.") It was not thought appropriate for women to go to bars or nightclubs or dances alone, so where *could* they go to amuse themselves? They could, of course, go to the movies, a socially acceptable activity. Women had always gone to movies, alone and in groups, but now they went more often, and they went more than once to

---

* Wayne Morris is not well known today, but he was a handsome young leading man at Warner Bros. during the 1930s. His war record was the most distinguished of any movie star who enlisted. A navy aviator, he was awarded four Distinguished Flying Crosses and two Air Medals, having been credited with shooting down seven enemy aircraft in aerial dogfights, and with sinking a gunboat and two destroyers. His return to films found him unable to regain his former popularity. He died in 1959 at age forty-five, ironically from a heart attack he suffered while he was watching aerial maneuvers aboard an aircraft.

the same film. Hollywood's job was to figure out what movies the home-front female audience wanted to see. What would lure them to the box office?*

Assessing their prospects, studios turned to an obvious topic: marriage, a subject that could not only help with the war effort but also connect directly to the women in the audience. Marriage could entertain and reassure them—and it could also teach them about their role in the war effort and thus comply with the goals of the Office of War Information. (Classroom films with movie stars!) The marriage movie could go to war. It could help save the country.

The movies made about marriage during World War II maintain the established story units of "the couple" and the familiar list of problems—the in-laws, the kids, the money problems, the infidelity pressures, etc. The difference was that the husband was now in uniform and probably overseas, and the problems were caused directly by a strongly presented external force, the war, which was in and of itself a bigger crisis, more important than a couple's own little problems. As Ann Sheridan says right out loud to her husband (Jack Carson) in 1942's *Wings for the Eagle*, "Whatever you and I feel about each other, there's a war job to be done." The national *situation* (war) outranked the personal problems a married couple might have.

The movie business was obviously already aware that during specific eras, current social issues and situations (a form of pressure) could be translated onto the subject of marriage with great success, but it was the era of World War II that really pinned down—and made full use of—this characteristic of the marriage movie.† During the war, the moviemaking business learned firsthand at the box office that the public could respond to crisis through familiar story patterns, and that marriage—that everyday old shoe—was just the ticket. Whereas the basic, "pure" marriage movie was isolated, during a national crisis that everyone shared, the usual troubles could be related directly to the crisis itself. The triumvirate of movie marriage issues—the couple, their problems, and the situation in which they lived, their marital context—shifted balance. The couple remained, but their problems, once dominant, took a backseat to their historical situation. This is a key milestone in the development of the history of the marriage movie. In fact, from then on, "situation"—or the background in which the couple struggled or lived—was almost always featured more prominently in marriage stories. Ramping up the "situations" of marriage movies made marriage more topical, more relevant, more modern. It had once been

---

* Movie attendance was at an all-time high during World War II.

† During the silent era, many movies addressed the changing moral structure, and during the Depression, many were about unemployment. The 1930s Depression, in particular, was an earlier "situation," in which movies about money problems in marriage increased, but many escapist movies provided a glimpse of wealthy marriages: the "other" view.

exciting enough just to picture a couple in glamorous clothes living out escap-ist marriages, but after World War II something more was needed: topicality.

As the war unfolded, there were many questions movies could use as plot lines. Wartime was hard on marriage, so the drama was there, and all of it eas-ily adaptable to the marriage format. What could a married woman who was left behind alone do with herself, and how was she to live her life without her husband (the "lonely wife")? Should a young couple rush to marriage before the man shipped out? (This "marry in haste" issue applied both to couples who had just met and to couples who knew each other well.) Should a woman left behind go to work outside the home ("Rosie the Riveter")? Should wives live together economically and share concerns (sisterhood)? Was it wrong for people at home to indulge themselves with black-market goods, keep their big cars, their comfortable lifestyles, in times of war ("Democracy for everyone on a fair basis")?

Most of these questions could lead directly to interesting plots for big-name female stars. It was easy to envision Loretta Young, Bette Davis, Myrna Loy, Irene Dunne, et al. coping with everything imaginable after her man decamped, or dealing with the challenge of sexual frustration, deciding to be unfaithful or not, or struggling to learn how to pay bills, or becoming a black marketer (temporarily, of course), or following her husband to camp. Kid stars like Bonita Granville and Jackie Cooper could run wild with no daddy at home to discipline them. And Betty Grable could show her legs and sing about it.

In its manual for Hollywood, the Office of War Information reminded filmmakers that "the men and women on the production line and the home front are as much a part of the battle front as the soldier in the battle zone." The "home front" section of the OWI's goals definitely endorsed the idea of the movies showing women enlisting in the armed services, taking jobs in war factories, and successfully taking the place of their men in the workforce. The American wife, the American woman, and the American girl were all to be sent the same message: you can cope without husbands, sweethearts, or fathers. Everybody had a role to play in gaining victory, and the motion-picture business was asked to participate with positive images. The goals of the govern-ment and the goals of the business were beautifully simpatico. So many issues, so many problems—and all of them ripe for Hollywood's picking.*

First, Hollywood faced the primary issue: how to tell a story about a mar-

---

* The Office of War Information had a list of seven questions as guidelines for the mov-ies during World War II, one of which was simply "Will this picture help win the war?" The OWI also stated that in addition to being shown "becoming war workers," American women in the movies should be "depicted as coping without their husbands or sweet-hearts."

riage without the husband at home to participate—a story about marriage with only 50 percent of the couple present. This was easy. A marriage without a man? Women's pictures had often been tales in which the man—husband, lover, father, or son—was killed off early so the heroine could have a few adventures of her own.

The absence of a husband was a staple of the woman's film genre. For anything to happen in a woman's life, screenwriters felt the need to liberate her from the home. Because so many of the great female stars of the 1930s and 1940s were mature women, they needed to be cast as slightly older. Still glamorous and youthful, of course, but nevertheless, "mature." Thus the story of a woman whose husband is already dead, or who is conveniently killed, or who disappears, or who just gets out of the woman's way by disappearing offscreen in an acceptable manner, was a Hollywood staple. Marriage did not need to be seen to be believed. What's more, there were often fanciful versions of how a woman could become married in some magical way. In *No Man of Her Own* (1949, starring Barbara Stanwyck), the heroine is an unwed mother whose brutal lover has dumped her, giving her a train ticket to nowhere. On the train, she meets another pregnant woman, a war bride on her way to meet her husband's in-laws for the first time. This happy woman (in a fur coat) lets Stanwyck try on her wedding ring, and bam! There's a train wreck that kills both the war bride and her husband. Because she's wearing the ring when she regains consciousness in the hospital, the in-laws think their late son's widow is Stanwyck. In *A Stolen Life*, Bette Davis plays twins. The evil one steals the boyfriend of the good one and marries him out from under her, as it were. When the twins go sailing, a huge storm comes up, washing the evil woman overboard while the good one clutches her hand . . . with its wedding ring, which conveniently slides off onto her own finger. When she wakes up, she's suddenly the bride of the man she loves.* This "magic of the rings" bestows marriage on a single woman who needs or wants love. No husband is needed. Audiences were familiar with this strategy, and accepted it.

Practically speaking, the war freed the movies to tell stories about a married couple without bothering to cast a male actor. Hollywood had already often suggested that a married man had about the same function in the home as a hat rack. (Plots often dictated that he just stand there and let people hang things on him.) Audiences had already watched Scarlett and Melanie have a baby in *Gone with the Wind*. (There *is* a father—their shared love, Ashley—but where is he when things are happening? It's Scarlett and Melanie who have the baby.) In *The Great Lie*, Bette Davis and Mary Astor, too, share a loved one

---

* This idea was copied for a 2011 television series, *Ringer*, starring Sarah Michelle Gellar.

(George Brent), and he had actually been husband to both of them, before he inconveniently flew off to South America and disappeared. The two marriages have overlapped so closely that Astor is pregnant with Brent's child. (He has disappeared too fast for Davis to keep pace.) Davis brokers a deal with Astor: they'll go off together into the desert, hide out, and have "their" baby. Who needs men?

Movies about marriage in which no men were prominantly featured had always been successful, most notably *The Women* (1939), in which there are literally *no* men, not even a photograph of one, not even a cabdriver. An ad for *The Women* in the October 1939 *Screen Guide* says, "135 women with nothing on their minds but men . . . Out of the boudoir and onto the screen! See women as they don't see themselves! Dowagers and debutantes! Chorines and mannequins! Countesses and cowgirls! . . . See 135 of them biting, kicking, scratching and kissing in the most hilarious battle over men ever screened!" There is no mention of marriage. Yet *The Women*, even without any men, is a marriage movie, albeit from only one side of the blanket. The women in it are trying to get married, trying to save their marriages, trying to wreck marriages, trying to figure out marriage, trying to put up with marriage, trying to look good for marriage . . . and constantly *talking* about marriage. Marriage is their profession, their blessing and their curse. A hilarious catfight, *The Women* talks about men and marriage nonstop, and its central story involves a loving wife who loses her husband to divorce, sees him marry a gold digger (played to comic hard-nosed perfection by Joan Crawford), and has to scheme and fight to get him back. It's all about *him*, but he's not important enough to have to be seen. Marriage is easily—and effectively—presented as a woman's story and a woman's game.*

---

* Similarly, the 1949 film noir *Reckless Moment* (remade in 2001 as *The Deep End*, with Tilda Swinton) depicts a married life in which the husband spends the entire film overseas in Germany on an important business trip. It's nearly Christmas, and his wife (Joan Bennett) is left alone to juggle her daughter's bad judgment in getting involved with a blackmailer (Shepperd Strudwick). Bennett lives in a household crowded by her father-in-law, a sympathetic maid, and her young son as well as the daughter, but the film actually shows how a typical housewife is really a woman alone. Bennett, while planning menus and reminding her son to put his shirt on, also has to dump a dead body in the bay, attempt to raise blackmail money with no collateral or money of her own, and indulge in a wild car chase with her maid riding grimly at her side. During all this, it's made clear she cannot find the words to write to her husband about it, nor speak of it to him on the telephone when he calls. She feels the need to keep things socially correct, and communicates only the safest, most reassuring and loving things to him. Even when the blackmail "collector" arrives (James Mason) and he sees her sympathetically, trying to help her, Bennett remains isolated emotionally. After enduring the car chase ending in Mason's death, she fights tears to cheerfully tell her mate when he calls: "We're getting a blue Christmas tree this year. Everything is fine, except we miss you terribly." Presum-

The war years, however, needed no clever devices (remove all male actors!) or reasonable excuses (he's off to Europe on business!) to justify the absence of men. The man's nonpresence was now vital to the country's survival. The husband was ennobled by his absence. He wasn't neglecting the little woman for his job or, worse yet, for another woman or another round of drinks at the country club. He was off saving the world for democracy. This absence was serious, and very real, and although the war inadvertently liberated the women left home alone, the main task of movies was to remind everyone to be faithful and respectful while "the boys" were "over there."

The first "marriage" issue to gain movie wartime focus was that of the wife left behind on the home front when her husband departs for war—"the lonely wife." She was defined early in the war by *Life* magazine. *Life*'s "Lonely Wife" appeared on the December 21, 1942, cover. She was wearing socks and flat shoes, smoking a cigarette, and slouched down in a patterned chair, looking less than happy with her fate. (She was, *Life* freely admitted, an actress named Joan Thorsen, hired to appear in one of their famous photo stories.)* "Lonely Wife" had been inspired by a book entitled *So Your Husband's Gone to War!* (a $2.00 purchase authored by Ethel Gorham, an advertising writer for the well-known department store Bonwit Teller). Both the original book and *Life*'s photo essay were designed as solace and education for the many American women who suddenly found themselves alone after their husbands joined the armed services. *Life*, like motion pictures, was aimed at a wide audience. Its cover story on the "Lonely Wife" shows her eating alone ("sad business"), sitting home alone, straightening up drawers alone, reading mail from her husband alone—and finally, about to "go mad" with doing everything alone, finding some solutions. She goes back to school at night and makes friends with a female neighbor in the same situation ("These two women understand each other, as both their husbands are in the armed forces"). Finally, she gets a job: she works part-time in a music store ("which involves meeting and talking to people") and spends the other half of her day in a volunteer civil-defense job. The author, carefully referred to as "Mrs. Gorham," is Helen Gurley Brown without the sex. "Mrs. Gorham" frankly warns that the day will come when "you want no more with books or lonesome beds, you are done with your vol-

---

ably he'll arrive home and never be the wiser that his daughter and his wife have been involved in criminal activities.

* Each of *Life*'s "photo stories" was a "story in pictures"—that is, photographs with captions designed to move a reader through a series of images that tell a story: a magazine version of a silent movie.

unteer work, and you feel high and dry. What you really want is an unwarlike interest in life, a little bit of the gay, friendly sociability you and your husband once enjoyed together." Gorham raises a red flag on that. She gives us an entire chapter on how to watch out for the too-helpful male who can lead to entangling alliances. She warns that men you know who are "towers of virtue" are the ones who turn out to be the "garter snappers." She advises that the company of other women is best. "Intelligent women add as much vigor to an evening as intelligent men," and "you can talk freely, honestly with them." She admits that women are of little interest when husbands are around, but, hey . . . there's a war on. Finally, Mrs. Gorham says that "in prayer" you can find "strength." It's a bit of an afterthought: God was in heaven, but garter snappers could be anywhere.

Life's article attracted the attention of the Hollywood studios. The concept of the Lonely Wife left behind to suffer bravely would be a perfect fit for movies with female stars, and would certainly attract a female audience. An endless variation of plots could be worked up out of the idea of a married woman suddenly on her own. Additionally, the shrewd bosses of the studios realized there was a big difference between leafing through a magazine to look at a few photos of a staged "wife" and sitting down in the dark of a movie theater to emotionally experience her story. If a Lonely Wife sat down to read about herself in *Life*, she could put the magazine aside to answer a ringing phone, get up to get a glass of water, or just fall asleep. She could lose interest and page ahead to read other, equally interesting stories. For instance, that December 21, 1942, issue offers photos of comedian Gracie Fields mugging; a serious think piece ("Geopolitics" by Joseph J. Thorndike Jr.); discussions of movies (*In Which We Serve* and *Random Harvest*); a photo of Admiral Nimitz dancing with a USO girl in a Hawaiian recreation center; and news that the Battle of Tunisia "has run into trouble." There is also a report on a troop of soldiers putting on a production of *The Women* at their camp with an all-male cast. (According to *Life*, they presented it straight, without burlesque.) Paging through the magazine, a Lonely Wife could also find shopping suggestions. It was just four days until Christmas, and although ads speak loudly about war worries, they speak equally loudly about buying Christmas gifts. Ginger Rogers sells Pan-Cake makeup. Santa Claus sells tires, toasters, Whitman's candy, and two brands of cigarettes. In an ad for bicycles, Santa tells a little boy, "I'm sorry, son, there'll be no new bicycle under the tree because of wartime shortages." His dad has bought him a war bond instead. (The kid is crying.) When the Lonely Wife went into a movie theater, she would not have these distractions. After the lights went down, there was a full immersion in a story in which a woman faced her loneliness. She would be lifted up out of her seat directly into a fictional experience like the one she was herself undergoing—now enacted by someone beautiful, well dressed, and empathetic. She could release what she was feeling—she could weep alone in the dark, in the privacy of her seat, if she so desired. And she could repeat the experience, coming the next night to watch the movie again. Hollywood jumped to embrace the lonely-wife concept, and lonely-wife movies, no matter how sentimental, show viewers even today just what it was like for married women left behind in the days of World War II.

A perfect emblematic example is the movie many believe best sums up the home-front story of World War II: Claudette Colbert in *Since You Went Away* (1944). Colbert was a popular actress, especially with women, and she was the ideal version of the mature "lonely wife" of World War II. She had been chic and soignée throughout the thirties, and by 1944 she had matured into an even more chic and soignée figure. Colbert, ironically, was French, but she represented the American woman in the way that American women liked to picture themselves. She exuded glamour, but not in a cheap or flashy way. Her characters were witty, intelligent, resourceful, and stoic. Colbert onscreen had American pluck, and the ability to withstand anything.

As *Since You Went Away* opens, Colbert has just been "left behind" by a successful and loving husband. Her home is beautiful, her children are beautiful, her life is beautiful, and she is beautiful. Her maid (Hattie McDaniel) is a fountain of wisdom and support. The film presents the absolutely perfect home (a seven-room brick colonial) and the absolutely perfect marriage as Hollywood defined it for the masses circa 1944. It's the American dream of married life. Colbert and her husband (seen only in a photograph beside her bed) have their own song (the treacly "Together," as in "We strolled the lanes, together,/ laughed at the rains, together," etc.). Their two daughters (Jennifer Jones and Shirley Temple) adore them, and even their bulldog knows his job: he poses in front of the fireplace, nestled close to his master's old pipes and comfy chair.

Since You Went Away will reboot this perfection. A title announces to viewers as the film begins, "This is the story of an unconquerable fortress . . . the American Home, 1943." The story begins early that year in an unnamed Ohio city, just as Colbert and her daughters return home from taking their man to the train station. Colbert assesses her situation as it has been so far. She is a wife. She plans menus and orders food to be delivered. She oversees keeping her house clean and socializes with a well-heeled group of friends. She makes sure her husband, a successful advertising executive, is happy, healthy, and comfortable, and she disciplines their daughters and raises them to be well mannered and to behave properly. Now, however, she is facing a marriage without purpose, because it's marriage without a husband. What is she supposed to do?

First, there's uncertainty. Even though Colbert is charming, witty, sophisticated, and not a weakling, she has depended on her husband to make decisions, pay the bills, and understand the larger world outside the home. Their marriage has been *traditional,* and thus representative. This wife must learn, and in so doing, she will teach the audience what women need to know now that they've been left behind. *Since You Went Away* is a kind of training manual for wartime marriage. Colbert begins by speaking on the sound track, saying what many women might be feeling: "I have no courage, and no vision."

As the film unfolds, Colbert will learn the following lessons: how to make ends meet by taking in boarders;* how to resist temptation in the form of a handsome old beau (Joseph Cotten) who still loves her; how to clean her own home and manage when her maid leaves to work in a war plant; how to let go and allow her oldest daughter to work as a nurse/volunteer; how to accept that same daughter falling in love with a young soldier (Robert Walker) and how to comfort her after his death; how never to cheat on the black market; how to break off from trivial, unpatriotic, and superficial friends; and, finally, how to go to work in a war factory and learn how the other half, especially immigrant workers, really live. Her family will plant a victory garden, gather salvage, buy war stamps, and cook nutritious meals without red meat. In the end, Colbert finds strength, courage, and a broader, wider understanding of life. She becomes a role model for her counterparts in the audience. She copes, she manages, and she makes decisions. In other words, she fights the female, married version of World War II. By removing the husband, the story of a woman in wartime can be told on female terms, which are marriage terms. (All the issues Colbert faces are the previously established issues of the marriage film: money, infidelity, kids, etc., just updated for the war years.) Her basic lesson is how to be married without being married, or how to be successful in her situation as a lonely wife.

Hollywood codified World War II's lonely wife in musical terms in *The Gang's All Here* (1943), a colorful, extravagant, and somewhat insane escapist entertainment directed by Busby Berkeley. If all the movies from the era crumbled into dust and there was nothing left but Alice Faye singing "No

---

* Men in service earned only their government pay, which meant a former executive or business owner with a family was facing a serious pay cut when called into the war effort. Colbert must deal with a major decline in household cash flow.

Love, No Nothin' " in glorious Technicolor, the war wife's feelings would still be clear to cultural historians. Faye wears a simple peasant blouse and skirt. She stands in a tiny little apartment with gray walls. She hugs a framed photo of her uniformed loved one. And she irons. While she irons, she sings: "No love, no nothin', / Until my baby comes home . . . / No fun with no one . . . / I'm gettin' plenty of sleep." There was a reason Alice Faye was a movie star. She couldn't act much, couldn't dance much, and she seemed passive, even immobilized in the frame. But she could put over a song like no one else, and her big blue eyes held honest pain and deep hurt. When she told Americans, "I'll wait for him until the cows come home," she didn't just tug on heartstrings; she ripped out guts, and furthermore made anyone who was cheating feel as guilty as hell. She was the lonely war wife musically personified, and her lonely-wife image had emotional power.

Not all war wives were depicted as lonely or unable to cope. They—both young and old—were also used to tell stories that "democratized" the home front and helped teach audiences they needed to pull themselves together as equals in the fight. *Over 21* (1945) was a successful Broadway play written by Ruth Gordon turned into a screenplay by Sidney Buchman, and it was a perfect starring vehicle for Irene Dunne. It's very sophisticated and witty and brittle, except that underneath it touched on serious issues. Its married couple, Dunne and Alexander Knox, are not ordinary people living in a small town and trying to figure out how to make things work now that the war has come along to shatter their status quo. They are smart-ass and highly successful—an escapist version of marriage that ordinary couples had often enjoyed watching in 1930s movies. But *Over 21* democratizes Dunne and Knox and brings them down to the same level as Mr. and Mrs. John Doe of Smallville, USA. Knox is a famous newspaper editor who ("on a schoolboy whim") enlists in the army. (He does this while his wife is out in Hollywood adapting her latest novel to the screen.) Since it's wartime, and everyone must do his bit, Dunne is thrilled by his gesture. ("Angel!" . . . "Darling!" . . . "I'll go with you!") She *loves* what he's done, telling her own editor that taking care of her husband ("the most important man I know") is "a full-time job." Just like that, she's off to Officer Candidate School in Tetley Field, Florida, to live in one of a series of tiny bungalows known as Palmetto Court. She arrives in a taxi—all hat and jewelry and luggage and clever quips. Dunne and Knox are a sort of Broadway version of Clare Boothe and Henry Luce, so when she shows up, all the other wives at Palmetto immediately know who she is. (Movies loved the idea that a book author would be recognizably famous out in the boonies.)

The situation that the famous couple face tells audiences they must all work together, living at the same level, so America can win the war. "Living at the same level" is literal. One of the most important units in any film about marriage is the home. Movie marriages are measured by furniture—and the size of the kitchen. A husband works to make the best and the biggest possible, and the wife suffers when the worst and the smallest are her lot. When Irene Dunne hops out of her taxi, she faces a great symbolic marker of just what a successful, happily married wife and husband are going to sacrifice for the war effort: she sees where she's going to be living—a bungalow in a cheap motor court. She will downsize for her country.

For one movie second, as Dunne exits her taxi, she is poised between prewar movies (her clothes and her luggage) and war movies (the bungalow court). Palmetto Court will become her barracks. The other women will be her fellow soldiers. And the incompetent handyman will be her form of the demanding top sergeant, an individual who just doesn't understand her problems and certainly doesn't cater to her personal needs. As Dunne moves forward from her taxi, she literally moves into World War II—and into her bungalow, the symbol of sacrifice. For instance, the bungalow doesn't have a sink in the kitchen, and there's no shower—but there *are* moths. The refrigerator bangs all night, and to turn the lights on or off, she has to go outside (in her negligee). And that doesn't include the comic window, which was apparently designed by one of the Ritz Brothers, because it operates as a punch line. It opens only when someone stamps a foot, but closes loudly whenever it feels like it. (As Dunne, ever a cheerful wisecracker, puts it when she learns about the window: "Where's the place where your skirt blows up?") *Over 21* is about a married *couple* at war. *Both* are being asked to cope with unfamiliar tasks in an alien world. In order to be together, because they love each other and because they are a married couple, they do it.*

The movie works out its main dilemma, which is Knox's difficulty in competing with younger men in training school. ("Over twenty-one, you don't absorb any more . . . you simply don't absorb a thing.") But the main point is the need for a democratic attitude, the need for sacrifice from both the rich and famous and the everyday people in the audience. Dunne says, "I want to be like all those other gals with their fellas." Her character undergoes a wartime learning experience. She bonds with other women, creating female camaraderie. Most importantly, she fills in for her husband, taking on his former job.

---

* And both husband and wife are over twenty-one, which in and of itself is news, even though Dunne is very sparkly and youthful in the chic lounge suit she wears for a little dinner she puts together (by getting someone else to help her cook).

World War II changed things for wives in marriage. Famous
Over 21 playwright Irene Dunne learns to mow the lawn (in high
heels and upsweep) while her publisher (Charles Coburn) and her
army husband (Alexander Knox) look on . . .

Unbeknownst to him, she writes a series of superb editorials over his byline.
(Never mind that the big one, "The World and Apple Pie," was obviously written by a woman.) *Over 21* says a woman can take a man's place . . . women can
work together as friends . . . no one should be richer than anyone else . . . and
women are needed for important jobs on the home front. The story becomes a
subliminal metaphor for a married couple's job during World War II: support
each other, replace each other, do whatever is necessary, and accept equality
with others who aren't part of your social set.* Their tasks as a married couple
lie *outside* their relationship, in a bigger situation.

Following a husband to camp to learn democracy was also the theme of *In
the Meantime, Darling* (1944), about a *young* couple played by Jeanne Crain
and Frank Latimore. Audiences meet Crain, the prospective bride, as she travels to an army camp on a crowded train with her wealthy parents. Mom is
leery: "Why not wait till after the war?" ("War . . . the great leveler," intones
Eugene Pallette, her father.) But Crain isn't having any. She's starry-eyed, and

---

* The basic situation came from the experience Ruth Gordon had in real life when she followed her husband, Garson Kanin, when he went to Officer Candidate School.

. . . while former sorority girl Jeanne Crain (with book) has to learn she doesn't know how to do anything useful, unlike the other war wives in *In the Meantime, Darling*.

she and her groom are obviously madly in love. Despite her parents' misgivings, the couple wed in a general store under a leaking ceiling in a rushed ceremony performed by a justice of the peace. They then go to the hideous rooming house where Crain will reside with other war brides, waiting for her husband to get a few free hours or perhaps a weekend pass until he ships out. (Mom sizes up the place at once: "No elevator.")

The purpose of *In the Meantime, Darling* (other than dubious entertainment) is again to show Americans the need to pull together across class lines. Everyone must find a way to contribute. Jeanne Crain is a naïve and coddled young beauty who comes to live among women who have always worked. She represents wealth and privilege, and she must learn. She is the audience surrogate. Step by step, with a somewhat jaunty, even cheerleading attitude, the film teaches her (and thus the audience) how to change and make sacrifices. At first, Crain doesn't know the rules. She comes down for breakfast at noon; she mistakes the colonel's wife for the cook; she gives orders about rearranging the furniture more to her liking; and she commandeers the only bathroom, taking someone else's scheduled time. Since none of this will do, she's quickly shaped up, a clever way of regimenting women the same way men are being regimented in an army camp. Crain is required to contribute to the household of women in some way, but she has no skills. ("She's a college grad," someone explains.) Since she can't do anything, the group decides to find her "something simple to start with." When she messes up even the simplest tasks, a housemate speaks the movie's basic lesson out loud: "That girl had better leave her throne and learn to mingle with the common people."*

The democratization of Jeanne Crain is a success. She learns to garden and clean, how to share, and how to put herself second. She comes to realize that romantic dreams aren't enough to make a marriage really work, ultimately admitting, "I'm just beginning to learn how much I didn't learn in college." By living with other women and discovering what she can do, Crain becomes *useful*, something required for everyone on the home front. Hollywood endorsed this message, and was adept at turning it into plots by using marriage as the metaphor.

Throughout the war, actresses portrayed married women on the home front in many strong and significant ways, including Greer Garson as the British Mrs. Miniver facing death and danger; Phyllis Thaxter as a young wife left behind when her husband flies the Doolittle Raid in *Thirty Seconds over Tokyo* (1944); or even Rita Hayworth as a bride who has to marry Lee Bowman by proxy in the Technicolor musical *Tonight and Every Night* (1945). These movies were not specifically marriage movies, but they worked off a useful concept that found great acceptance and a sense of authenticity: the lonely wife, or more broadly, the woman who has to face reality standing on her own two feet.

World War II marriage movies clearly endorse sisterhood as an alternative to marriage.† In *Music for Millions* (1944), a group of female musicians band together to help a cellist (June Allyson) who is married and pregnant. The members of the orchestra (led by José Iturbi, playing, as always, himself) are almost all women, because "that's the condition we're in," says Jimmy Durante. All the men, including Allyson's husband, have gone to war. The musicians live in a rooming house together, sharing everything, including Allyson's pregnancy. She even reads her letters from her husband aloud to them, and engages their help in caring for her little sister (Margaret O'Brien). When it's all too much for Allyson and she breaks down and weeps, saying, "I'm just a coward,"

---

* Similar movies about the lesson to become democratic did not involve marriage. For instance, in *Meet the People* (1944), Lucille Ball plays a famous movie star who goes to work on an airplane assembly line as a publicity stunt. After not fitting in at first, she becomes a real riveter, and just one of the gals.

† Sisterhood also appears in movies in which women join the armed forces. Lana Turner plays a society girl who joins the WACs in *Keep Your Powder Dry* (1945), and she has to learn democracy, too. In women-in-combat films such as *Cry "Havoc"!* (1943) and *So Proudly We Hail* (1943), the women become the men, as it were, and undergo combat conditions on Bataan. In both these military movies, there's a married woman at the center of the issue.

she is reassured by Iturbi with the mantra of the times: "No. You are a woman. A wife. A mother"—and thus, by implication, not only important, but essential for the war effort.

In *Tender Comrade* (1943), Ginger Rogers joins up with other women who work in a defense plant to rent a house in which they can live while they await the return of their men. The women are again being asked to do something similar to what their men are being asked to do: bunk together in a barracks-like situation while they work all day (and/or all night) on behalf of the war effort.* The women, like their husbands, sacrifice home, comfort, and leisure time to give all they've got for defense. The marriage movie was the most useful story form for such efforts, because it linked not only the husband and wife on film, but also the husband and wife in the audience. Such plots had the highest degree of audience emotional response, and thus the highest box-office-return potential.

Tender Comrade is one of the most representative of the war films about the married woman left behind. It serves two masters: it tells in flashbacks the story of the marriage between Rogers and Robert Ryan, and it tells in present tense the story of women left alone to work in war plants while their husbands serve. It first establishes the prewar model of the marriage movie with a couple and their problems, and then overtly reconstitutes their story in the new "situation." If the marriage section were shown on its own, the marriage would not be a picture of happiness. Rogers and Ryan quarrel, shout at each other, and disagree. Rogers is bored and unhappy, because she works hard all day cooking and cleaning and Ryan ignores her when he returns home. She threatens him by saying she'll go out and get a job—the era's ultimate rejection of male domination. Because it's wartime, however, this dreary picture (actually the portrait of a bad marriage) is tarted up with a wink-wink attitude that says, "We all know they really adore one another." When the war breaks out and Ryan must leave, all these earlier issues are swept away as trivial. Of course he will now pledge his love, need Rogers, pay attention to her, and of course she will go out and get a job with his approval—in a war plant. *Tender Comrade* uses marriage to teach in an obvious manner, but teach it does. Furthermore, it will pull no punches about the sacrifice. Ryan is killed in action, leaving Rogers alone with a baby to raise.

Like *Over 21* and *In the Meantime, Darling, Tender Comrade* also presents

---

* Even in a musical, women are forced into community living. In *Tonight and Every Night*, which takes place during the London Blitz, the showgirls decide to live at the theater together, dormitory-style, rather than risk going home in the blackout.

women banding together, forming a commune of sorts.* These patriotic sororities were linked closely to what was actually happening offscreen. There was an acute housing shortage during the war, and women did rent houses, or bungalows, or hotel or boardinghouse rooms, and share expenses, friendship, and tragedies. World War II was one of the few times—if not the only time—women were seen in numerous films as if they, too, were men, regimented into barracks life and serving side by side.

The experiences depicted in these films (and in *Life's* "Lonely Wife" article) were by no means the inventions of screenwriters. They are verified by *Washington Post* publisher Katharine Graham's autobiography, in which she writes vividly and eloquently about her years as a wartime wife. In particular, she sketches her husband's departure to service on the morning of July 27, 1942, with a poignant simplicity: "The dreadful moment of our parting came at the Greyhound bus terminal in downtown Washington, already a depressing place, but made more so by the sight of nervous recruits huddling together . . . I embraced him, turned, and fairly dove through the door of the terminal as he joined the group of jittery inductees. I happened to look down just as I fled, discovered that my slip was showing." Her memory could easily be translated into a screenplay. It's visual, detailed, and contains a wonderful subtext, including a moment for a significant cut to represent her helplessness and her loss: her slip sticking out underneath her dress.

Graham's autobiography included other experiences similar to those seen in *Over 21, In the Meantime, Darling, Tender Comrade*, and *Since You Went Away*. "After a short time at Fort Meade, Phil [her husband] was sent for basic training to Atlantic City, where I joined him and began my life as a camp follower. I found a room in a boarding house not far from the Boardwalk, where we shared a nightly two and a half hours. Much of the rest of the time I spent watching the men marching up and down the Boardwalk in the humid heat." Graham and her husband end up in Sioux Falls, South Dakota, where the newly set-up army camp has a population of 45,000, grafted onto a town that itself only has 15,000 people. Graham portrays the physical problems wives faced: overcrowding, housing shortages, rationing. She talks about the brief hours of togetherness any couple could expect, and confirms the lonely-wife scenario of how she and the other women coped. Graham enrolled in a typing-and-shorthand class, worked for the Red Cross, and joined a club for the wives of privates (the "Mrs. Private" club, which had the slogan "Hap-

---

* During the HUAC hearings, *Tender Comrade* came under suspicion for its possible "Communist" propaganda. One era's plot point is another era's poison.

pier Lives for Privates' Wives"). She sought out the company of other wives to attend movies, church suppers, lectures, and various other social events designed to keep the women busy. Her wonderful book demonstrates how the marriage movies of World War II were grounded in honest experience. Today, these movies may seem treacly or even false, but they were all too real for women in the audience at the time.

Films like *Tender Comrade* and *In the Meantime, Darling* that assembled married women as roommates, learning to support the war effort, were successful. Everyone endorsed the message, not realizing it actually represented big changes for women that would have to be dealt with later on: females embracing sisterhood, working outside the home, gaining independence, and becoming more flexible socially, intellectually, even morally. Wives such as the ones in *Since You Went Away* and *Tender Comrade* entered the workforce to work in war plants. They became "Rosie the Riveter," a female icon generally presented as an unmarried woman.* The lonely wife being democratized was also being redefined as a single woman who would live without depending on men. The marriage-without-the-husband movie was setting up the wife at home as a parallel hero to her husband overseas—an equal in service to her country. This would ultimately become a source of social change—and the marriage movie had played a role in making it happen.

During the war, couples who barely knew each other married in haste, and some lived to regret it. This became a popular wartime marriage story line. (The issue was so much on people's minds that Vaughn Monroe even had a hit song that asked, "Is it love or is it conscription?") Marry-in-haste movies helped an audience understand the pressures of war on young couples. Time was always spent discussing why getting married without really knowing each other was a bad idea, followed by the sudden shift to why it was a good idea: love.

---

* Rosie the Riveter first appeared in a 1942 ad campaign for the Westinghouse Company. "Rosie" was a nameless image modeled after a Michigan factory worker named Geraldine Doyle and designed to be the symbol of the industrial, working American woman of World War II. Norman Rockwell's version of Rosie, the one most people remember, appeared on the May 19, 1943 cover of the *Saturday Evening Post*. The use of Rosie in World War II encouraged women, both married and unmarried, to do jobs traditionally performed by men, because their country needed them. Women in American movies had previously been commonly pictured doing work, but seldom working the assembly lines alongside other women, or even men. Rosie was unique. There was also a real Rosie, Rose Monroe, who was a riveter at the Willow Run Aircraft Factory in Michigan. She wasn't the inspiration for the ad campaign, but she fit its image well, and she was chosen to play Rosie in the promotional movies made during the war to recruit workers. The Rosie the Riveter ad slogan was "We Can Do It!" and a popular song, "Doin' It for Defense," had a female singer singing, "This ain't love, this is war, / I'm doin' it for defense."

True love would make it okay, just as the war justified it happening. Some films told only of the rapid courtship, such as *The Clock* (1945) with Judy Garland and Robert Walker. The film devotes its running time to their meeting and deciding to wed, and to the rush they must undergo to get their required documents so the ceremony can be performed before he ships out. The film talks out loud about whether this haste is good or not, but it endorses the concept that life must be lived. He may be killed overseas and is entitled to . . . what? Love, says the movie. (Sex, thinks the audience.) In order to remove any sense of smarm from the proceedings, Garland and Walker are presented as decent, wholesome, innocent, and really in love with each other.*

In *Marriage Is a Private Affair* (1944), things don't go as smoothly. The movie opens up on a big, glamorous wedding in which Lana Turner is walking down the aisle, saying to herself on the soundtrack: "What on earth am I doing here? How did I get into this, anyway?" She's marrying John Hodiak, a man she knew only three days when he proposed. ("But I don't know you. You don't know me.") He counters with the argument of the war years: "We have so little time." (Turner's mother, herself wed three times and on the way to her fourth, warns: "The guy's from Boston.") Everyone else, however, tells Turner that it's *love* that matters, and she says she *knows* she loves him. Mom accepts the situation: "Well, the first marriage *should* be romantic." By the time the wedding is planned and under way, and Turner and Hodiak are saying their vows, they have known each other only two weeks.

Marriage Is a Private Affair was designed for two things: to show Lana Turner in a spectacular wardrobe, and to recognize that young couples were marrying on short acquaintance. However glamorized by Turner's presence, it tells a story of a hasty marriage under wartime pressure. A baby is born,

---

* In the early months of the war, one movie upgraded a familiar marriage plot line, the "without love" marriage. On October 8, 1942, about ten months after America entered the war, *Seven Days' Leave* opened. It was the story of an army private (Victor Mature) who, by the rules of his grandfather's will, can inherit $100,000 if he can marry a specific heiress before he ships out. Mature has less than a week—his seven days' leave is already under way—to chase down, woo, and marry Lucille Ball for all the wrong reasons. Since Mature is going overseas, a hasty marriage is understood to be not only necessary but prudent. *Seven Days' Leave* has no particular message about anything, but slyly reboots the idea of the "without love" marriage for wartime haste.

Various former screwball plots were also harnessed to the wartime years. In *The More the Merrier* (1943) the housing shortage forces Jean Arthur to share her tiny apartment with Joel McCrea and Charles Coburn. In *Make Your Own Bed* (1944) Jack Carson is a comic detective on the trail of a racketeer. In order to solve his case, he and Jane Wyman pretend to be a married butler and maid in crowded Washington, where there's a shortage of servants. These films update old formats to the circumstances of the home front at war.

What was happening in marriage during World War II made excellent plot material. When Lana Turner marries John Hodiak in haste, her mother-in-law (Virginia Brissac) steps in to help with the problems, forgetting that *Marriage Is a Private Affair.*

troubles arise, and everything goes wrong. The movie says there's a wartime law that prevents a woman from divorcing a soldier who is overseas without his consent. Since her mom is hardly a source of wisdom, Turner consults her father about what to do. He's a man she didn't recognize at her wedding because he was her mother's *first* husband from way back when, but he's rich, and therefore, by MGM terms, very wise. He tells her, "Just because everyone gets married, it doesn't mean that it's an institution . . . It's your own private affair." This puzzling observation settles Turner down, and she and Hodiak reunite. What the film accomplished for audiences was *reassurance.* This time that reassurance comes attached to star power, a fantastic wardrobe, and lavish set decoration, some humor and sexiness, but no real information. It's the reassurance that can be obtained when a familiar story—two people run into trouble after marrying—is grafted onto a topical film of an era: situation triumphs over individual problems for the couple.

There's a tendency today to assume that everything Hollywood presented about the home front and marriage during wartime was positive. This is not the case. Everyone in the audience was living through the war, and however much they might have wanted to escape or forget, they weren't fools. Hollywood had to mix some reality into the stories they were telling. That had always been their filmmaking policy—take off from a ground base of realism where possible or required. They kept that policy alive even during the darkest days of the war. For instance, *Allotment Wives* (1945) presented a crime peculiar to wartime: women ruthlessly married men who were shipping out in order to gain control of their paychecks, known as "allotments." (During the war, the Office of Dependency Benefits provided allotment checks and family allowances to women whose men were serving in the armed forces.) The film concerns the ODB discovering a high level of fraudulent claims made by women who were marrying multiple times to different men and then claiming their checks. The woman who runs this racket is the very well-dressed Kay Francis, who operates a high-class beauty salon as her front. A low-budget movie from Monogram, *Allotment Wives* disintegrates rapidly into a story of gangsters, racketeering, mother love, and suitable punishment for Francis, who is gunned down close to her hair dryer, but the movie pulled no punches. There was ugly fraud being committed on the home front, women were involved in it, and marriage was their ruse.

A good example of a movie that presents an American family, the topic of marriage, and the problems of women on the home front in a negative—although ultimately redeemable—way is the little-known *The Very Thought of You*, made in 1944 and starring Dennis Morgan, Eleanor Parker, Dane Clark, and Faye Emerson. The film contains a roster of World War II marriage-movie concepts: a lonely wife, the should-we-marry-or-not? question, the hasty wedding, the unfaithful wife, the war-plant female worker, the baby born while Dad's overseas, the husband injured in war. It throws in everything, but it's also a rare example of how movies, designed though they were to uplift Americans, could also get down pretty mean and low . . . and honest.

The movie features four levels of marital connection. First, there's the central story about a young soldier and a girl (Morgan and Parker) who happily fall in love and wed inside a brief time frame. Second, there's the failure of a marriage between Parker's parents, Henry Travers and Beulah Bondi. Mom is resentful, bossy, and scornful of her husband because he was just "a WPA worker who then became a clerk." He's never amounted to much by Mom's standards, and she openly says, "I wanted my daughters to marry well. That's all. I wanted them to profit from my mistake." The third marriage is one hanging in the balance, the cautionary tale for viewers. Parker's older sister (Andrea King) is married to a sailor who has been overseas so long that she's forgotten "what Freddie looked like." King is embarrassing everyone by being openly unfaithful, never writing to Freddie, and constantly bad-mouthing the concept of the wartime marriage. (Censorship of the day puts a decent spin on her activities, but when Freddie comes home and Molly has to confess, she says she was especially bad with one wealthy older man: "I let him kiss me." Audiences knew what that meant.) The fourth marriage is not a marriage but a reflection of the romantic comedies of the prewar era—the "funny" relationship between Clark and Emerson, which is played for laughs, sexiness, and a soldier's "wolfish" nature. (At the end of the film, they unite and will marry.)

Parker's "typical American family" isn't very inspirational. There's her 4-F brother (a goldbricker), her disobedient teenage sister, the aforementioned adulterous sister, her weak dad, her brother's repressed wife . . . and, finally, Mom. Most people think the moms of war movies were all swell creatures, keeping those V-mails going overseas and those apple pies coming out of the oven. This mom is mean. (Later, she'll go googly over her grandson, but early scenes show her for what she is.) The audience is frankly shown a dysfunctional family. They quarrel, resent one another, and don't support one another's emotional needs. Before she brings Morgan home for dinner, Parker pleads, "Please, everyone, be nice to him." But they aren't. Uncomfortable silences reign at the table, and since no one has heard about Morgan previously, King wonders if "our own little Jannie has been having herself a fling." The brother grouses, "A fine sister, picking up soldiers in the street." King points out that her brother is "a filthy, draft-dodging heel." After Morgan leaves, Parker runs upstairs, yelling, "I hate what you've done," to her family, and Dad comments that they treated their guest about the same way they would treat "a Jap."

Parker and Morgan are unquestionably in love, and no conflict arises between them. Parker's character represents three important issues for women in war: she works in a parachute factory, becomes a lonely wife, and gives birth without her husband at her side. Everything ends well, after both Morgan and Clark are wounded and shipped home, but along the way, things are shown and said about the American family and women left behind that are shockingly unsentimental and certainly not patriotic. There is no endorsement for these remarks—or for bad behavior—but the misery and anger are not hidden from the audience.

It's startling to hear these remarks, which are not usually associated with a positive portrait of the American home front. When Parker returns home at three a.m. after a date with Morgan, the family is waiting up. Mom: "You lied to me . . . Did he make love to you?" She slaps Parker hard and adds, "You set a filthy example for Ellie [the teenage sister]." King says all a woman gets from a wartime marriage is "a swift kiss, a swift kick, and bingo, you're a war widow." Morgan says the home front is a difficult situation: "It takes more gizzard to be a soldier's wife than it does to fight." When King's husband returns home unexpectedly, he bitterly discusses what the patriotic "sell" of the war effort

All the visual details of the marriage movie were adjusted for the war. Because of the shortage of hotel rooms, Eleanor Parker and Dennis Morgan spend his only night before he goes overseas camped out on a beach in *The Very Thought of You*.

really is: "They don't show what home really is. It's not all Mom and apple pie." He adds that, furthermore, they don't show what combat is, either. "It's not all fighting . . . it's waiting." He says that he kept himself going by hanging on to what he could believe in. "It wasn't like in the ads with me. It was home." He accepted all its flaws. Such bitterness and disappointment—and definite questioning of the surface portraits of Americans at home—found its own acceptance with the audience, and in the end, all is resolved. *The Very Thought of You* ends in the bright California sunshine, with Clark and Morgan disembarking from a troop train in Pasadena to embrace their loved ones. Parker's mom and dad are now apparently happy as clams together, and especially fond of their fat little grandson. (The audience wanted at least some connection to reality, but didn't want things to end in tragedy if it could be avoided.) In showing negatives but reaffirming positives in the end, *The Very Thought of You* followed the tradition of the marriage film from its very roots, but its very strong negatives stood out in wartime.

As the war moved to its close, more and more movies began to stress problems married couples would be facing in the postwar era. Soldiers developed severe psychological and physical difficulties, as in *I'll Be Seeing You* (1944) and *Pride of the Marines* (1945). Infidelity on the home front surfaced. *The*

Unfaithful, actually made in 1946 and released in 1947, illustrates how rapidly attitudes were shifting. From 1941 to 1946, marriage movies had taught that women should be faithful to husbands who were overseas, but *The Unfaithful* defends a wife who committed home-front adultery. Ann Sheridan plays a wife who had an affair while her husband was overseas. When her lover blackmails her, she stabs him. Sheridan's lawyer excuses her, pointing out that, had there been no war, which upset everyone's lives and sense of order, she would not have strayed. Even more significantly, Sheridan's bitchy friend, brilliantly played by Eve Arden, stands up for her to the wronged husband (Zachary Scott), telling Scott that the two years he was gone were a long time (to go without sex, it is implied). "I managed it," he tersely replies. "In the South Pacific," shoots back Arden. "Try it on Wilshire Boulevard." Arden also tells him it's only his "manly pride" that is really hurt.* Ads for *The Unfaithful* spelled it right out: "It's so easy to cry 'Shame' . . . If she were yours, could you forgive?" "Could you for- give?" was now a useful postwar question for a marriage movie—where before, the rule was "You shouldn't have cause to forgive."

By late 1944 and early 1945, and even into 1946, the motion-picture business adjusted its home-front movies and began to point them toward the postwar period. A series of such movies presented tales in which a husband returns home and his wife has to readjust to his presence. These films address the postwar problems of hasty marriage—now you have to live with each other even though you're barely acquainted. Because it was still wartime, however, the stories are optimistic. They're sober in presenting the problems, but suggest that everyone must live with the decisions they made.

One of the most representative of these stories was *The Impatient Years,* released in late 1944. Jean Arthur and Lee Bowman play a couple who married during the war after a whirlwind courtship, and when he left her behind, he left her expecting their child. Now he's home and finds himself living not only with a wife he hardly knows, but also a demanding one-year-old son *and* his wife's father.

Demonstrating that this was a real issue, well understood to be more than a fanciful plot—that it was an honest problem couples would be facing more and more—the advertising for the film laid the dilemma right out in front of poten- tial audiences. "Mr. and Mrs. Soldier—This Is Your Love Story!" screamed the posters, and the prevues carried this copy: "Charles Coburn is the wise old

---

* Within less than a year, Hollywood has shifted ground in its attitude toward women at home, and in less than another year it will shift again to begin presenting married women as little homemakers in late-1940s and early-1950s movies.

Cupid who knows his daughter's problem was the problem of millions!" "The problem of millions" was looming on the horizon—a postwar phenomenon of returning GIs who had married in haste. *The Impatient Years* was designed to show the audience that phenomenon.

After a very short time, Arthur and Bowman discover they can't stand each other. Into the divorce court they go—but the judge isn't having any. He's seen enough wartime marriages go on the rocks. He orders them to "relive" their romance, scene by scene, to find out what happened. What did they see in each other, and why did they marry in the first place? In showing Bowman and Arthur the answer, the movie shows it to an audience and also updates the familiar prewar marriage format of the divorce movie, now designed as a postwar training manual with laughs. What drew audiences to the train-wreck concept of a hastily married couple who want a divorce but are forced to remember what they once had but can no longer recall? Obviously, movies of this type are speaking directly to those in the audience who are in the same boat, and perhaps there was romance in asking postwar couples to try to put themselves back into the wartime frame of mind. They're expected to believe that love, hopes, and dreams can all be regenerated, like the arm of a starfish. *The Impatient Years* is a return to the romantic comedy of the past, dressed up in new clothes.

Janie Gets Married (from early 1946) was designed to capitalize on the success of 1944's hit film *Janie*, which starred Joyce Reynolds in the title role. *Janie* was based on a highly successful Broadway play, the kind of little topical play that's never seen on Broadway today: a pleasant ramble about a small-town girl who's crazy about the soldiers billeted in her small town. (Her dad [Edward Arnold] sees the nice young GIs as love-starved predators.) *Janie Gets Married*, a postwar sequel, begins with the premise that Janie (now played by Joan Leslie) has at war's end quickly married the nice guy she met in the first film (Robert Hutton). Janie's job will be to become a good wife and help her husband adjust to civilian life. Everything about the movie is designed to connect to the arrival-home experience and to reassure everyone that it's all a hoot and will turn out just swell. The narrator tells us "two years ago, the boys went off to war . . . And now these boys are coming home" to their "average, homey little American city."

Yet for a movie that wants to reassure everyone, there's a lot of negative dialogue. ("There are times when you'll want to *cut her throat*," the groom's stepdad tells him. "Just expect the worst and you can't be disappointed." And: "Marriage . . . they ought to give a Purple Heart for it . . . It was never an easy deal.") An audience sits (grimly) watching everything go wrong. Hutton is working in a job Leslie's dad arranged for him, and he's no good at it. Leslie

Postwar marriage movies dealt with the adjustment necessary when couples who married in haste faced each other after the war. In *The Impatient Years* (released in late 1944) Jean Arthur tells her dad (Charles Coburn) she doesn't know why she ever married Lee Bowman. Bowman seems equally dubious.

can't manage the home, and her maid bosses her around. (Since Margaret Hamilton is the maid, this is believable.) His mom is paying half their rent so they can live beyond his salary. Both their mothers want to buy the drapes for their new house, resulting in an in-law war of window treatments. Janie tries to cook (in apron and pearls); his old army buddy turns up and she's a gorgeous WAC (Dorothy Malone), so jealousy rears up. What a mess! All the old prewar issues of marriage movies are on display—money, incompatibility, in-laws—illustrating how the established format will now return for the postwar era. (In the end, Joan Leslie cheerfully embraces her husband and says, "A girl can't learn to be a wife all at once.") Like *The Impatient Years*, *Janie Gets Married* is a return to an old marriage-movie format. The "situation" (World War II) has ended. Movies like these are about the need for everyone to adjust to change (it's good for you), to come together in postwar unity (we've won the war, now let's win the peace), and to get things back to where they were, if possible (although both movies admit that things *are* different now).

But sunny movies like *Years* and *Janie* were not the only presentation of the married-in-haste issue. Running alongside such optimistic comedies were films that would later come to be known as "film noir," dark stories that had something different to say about wartime marriages. Often the day-to-day of a couple's conflicts wasn't actually presented, but the story would be grounded in marital strife and disappointment. A typical example is *The Blue Dahlia* (1946), starring Alan Ladd and Veronica Lake. Ladd is a veteran returning home from combat in the South Pacific. He finds his wife (Doris Dowling) living in a hotel bungalow, togged out in gold lamé and tanked up on scotch. He arrives during one of her riotous cocktail parties and finds her more or less in the arms of a married nightclub owner (Howard Da Silva). When Ladd finally gets her alone, a vicious (and violent) quarrel erupts, and she tells him the truth. While he was away, she got bored and started partying. She was driving drunk with their little son in the car and he was killed when she lost control of the vehicle. (She had written Ladd in the Pacific that their son had died of diphtheria.) Now she wants rid of Ladd, too, and can't turn back time to become a little housewife after loose living, good clothes, and nightclub excitement have permanently changed her. Dowling ends up dead, and Ladd ends up with Lake, and no one tries to convince the audience that a wife who found a different way of life during the war was likely to want to go back to the old ways. ("How ya gonna keep 'em down on the farm . . . ?")

For Hollywood, the postwar years would be the beginning of the end of the golden era known as the studio system, and changes would occur to the marriage movie as a direct result. By 1948, the basic elements that would ultimately kill old Hollywood were in place: antitrust laws that forbade the studios from both making films and owning the theaters that showed them; the defection of big-name movie stars from studio long-term contracts; wider distribution of foreign films that created new appetites in audiences and provided new sources of competition; the House Un-American Activities Committee, which decimated and divided Hollywood talent; and, of course, the one that most people think killed the system all by itself: the arrival of television.*

Hollywood had to come down from the all-time high of movie attendance during the war years and face these changes, and as always, the business was flexible. To offset the arrival of television, it initially advanced new technologies (stereophonic sound and wide screen would both take hold in the early 1950s). Movies became bigger, much bigger, but at the same time, in order to compete with the new foreign product, films were made that were grittier, more realistic. Movies also got smaller, much smaller. (Hollywood films began to polarize into large, wide, and colorful versus small, narrow, and black-and-white. As

---

* The film business fought TV initially but soon enough embraced it, creating its own TV shows and stars and selling both old and new movies for showing at home on the small screen.

far as television was concerned, the business initially was content to ignore it, lampoon it, and warn its stars against it.)

What was the role of movies about marriage for this period of time? It was obvious that movies about marriage didn't need to be "bigger and bigger" but would more likely fit the "smaller and smaller," money-saving strategy. By the start of the 1950s, the majority of marriage films being made and released by major studios were of a type known in the business as "programmers." Programmers were a low-cost form of an A-level movie and are often erroneously called "B pictures."* The "programmer" was *not* a B—it was an inexpensive way for a studio to use its A-level stars and make money at the box office without a lavish production budget. Programmers were often written and directed by top-of-the-line talent, and they were well advertised in fan magazines and newspapers. As the studios faced losses of profits in the 1950s, the low-cost programmer became more and more important to profitability—and more and more the format for marriage movies. The onscreen "situation" was dictated by necessary budget practice.

The programmer was a perfect format for a small black-and-white film about marriage designed to connect to the postwar audience, and a comparatively large number of marriage programmers were released between 1947 and 1960. Such quick-and-easy dramas were not only affordable but found a direct connection to the viewing audience. Without much money, and often with small children, young American couples were looking for cheap entertainment, and as always, it was the movies that could best provide it. The movie business acted rapidly to start creating films about these young couples and the situations they were living in. The return of the men who had fought the war brought a parallel emphasis on home, wives not working, family, togetherness, and, inevitably, marriage. Just as marriage in the 1930s was often escapist and glamorous, and during the war it had been full of patriotic purpose, it was now time for ordinary, low-key, "realistic" postwar married life. In other words,

---

* A B movie was specifically designed for the bottom (or B) half of a double-feature bill. "B" was not an evaluative term but a budget term. B films had low budgets, with no new sets being built. They had running times of under seventy minutes and featured no established A-level movie stars. (It *was* possible a former star could sink down to B level, or an up-and-coming player who would later become a star might appear in a B. For instance, Rita Hayworth, as yet unknown, was in *Charlie Chan in Egypt* in 1935, early in her career.) There were also B-level studios, such as Monogram, an organization that made movies for the bottom half of the bill or for the very, very small-town market. Major studios (such as Warners, MGM, Paramount, et al.) had B units with specific personnel hired for that purpose. The decision about what films would be A or B level was made in advance, before the picture was shot.

the postwar era deglamorized marriage, brought it down in size, and put it in the kitchen (which no longer was the size of a football field or populated by witty servants). Where once Clark Gable, a loving husband, had presented his perfect wife, Myrna Loy, with a surprise anniversary gift—a diamond bracelet hidden in her breakfast kippers—now a man bought a woman a washing machine purchased on the installment plan. In *Topper* (1937), the young married man-about-town and his wife were Cary Grant and Constance Bennett. Now they were Van Johnson, with his freckles and gee-whiz personality, and Janet Leigh, with her fresh-faced beauty. Grant was a rich playboy; Johnson is a veteran. Bennett shook a cocktail shaker; Leigh scrambles eggs. Bennett and Grant drove a fast roadster and stayed out all night, showing up for important bank meetings in tuxedo and evening gown. Johnson and Leigh, thoroughly domesticated, go to bed early in sensible pajamas and quilted robes.

When moviemakers looked out their windows onto the California landscape, they saw tract after tract of low-cost homes being built and bought up by young couples who financed them through GI war loans. Movie settings shifted accordingly, from Long Island mansions, gambling dens, and cocktail bars to these little houses, usually set in small midwestern towns or some vaguely located suburb. These movies were mostly comedies, because no one in postwar America was in the mood for any more tragedy on the home front if they could avoid it. Marriage movies were stories about a young couple, maybe with kids, whose friends were other GI couples. Because the husband had served his country, he was no longer to be treated as if he were a silly fool. This responsibility was shifted over to his wife, tying in with a culture in which women who had just been out riveting airplanes were now told to go back into the kitchen and let the men do the thinking. The wife was supposed to listen to her husband (he had survived the war, after all) and to stay home before she went out and created some big mess. The problems the couple faced were the same ones as before—money, relatives, infidelity, etc.—because the postwar marriage movie was built from parts from the recycle bin. It was all just redecorated, reduced in size, and made cute. The new marriage movie was designed to reinforce "American" values (the ones we'd all been fighting for), stress togetherness in the home, ennoble family responsibilities, and celebrate the sheer glory of the ordinary over the glamorous. It was designed to bring things back to normal; its "situations" were directives.

Examples of the programmer marriage movie that provided postwar transition are found in abundance in the eight-year period between 1948 and 1956: *Apartment for Peggy* (1948), *Sitting Pretty* (1948), *Father Was a Fullback* (1949), *The Big Hangover* (1950), *Father's Little Dividend* (1951), *Young Man with Ideas*

(1952), *The Lady Wants Mink* (1953), *Confidentially Connie* (1953), et al. There were colorful musical versions (*Everything I Have Is Yours*, 1952) and film-noir versions (*Cause for Alarm*, 1951). Three apt examples that demonstrate how old marriage formats were both used and updated are *Dear Wife* (1949), *Phffft* (1954), and *Full of Life* (1956).

Dear Wife was a sequel to the wartime hit movie *Dear Ruth*, which had been a smash Broadway play. The original, written by Norman Krasna, told a topical wartime story about a bouncy teenager who pretends to be her older sister (the Ruth in the title) when she writes to a soldier overseas. The play and the resulting film brought welcome laughter to home-front audiences. (In fact, the characters were so popular with filmgoers that another sequel was made, *Dear Brat*. Neither of the sequels reached the same height of success as the original.)

Dear Wife (written directly for the screen) is a typical postwar marriage programmer. The lovebirds from *Dear Ruth* (Joan Caulfield and William Holden) are now married. The war is over, and Holden is out of uniform. The couple are living with her parents in her old room, because they haven't yet been able to find affordable housing. Holden *does* have a job—but it's the very same job his wife occupied during the war: she has had to vacate it as her patriotic duty to make room for her husband. (Where once her patriotic duty was to work to take a man's place, now it is her duty to walk away. This uncomfortable situation is made worse by the fact that his new boss, the inexplicable Billy De Wolfe, used to be his wife's boyfriend.) The movie has thus connected to two major issues for the audience's real-life situation: women in the workforce being sent home, fired or demobilized to create jobs for returning GIs, and the serious postwar housing shortage. *Dear Wife*, set in "Van Buren Heights, New York, twenty miles from Manhattan," also creates two plot points for the postwar era: expansion and media influence. The town is considering building a new airport in the community and facing the role the rise of advertising is playing in politics. (Since *Dear Wife* was released in 1949, it was too soon historically for the advertising to be on television. The movie uses radio, but clearly demonstrates how commercials would intrude into peaceful homes and exert strong media pressure both in creating consumer desire and in determining political winners.)*

Dear Wife is an amalgamation of old marital woes (jealousy, suspected infidelity, money—her dad buys Ruth a dress her husband couldn't afford) and

---

* The son-in-law is pitted against his father-in-law, an accomplished townsman, in an election. When asked what experience he has that would entitle him to hold office, the son-in-law firmly replies, "Four years overseas."

new, more topical ones (putting the wife back in the home, media dominance, suburban living, and the return of the GI). Its events are episodic—and situational. *Dear Wife*, in fact, looks like a cheap television sitcom, even though Ruth's parents are well off and have a long-suffering maid to wait on everyone. The film is obviously pared down, less glamorous, with a lower budget for production values. It's a classic example of the marriage film in transition, with everything solved happily, leaving the teenager of *Dear Ruth*, still in the picture, to intone, "In the battle of the sexes, nobody ever wins." The final image shows Caulfield and Holden moving into their very own little tract house.

*Phffft** takes the marriage movie back to its divorce roots, but with a new kind of sexuality. It provides the new version of 1930s romantic comedies like *The Awful Truth*. The *Awful Truth* couple (Irene Dunne and Cary Grant) were wealthy sophisticates without any apparent means of income. Money? They just have it. The stars of *Phffft!* (Jack Lemmon and Judy Holliday) have jobs. Lemmon's a former navy lieutenant who's become a partner in a law firm, and Holliday's a former magazine writer and now a highly successful ($40,000 per year) writer of a television soap opera, *Serena Noble, Doctor's Wife*. As the movie opens, they're wed, living in the postwar idea of a perfect home in the country, and enjoying the 1950s good life (by *Good Housekeeping* or *Ladies' Home Journal* standards). Everything *looks* ideal: a fire in the fireplace, a maid serving after-dinner coffee in china cups, and Holliday in a lounging outfit. Lemmon is reading a sexy murder mystery of the Mickey Spillane type (*He Stooped to Kill*) while Holliday sits nearby, bored to tears and very unhappy. She finally says out loud the very first lines of meaningful dialogue: "Robert. I want a divorce." To her surprise, he agrees, and the entire first scene plays out as a terrible quarrel between them as they get ready for bed. Their argument? Which one of them first had the idea to divorce. Sounding melancholy, Lemmon (in voice-over) says, "It was just like a movie. They got married and lived happily ever after—until eight years later, when they got divorced."

Within seconds, she's in Reno, and it's over. ("Wasn't that a beautiful, beautiful divorce?" asks her lawyer. "A lovely ceremony?") The movie is now free to tell the story of their divorce, which is not just the story of how they have to rediscover their love for each other, but also the story of how nothing will work for them *except* the boundaries of marriage. Their problem is that they are old-fashioned. (They should be in a prewar marriage movie.) The new part

---

* "Phffft" was a well-known expression of the day, used by Walter Winchell in his gossip column when he wanted to tell his readers that a couple had split up: they've gone phffft. (Sometimes the title is seen with an exclamation point, but there's none in the actual onscreen title.)

is the presentation of the freer morality by which the couple is surrounded, the possibility of easy sex and an introduction to the world of the emerging "swinger," à la *Playboy* (the brand-new sexy magazine that published its first issue in December 1953). Written by George Axelrod, a man who really had the number of the 1950s, *Phffft* stresses money, accepts the presence of TV, plays lightly with the swinging bachelor world, and says everyone ought to drink martinis and have more fun. It even dares to put into the mouth of Holliday's *mother* the ideas that are beginning to float around: "You've got to stop thinking like a high-school girl. Love—whatever that is—occurs rarely . . . Meanwhile, life must go on." Obliquely telling Holliday to just go out and get laid, she suggests her daughter think of sex as "medicinal." Jack Lemmon (in his early comedy phase) is set up to be a perfect identification figure for most men in the audience—he gets to party with Kim Novak—as well as a perfectly reassuring figure for the women: he turns out to be a homebody who loves his wife.

Phffft's married couple find themselves lost in the emerging world of sex, consumerism, quickie divorce, loose morals, and cocktails. (Martinis are made, discussed, and consumed so often they are practically co-stars. In the 1950s, martinis are signposts to sex.) Lemmon, always perfect as a schlemiel, *wants* to swing—he really does. He *tries* to learn. But he just can't do it, even when Kim Novak* shows up. Her cheerful let's-do-it attitude scares him witless. (Postwar America might have new issues, but Hollywood still knew how to work its old formulas: give them what they want to see, but pretend it's naughty and reinforce old values. *Phffft* is a DeMille movie without a sunken bathtub.) Holliday also tries hard to be modern. She says she'll be "a combination of Sadie Thompson, Amber St. Claire, and Scarlett O'Hara . . . passion's plaything," but she can't do it. She takes French lessons; he takes painting lessons. He grows a mustache; she lets her mother redecorate her bedroom with a round bed. He buys a sports car and flashes a new wardrobe; she buys furs and uses a long cigarette holder. They buy, but they don't really consume. Unbeknownst to each other, they both take rumba lessons, which leads to a dance-off when they show up at a nightclub with other dates. Inevitably, they try to out-rumba each other, but when the band switches to a hot mambo, they grab each other (familiarity needed) and go wild, the perfect metaphor for how they really feel about one another—and about the frightening changes that have occurred in their lives. This mambo scene defines the typical early

---

* Novak is at the very start of her successful career. In a tight, low-cut sweater, she more than holds her own, showing comic skills that were never fully utilized because of her sensual, passive quality, which her studio felt would sell more tickets.

1950s marriage: the couple want all that bad stuff *Playboy* is telling them about, they can even buy it and wear it and dance it, but what they really need is an old-fashioned ending, the DeMille kind of reassurance. And soon enough they get it, back together, clinking martini glasses, sitting on the round bed, all the old verities restored.

Full of Life represents the new in marriage movies because it's the story of a pregnant woman. Up until the postwar period, the condition of pregnancy was never really seen onscreen. A woman became pregnant. Cut. A baby was born. Or a woman who was pregnant stood around briefly in a well-cut maternity frock, flat-tummied, with no apparent bump on her front, and someone had to tell us she was "expecting." (Women on film who were pregnant never showed. It was one of the perks of stardom.)

Full of Life was one of the movies that changed that. It opens right up into a pre-credit nighttime sequence in which Judy Holliday pads downstairs and makes herself a Dagwood sandwich (bologna with gobs of mustard and onions). The audience is allowed to see her feet, her face, and then a strategic camera pullback to reveal her situation: she is *hugely* pregnant. (Audiences actually gasped in the theater I worked in at the time.)* It was a new presentation of "realism" for the postwar baby boom.

The movie develops a small story that could easily have been presented as several short episodes in a TV sitcom. Richard Conte, Holliday's husband, is an ex-GI now working as a writer at home, struggling to finish a second book while they live on his savings from the first. It's a sitcom situation—husband at home every day, man and wife getting in each other's way. There are neighbors to drop in, a black maid to make sarcastic comments (the couple have no money, but they have that kind of money), workmen who come by to over-charge them and make smart-ass remarks, and the inevitable in-laws. In particular, there's a colorful character, Conte's father, played by the former opera star Salvatore Baccaloni. He's a stereotypical Italian, with his own ideas about family, religion, male/female roles, houses, fireplaces—all of it irritates Conte. The primary setup occurs when the kitchen floor of the old house they've purchased collapses under Holliday—it's termites—and as she hangs in the hole, they figure they're going to need his father to move in and help them repair

---

* The movies were following the lead of *I Love Lucy*, which had frankly presented Lucille Ball as a pregnant woman when she was expecting both in her private life and in the main story line of the show. Putting Lucy on TV—and thus in the American home—as openly pregnant was a very big deal, and partly made acceptable by the fact that she and her co-star really were husband and wife. (They weren't allowed to use the word "pregnant," however. Lucy was "expecting.")

things. For any sitcom, this opens the door to weeks of episodic storytelling, with daughter-in-law and father-in-law becoming close, husband getting more and more irritated, things getting done that aren't wanted and things not getting done that are wanted—it's a whole season. *Full of Life*, however, is told on screen in ninety-one minutes. It straddles the two formats, and thus reflects a new kind of marriage movie. There is no single, focused crisis for the narrative to resolve; instead, there's a series of issues that hang on so that characters can meander around and through them, day by day.

Full of Life understands what it has that is unique for moviegoers: there's a constant conversation about Holliday's pregnancy, its effect on Conte (no sex, he's cranky) and on her (she's uncomfortable, afraid, and jealous when he looks at another woman). She says, "It takes a long time to have a baby," and he says, "When I think of you being slender again I almost pass out." She expresses what young wives in the audience might be feeling: "Look at me! I'm a cow, a big fat cow. No one loves a pregnant woman." Holliday and Conte show audiences a new kind of young couple—they are pregnant and having to cope with it. Additionally, *Full of Life* talks about the expenses of home ownership, needing help from families, birth control, pressures from parents to behave the same way they did, etc. Every attempt is made to suggest to audiences that this movie, because of the pregnancy, will be honest with them.* When the time comes for Conte to take Holliday to the hospital, she just says, "Don't get excited—it's time," and they go. There's no bug-eyed husband falling over his feet. No mad dash to the hospital with Irish motorcycle cops. No fainting, no slapstick reaction,† just a simple realism. As Holliday feels her first serious pains, she calmly sends her husband away from her in the style of the times; and in the end, they come home with their new baby.

---

* Today, it's a bit of a shock to see Holliday as a pregnant woman smoking and drinking wine. Times change.

† Not all the small programmer films of the era were situation comedies. There were low-budget, black-and-white marriages that were tragic but still fit the format of the returned GI, the little tract house, and family and adjustment issues. Three examples are *No Down Payment* (1957), with Joanne Woodward, which presented an amalgam of postwar marriage problems, all located in one of California's tract housing developments. (There's racism, rape, sexual immorality, money problems, and alcoholism.) In *Japanese War Bride* (1952), a sensitive story about a GI and his war bride, the couple face racism in California's wine country. In *Pitfall* (1948), an outstanding film noir, a bored insurance salesman (Dick Powell) has a fling with a model (Lizabeth Scott) mostly because of his boredom. The violence he's drawn into enters his cozy little tract home, and his wife (Jane Wyatt), who's willing to forgive him murdering someone, turns angry when she learns of the infidelity. In the end, they are stuck with each other and agree to tough it out. ("We'll *try*," she says.) No one seeing the film could possibly believe it will work.

None of these little comedies that introduce fresh takes on old material are remembered today. The definitive postwar marriage film that addresses the return of the husband to his half of the American married couple is *The Best Years of Our Lives* (1946), one of Hollywood's finest films of the postwar period (or any period), and it defines the marriage film's new social awareness. It showed audiences that change is change, and there are few laughs to be had. Some married couples can adjust and some cannot. Presented partly from the male point of view, it tells the story of three men who are each in his own way afraid to return home, knowing they've changed, afraid of what they'll find. The war has redefined each man's social status. Dana Andrews, a former drugstore employee, became an officer and a bombardier. Fredric March, a banker, became an infantryman. The character "Harold Russell," famously played by a non-professional, lost his hands (for real) in the service and now uses hooks for normal activities. Each man must face a woman on return: Virginia Mayo, who married Andrews for his looks, his uniform, and his paycheck; Myrna Loy, faithful companion to March, who has nevertheless gotten comfortable not having him around; and Cathy O'Donnell, engaged to Russell before the loss of his hands.

Best Years of Our Lives plays out a story of acceptance and adjustment, a life-must-go-on scenario. Everything that should be right becomes right again, and negatives are overcome. Loy and March love each other and are able to recover their former relationship (good marriage restored). O'Donnell sincerely loves Russell and overcomes his fears and reluctance so they can wed (good marriage undertaken). Andrews ditches Mayo and teams up with March and Loy's lovely daughter, Teresa Wright (bad marriage abandoned, possible future good marriage). There are many side issues—housing shortages, etc.—but the audience is given an uplifting story about what the sacrifices of the war have done to the lives of "ordinary" people, and how those sacrifices were worth it. It also teaches them that they can't turn back the clock; they must live with the consequences of war, realize that the war years were a time of unshared, unspoken experiences, and accept the changes in their partners.

The charming British film *Vacation from Marriage* (1945) is more of a comedy than *Best Years of Our Lives*, but it taught a similar lesson, and proved a hit when released in the United States.* Basically, the plot seemed to say that what most marriages need is a jolly good war to shake them up. Deborah Kerr and Robert Donat are a bored and boring, totally uncommunicative married

* *Vacation* was produced and made by MGM in England through their London Film Productions wing.

couple when the film opens on April 4, 1940. She has no glamour, no pizzazz. He's a clerk among clerks. Together they make a totally unromantic pairing. And then he joins the navy . . . and she becomes a WREN. Away from each other, they blossom, and they dread getting back together on leave. When they reunite, each determined to divorce the other, they meet outside during a blackout. They can't see each other, and in the dark they agree to divorce. Later, inside in the bright lights of a pub, each is shocked by the sight of the other. He's handsome and fit, and she's Deborah Kerr! (During their ten-day leave, they will, of course, reunite.) What *Vacation from Marriage* suggests is that the changes everyone has undergone are a good thing. We're all better for having suffered and served. The postwar message about marriage via the motion picture was that everything will be all right if people can live with the changes.

By 1950, it was clear that World War II had been a turning point regarding the context (or situation) in which marriage movies were set. The war solidi- fied the use of marriage as an explanation of and primary location for social change. What was learned was the power of marriage as such a catalyst. The subject still had its familiar internal problems and its couples, but now it took on more fully than ever before in movie history a development that almost moved marriage into the "social problems" movie category. After World War II, the "social purpose" form of the marriage movie became more common than the pure marriage movie. In the decades that lay ahead, marriage would be used to showcase the issues of communism (*I Married a Communist* [1949], *Conspirator* [1949], *The Iron Curtain* [1948]), the threat of nuclear weapons (*I Married a Monster from Outer Space* [1958]), postwar adjustment (*No Down Payment* [1957]), the Sexual Revolution (*Bob & Carol & Ted & Alice* [1969]), race relations (*Guess Who's Coming to Dinner* [1967]), and many others. By 1950, however, there was a new factor influencing what would happen to sto- ries about marriage for the American public, which Hollywood was not fully prepared for: television, the home of the sitcom marriage.

Marriage stories took place in the home and were always, in some funda- mental way, about furniture. Television sat in the home and *was* furniture. Over the 1950s, the marriage story largely left motion pictures and moved next door, to television. This constituted a significant change. Movies were an escape; television was a distraction. When you entered a darkened motion-picture the- ater, often into icy-cold air conditioning (or cozy warmth, depending on the season), you left behind the outer world and sank into a plush seat, ready to soar away from everything known. When you watched TV, you were in your own home, possibly doing another task, subject to interruptions from the telephone,

The most celebrated movie about postwar adjustments for veterans and
their families was *The Best Years of Our Lives*. Air force glamour boy Dana
Andrews finds a dissatisfied spouse (Virginia Mayo) who doesn't like him
without the uniform and the wings and the money . . .

the doorbell, family members, etc. Television even interrupted itself—with
commercials. Whatever was happening on TV also happened in your living
room, or bedroom, or wherever you were watching. The screen was smaller
than you were, and you looked downward toward it, not upward as you did for
the gigantic movie show. What you saw on TV could be anything—local and
international news, weather, game shows, variety shows, westerns, sitcoms—
but they were all there in front of you at the same time. You could control
them, moving up and down on the dial; no longer did the image take over and
dominate you. The reverse happened: you dominated it, easily eliminating
anything you didn't like and changing to something else. The TV shows that
were narratives were not lavishly decorated or detailed. They were usually set
in one main room where the majority of the action took place, with side trips
to other cheap-looking places—a bedroom or two, the kitchen, or a yard. There
were no long sequences without dialogue in which the camera lingered over a
star's face, allowing a viewer to feel, think, and empathize with the character,
imposing his or her own feelings onto the actor. Audiences just sat and listened,
because everything was dialogue-driven: an actor and talking was what the
little set could provide. Movies featured stars who were bigger than life and
who audiences imagined were playing themselves, but television developed

. . . while former infantryman Fredric March returns home to his sympathetic wife (Myrna Loy).

stars who played the role they were cast in. (Gable is Gable; Dennis Franz is Andy Sipowicz.)

Despite these significant differences, or perhaps because of them, the little television box turned out to be an excellent place to set the kind of small marriage/family drama that would come to be known as a "sitcom." The television sitcom about marriage had the same essential goals as the movie about marriage: to connect to what the audiences knew and understood. The difference was that the movies expected to move away from the known and off into someplace exciting or dangerous or funny to release the audience from its doldrums. It then expected to return, with everything restored. The television marriage, by comparison, was never going anywhere except to the next episode. It maintained a balance, a status quo, that could be amusingly threatened within its half hour ("Oh no, the maid is quitting!" or "Oh no, we accidentally gave Daddy's favorite sweater to Goodwill!" or "Oh no, little Billy's softball game conflicts with sister Mary's spelling bee!"). In the movies, marriage was a roller-coaster ride; on television, it was a merry-go-round.

In a movie marriage, everything goes wrong. In the TV version, little things happen. The former is a two-hour build to crisis, followed by resolution. The latter is a forward movement with little ups and downs that surface and disappear. They are dissimilar because the media they appear in are dissimilar.*

---

* One thing they do have in common is the rhythm of lying and confession, whether comic or tragic. Married people in the movies and TV—and their kids and relatives and

292 · I DO AND I DON'T

The sitcom families of 1950s television are an indelible part of American pop culture and are now the subject of courses in colleges and universities, but the "sitcom family" wasn't necessarily something new to American audiences, or even something originally defined by the small box in the living room. Movies had already established the template—low-budget movies that featured families in ongoing serial form: the Hardys, the Joneses, the Aldriches—and, of course, the Bumsteads, originally of the comics. Just as the television sitcom family appeared often—every week over several months—the serial movie family could appear as often as three or four times a year in films telling continuous stories, often picking up at the exact same moment where the previous release ended.*

In fact, looking at the low-budget programmer marriages in movies from 1948 to 1956, one can see how very much like the television sitcom they are. Slice them apart, and they become several episodes of a sitcom. Condense them down to their basic setup, and there's a half-hour sitcom pilot. These movies are often forgotten today, and their link to the development of—and inspiration for—the television sitcom is forgotten. Besides redefining the marriage movie, the late-1940s/early-1950s marriage programmers represent a transitional era in media history, the link between movies and television.†

A perfect example of the connection between the TV sitcom and the marriage-movie programmer is 1949's *Father Was a Fullback*. Its format proves the point. Well directed by John M. Stahl, it *is* a sitcom; it's just an hour and a half long. The characters include Fred MacMurray, the father of the title, a

---

friends—lie to one another about things big or small, and the lie will ultimately have to be confessed. Confessing in the medium of the moving image is an American ritual. After TV took hold, public filmed confessions became familiar and very popular as a form of absolution. Politicians, movie stars, TV stars, celebrities, sports figures—everyone started confessing on television what bad things they did. Now "sinners" just cut right to the chase and tell us on TV they're sorry for what they did. No confession needed, only the apology. The tabloids have already revealed the sin that was supposed to be their secret.

* Hollywood knew that repeating characters in movies was good business. Sometimes movies were built around a single character—Nancy Drew, Tarzan, Sherlock Holmes, the Whistler, Boston Blackie, Charlie Chan, Mr. Moto, Mr. Wu, Torchy Blane, and others. These characters were surrounded by their own "families" of familiar characters, but they usually weren't about a married couple. They were also, however, very similar to what television would provide. There were also weekly movie serials that appeared in chapters, one per week, with such characters as Buck Rogers, Flash Gordon, Ace Drummond, Superman, and others, going all the way back to silent days with *The Perils of Pauline* and *The Exploits of Elaine.*

† Radio shows are the usual parallel drawn to the TV sitcom, because they were often fifteen-minute or half-hour shows dominated by dialogue and featuring married couples, but the movie parallels are significant as well.

football coach at "State U" in "Riverville" (second only to "University City"); his loving wife, always calmly doing her mom/wife job (Maureen O'Hara); a teenage daughter (Betty Lynn) with boyfriend problems and a great sense of personal drama; a nosy, bratty little sister (the young Natalie Wood), who is a wise-ass and always knows what's going on; a snappy, outspoken maid (Thelma Ritter); a next-door neighbor who's a sounding board across the fence for Mac-Murray (Jim Backus); a fussy, impossible nemesis for MacMurray in the form of the president of the Alumni Association (Rudy Vallee). What more does one need for a sitcom that could run for years? The plot is made up of the kind of small, quickly resolved misunderstandings that often become the "sit" of the thirty-minute sitcom: MacMurray erroneously thinks O'Hara is pregnant; both parents erroneously think Betty Lynn is pregnant; Dad and his next-door pal hire a guy to date Lynn; Ritter places bets against MacMurray's football team; a "secret weapon" player to win a big game backfires on them and they lose anyway; Lynn gets a story published in *True Confessions* in which she claims to be a fifteen-year-old bubble dancer. The movie takes place almost totally in the family living room, with excursions to a football field, the yard outside their home, the house next door, a gas station, and a banquet hall. It's low-budget, focused on cheap sets with a minimum of variety, and based on small, intimate family issues, with the larger context being the genuine pressures MacMurray is under to win football games.*

As the movie business struggled with changes and the studio system collapsed, from approximately 1950 to 1966, television presented its golden age of the marital sitcom and took ownership of the concept of the moving-image marriage. Nobody really needed marriage movies anymore: marriage was all over TV. *I Love Lucy* was the Rolls-Royce of the type, but besides Lucy and Ricky Ricardo, there were the Kramdens of *The Honeymooners*, husband Ralph and wife Alice, a great pair of frustrated (her) and exasperated (him) characters—two people destined never to be *really* together but nevertheless locked step by hilarious step unto death . . . or unto the moon. There were also Ozzie and Harriet Nelson, who, like Lucille Ball and Desi Arnaz, were a real-life married couple. Their show, entitled *The Adventures of Ozzie and*

---

* MacMurray, an underrated actor, was a top-of-the-line film personality who would go on to become one of television's greatest sitcom stars in the long-running hit *My Three Sons* (1960–1972). *Father Was a Fullback* has an uncanny parallel to a serious film version of the pressures of being a coach released in 2004, *Friday Night Lights*. That *Friday Night Lights* would itself be turned into a superbly written and acted one-hour TV series of the same name is a further interesting development of how a story of this nature can fit well into both media.

Harriet, was a fourteen-season success. Ozzie was a big-name bandleader, and his wife, the former Harriet Hilliard, had starred in such hit movies as *Follow the Fleet,* with Astaire and Rogers. (She played the love interest for Randolph Scott.) The Nelsons were the parents of teen idols Ricky and David Nelson. In their highly successful series, which gives an idealized portrait of suburban life of the 1950s, Ozzie was an understanding father, slightly bumbling, standing around in a cardigan sweater, and Harriet was a patient, all-knowing, all-accepting wife.*

There were *I Married Joan* and *Blondie,* shows that were essentially grounded in marriages, and also *December Bride* and *The George Burns and Gracie Allen Show, The Life of Riley, Make Room for Daddy,* and others. Shows that were domestic but not really "marriage situations" were also popular. *Bachelor Father* was, obviously, missing the wife. *The Real McCoys, Leave It to Beaver, Dennis the Menace,* and others were focused more on the family or the children. *Lassie* focused on the dog. *The Thin Man* was about solving mysteries, and the couple were not a typical suburban marriage. *Mr. Adams and Eve* was about two movie stars married to each other, but who got along better onscreen than off- (played by Howard Duff and Ida Lupino, two married movie stars who also, as it turned out, got along better onscreen: they were soon divorced). TV became the pop-cultural home of the American marriage, and its definition began to lie there, not at the movies, where increasingly the marriage story began to fade away. What did the TV marriage give viewers?

When people talk about the TV marriage sitcoms of the 1950s, 1960s, and into the 1970s, there's a tendency to lump them together as if they were all more or less the same. This ignores a fundamental issue: some marriage (or family) sitcoms were designed to be "realistic," while others were clearly a form of exaggerated comedy that grounded action in a marriage strictly for laughs. The former type offered viewers an ideal model for their own lives, a romanticized world in which all parents were understanding and sympathetic and all children learned the lessons they were supposed to learn. (These sitcoms are much criticized for these qualities today.) The other format tended to poke fun at marriage in a sympathetic and larky manner; marriage is used for a background to fun, and as a way to siphon off negative feelings and complaints about the spouse. (These sitcoms are usually beloved today.)

The "realistic" sitcom of the 1950s is exemplified by *The Donna Reed Show,*

---

* Behind the scenes, Ozzie wrote, produced, and directed many of the episodes. His great achievement was figuring out how to incorporate the Elvis-like celebrity of his son Ricky into the plots. The presentations of Ricky's musical performances in the show are considered by many to be the forerunners of today's music videos.

which first aired in 1958, and *Father Knows Best*, which went on even earlier, in 1954. Reed was an Oscar-winning movie star with nothing to prove. She moved into television to continue her career when the studio system began to collapse and she began to age. This was typical of many other actresses of her generation (Loretta Young, who pioneered television in its earliest years; Barbara Stanwyck; Jane Wyman; and others). Reed, a beautiful woman, looked young and fresh and slender, and had no need for special lighting and careful handling to be recognizable as Donna Reed. Her show presented her as a typical housewife and mother. Her husband, a successful pediatrician (who makes house calls), was played by the handsome Carl Betz. They lived in a small midwestern city with their two children, played by Shelley Fabares and Paul Petersen.

The Donna Reed Show presents a marriage that is happy, with parenting that works. There is a strong attempt at simplicity and honesty, no matter how sentimental. Since it's supposed to be a reflection of the audience's "real" world, it addresses basic problems that were "out there." Its little problems—and they *are* little—are ones any family could have. The very first episode, "The Vacation," shows the father as too busy to spend much time with his kids—or his wife. No one is happy about this, including him, but he seems to be bothered by it the least. Donna solves the problem, cleverly eliminating all the obstacles to a family vacation and establishing who the central character is going to be. Reed's TV family also faced problems about budgets, nosy neighbors, sibling rivalry, challenges at school, report cards, and growing pains—but nothing heavy, nothing seriously threatening. The children are well behaved, although the son is sometimes the voice of cold truth. ("I thought she stunk" is his opinion of Mom's performance of Nora in Ibsen's *A Doll's House*.) The couple are comfortable but not rich, and their home appears modest, not lavish. The episodes usually ended with the husband and wife, who clearly love each other, happily alone in their bedroom together. It's made abundantly clear to viewers that Dr. Stone likes Mrs. Stone a great deal, and that she returns the favor. They're always happy to find themselves alone, although naturally there's nothing even remotely salacious about it. They love each other—that's it.

Although people remember Reed as always attired in pearls and high heels, she is often wearing jeans and sneakers. She doesn't *just* cook and clean, though. She acts in plays in her community theater, visits her husband's hospital for various reasons, and influences everyone around her with her own little plots and schemes. She would not, however, be found stuffing chocolates into her bosom on a candy-factory assembly line. Her world is designed to be *recognizable*—not any truer than any plotted piece of entertainment ever is, just recognizable. Reed is often self-deprecating, and whatever plans she gets up to, her husband always wisely sees through them. (He seldom says anything about it, but an audience is allowed to understand that, as a children's doctor, he's able to pick up on anything concocted to fool him.) Everyone pays tribute to Donna Reed's looks—and her sweetness—and her success as wife and mother. She smiles gratefully, gives thanks, and moves on. If things get too sticky-sweet, Reed cuts them back with a wry look or word. When they get too harsh, she's there to bring things back yet again with a soft touch. Reed is lovely, a skilled actress who handles her character well. One of the reasons *The Donna Reed Show* gets a bum rap is because she *is* so effective. She works so well that everything begins to seem too perfect, which sometimes became irritating to people whose lives were not perfect. Most audiences loved the show, but many felt burdened by its ideal standards. If Reed had been less charming, more strident, and not as beautiful, this might not have happened. The truth is that Donna Reed deserves a break. She's effective, and her little low-key sitcom was just trying to entertain while presenting some wholesome values. Let's let her out of Pop Culture Jail.

Father Knows Best first aired on October 3, 1954, and concluded its run on May 23, 1960. Like *The Donna Reed Show*, it was the story of a family in the Midwest—in the fictional town of Springfield. The parents were Robert Young and Jane Wyatt, both film veterans, and their three children were played by Elinor Donahue, Billy Gray, and Lauren Chapin. Young was an agent for the General Insurance Company, and Wyatt was a stay-at-home wife. The three children ("Princess," "Bud," and "Kitten") ranged in age from sixteen to nine when the series began, and the stories of their growing up formed a large portion of the sitcom's action. *Father Knows Best* is structured similarly to *The Donna Reed Show*, but centered on the husband rather than the wife (although, as always in sitcoms, every character gets to be featured as central to the story from episode to episode). *Father Knows Best* presents problems of money, school, job, friends, and teenage adjustment, and like *The Donna Reed Show*, it attempts to be as low-key and honest as possible, never suggesting marital discord of any serious nature. It took itself very seriously, and its goals were often lofty in terms of ethics, morals, and civic duty.

Taken together, these two shows define what happened to the media portrait of marriage. It was desexed, made familial. It became completely *situational*, week to week, with easily solved problems and an idealized, elevated status, held up as a role model most people felt they couldn't live up to because it seemed dishonest. The old horrors presented by movies, however easily swept away in happy endings, had more guts; under the movie surface always lurked the monsters. Under the TV sitcom marriage lurked the sponsors.

Television presented marriage mostly as a family story, as in *Father Knows Best*, with dad Robert Young and mom Jane Wyatt and their three kids.

As popular as *The Donna Reed Show* and *Father Knows Best* were, the show that claims the sitcom crown in the marriage sweepstakes—and that is running somewhere today on some channel if you just turn on a television and look for it—started out inauspiciously. In March 1951, Desi Arnaz and Lucille Ball made a half-hour comedy about a married couple that they hoped to sell to CBS. This "pilot" was subsequently lost and not found for years. It finally aired as a big event on August 30, 1990. Where once it had been a hasty, on-the-cheap little playlet designed as a smart sales pitch, it was exhumed and presented to America with all the reverence of a new opening of King Tut's tomb. That's because the "little show" had become one of the most beloved—if not *the* most beloved—television shows in the history of the medium. It was called *I Love Lucy* and it was about a married couple.

It is fashionable today to say that the leading lady of *I Love Lucy*, Lucille Ball, was never a real movie star, but she had a long career and her name appeared over the title in numerous films; her face adorned the covers of movie magazines, and she even had her own endorsed set of paper dolls for little girls to play with. She *was* a star, just not a legendary one.* It was her husband, Desi

---

* Proof that Ball was considered a star lies in *A Woman of Distinction* (1950), starring Ray Milland and Rosalind Russell. When Milland arrives in the United States on a transatlantic American Airlines flight, a crowd of news photographers push forward, yelling, "Look, fellas, there's Lucille Ball!" Ball deplanes with Milland, handing him her fur coat, her giant hatbox, and her little dog, in order to pose. This type of star cameo—the

Viewers of the small screen could see shows that purported to be realistic, as in *The Donna Reed Show*, with Reed as a typical 1960s housewife . . .

Arnaz, who didn't reach the level of movie stardom that his looks and talent might have guaranteed him. During the mid- to late-1930s, Ball emerged as the headliner of inexpensive black-and-white movies at RKO. (It was at RKO that she first met Arnaz, when they co-starred in the 1940 musical *Too Many Girls*.) Ball was glamorous and hilarious in comedies such as *The Affairs of Annabel* and *Annabel Takes a Tour* (both 1938). She was glamorous and dramatic in *Beauty for the Asking* (1939) and *Dance, Girl, Dance* (1940), and highly effective in a serious role in *The Big Street* (1942), opposite Henry Fonda. In late 1942, her considerable RKO success led to the offer of a contract from the all-powerful star factory Metro-Goldwyn-Mayer, proof she *was* seen as a real star. It also meant something else, which would ultimately derail her potential: MGM, the studio of glamour, was hiring Ball to be one more of its glamorous female creatures. (MGM had under contract Lana Turner, Hedy Lamarr, Greer Garson, and others.) Whereas RKO had been developing Ball as a sophisticated comedienne who could do slapstick as needed, MGM introduced her as

glamour arrival—was reserved for real movie stars, as when Ava Gardner gets off the same train as Fred Astaire in *The Band Wagon*. In 1950, Ball had not yet begun *I Love Lucy*. Her earlier film career is much more solid and varied than she is usually given credit for; it's by comparison to her huge success on TV that it's been underrated.

. . . or shows that bounced off that wall, as in *I Love Lucy*, with Desi Arnaz, Lucille Ball, and Vivian Vance. There was nothing typical about Lucy.

"the Queen of Technicolor" in a huge *Life* magazine spread. MGM had Ann Sothern under contract, and she was their resident good-looking female with musical ability who could do comedy, verbal and physical. MGM didn't need (or so they thought) what Ball could offer in comedy. The studio didn't ignore her comic abilities; it just didn't build them up. For instance, they cast her as the romantic and glamorous leading lady in such musicals as *DuBarry Was a Lady* (opposite Gene Kelly and Red Skelton) and *Best Foot Forward* (1943, in which she plays Lucille Ball, a movie star). Both films stressed her glamour and sex appeal, but also allowed her to do a little comedy rather than just be a standard romantic lead. Ball was a beautiful woman, tall and thin, and she wore clothes well, but she was never made to be a clotheshorse. Although she was at a top studio, her career began to languish. MGM began to use her as a kind of Eve Arden clone, casting her as the sharp-talking second lead in such films as *Without Love* (1945) and *Easy to Wed* (1946). She found welcome success away from MGM as a wisecracking secretary to a private eye in *The Dark Corner* (1946) and as a model menaced by a murderer in *Lured* (1947). She began her real work as a slapstick comedienne in *The Fuller Brush Girl* (1950) and in her pairing with Bob Hope in *Sorrowful Jones* (1949) and *Fancy Pants* (1950). In 1951, both her life and her career changed course, when *I Love Lucy* debuted.

Lucille Ball and Desi Arnaz got married on November 30, 1940. Arnaz then served in the armed forces during World War II, and despite excellent earlier appearances in such movies as *Bataan* (1943), at war's end he found he could not jump-start his film career. He went on the road with his band, and the Arnazes experienced serious marital troubles. After a reconciliation, he began to look for ways he and his wife could work together in a show that would keep him at home. He wanted to find something to utilize both her considerable comic skills and his musical knowledge, and he came up with an idea. Ball had been appearing regularly in a successful radio show called *My Favorite Husband*, and radio had always been a good locale for the short-form comedy featuring married couples. There were Fibber McGee and Molly, Burns and Allen, *I Married Joan* with Joan Davis, and a model that may well have directly influenced Arnaz: *The Phil Harris–Alice Faye Show*. There was also a wonderfully funny radio act called *The Bickersons*, starring Frances Langford and Don Ameche, which stands today as a yardstick by which all shows about bickering married couples can be measured. The radio show gave Arnaz an idea for television.

Arnaz's thinking resulted in the pilot that ultimately sold the idea of *I Love Lucy* to CBS. *I Love Lucy* (1951–1957) and the subsequent thirteen hour-long comedies set in their country home in Connecticut (*The Lucy-Desi Comedy Hour*, 1957–1960) were unprecedented hits. In all of them, Ball and Arnaz played a married couple called Lucy and Ricky Ricardo.* There weren't really many imitators of *I Love Lucy*, because there weren't many Lucille Balls. She was a brilliant physical comedienne and possibly the greatest female slapstick artist ever to be seen in the media. (We don't have enough footage of Mabel Normand for a solid comparison.) Her comic timing was precision-perfect. She was physically agile and apparently fearless. Although really a tall, slim, and beautiful woman, she wasn't afraid to let herself look silly, or even bad. She was a treasure, and her husband of those years, Desi Arnaz, was not only her perfect foil and an equally brilliant straight man, but also a smart businessman who understood what to do with her.

Most people think of *I Love Lucy* as a typical 1950s married couple. Lucy, in particular, is thought of as a 1950s housewife (God help us!). But nothing about *I Love Lucy* is really "typical" the way *The Donna Reed Show* and *Father Knows Best* are. *I Love Lucy* merely uses a real marriage as a springboard to hilariously off-the-wall (and totally unrealistic) comedy adventures. Yes, it's

---

* Although Ball continued in television after her divorce in 1960, her shows featured only herself, not Arnaz, and she always played a woman without a living husband.

true that Lucy is a 1950s housewife, and she and Ricky are happily married. They even become parents when Little Ricky is born. Yes, it's true that Lucy wears comfortable clothes around the house—flats, pants, simple dresses, even aprons—and yes, she cooks, she irons, she keeps house, she shops for groceries. But—and it's a very big "but"—when Lucy cooks, the bread she's baking (with too much yeast) fires out of the oven like a battering ram and knocks her out the door. When she irons, she burns. When she cleans, she crams everything into one closet and opens the door in time to bonk her mother-in-law on the head. And when she shops for groceries, she turns it into a Ponzi scheme in order to bilk her neighbors.

Why would anyone imagine that the Ricardos were the role model for American married couples? The Ricardos give audiences two contradictory things: wedded bliss and resounding discord.* They aren't even like other sit-com families. Ricky and Lucy live in an apartment in New York City, not a house in the suburbs or some vague midwestern locale. They have no relatives living with them, and, initially, no children. Their best friends are their landlords, Fred and Ethel Mertz, and he's an ex-Vaudevillian. Lucy dyed her hair, and Ricky was a Cuban bandleader, for heaven's sake! *I Love Lucy* was not about the neighborhood, the children, and their troubles at school. It was not about the husband's challenges in his work as lawyer or doctor, or the wife's management of her home or her problems at the PTA meeting. *I Love Lucy* was a slapstick musical comedy about show business. The wife's frustration was that she wanted to get out of the house and into her husband's act. Instead of a Blondie/Dagwood situation in which the ever-reliable Blondie bailed out the bungling Dagwood from his mismanagement of day-to-day activities, the beleaguered Ricky—supported by the cheapskate Fred Mertz (William Fraw-ley)—had to survive the tactics of his scheming wife. In her various shenani-gans, Lucy was herself supported by her faithful Sancho Panza, the equally numbskulled Ethel Mertz (Vivian Vance).

The truth is that Lucy is dangerous—comically dangerous, but dangerous. She's not the all-American wife and mother; she's like the movies' mad doctor who invents things: he can get the plan off the ground, but then it goes wild

---

* Because Ball and Arnaz had careers that began in movies, they often grounded their show inside issues they had seen in movie marriages. For instance, Lucy's mother-in-law comes to visit, confirming the basic mother-in-law-as-punch-line concept. (Ethel says, "A mother-in-law is a mother-in-law . . . Mine comes once a year all the way from Indiana just to look under the rug . . . If I thought she'd stay home, I'd send her the rug and a box of dirt.") Lucy overspends her budget (money), Lucy gets jealous when she fears Ricky has a girlfriend (infidelity), Ricky forgets their anniversary (communication), and Lucy thinks she and Ricky aren't really married (oops!). These are old problems, old issues.

and destroys civilization. Lucy has an endless fountain of crackpot ideas to further her goals, but also an indomitable spirit to keep her plugging away at them when they obviously aren't working. Who has forgotten Lucy eating the chocolates on the assembly line? Stomping the grapes in the wine vat? Gamely coming down the stairs in high heels and a "Follies girl" hat that is tipping her dangerously backward? None of these enterprises goes right for her, but she presses onward, never relenting, never stopping, and always acting as if she can master her fate if she just keeps going. (This is why Lucy became emblematic of the 1950s American woman: not because she's "normal," but because she's *determined*. She treks ever onward, confident there must be a better life somewhere up there ahead.) Furthermore, Lucy's got a mean streak. When she reads about a wife who's conked her mate on the head with a baseball bat, she bursts into hysterical laughter: "The idea of someone letting go and doing exactly what they want after twenty years just kills me!"

Lucy accompanies Ricky to Europe, where she teaches Charles Boyer how to be Charles Boyer and where she stomps some eternal grapes. Lucy and Desi also go to Hollywood, where Lucy (with the help of the ever-wary but ever-reliable Ethel, of course) steals John Wayne's footprints from Grauman's Chinese Theatre. She sets William Holden's nose on fire at the Brown Derby, and burgles Richard Widmark's house. In each case, she directly encounters the famous star (guesting on the show). Lucy is thus no ordinary housewife, and no ordinary sitcom wife. (She's Lucy, she's out there, and look out if you run into her! Out on the street, Lucy and Ethel were a menace. In the home, their own turf, they were atomic.)

Lucy and Desi are *exaggerated*. The difference between *I Love Lucy*'s marriage and a more conventional sitcom marriage is illustrated by the episode "Lucy Does the Tango." Now living in their Connecticut home, with the Mertzes still next door, the Ricardos are carrying on in their usual manner. Lucy wants to keep chickens and sell the eggs to make some money for herself. Ricky is totally opposed. Naturally, with Ethel's help, Lucy secretly raises chickens and hatches eggs. When she and Ethel bring several dozen eggs into the house, Ricky comes downstairs unexpectedly and tells Lucy it's time to rehearse their tango. Tango? Here's where the marriage of the Ricardos can be marked out as an "unrealistic" situation. The chickens are acceptable, and certainly the eggs; telling a lie to a husband is standard sitcom behavior. But the *tango*? It's the tango that marks the Ricardos out as the married-sitcom "other." In a normal family, the husband is not a bongo drummer, and he does not need to rehearse the tango—and if he did, his wife wouldn't know how to do one. It's perfectly "real" for the marriage established for the Ricardos in the Ball/Arnaz sitcom universe, but it is not realistic in the everyday world of the viewers.

What happens moves from "let's rehearse" (which *might* be normal) to the tango (which is becoming esoteric) to the bizarre. To hide the eggs, Lucy stuffs as many as she possibly can into her blouse. To keep Ricky from finding out what she's doing behind his back (raising chickens), she must tango very, very carefully. In particular, she must *not* let him sweep her close in a passionate chest-bumping embrace that would break the eggs and reveal her lie. And so the viewer is drawn into the world of show-business professionalism, inhabited by two people who know one another's rhythms and moves, and who both understand their half of the pairing. Desi Arnaz, underrated in his ability to handle Lucy and enhance her comedy, spins her, twirls her, and tries to embrace her, innocently unaware that there's anything more at stake than a good tango. Lucy, a physical genius, blocks him at every turn but with a shaky smile and a worried look that she glosses over. Time and time again they almost crash, until the final punch line—smash go the eggs!—and the aftermath of chagrin for her and startled questioning for him.

This tango-of-the-eggs is more than a funny slapstick comedy routine; it's a classic marriage metaphor played out by two people who are married in real life. It's about everyday deception of a practical nature paired with the awarenesses of years lived together. Nobody needs to be a cultural analyst to get it; one only has to be married. There was more than comedy to Lucy and Desi; there was marriage—*real* marriage, and a complicated one at that. This element is strongly layered over everything they do, and probably accounts for why people remember their shows as typical rather than exaggerated. It is significant that audiences could feel the real tension in Lucy and Desi's marriage via a dozen eggs, and decide as a result that here was a real marriage, and also know that, at their core, the marriages of Donna Reed and Robert Young were false.

When Desi Arnaz chose to expand *I Love Lucy* to the one-hour format, the strange reality/unreality of the televised union between Ball and Arnaz became even more apparent as they interacted with four other real-life show-business couples: Betty Grable and Harry James, Edie Adams and Ernie Kovacs, June Haver and Fred MacMurray, and Ida Lupino and Howard Duff. Ball and Arnaz are playing Lucy and Ricky Ricardo, but the other four couples play themselves. The real-life couples act as if Lucy and Ricky are, like themselves, a real married couple at work in show business. The strangeness of this blurring of marital reality is compounded by a fifth complication: Danny Thomas and his fake television family from *Make Room for Daddy* also do an episode. (*Make Room for Daddy* was a Desilu-owned and -produced sitcom.) Was it any wonder that confusion about identities, marital responsibilities, and role playing emerged? When Ball gave birth to a son both onscreen and offscreen

Lucille Ball and Desi Arnaz also made movies together. They start
out happy after their big wedding, driving off in their brand-new
Long, Long Trailer . . .

in 1953, the fusing of the Arnazes (real people) and the Ricardos (fake people)
became forever set in the minds of their audiences.

Lucy and Desi were an enormous success on television, so much so that the
movies suddenly wanted them again; they both became movie stars by default.
Since they were totally associated with marriage, MGM hired them to make
two movies about marriage: *The Long, Long Trailer* (1953) and *Forever, Darling*
(1956).* Both these films were hits, and in them, the Arnazes essentially played
the Ricardos. These movies were an extension of their television show, with
The Long, Long Trailer providing a perfect visual metaphor for marriage: the
title vehicle. As newlyweds, Lucy and Desi disagree on things right from the
start. In particular, Lucy thinks it would be grand to buy a trailer—a long, long
trailer—and make it their new home. As they drive to their new living location,
that metaphor for marriage—a long, long, and unwieldy trailer—rides behind
them like a rigid beast that at any moment may charge forward and destroy
them. The ability to move easily from TV to movies was characteristic of the
work of Lucy and Desi, for whom the movie was always the gold standard, the
place where they had learned their techniques.

* In *Forever, Darling*, Lucy's imaginary mentor (embodied by James Mason) defines who a
  husband should be: "father, brother, friend, sweetheart, guardian angel . . . with a touch
  of Prince Charming."

. . . only to end up in a cheap roadside diner, bandaged, bewildered, and brokenhearted.

In 1993, after both her parents were dead, Lucie Arnaz Luckinbill made a poignant and intelligent documentary about them that addressed their real-life marriage from the point of view of a child in the family. It turned out to be an amazingly honest marriage movie. Sitting alongside her brother, Desi Arnaz Jr., and with her own children around her, Lucie Arnaz asked herself (and thus her viewing audience) the familiar question: "Why couldn't they stay married?" Using archival footage, home movies, and interviews, Arnaz explored what she called "the personal side" of her parents' union, by which she means, of course, *not* the Lucy and Ricky Ricardo side. "Things don't just happen," she says, as she goes back to look for an answer that can help her (and her brother) come to terms with their background. (Imagine being Desi Arnaz Jr., who became a TV character known as Little Ricky on TV the day he was born, played by another child. Throughout his life Desi Jr. was approached by strangers with the words "You're Little Ricky!" "No, I'm not—I'm not who you think I am!" he tells viewers in the documentary.)

Working with childhood friends, cousins, Lucy's brother, celebrity friends such as Bob Hope, business connections, etc., Lucie Arnaz searches—and finally ends up with a story that could have been a typical 1940s marriage movie: two people from very different backgrounds (class) meet and fall immediately in love (romance and glamour) while appearing in a movie together. They wed, become successful (money), but he is unfaithful (adultery). She plans to divorce him, but on the way to the courthouse she stops to see him and they reconcile. (That is movie number one, the "I do!" version. It is the true story of the Arnaz marriage prior to their sitcom success.)

In movie number two, the inevitable "I don't!," the couple become rich, rich, rich and famous, famous, famous (money), and issues of competition and control emerge. They stop communicating (incompatibility), and as they live together children are born, Lucy's mom never likes Desi, and Desi's mom is imperious toward everyone (kids and in-laws). Pressures arise for both, and Desi becomes increasingly unfaithful and a serious alcoholic (addiction). They do not kill each other, although Lucie recounts a horrific story of how, as a child, she heard her parents screaming at each other. She peeked in at them: "My mother was leaning over him with her long red nails. [Her hands] were poised at him like that [makes murderous gesture] and she said with her teeth gritted and her mouth in a horrible expression: 'I wish you were dead.' " In the end, they divorce—the "I don't" variation, this time played as "I really don't."

Sadly, Lucie Arnaz says to the camera, "They would have loved to have been the Ricardos," but like so many others, they couldn't manage a sitcom life offscreen, only on. "We're haunted by The Donna Reed Show or Father Knows Best . . . There are no perfect families out there . . . We're all struggling." She remembers how she and Desi Jr. started showing The Parent Trap to their parents in the hope that it would influence them to reunite. (This illustrates the power of the motion picture even in the world of people who should know better.) Lucille Ball is shown on camera saying, "They must have shown us that movie about seven times before we had to sit them down and explain things."

In the end, says Lucie Arnaz, her parents did the I Love Lucy show in order to be closer together in their work, and to be able to have kids and raise a family. The show worked, but the marriage didn't. ("Why couldn't they stay married?")

Touchingly, Lucie is both willing and able to give her father and mother the happy ending life denied them. The final images of her unique documentary are those of her aged parents, happily splashing with their grandson in Lucie's swimming pool. Lucille smooths Desi's wet hair. They laugh, sing, and paddle around. Their plump little grandson bangs the water like a bongo drummer. On the sound track can be heard the old lyrics from I Love Lucy: "I love Lucy and she loves me. / We're as happy as we can be . . . / Lucy kisses like no one can. / She's my missus and I'm her man." The film becomes a marriage movie, a TV movie, a real-life movie, and a documentary—but no answer to the question "Why couldn't they stay married?"

As the 1950s and 1960s unfolded, the TV marital sitcom continued to be dominant. There were many examples, such as Green Acres, a "class" marriage with him (Eddie Albert) a farmer type and her (Eva Gabor) a woman dripping diamonds and feathers; and *The Dick Van Dyke Show.* Based on the *I Love Lucy* model, Van Dyke worked as a comedy writer in show business, and his wife, Laura (Mary Tyler Moore), wanted to be a part of his working life. *The Dick Van Dyke Show* was a cleverly constructed variation on *Lucy,* set 50 percent inside a typical at-home sitcom marriage and 50 percent inside the world of writing jokes for an egomaniacal comic. It was a smart format that offered viewers two different kinds of entertainment. (*The Dick Van Dyke Show* was different from *I Love Lucy* in that, although Ricky worked in show biz, the balance was always toward Lucy's half of the show. Any episode that moved her out of the house and into Ricky's world was still essentially about her.)

Meanwhile, as TV presented perfect marriages on a week-by-week basis, the subject became an irrelevant topic for movies, especially in an era in which movies were male-dominated. It would be years before marriage would make a comeback in the movie house. By making itself socially relevant, grounded in topicality, the marriage movie had made itself obsolete in the era of the TV sitcom—and in the new reality. Throughout the 1970s and 1980s, movies polarized into either studio product or the emerging, more independent movie. Films began to be more and more about men, with fewer great female stars and fewer roles for the ones that existed. By the mid-1980s, newspaper and magazine articles were lamenting the paucity of good roles for actresses, and this meant fewer and fewer marriage movies were going to be made. A general reduction in audience interest in the topic also caused the decline. Who needed to say "I do" with the new morality? And who needed to say "I don't" if they hadn't promised "I do"? *Everything* changed.

PART THREE
THE MODERN ERA

In his sister's documentary about their parents, Desi Arnaz Jr. defined the purpose of married life in the 1940s and 1950s. "Keeping secrets," he said, was the code of the proper American marriage. "People pretended things were okay." By the mid-1960s, however, "keeping secrets" was becoming less and less necessary. People began to live their secrets openly. The Sexual Revolution came along, with the pill to prevent unwanted pregnancies. There was a new attitude toward divorce and marital fidelity. Couples began living together without being married, even having children if they wished. Money issues diminished—easy credit was available for the wife who wanted that fur coat and all that new furniture *right now*. In-laws were having their own open secrets, and nobody had to live with them anymore anyway. In such a world—which was also the world of TV marriage—was there any role for the marriage movie? As I had tracked it historically, it had first needed to find a definition for itself (couples, etc.), then a purpose (showing the problems of marriage), and then a further purpose outside itself to remain relevant (its "situation"). Now what?

The social changes affecting the marriage format and the competition from TV were not the only challenges movies faced. In the mid-1950s and onward, the motion-picture business in America had also begun to change. These changes have already been mentioned: the studio system collapsed, to be replaced by a more international business ultimately controlled by large conglomerates; stars defected or were fired from their home studios; television became popular and prevalent, with many kinds of news programs, events, and genres; more foreign films were imported. Everything was different, and the number of people who went regularly to the movies decreased greatly, which meant fewer and fewer films being made. In the new, tighter market, with more competition from other sources, any type of movie had to have a wide appeal. This combination of a new social climate with the new moviemaking and marketing challenges inevitably made marriage uninteresting as a topic for a movie story. The issues of marriage seemed not only dated, dull, or possibly even quaint, but somehow irrelevant. Nobody needed any help with its former "secrets." Slowly but definitely, from 1960 to 2000, the marriage movie settled into a small rut, with only a few interesting innovations. It struggled to find its purpose more than it ever had, and more than ever before its purpose was directly defined by current social situations.

Doris Day and Rock Hudson were one of Hollywood's
best onscreen couples. They played married impeccably
in *Send Me No Flowers*, perfectly capturing an
argument . . .

As the 1960s began, audiences could—and did—still go out to traditional
stylish comedies about marriage. Two popular Doris Day vehicles illustrate
the point: *The Thrill of It All* (1963) and *Send Me No Flowers* (1965). In the
former, Day is the wife of James Garner, who becomes a neglected husband
when she stumbles into a big-time career as a television ad woman. In the latter, the husband is Rock Hudson, a hopeless hypochondriac. Convinced he's
dying, he enlists the help of a lecherous friend (Tony Randall) to select a suitable new husband for Day, but without her knowledge. The latter script is witty,
and Hudson and Day were a delightful screen couple, but neither of these
films breaks any new ground for marriage comedy. They *are* topical (wife working and wife flirting with an infidelity pimped by her husband), but they only
seem rakish; they really aren't. Instead, they follow the familiar formula: induce
problems and then solve them, remembering to show audiences plenty of wardrobe changes, well-appointed homes, and consumer goods along the way.

... and perfectly depicting the make-up scene to follow, realistically depicted with hair curlers.

In the second half of the decade, these tired comedies continued to appear, but in smaller numbers: *Marriage on the Rocks* (1965), *That Funny Feeling* (1965), *Not with My Wife, You Don't!* (1966), *Buona Sera, Mrs. Campbell* (1968), *With Six You Get Eggroll* (1968), and others. There were also the usual melodramas about adultery (*The Sandpiper*, 1965; *Reflections in a Golden Eye*, 1967), some interesting horror-film variations (*Rosemary's Baby*, 1968, and *The Stepford Wives*, 1975), and an attempt to rework the old murder-your-spouse variation with comedy, as in *How to Murder Your Wife* (1965), in which Jack Lemmon marries Virna Lisi while drunk and spends the rest of the movie trying to kill her—until, of course, he falls in love with her. There were also prestigious "serious" marriage analyses based on Broadway dramas, such as *Who's Afraid of Virginia Woolf?* (1966), as well as the adaptation of successful Broadway comedies like *Barefoot in the Park* (1967), in which Robert Redford and Jane Fonda play newlyweds.

There were some minor harbingers of possible changes, pointing to the future, but still housed in the old formats: African-American marriages (*For Love of Ivy*, 1968); interracial marriages (*The Great White Hope*, 1970); the old Laurel and Hardy two-men-as-married-couple idea (*The Odd Couple*,

1968); the hint of feminist issues (*Penelope*, 1966, in which Natalie Wood, as a neglected wife, makes a statement by robbing her husband's bank). One comedy in particular linked itself to the changing morality regarding marriage: *A Guide for the Married Man* (1967). Robert Morse, always an appealing little-devil surrogate, tries to teach the faithfully married Walter Matthau to become a swinger by providing him with a series of lessons on how to get away with infidelity.

Of all the 1960s marriage movies that repeat a familiar pattern, the two best and most significant are *Divorce American Style* (1967) and *Yours, Mine and Ours* (1968). *Divorce American Style* is the updated version of movies like 1937's *Awful Truth*. A couple who basically love each other have a misunderstanding and get a divorce, so the rest of the movie can be spent enjoying the comedy of their misery as they grope their way back to each other. The movie shows the difference between the Americas of 1967 and 1937 in all ways: style, clothes, and mores. *The Awful Truth*, as has been pointed out, is not really a marriage movie; it's a romantic comedy that uses the divorce to unleash a new courtship period for two older, more sophisticated mates. The stars, Irene Dunne and Cary Grant, do not lead a domestic life and are never seen cohabiting in any sort of married tradition. They're all glamour, nightclubs, tuxedos, and fur-trimmed evening wraps. The stars of *Divorce American Style*, Debbie Reynolds and Dick Van Dyke, are married by suburban rules. Like couples in the first postwar marriage programmers, they live in a ranch-style home, have kids, conduct an ordinary set of social gatherings with others in their neighborhood, and are thoroughly domesticated. They eat breakfast in their kitchen, they put their cars in the garage, and they brush their teeth, put on their pajamas, and go to bed. After they divorce, they both try to date, but inevitably end up back together, confirming the pattern of "affirm, destroy, reconcile" that is traditional to the marriage-movie format.

What *Divorce American Style* has to offer that's fresh is a little peep at the new morality that's in play alongside the new credit-driven economy. It presents a story about the problem of increasing divorce.* The couple represent an old-fashioned boy and girl who married for love and who now face the upheaval of their original universe. There are new values out there, easy divorce being one of the most prevalent. Van Dyke has to learn that his wife will keep the house, the car, and most of the money, and he'll see his kids only on weekends. Reynolds has to learn to date, and most men will expect that to mean pay-

---

* According to Andrew J. Cherlin's book, *Marriage-Go-Round*, today nearly half of American marriages end up in the divorce court, which is even more than in liberal Sweden.

ing for dinner with sexual favors. She has to cope with loneliness and loss of self-confidence. One of the movie's main points is made when Van Dyke meets another divorced and penniless man (Jason Robards), who sets him up with his ex-wife (Jean Simmons) because if he can just marry her off, he can get out of his own alimony dilemma. (*Divorce American Style* is largely about the economics of alimony.) In the end, when Van Dyke sees Reynolds volunteer to be the victim of a hypnotist's act in a nightclub (it's the 1960s!), and he watches her sincere but free-spirited release of herself, giving everything she's got, he realizes how much he loves her and how crazy they've been to surrender to the new morality. It's déjà-vu Cecil B. DeMille, but with station wagons, patios, grocery stores . . . and alimony.

As I've stated, few movies present older people in a mature marriage. Proof that when such movies occur they are often better than usual (*Dodsworth, Mr. and Mrs. Bridge*), is the somewhat silly yet tenderly enacted *Yours, Mine and Ours*, starring Lucille Ball and Henry Fonda as a middle-aged couple who decide to marry in spite of their initial misgivings. Oh, they love each other all right; it's just that they have a problem: she already has eight children and he has ten. *Yours, Mine and Ours* gives Ball moments for displaying her comic genius and gives Fonda time to be the excellent actor he is without either one suffering. The movie lurches from typical Ball comedy (a false eyelash that goes astray in a nightclub scene) to a typical Fonda "important speech" (when he discusses sex with one of their teenaged boys and tells him to watch carefully what Ball is going through as she begins to experience birth pains: "This is the end result of all that"). Fonda and Ball are good together, despite seeming to come from two different movie universes. (They had been paired in *The Big Street* in 1942 to good effect.) The movie is an update on the old kids-will-kill-you-and-destroy-your-marriage ploy, but despite its flaws it was a box-office success. It plays honestly and credibly with an authentic presentation of daily marriage, life, and problems with kids, and it opened the door for the possibility of modern marriage movies to become more honest, more detailed—possibly even *duller*—to reflect reality.

By the end of the 1960s, marriage movies *did* overtly ask audiences to question the institution by using current social terms. One was a huge box-office and award-winning success, *Guess Who's Coming to Dinner* (1967); one was an independent feature directed by John Cassavetes, *Faces* (1968); and one ushered in a new sexual morality, *Bob & Carol & Ted & Alice* (1969). The first, well-embraced by moviegoers and awarded Oscar wins and nominations, juxtaposed a happily married upper-middle-class couple (embodied by the aging Spencer Tracy, in his final film, and Katharine Hepburn) alongside a new kind

The hippie-era movie marriage: *Bob & Carol & Ted & Alice*. (Eliot Gould, Natalie Wood, Robert Culp, Dyan Cannon). It's a group thing.

of couple (Katharine Houghton and Sidney Poitier). Since Houghton, playing the daughter of Hepburn and Tracy, is white, and Poitier is black, when the daughter shows up to present her parents with the man she wants to marry, their liberal ideals are put to the test. (But not too much: the future son-in-law is a famous doctor, and he's also Sidney Poitier.)

Faces frankly faces infidelities in various marriages with a new style of film-making that stressed honest emotion over easy solution.* Cassavetes called his type of filmmaking "actor's cinema," because he brought together his own actor friends and let them improvise before the camera. Working from the blueprint of his script, actors such as Gena Rowlands (Cassavetes's real-life wife) presented an in-your-face kind of realistic look at marital relationships. The actors were free to unleash any level of emotional intensity they could bring forward, and the result is not only an amazing demonstration of acting skill, but also a free-form telling of the marriage story, warts and all.

Bob & Carol & Ted & Alice was one of the most talked-about movies of 1969. Both Elliott Gould and Dyan Cannon were nominated for Best Supporting Actor and Actress Oscars for their performances, and the movie's hipster take on the values of middle-class marriage made it a daring, cool conversation topic at suburban cocktail parties. The script was loaded with hot lines of dia-logue that wrenched guilty giggles out of everyone before order was restored.

---

* The film was shot with a handheld 16mm camera and later blown up to 35mm.

("I want a better orgasm" resides right alongside "The gazpacho was amazing.") Gently but specifically poking fun at the "new" take on living taught by such California-based centers as the Esalen Institute, the movie presents an audience with two married couples: Bob and Carol . . . and Ted and Alice. One couple has already crossed the boundary from old-fashioned to clued-in (Cannon and Gould as Alice and Ted), but the other is only starting to learn the new lifestyle. The mantra for the new marriage is that what matters is "not what you think, but what you feel."

Bob & Carol & Ted & Alice is a key transition movie in the marriage format. It's slightly ahead of its time for the average moviegoer, but slightly behind the times re the morality that the younger college generation had already embraced. Changing partners, having orgies, learning to smoke dope, and doing what pleases you with the tennis pro became the topic of sly social humor. The movie says this is what's happening, but also says this is what's done by silly people who follow trends. In that regard, it presents the usual marriage trajectory for movies: say and do one thing, but suggest another. It also begins another tradition—that of *discussing* marriage in an ongoing dialogue. Where older movies moved toward a final scene in which one big spoken summary of wisdom is laid down for the audience about what the role of marriage is in the lives of a man and a woman—that is, in the lives of the ticket buyers—this movie shifts focus and does nothing *but* discuss . . . and discuss . . . and discuss. Discussion (and analysis) of what was once taken for granted begins to be one of the most important things about marriage in movies. Since we don't *have* to do it, let's debate it. In fact, analyzing it is pretty much the only reason to keep it around. Everything else about it that mattered—fidelity, companionship, family, an economic support system—is no longer necessary.

And so Bob and Carol and Ted and Alice "learn to open up" and *tell* each other everything they are thinking or feeling or wondering. They do the touchy-feely things, lots of group hugs, and generate tears and confessions. "I had an affair in San Francisco," Culp tells Wood, so they can just discuss an issue that would have once been the central crisis in a marriage movie. ("You're sharing something!" exclaims Wood happily in response, turning a potential disaster into a positive. She then promptly heads for the tennis pro to grab some sharing for herself.) The marriage story has become analysis and discussion. In this film story, freedom of choice and looser morality has led to paralysis, boredom, and selfishness. The Sexual Revolution for the older set is apparently mostly conversation that addresses experimenting in the field of sexual freedom.

In its day, *Bob & Carol & Ted & Alice* seemed racy, and it is intelligently satirical. Culp and Wood don't seem comfortable playing this type of modern screwball comedy, but Gould and the underrated Dyan Cannon are very good at it. Seen today, the movie seems to apply a European style of filmmaking to a very American attitude toward life. It's the boredom of Antonioni's jaded set of sophisticates presented in an upbeat tempo, and the heritage of Puritanism and the new definitions of marital responsibilities clash with each other. ("You've got the guilt anyway . . . don't waste it" is one line of advice.) In the end, the two couples go to Las Vegas, the American Temple of Sin, to party together. ("First we'll have an orgy and then we'll go see Tony Bennett.") For today's moviegoers, it's a long wait for a peep at an orgy (which never appears)—and they don't get to see Tony Bennett, either. As the movie ends, the lyrics of "What the world needs now is love, sweet love" provide an ironic counterpoint.

By the beginning of the 1970s and throughout that entire decade, marriage movies practically disappear. For one thing, movie audiences were growing younger and younger, moving toward the heaviest attendance coming from teenage boys, who presumably were the least viable market for a story about married life. For another, it was a decade of renaissance for young filmmakers who had been trained in colleges. They brought new ideas, new styles, new attitudes, and new problems to the screen, and they were mostly young issues—young *unmarried* issues. The 1970s were the historical bottom of the marriage movie pit. Researching lists of American films released, the hundred top box-office draws, and the decade's award winners turn up the fewest marriage movies ever made in America in a single decade. Of the sixty or so movies that even touch on marriage between 1969 and 1979, very few have remained significant. *The Way We Were* and *New York, New York* have already been discussed. In retrospect, we can see that the most significant other titles all have feminist messages.

A British film of 1964 laid the groundwork for the 1970s feminist marriage movies, which ask the question "What's in it for women in marriage?" *The Pumpkin Eater* was directed by Jack Clayton, starred Anne Bancroft, Peter Finch, and James Mason, and was written by Harold Pinter from a Penelope Mortimer novel. These heavy-duty credentials sent a serious message to the moviegoing public: if it's a marriage movie you want, prepare to step up and suffer. Bancroft plays the mother of eight children. She just can't stop marrying and she just can't stop giving birth. Her world goes awry when she finds out that her third husband (Finch) is unfaithful. *The Pumpkin Eater* is an intelligent film, but a grind, sending a message about the emotional confusion of traditional motherhood, marriage, fidelity, and the woman's lot in life as an alert to what lay ahead in the next two decades. Everyone—that is, everyone who went to see it—had full warning.

The 1969–1979 feminist marriage movies were not so much stories about marriage itself as they were about how marriage was not working for modern women. Such movies demonstrated how unfair marriage was to women, how it stunted their lives and creativity, blocking them from the successes they could otherwise have had, and how the men they married were fundamentally a bunch of selfish idiots.* In that sense, they are women's films. Some of them, such as *Alice Doesn't Live Here Anymore* (1974), don't present anyone living in a real "marriage" day by day, but most of them set up the status of marriage, and the couple undergoing it, with clarity. These feminist movies make a serious point, and they answer their own questions by saying a woman is better off alone than unhappily married, and that love doesn't have to be eliminated from an unmarried woman's life any more than a career should be eliminated from a married woman's.

The feminist marriage movies of the late 1960s and early 1970s are few but significant, and they carried a large impact in their day. They have subtle variations. For instance, *Petulia* (1968) is about a divorced man (George C. Scott) and his romance with an unhappily wed free spirit played by Julie Christie. *Kramer vs. Kramer* (1979) confronts the new issue head-on from the man's point of view. A feminist wife who needs her space (Meryl Streep) walks out on a hard-driving, up-and-coming executive (Dustin Hoffman), leaving him alone to care for their small son.† The presentation of women who want to be free is the raison d'être of these two films. Three other movies focus more exclusively on the female character and tell real stories about marriage: *The Happy Ending* (1969), *Diary of a Mad Housewife* (1970), and *An Unmarried Woman* (1978).

The Happy Ending is about an unfulfilled housewife (Jean Simmons, nominated for a Best Actress Oscar for the role) who is slowly sinking into alcoholism, sitting around by herself watching *Casablanca* on late-night television. The story of how she suddenly finds the courage to walk out on her husband (basically a nice guy) and return to college in an attempt to find the youth she lost is a woman's film with a detailed picture of married boredom and

---

* This in and of itself is not necessarily new. Blondie and Dagwood are only one example. The difference is on the basic focus and the attitude taken toward it.

† In the July 10, 2011, *New York Times Sunday Magazine*, Heather Havrilesky, a shrewd observer of the cultural scene, compared *Kramer vs. Kramer* to the current television sitcom *Happily Divorced*, starring Fran Drescher: "If you want to get a sense of how drastically the mood around divorce has shifted in American popular culture in the 30 years since *Kramer vs. Kramer*, spend a half hour with Fran Drescher's new TV Land sitcom *Happily Divorced* . . . These days, divorce doesn't sob and drink to excess; it dons a joyful Kabuki mask to obscure the anguish of marital bliss gone sour." *Happily Divorced* is about a wife who finds out her husband is gay, although after their divorce, they continue to cohabit for financial reasons while still trying to find new mates. The idea is based on Drescher's real-life experience.

how destructive it can be. *Diary of a Mad Housewife* shows Carrie Snodgress stuck inside a dull marriage to a fool of a husband and finding release in an affair with an equally dubious, self-centered man (Frank Langella). *An Unmarried Woman* shows how a woman (Jill Clayburgh in an excellent performance) copes when her husband walks out on her. Well written (and directed) by Paul Mazursky (who also did *Bob & Carol*), the movie's presentation of Clayburgh's bonding with her female friends is significant. As the women sit at lunch together, giggling and letting their hair down, they openly discuss their sex lives. These scenes are the forerunners of the latter-day *Sex and the City* scenes, but they're funnier, better written and acted, and carry more honesty.* *An Unmarried Woman* is a fitting end to the few marriage movies of the 1970s, and it helps explain why there were so few of them. Women moved on—and as moviegoers, they moved on, too. The films existed to explain what was happening to marriage in the culture, and they're couched in female terms because it was the women who were calling the shots, the women who were questioning the point and asking themselves if marriage was a fate they really wanted.

In 1973, one interesting film about how both a woman *and* a man could be blocked and live together without real fulfillment or communication was released. *Summer Wishes, Winter Dreams* is another of the rare films about a marriage between two older people—in this case, Joanne Woodward and Martin Balsam. They play a couple who've been married for over twenty years. Woodward is unhappy, estranged from her beloved son, always quarreling with her daughter, intimidated by her mother (Sylvia Sidney, in her last great role), and cold and unresponsive to her husband. "You don't have enough to occupy your brain," Sidney tells her. Woodward lives in the past, dreaming of her childhood, of a youthful crush she had on a farmhand who was killed in World War II. When her mother unexpectedly drops dead of a heart attack while watching an Ingmar Bergman movie (someone had a sense of humor!), Woodward goes into a tailspin. Her daughter tries to shake her mother out of the past: "It's all gone . . . your childhood, the hired hand, your plans for the future, Grandma and Grandpa . . . It can't come back with a taste of raspberry jam with the label 1940 on it." To help her and, he hopes, distract her, Balsam takes Woodward on a trip to Europe.

As the couple make the obligatory visits to monuments and shops, Balsam asks Woodward the familiar marriage-movie question: "*Why* did you marry me?" He demands an answer, but never gets one. Ultimately, they visit the site

---

* Indeed, the commonly accepted, oft-repeated view of *Sex and the City* is that it's not about women at all, but "gay men with vaginas."

of his World War II service during the siege of Bastogne. During his emotional meltdown there (as he tells her of the horror of combat), a kind of connection occurs between them. Later she tells him she knows she's undemonstrative, but it's not because she's *really* cold—but they then fall back into playing their familiar roles of concerned husband and neurotic wife. The movie ends, however, on a small, hopeful note: "When we get home," she says, "I'd like to move into a smaller apartment." For her, as is always true for a woman in a woman's film, the home is everything. Her willingness to move is a symbol of her possibly being able to let go of the past. The movie tries hard to be European and sophisticated, and falls short, ending up rather muddled and clichéd; nevertheless, it remains one of the few honest portraits in its time of the mystery of a decades-long marriage between two people who have never really communicated with each other.

During this period, the marriage film struggled to find fresh takes on old ideas. The most common ploy was a simple update that reversed former attitudes. An example of the shift that held on to the original format is provided by comparing 1952's *The Four Poster*, starring Rex Harrison and Lilli Palmer, and 1978's *Same Time, Next Year*, with Alan Alda and Ellen Burstyn. *The Four Poster* is based on a successful stage play by Jan de Hartog (which later was translated into the hit musical *I Do! I Do!*). It's the story of a marriage, decade by decade, issue by issue, as a couple experience bliss, survive infidelity and aging, etc.* *Same Time, Next Year*, on the other hand, is the story of an adultery. Two married people meet each other for one weekend per year over a twenty-six-year time frame. The structural idea is the same, but where Harrison and Palmer faced changes in themselves as they aged, Alda and Burstyn face changes in America: loosening morality, hippiedom, and drugs. The shift is away from a couple and their personal problems over to a couple and their social situation—and, of course, from a legally married couple to an adulterous couple as protagonists.

The 1980s seemed to restore some interest in the subject of marriage, but without generating any real changes. During that decade, there were quite a few comedies about marriage: *Overboard* (1987), *The Four Seasons* (1981), *The Incredible Shrinking Woman* (1981), *Ruthless People* (1986), *She's Having a Baby* (1988), *Seems Like Old Times* (1980), etc. They were a form of retreat, hoping to regenerate a romantic context for marriage or rework old themes

---

* The transitions in time are marked by wonderful animated UPA cartoons, which are valued by animation historians.

A reliable pattern for a movie story about marriage appears in *The Four Poster*. Rex Harrison and Lili Palmer (wed in real life at the time) enact a marriage in scenes that move forward through time, from wedding-night innocence . . .

about divorce, murder, money, and the battle of the sexes. *Irreconcilable Differences* (1984) tarts up the old format of the divorce movie by presenting the story of the love affair, courtship, marriage, and ultimate collapse of the relationship of Shelley Long and Ryan O'Neal as a story being told by their ten-year-old daughter (Drew Barrymore). The twist? *She* is suing *them* for divorce.

Comedy seemed to be the major draw for marriage during these years, particularly since it maintained the staple that had been in place since the days of DeMille: the opportunity to present beautiful kitchens and bathrooms. There were fewer melodramas made, and most did not present a portrait of the daily life of marriage in any new way.* *Falling in Love* (1984) was an American version of the British *Brief Encounter*, starring Meryl Streep and Robert De Niro as two married commuters.† *Shoot the Moon* (1982) told the story of how a divorce affected the emotional lives of a couple (Diane Keaton and Albert Finney) and their children. *Honeysuckle Rose* (also 1980) was yet another ver-

---

* *On Golden Pond* (1981), an adaptation of a successful play, found Oscars and box-office gold largely due to its star casting of Katharine Hepburn, Henry Fonda, and Jane Fonda. Ostensibly a movie about a long and loving marriage, it was more a story about the reconciliation of a harsh parent and a rebellious daughter.
† In keeping with the new morality, Streep and De Niro very definitely have an affair, unlike the oblique did-they-or-didn't-they? presentation of *Brief Encounter*.

. . . to sophistication across a variety of troubles and temptations, through boredom and disappointment, to the ultimate stability and appreciation.

sion of the triangular infidelity story, this one with a country-music setting, with Willie Nelson, Amy Irving, and Dyan Cannon.

A little-known but touching film, *Twice in a Lifetime* (1985), put a new twist on the adultery theme. The movie is realistic, with no neatly wrapped-up happy ending. Gene Hackman plays a middle-aged man who falls in love with a younger woman (Ann-Margret). For once, the terrible pain and anger that all the participants must endure as a result (including Hackman's wife, played by Ellen Burstyn, and daughter, Amy Madigan) is not simplified or even settled. The story is an old one, but the approach (including superb acting) is original and the ending unpredictable.

Another exceptionally honest portrait of marriage was *Heartburn* (1986), the screen adaptation of Nora Ephron's best seller about a sophisticated couple (disguised versions of herself and her former husband, Carl Bernstein). The marriage looks from the outside like the ideal mating of brains, talent, and wit—Meryl Streep and Jack Nicholson—as they host fabulous dinner parties in their chic Washington digs. Everything goes to pieces when the wife discovers her husband is being unfaithful to her while she's pregnant. ("If you want monogamy, marry a swan," her dad tells her.)

Heartburn is the updated story of marriage from the woman's point of view. It presents the wife's side, but without being a screed against the husband. ("Marriage doesn't work," she says. "You know what does? Divorce.") The movie is intelligent, human, and genuinely funny, and it doesn't hurt that its married couple are played by Streep and Nicholson in their prime. Looking at *Heartburn*, it's easy to see how movies that want to tell stories about marriage have changed. During the heyday of the studio system, marriage was dramatized. Its daily world was shaped into an arc of events that built from ordinary and recognizable, into an emerging set of problems, toward a crisis and some final reconciliation. Marriage was *the* social contract of those years, and although in real life it might be a bit dull and dramaless, on screen it had to pop—it mattered too much not to be made dramatic. By the time of *Heartburn*, couples could marry or not marry, and the importance of marriage, though not eliminated, was nevertheless greatly reduced. Thus *Heartburn*'s story has no single high point, no true crisis. It moves from a random wedding (where the couple meet) to courtship (in a bar, kissing under a marquee for a theater that's showing *Mephisto*, surely a bad omen), to their own wedding, and then dinner after dinner after dinner. Marriage becomes about being with other couples, having babies (two), and consuming excellent food.

Once marriage movies took place in nightclubs, country estates, or around dinner tables (the servants were in the kitchen). If the couple weren't that wealthy, they were in their living room or bedroom in a little cottage, and if poor, perhaps in their tiny cramped apartment; but the new movies suddenly located almost everything about married life in a gloriously updated kitchen. It's ironic to think that just about the time people started eating out in restaurants because both the husband and wife worked, movies about the husband and wife started living in kitchens. And not just any kind of kitchen: giant kitchens; stainless-steel kitchens; granite-topped kitchens, with yards of spice racks, double and triple sinks, wine coolers, backsplashes, and decorating schemes to die for. (Contractors reported that clients often asked them to re-create movie kitchens, particularly those of Diane Keaton in 1991's *Father of the Bride* remake and 2003's *Something's Gotta Give*.) In the old films, if the people were in kitchens, they were stirring pots on top of a stove or opening the oven to pull out a turkey to baste.* In these new movies, people were chopping things—

---

* Even Jane had her jungle kitchen. In *Tarzan Escapes* (1936), she proudly tells a visitor, "I designed the kitchen myself."

The very modern marriage movie *Heartburn* puts the couple (Jack Nicholson and Meryl Streep) into a sophisticated group that talks incessantly about the status of their relationships.

chopping, chopping, chopping, with expensive German knives. The work of the kitchen was yuppified and given a vague anger.* Since women don't have to cook, they cook because they have a superb palate, and because inside their career-driven hearts is the soul of a nurturer. (She used to nurture—now she cooks fancy dishes on the weekend.) Couples who both work have chic, tony jobs. They gossip and exchange pleasantries and information around tables laden with excellent food in restaurants and homes, and on picnics. Marriage continues its modern trend of being about discussion, if happy, and debate, if unhappy. Since nobody has to be married to meet social standards, how could it be otherwise? The marriage movie had to become a slow-moving conversation, a set of observations about events that are happening (largely offscreen) in an undramatic way. *Heartburn* presents Meryl Streep's debate with herself about why she shouldn't marry (because it didn't work for her the first time, and it never worked for her parents), why she is so terribly happy after she does it again (especially when she becomes a mother, which she loves), why she should not stay with her husband after discovering his infidelity (his "I'm going

---

* A cartoon in the *New Yorker* by P. C. Vey suggested another purpose: as a husband reaches for his wife, who's occupied at the stove, she's saying, "Not now. I'm cooking to avoid intimacy."

shopping for socks" excursions), why she should go back to him (he comes to get her and bring her back), and ultimately why she should leave him for the final time. (He's unfaithful and always will be.) *Heartburn* rolls out, rather like marriage itself, in a series of daily chores—shopping, cooking, cleaning—until the light bulb goes on in Streep's head. The shape of the marriage story is no longer a dramatic arc.

Heartburn and *Twice in a Lifetime* both give the viewer the feeling that he or she is watching a real marriage unfold. Little touches, little insights, little details reveal to any married person what is recognized as the day-to-day of married life. *Heartburn* is witty and amusing, but it contains great anger and pain. *Twice in a Lifetime* has compassion, deep regret, and the sense of loss that accompanies any kind of divorce action. These two movies prove that the audience for the marriage story existed, and the people who could write intelligently about marriage still were out there. Perhaps they stand out of the period 1970–1990 as two unusually solid marriage movies for one simple reason: both are the stories of real people's marriages and divorces: *Heartburn* was Nora Ephron's, and *Twice in a Lifetime* was that of Bud Yorkin, its director.

Two other movies set inside marriages in the 1980s found their "modern" twists: *Mr. Mom* (1983) and *Married to the Mob* (1988). The former has a sitcom setup. When the husband and father of the family (Michael Keaton) gets fired, the wife and mother (Teri Garr) has to go out and earn the living, which she turns out to be super-good at. Dad has to stay home and learn how hard it is to run a household. The latter film follows the old idea of using the word "married" in the title in a clever way that skirts the issue, but it presents no real sense of married life. Rather, it's a comedy in which the wife of a hit man has to escape the clutches of the mob after his assassination.

None of these films inspired new waves of marriage movies, although there were always movies that found ways to incorporate marriage into a larger context in a clever way. *Prizzi's Honor* (1985) is a hilarious and terrifying gangster film grounded in the problems marriage can bring into your life—especially if you're a hit man and you marry a hit woman. One movie about marriage in the 1980s, however, generated great debates among moviegoers: *Fatal Attraction* (1987). It was a riff on the adultery movie, and old-fashioned in that sense, but as a riff it was really only a riff. Michael Douglas has a one-night stand (in a freight elevator, riding up to her loft) with a pickup (Glenn Close). He goes home happy—and has to wake up scared. (*Fatal Attraction* was really a ripoff of Clint Eastwood's 1971 directorial debut, *Play Misty for Me*. The main difference was that Eastwood's character, menaced by former girlfriend Jessica Walter, is not a married man.)

The 1990s just kept following the old paths, with an occasional hit that involved marriage, but with an astonishingly small list of major movies on the subject. There were the usual comedies, making an attempt at being romantic: *Honeymoon in Vegas* (1998) and *So I Married an Axe Murderer* (1993). Men continued to either kill their wives or try to kill them, mostly for money: *A Perfect Murder* (1998), *Reversal of Fortune* (1990), and *A Shock to the System* (1990). Wives became alcoholics and ruined everything (*When a Man Loves a Woman*, 1994), and in-laws disapproved of the choice in mate, spoiling things (*Only You*, 1994). Husbands died and had to be reached through mediums (*Ghost*, 1990). Women still have to enlist the aid of some stranger to pretend to be their husband when they go home to their families (*A Walk in the Clouds*, 1995); women still take revenge on their exes (*The First Wives Club*, 1996); and old marriage movies start being remade: *Father of the Bride* (1991); *The Preacher's Wife* (1996).* Real-life stories are presented as cautionary tales (*What's Love Got to Do with It*, 1993). All-black casts appear in *Waiting to Exhale* (1995) and *How Stella Got Her Groove Back* (1998). *Corrina, Corrina* (1994) focuses on an interracial couple.

As had always been true, marriages also pop up with little yoohoos of honesty in movies that are technically about something else. The darkly violent 1996 comedy by the Coen brothers, *Fargo*, puts onscreen one of the best movie marriages. The lumberingly pregnant Marge Gunderson (Frances McDormand) and her husband, Norm (John Carroll Lynch), who paints duck decoys, hoping one will be chosen by the postal department for reproduction on a stamp, are an authentic example of an everyday married couple. Marge is a sheriff, and she gets her man. Meanwhile, her husband stays at home painting, but is always thinking of her, whether he's giving her frozen car "a jump" on a cold morning, bringing her junk food for lunch, or just snuggling up to her in bed. Marge and Norm ring true. As the gay couple in *The Birdcage* (1996), Nathan Lane and Robin Williams are the perfect example of two married prima donnas who drive each other crazy, but who'd die for each other should it become necessary—die onstage, perhaps, under a spotlight, wearing spangles, but die for sure. Lane and Williams are very married even though the legal system said they couldn't be.

During these decades of decline—years that seemed to be transitional but were apparently transitioning to nowhere—television soldiered on as the

---

* These films were originally *Father of the Bride* (1950) and *The Bishop's Wife* (1947). In 1986, *Mr. Blandings Builds His Dream House* (1948) also had been successfully remade as *The Money Pit.*

show-biz world of married folks who had kids, in-laws, neighbors, and money issues. Throughout the 1970s, there were homespun family shows like *Happy Days*, *The Partridge Family*, *Family Ties*, and *Little House on the Prairie*. There were mystery shows with charming married couples, bringing back the glamorous world of the Nick and Nora Charles (*Hart to Hart*, *McMillan & Wife*). There were prime-time soap operas with glamorous settings and all kinds of up-to-date marital issues (*Dallas*, *Falcon Crest*, *Dynasty*). There was the groundbreaking *All in the Family*, which attacked political issues with comedy, as did its spinoffs *The Jeffersons* and the innovative *Maude*. Television paraded marital shows, making them more and more honest in some way: *Roseanne* (about a lower-middle-class couple), *The Cosby Show* (an upper-middle-class black couple), *Mad About You* (yuppies without kids), *Married with Children*, *Growing Pains*, and others, moving on toward *Everybody Loves Raymond*, *Evening Shade*, *Dharma and Greg*, *Kelly Kelly*, and, of course, *The Simpsons*.

Soon enough, however, even the marriages on TV slowed down; by the year 2000, there was little left. *According to Jim* and *Malcolm in the Middle* kept up the sitcom tradition. Brilliantly written and acted hour-long dramas such as *The Sopranos* and *Mad Men* appeared, and both shows contained significant portraits of marriage within their respective arenas (the Mafia and 1960s Madison Avenue advertising).* Yet neither show focused on *marriage* as its dominant topic, although hour-long drama *did* bring one of the finest shows ever presented on marriage: *Friday Night Lights*.

Writing about the high quality of the underrated *Friday Night Lights* in the *New York Times Sunday Magazine*, Heather Havrilesky perfectly described the show's magic: "The real message of *Friday Night Lights* is a message about the joy of little things: the awkward thrills of a first kiss; the strange blessing of an unexpected rainstorm on a lonely walk home from a rough football practice; the startling surge of nostalgia incited by the illumination of football-stadium lights just as the autumn sun is setting; the rush of gratitude, in an otherwise mundane moment, that comes from realizing that this (admittedly flawed) human being that you're squabbling with intends to have your back for the rest of your life." In her last example, she's referring to the core relationship of the series, the marriage of Coach Eric Taylor (Kyle Chandler) and his "hot coach's wife," Tami (Connie Britton). It's possible that there's never been a more honest and natural marriage portrayed in film or television.

When *Friday Night Lights* opens up on its first episode, the local radio sportscaster blares out, "Sit down and shut up, it's game time, people!" It's

---

* *Mad Men* turned back the clock to depict a 1960s marriage from a 2000 point of view.

early on a Monday morning. The coach is watching game tapes and field-ing reporters; his wife is reading house-sale ads and dreaming of his-and-hers closets; and their teenage daughter, Julie, is reading *Moby-Dick* and rebuffing guys who want to date her. They are living in the small town of Dillon, Texas, where winning in football is the definition of success over failure. The Taylors are from the get-go defined as *real*.

They have money problems. They struggle with their rebellious teenage daughter, cope with the unexpected birth of a new child, survive a live-in visit from her sister, and always endure the challenges of Dillon, Texas, and the pressures of football. They have each other. He's tight-lipped, a man of few words. She's communicative, outwardly social, but in her way as self-contained as he is. She's loving, but so is he. He's tough, but so is she. He stands up for his football code of behavior, and she, all southern charm and sex appeal, knows how to "stand up," too. She breezes into the Booster Club meeting to let the old boys know she's on to their game ("Hi, y'all!"). Both are very good at their highly stressful, always precarious jobs (she's a high-school guidance counselor and sometime principal). The Taylor marriage is a wedding between two strong and independent individuals who know what is expected of them by the town, by their jobs, and by each other. While he endures endless and useless downtown quarterbacking and the constant threat that he'll lose his job if the Dillon Panthers don't win State, she makes two hundred Rice Krispies treats (with M&M's) and prepares a football party for over one hundred people with two days' notice. They smooch on the couch, obviously enjoying a full and rewarding sex life, and navigate their too-small house as best they can. ("Room in the bathroom has saved more marriages than Oprah and Dr. Phil combined," a real-estate agent solemnly informs Tami.) The Taylors are under-paid and overworked, so they do what real couples do—they quarrel a lot. The Taylors cope and they juggle and they stay focused, but they're not afraid to let each other have it. Their quarrels are the greatest validation of the honesty of their relationship, because what comes out is an endless river of daily woe every married person in the audience recognizes. He forgot to do this, and she forgot to do that. He wonders where his clean socks are, and she already told him. She's trying to talk to him about something important; he's not listening. One of the gems of this realistic presentation is a moment when they fight over garbage cans. He drives up just as she's struggling to get them out to the curb for pickup, and she gets on him about it. In a huff, he insists on taking over and doing it himself, but she's not having that: it's *her* issue of complaint, and she's going to see it through. They grapple for control over moving the cans until someone connected with football suddenly drives up and needs the coach's

One of the most honest marriages seen in either movies or television is
that of the five-year series *Friday Night Lights*, in which Kyle Chandler
and Connie Britton play a Texas high-school football coach and his wife.

attention. He immediately drops the can he's commandeered and walks away,
leaving her right back where she started. (All audiences know that one of a real
marriage's biggest issues is who's gonna take out the garbage.)

When the quarreling turns serious, as it often does, they are quieter and
more careful with each other. They know negotiation is possible, but that compromise will be necessary. Who will come out with the short stick, because
neither of them is really going anywhere else? ("You know your father and
I love each other very much, don't you?" Tami asks their daughter during a
particularly difficult crisis. In other words, she says, it may look as if this latest
problem is hopeless, but they *will* work it out.) They are committed. "I'm sorry
that you're mad at me," he says. "I'm not sure that counts as an apology," she
replies. Things stay touchy between them for periods of time, but he's a man
who knows he doesn't understand women and never will, and he's also a man
who knows he's got a fabulous wife and he loves her. He's learned the basic
rule of marital survival: "I was wrong," he tells her. "Of course you were," she
replies. "Friends?" he asks, and they kiss. And that is the answer to why their
TV marriage is so honest: they are friends. They *will* survive, and he knows to
apologize because she's the one who most commonly gives in. (And yet, she's
no doormat. Shortly after the birth of their new baby, when he's eager for sex
and all she wants is a good night's sleep, she resists his advances and tells him
flat-out, "You know what, honey? I don't want to.")

When Tami is invited to become dean of admissions at a Pennsylvania college, she carefully reminds her husband that she's been a coach's wife for eighteen years. It's her turn now. When school representatives come to their house to offer him a new job with all the support he deserves, she lets them in, again with her cheerful "Hi, y'all!," but as she passes her husband in the hall, she quietly says only two words: "Eighteen years." (He doesn't take the offer. When the series ends, they have relocated, starting new jobs with a new life—as always, together.)

The Taylors' marriage plays out with ups and downs, highs and lows, crises and triumphs, all presented with a kind of quiet honesty and impeccably acted by Chandler and Britton and a superb supporting cast. The marriage in *Friday Night Lights* has time to develop, played out over five seasons in multiple episodes, which helps its credibility, but its bottom line is in the ability to present life as it is actually lived by ordinary people in a small Texas town. *Friday Night Lights* is not really a show about football. It's a show about how marriage works when it actually does work.

In all the movies about marriage I watched, I observed a constant attempt to find the best strategy to tell what was, as I said in the beginning, a story that the audience already knew. Satirize it, romanticize it, criticize it, idolize it. Pretend the couple weren't really married. Tell the story in flashbacks. Reverse the roles so the woman was smarter, richer, higher ranked than the man. Make it really about divorce, etc., etc., etc. These constant strategies made it necessary to shape a marriage story into something constructed, plotted, designed. When I thought about all the marriages I viewed in movies—and television, too—the *Friday Night Lights* marriage stood out for its lack of such strategies. Over the five years the show was on the air, there was no "strategy" for their marital story: no clever plot twists, no dream episodes, no other woman or man, no cheap theatrics or misunderstandings. The "big seven" problems that I could clearly identify in marriage movies didn't swamp the Taylors or interfere with their daily lives. The Taylors were not rich and had to plan their budgets, but they both had jobs, a nice home adequate to their needs, and enough money to feed the football team steaks if it was necessary. The thought of infidelity was ludicrous; they were totally committed to each other. The one time a colleague just up and kissed her, Tami Taylor was deeply shocked, and really embarrassed by his lack of judgment. The couple has problems with their daughter of the sort all parents face, and they coped with Tami's unexpected pregnancy, but neither children nor in-laws undid them. (A sister overstayed her visit, but that got sorted out.) Neither Coach nor Tami became an alcoholic, and they didn't try to kill each other. (They just yelled a lot.) The Taylor marriage was a marriage not governed by genre rules or assaulted by plot development.

Friday Night Lights was a one-hour continuous series on nighttime television about the everyday lives of real people. Yet it wasn't a soap opera. Soap operas (god bless 'em) have drahhh-ma. *Friday Night Lights* had emotional truth, ladled out a drop at a time so viewers could recognize it, absorb it, and be nourished by it. The marriage of the Taylors was the driving force, but when the series ended, five new potential relationships between a man and a woman sat unresolved, each with the possibility of becoming an honest story about marriage. One couple *was* married: the somewhat dim-witted and hapless newlyweds with a small baby who were expecting twins. The other four couples were young and unwed, with stories that had not grown out of romantic comedy. The Taylors' young daughter and her high-school boyfriend had reunited, living together in Chicago, with plans to wed. The town's James Deanish, tender-hearted sex symbol was staying behind to wait while the girl who truly loves him went out into the world to prove to herself that she's not the trailer trash she was born to be. The high-school-senior football hero was at fall practice while the girl he loves, already graduated, has gone to work in Dallas. The sadly neglected young girl who found love with a rancher's son says goodbye to him at the bus station when he leaves for military service. If *Friday Night Lights* had continued, each of these relationships could have played out honestly, week by week, with no need to hold the interest of viewers through jumped-up strategies that could later be easily resolved. The Taylors had set the tone, their marriage creating a trickle-down effect, their honesty dripping over onto the rest of the story and characters. Viewers accept that, for whatever inexplicable reasons, two people have been drawn together and will try to make a life together if they can.*

Taken all together, most of the hit TV shows of the later decades were less and less about marriage.† It was big news when a fresh new show, still a variation of the half-hour sitcom, appeared in 2009. *Modern Family* tightly linked three families: one traditional, with husband, wife, kids, and house; one with a

---

* The key character of the football star who became a paraplegic had already been completed with his marriage to the mother of his little son. The couple are happy; he's a devoted father; and they live in New York, where he is successfully employed. Interestingly, two other key characters from the series aren't included in the final wrap-up of relationships: the smartest boy and the prettiest girl. These two have left their small hometown to attend college at Rice and Vanderbilt, respectively. They are out of the marriage mix, a somewhat sinister and subtle class distinction.

† In 2010, one of the strangest shows about marriage ever conceived was launched by Jerry Seinfeld: *The Marriage Ref*, in which a panel of celebrities listens to the fights of real-life married couples and then vote on who's right. Seinfeld commented, "All marriages are based on a sitcom premise: what if you and I tried to stay together for the rest of our lives? . . . The joke of marriage is that you can't leave."

gay male couple who adopt an Asian daughter; and the last with an older man, his sexy young Colombian wife, and her son from an earlier marriage. When, at the end of the first episode, the three families turn out to be one larger "modern" family, it was a wonderful surprise—and a big hit. New hit TV shows were often about family dynamics, raising children, the issues teenagers face, and romance and solving mysteries, but sitcoms that focused on marriage alone had become rare. Even the early prototypes, *The Donna Reed Show* and *Father Knows Best*, were family dramas, because TV had the time to develop multiple characters. "Marriage" became "family." (A situation comedy was going to run for years and have between twenty to twenty-four episodes a season. To find enough plots for only two people—a husband and wife—was difficult. Adding on children, relatives, co-workers, and neighbors opened up the plot possibilities for harried sitcom writers.)

Television's episodic quality, however, makes it ideal for developing marriage stories played out over time, set inside a larger narrative context. Such shows as *The Sopranos, Mad Men,* and *Homeland* (among others) offer viewers a slow revelation of the complicated power dynamics that shift back and forth between two married people. There's time to incorporate small but significant marital moments that provide big insights: the Sopranos in their kitchen, Carmela repeatedly offering her man endless choices of food out of her well-stocked refrigerator; Betty Draper, alone at night in *her* kitchen, drinking white wine, smoking, waiting for her husband to come home; the uneasy wife of an Iraq War vet, nervously moving around the kitchen, trying to make conversation with her unresponsive, brooding mate.

The Danish series *Borgen* (the popular nickname for Denmark's parliamentary building) appeared in 2010, just as Hollywood had begun to produce more and more false portraits of marriage in a pseudo-comic mold: *Date Night,* in which a couple go on the town and have exciting "adventures" that reunite them; *Hall Pass,* where new strategies for pepping up dull unions include letting the husbands feel free to have affairs; *It's Complicated,* with a titillating "rethinking" between a divorced couple; and *Hope Springs,* in which a bored husband and wife go for supposedly hilarious marriage counseling. *Borgen,* by contrast, presents an intelligent, thoughtful, and engrossing version of marriage. It's beautifully acted and written, sobering in its clarity about the difficulties of two people staying together when they move far apart in the ordinary daily sharing that makes a marriage work. A happily married career politician (Sidse Babett Knudsen) is elected to the office of Danish prime minister. She lives with her husband (Mikael Birkkjaer) and their two children in a charming cottage surrounded by flowers. The couple pledge to each other that, despite her new high-powered position, they will maintain "a normal family life." No matter what is happening in Denmark, Mom will get home in time for dinner and put the kids to bed. Nothing will really change, because she has always worked, the children understand the situation, and her husband (a professor) has a flexible schedule.

This family's "normalcy" doesn't make it through the first season. *Borgen* lays it down cold. Week after week, it shows how things in a marriage can slowly, but irrevocably, change. The wife is caught between two power structures: the Danish government and the average marriage. In the first, she is allegedly the designated leader with the ability to wield power. In the second, she is allegedly in a world of equality in which she and her husband will share decisions. Both structures are, in reality, deceptive. She finds that as prime minister she is forced to fight for her implied power. This means becoming tougher, ruthlessly seizing hold, and giving full attention to all aspects of her job. She begins an inevitable wheeling and dealing, making the hard decisions she has to make, betraying old friends and threatening new ones. She accepts the subtle corruption required to *own* her position. As a viewer watches—and it's like watching a beautiful statue crumble to dust—she becomes a different person. Meanwhile, as her grip on politics sharpens and strengthens, her marriage disintegrates. The person who is in the home on a regular basis—formerly herself, now her husband—is actually a person with daily power. Since she arrives home too late for dinner, the kids are already in bed, she's distracted and certainly too tired for sex, so her husband begins to make all the key decisions. The children turn increasingly to him, and he, lonely and unhappy, turns to another woman. The Danish prime minister might as well be Ann Carver or Mildred Pierce.

Looking back on 1960–2000, four decades of movies, reveals how little there was on the subject of marriage since the institution itself had become increasingly socially irrelevant. For the forty years of 1970 to 2010, the audience seemed not to need marriage in the movies at all, except where some new twist might be brought to bear, however briefly. There are four things to be learned; two are traditional, and two are new. The two traditional lessons are:

1. Television carried on, becoming more and more the place where those who wanted to understand marriage went to learn about it, whether comic (*All in the Family*), ethnic (*The Jeffersons*), realistic (*Roseanne*), or cautionary (*The Sopranos, Mad Men*).

2. Movies continued to use marriage, although rarely, to tell about cutting issues ("situations"), with an increasing emphasis on divorce

(*Divorce American Style*), feminism (*Diary of a Mad Housewife*), and shifting morality (*Bob & Carol & Ted & Alice*).

The two new things that appeared, both fairly unsettling, are:

1. Marriage movies went nuclear. The battle of the sexes armed itself, and married couples literally began shooting: *The War of the Roses* (1989), *Mr. and Mrs. Smith* (2005).

2. Everyone lost interest in the events of married life, eliminating its reflective purpose for audiences. Hollywood kept only the ritual, making movie after movie about weddings. Since no one felt the need for marriage—you could have sex, children, and cohabitation without it— films elevated the event and made it the main point: the Big Wedding in which you could have the decorations, the food, the booze, and the outfits without having to be bored by marriage problems.

The nuclear couple—that is, the married nuclear couple—appear in a peculiar form of movie: the marriage in which things explode, and not because someone left them in the microwave too long. It's a situation in which the battle of the sexes literally arms itself, but more importantly, in which the couple enact the tensions of marriage by shooting at each other and/or destroying the home in which they live—literally. As is appropriate for something atomic, the nuclear marriage was a brief, sudden, and deadly trend that self-destructed. After all, how many ways are there to blow up a kitchen, and how many times would audiences really want to see a couple take up arms against one another? There is a finality to the marriage movie implied in films that blow everything up. The nuclear marriage was a gimmick, but a clever one.

Combat in the hands of a married couple surfaced in a minor film, 1993's *Undercover Blues*. Kathleen Turner and Dennis Quaid play a revved-up Nick and Nora Charles (with no progress in the charm department). They are retired spies, married with a baby daughter, and are reluctantly forced back into service. There are jokes about having to toss the kid back and forth while escaping and having to engage in fisticuffs and explosions rather than bottle warming and breastfeeding. Two other movies of the decade were variations on the idea: *True Lies* in 1994 and *The Long Kiss Goodnight* in 1996. Both of these films use marriage as a background conceit, and they don't really tell marriage stories. *True Lies* comes the closest, as its premise is that Jamie Lee Curtis is a normal everyday housewife with dreams of adventure who is married to a computer nerd, Arnold Schwarzenegger. The surprise (some surprise!) is that *he* actually is a high-tech, danger-addicted James Bond secret agent. She has no idea. He, in his own way, also has no idea. Neither of them has any real understanding about what is going on inside the other, until he discovers accidentally that she is longing to have some adventure in her life. He starts to woo her from "behind the curtains" by pretending to recruit her as a spy, only to find out what smolders inside her, but also to accidentally endanger her. *The Long Kiss Goodnight* puts the secret life of a housewife on the screen by tugging out the insides of a "normal" young mother, Geena Davis, who wonders exactly why she can suddenly zing a paring knife at a fly and nail it to the wall. (It's because, in her earlier identity, she was a hotshot commando-style secret agent.)

The two best nuclear marriages, however, are in movies separated by sixteen years, a "first and last" set of atomic parentheses in which the couples actually *do* try to destroy one another: *The War of the Roses* and *Mr. and Mrs. Smith.** Each of these movies presents a handsome couple played by major stars (Kathleen Turner and Michael Douglas in *Roses*, Angelina Jolie and Brad Pitt in *Smith*). Each shows the couple living in an idealized, upscale suburban home, with two cars, closets full of clothes, high-paying jobs, and plenty of yuppie friends. Chandeliers hang. Walls of ovens are ready for baking. And disaster lurks. The difference between the films is that Turner and Douglas are simply "the Roses," an allegedly normal couple living the American dream as suitably defined by movies and women's magazines. The Smiths, on the other hand, are merely posing as such a couple. (They are, in effect, posing as the Roses.) Secretly, the Smiths are superagent assassins, both very good at their jobs.

As *The War of the Roses* opens, a divorce lawyer blows his nose into a snowy-white handkerchief and says to an unseen couple, "You have some valid reasons for wanting to divorce." He's actually talking directly to the audience, and apparently they were never more receptive. The lawyer (Danny DeVito) proceeds to tell the couple—audience surrogates—the cautionary tale of Barbara and Oliver Rose (Turner and Douglas). At the price of $450 per hour, he calmly relates in detail what is by now a typical American story of movie marriage. "They *met* great. They agreed on that. But the way I saw it, the poor bastards never had a chance."

DeVito has, in effect, summed up the history of romantic storytelling in motion pictures. They always *do* meet great, and if it ends there, it's a happy romance; but if events (that is, the movie events in particular) proceed further, his observations of their chances are pretty much accurate.

---

* This movie should not be confused with the 1941 film of the same name, directed by Alfred Hitchcock and starring Robert Montgomery and Carole Lombard as a couple who discover they aren't legally wed—one of the "we're not married" films.

The Roses *are* brought together in a "meet cute" manner. During a nor'easter on the island of Nantucket, they are two strangers who both attend an estate sale and bid on a Japanese carving (circa 1700). It's a Shinto goddess, who will then preside over their future relationship. Turner wins at fifty dollars. This sets up what will become the basic definition of their relationship: she's smarter than he is about everything, including money; she has better taste; and furthermore, she always wins, but he's a Harvard Law scholarship student, and she's only a gymnast. From day one, he feels superior, and she agrees he's right . . . although he *is* captivated by her ability to execute a V-shaped head-stand.

Their romantic courtship is brief. He runs after her in the rain, and they have hot sex, and she says, "This is the most romantic day of my life," and he says, "This is a story we're gonna tell our grandchildren." Boom. That's the "they met great" romantic comedy part of *The War of the Roses*. As the movie cuts ruthlessly ahead, Turner and Douglas are married and have two children (a boy and a girl). He's working on an important brief and she's bought him a Morgan as a surprise Christmas gift. He exults, "I'm more than happy. I'm way past happy—I'm married!" DeVito tells his listeners that it "sounds like a fairy tale, doesn't it? And it was." After sharing further folk wisdom about how his dad always said there were four things that defined a man—his house, his car, his wife, and his shoes—DeVito moves forward to present us with the generic truth about the marriage of Barbara and Oliver Rose. It's a horror film.

As Oliver moves up in the world, Barbara sets a fabulous table and entertains exquisitely to further his career. (Fresh figs with cognac, crystal on the table, and two very fat kids to be shown off.) Only a few more minutes of running time are needed for this modern marriage to bottom out into a presentation of discouraging truth: he's a prick, and she's treated like a servant. They quarrel their way forward toward a marital Armageddon, and six years later, Turner has turned their home into a spectacular showplace. The kids are going off to college, so she starts her own catering business. Douglas is uninterested in any of this—he swats a fly with her contract—and they begin their first real physical battle. It's one thing to bicker, or to seriously quarrel, but the Roses take up arms and go to war. Their war, of course, must be fought with household items. Turner begins it by turning on all their small appliances, including the garbage disposal ("Oliver was a sitting duck," intones DeVito), and the movie begins its presentation of the disintegration of a modern marriage, as well as its decline from a realistic presentation into one of exaggerated serio-comic combat. Since it *is* 1989, the movie feels no need to hold back insults or pretty things up. The ultimate denunciation of marital love is clearly, cruelly, and calmly uttered by Turner to Douglas, and hearing it aloud is shocking: "When I watch you eat, when I see you sleep, when I look at you lately, I just want to smash your face in." Finally, in the divorce court, they focus on the house, the central setting of any marriage, and the symbol of their union. All she wants is the house, but he claims all the money he's made has gone into it. They face each other in a death stare: "*You will never get that house*," he says. "We'll see," she says. (DeVito observes, "Women can get a lot meaner than we give them credit for.")

As *The War of the Roses* reaches its peak, the couple have been married for eighteen years. A legal loophole allows them both to live in the house while they quarrel over it, and as the holiday season arrives, the house becomes a battlefield. They define a red zone (hers), a yellow zone (his), and green areas (neutral). Barbara and Oliver Rose begin a dance toward death that is not unlike one of Laurel and Hardy's hilarious scenes of slowly paced, carefully thought-out ballets of destruction. He runs over her cat, and she nails him into the sauna. He cuts the heels off all her shoes. She pretends to want a truce and feeds him a pâté, which he loves, and then she tells him it's made from his dog. (She lies: the dog is really okay.) At one of her elaborate dinner parties, he urinates on the fish course waiting in the kitchen. She throws a copper pot at his head, and wrecks his prized Morgan by backing over it in her catering van. (DeVito: "So far, it's a pretty normal divorce proceeding.") In the end, they both go totally nuts, and she drops a chandelier on him. The film becomes demented, with physical fighting that ends up in sex, after which she bites him and throws him out of the attic. They begin playing baseball with the little statue that first brought them together, swinging the fireplace poker at it. The film ends with both of them on top of the chandelier, swinging back and forth, until it crashes to the floor, taking them both down. Before they die, he admits, "Through all that's happened I still love you," and she reaches out her hand toward his.

Where's Preston Sturges when you need him? What is an audience to do with such a presentation of marriage? After destroying the concept and presenting the physical metaphor of the demolition of the typical yuppie suburban home, the movie ends with DeVito offering a discussion of marriage, again delivered in direct address to an imaginary couple but really to the audience. "What's the moral? Other than dog people should marry dog people and cat people should marry cat people? Maybe it's because of what I've seen that I've stayed married to one person for life. Maybe it's not natural, but my parents did it—sixty-three years . . ." He advises the couple to "get up and go home to find some shred of what you once loved about the sweetheart of your life. Take a minute." (His clients leave.) DeVito then calls home and tells his wife he's on his way. "Love ya, sweetheart."

Kathleen Turner and Michael Douglas end up hanging off the chandelier, trying to kill each other in *The War of the Roses*, which was billed as "a black comedy about love, passion, divorce, and furniture."

In other words, DeVito is telling us what the marriage movie claims: just tough it out. Find the positives. There's nothing new here except physical destruction and death. (Douglas's dubious dying statement and Turner's hand reaching out toward his as they expire is no real reconciliation.) Since *The War of the Roses* has invested in so much negativity, and the total devastation of *everything*, an audience has merely visited a violent comedy with its twist simply being that it's about marriage.

A *Good Housekeeping* home—once the dream of movie marital unions—was literally wrecked in *Roses*, and the format is confirmed by the other key example of the type. *Mr. and Mrs. Smith* opens up in a marriage-counseling session, with an uncomfortable-looking couple (Pitt and Jolie) carefully avoiding eye contact and answering the therapist's questions as briefly—and as evasively—as possible. How long have they been married? "Five years," says Pitt. "Six," corrects Jolie. "Almost six," adds Pitt, needing the last word. And why are they there? Pitt answers with a mechanical metaphor about "time to change the oil." How and where did they meet? "In Colombia," says Pitt. "In Bogotá," says Jolie. Even when they agree, they can't agree. "Five years ago," adds Pitt. "Six," corrects Jolie. "Five *or* six," shoves in Pitt as the image of the film returns a viewer to a steamy, revolutionary-fueled Bogotá, Colombia. Pitt is at the bar, and Jolie whirls in from the dangerous streets. As she stands in

front of him, and he eyes her top to bottom, he moves toward her like a hom-
ing pigeon. After gunfire and explosions rock their room, "I'm Jane," she says,
and "I'm John," he adds. Then they dance—and, of course, wake up together
the next morning.

Back in New York City, he's a "big-time contractor" and she's a "Wall Street
success," and they both tell a friend they're going to get married. So far, everything seems reasonably normal to any viewer. Despite the steamy streets of
Bogotá, where few would go to vacation, this could be a typical couple embark-
ing on a romcom. Never mind the fact that when they visit a shooting gallery
at Coney Island, both of them are remarkably adept at hitting every target,
winning the largest teddy bear on the site. Everything seems low-key, familiar,
and traditional.

As a married couple, they have a beautiful colonial house in an upscale
suburb, with elaborate landscaping and magazine décor. He's first seen out in
front of the place, in his pajamas, picking up the newspaper off the curb. She's
in the kitchen, making the coffee. As they dress for work, going about their routines like robots, talking but not really saying anything ("Dinner's at seven"),
they could be Mr. and Mrs. Blandings from 1947. They get in their cars to go to
work, driving out and turning in opposite directions. At night, as she's making
dinner, she tells him sweetly, "I got new curtains." There are other small hints,
of course, besides the shooting gallery. When Jolie is plumping up the top of
her curtains, she's standing on a small dining chair in high heels, perfectly
balancing the chair on its back legs. (As Pitt approaches, she carefully lowers
it back down to the floor so he won't see.) When they drive out of their garage,
they both roar forward at high speed, one having to cut back to allow the other
to go first in the one lane they have. But, on the whole, it is Mr. and Mrs. Blandings in a suburban house. In her solo session with their counselor, Jolie says,
"There's this huge space between us," which she defines as the fact that she
knows they don't say what they really think to each other. "What's that called?"
she asks. "Marriage," answers the counselor.

A viewer is set up to be watching a traditional marriage movie, with a couple
who have lost touch with each other and are seeking help. The twist comes
when she has to go back to work one evening ("a problem in the office") and he
takes advantage of her absence to go out alone. Jolie goes to a hotel, dresses up
like a dominatrix, and starts whipping a handsome young man. (Is she an adulterer? A sex worker on the side?) Pitt goes to a seedy dive, stumbles drunkenly
into the back room, and bulls his way into a closed poker game. (Is he secretly
a lush? A gambler?) No. That, after all, would not necessarily be news. They
are both assassins, working for rival firms. She twists the head off her trick and

It's another day at work for *Mr. and Mrs. Smith* (Brad Pitt and Angelina Jolie). Playing a married couple who find out after the ceremony that they are both assassins may seem bizarre, but it's not really different from what happened in many marriage movies in the past: they didn't really know each other when they wed.

plunges out the window, down the side of the hotel on a flexible wire, hailing a cab as she lands on the sidewalk. Sober as a judge, he shoots everyone at the poker table and sashays out the door. Back home, each of them puts away his secret weapon. His stash is underneath the garage, and hers in a secret compartment behind one of the wall ovens.

Mr. and Mrs. Smith is a story about what happens when the escapist dream life of a couple is their real life. After an assignment goes wrong, they find out about each other, and everything changes. At first, he still comes home for dinner at seven. She still greets him with a smile, a cocktail, and his favorite pot roast, but when she slices the bread, and when he cuts the meat, there's danger in the air. They are both not quite able to believe what they've discovered, so he tests her, casually walking by her chair and dropping a bottle of wine. She instinctively catches it without a moment's hesitation . . . and then remembers (too late) to let it "slip" through her fingers. Then they both know.

From this point on, *Mr. and Mrs. Smith* is a gun battle of the sexes. Each is assigned to kill the other, and off they go. As they duke it out, she asks him, "Did you expect me to roll over and play dead?" and he says, "I should have been used to it after five years of marriage." "Six!" she yells back. "Any last words?" she asks him. "Your curtains are hideous," is his reply.

The movie then enters a round of car chases, gun battles, exploding buildings, and hand-to-hand combat. During all this, the couple speak lines to each other that, if separated from the action, would be typical of a marriage movie or a session with a therapist. "Satisfied?" she asks him. "Not for years," is his reply. "Why do you think we failed? Because we led separate lives?" and "We approached our marriage like a job." After she has failed to kill him on her second try, she sits alone at the elegant restaurant where he first proposed to her. When he shows up, maddeningly alive, they dance a hot tango during which they also cleverly disarm each other. Driving home in separate cars, they talk on the phone. He tells her the first time he saw her, he thought she "looked like Christmas morning . . . I guess in the end you start thinking about the beginning." This is the traditional format of the marriage movie—to reach the end, look back to find the lost love, the original purpose and meaning to the relationship. (Jolie undercuts this by telling him that the first time she saw him, "I thought you were the most beautiful mark I'd ever seen.")

Once they're home, they engage in a detailed and lengthy shootout, the visualization of the subtext of any marriage movie. They're full of disappointment, a sense of betrayal, and anger. They trade insults—"Your aim's as bad as your cookin', sweetheart"—and give each other challenges. "Come on, honey, come to Daddy," he taunts her after knocking her down, but she beans him with a frying pan and says, "Who's your daddy now?" During this melee, which gets really ugly, the house is totally wrecked. They finally stand off, gun to gun, each ready for the other to fire, but Pitt lowers his weapon first: "I can't do it." They embrace, kiss, and knock each other around the house, through the wreckage and over the broken glass, in a display of hot sex.

The next morning they are united, but under attack from both of their employers for having violated the rule never to marry inside the business. (They didn't know.) From this moment forward, the film is nothing but action, and it begins with the complete blowing up of their suburban home. *That* marriage is over, shattered to smithereens. They steal a neighbor's car and roar off in an elaborate chase in which, as they run, they are followed by a fleet of well-armed black cars. Having been caught in early-morning deshabille, Pitt battles in his underwear, shooting, grappling, tossing weapons, while she drives at high speed, skillfully maneuvering the freeway (but only after she's insisted he let her take over and drive, a marital moment). As they engage in combat, they have another conversation about marriage, slowly revealing the truth to one another. ("I was never in the Peace Corps . . . I was married once before . . . I went to Notre Dame and was an art history major . . . I'm Jewish . . . My parents died when I was five"—this means her parents at their wedding were really actors—and as for her bad cooking? She never actually made any of it.) When it's all over, and they've vanquished their foes, she comments that "We have to do every conversation we've ever had over," and he laments, "I can't believe I brought my *real* parents to our wedding."

Mr. and Mrs. Smith sets a rhythm—action, destruction, and chaos—over which are laid traditional marital quarrels and nags. As the couple work together to save their lives, they do what the movie married couple has always done: they bicker. (A co-worker, Vince Vaughn, says, "You're Macy's and Gimbel's.") In the end, they remain consistent. Their lives in danger, they work together and win out. How different is this from *Made for Each Other* in 1939? A crisis saves the marriage of Jimmy Stewart and Carole Lombard when their little son falls ill. A crisis saves the marriage of Pitt and Jolie when people start shooting at them. Their final gun battle takes place in a suburban store full of things that married couples would buy—clothing, furniture, household goods. As is always the case, marriage is destroyed and restored, shown to be unworkable, and then worked out. In the end, they're back at the marriage counselor, this time looking radiant and fit, explaining that there were times when they just wanted to kill one another, but . . .

Bickering, arguing, and exchanging snappy—even insulting—repartee had always been the language of love in American movies, and one of the basics of the marriage-movie relationship. These modern films brought an escalation of that bickering into hideous argument and finally revealed it for what it was: the battle of the sexes, well armed and deadly. Just listen to a scene from *Who's Afraid of Virginia Woolf?*, in which George and Martha try to kill each other with verbiage, and then watch Mr. and Mrs. Smith shooting at each other from dining room to kitchen, and you realize it's all the same thing. George and Martha kill with words; Mr. and Mrs. Smith just kill.

In the case of *Mr. and Mrs. Smith*, a couple of killer assassins each found the perfect mate—another killer assassin, someone with shared interests, skills, and hobbies. It's amusing, and one of the most original commentaries on marriage, the marriage movie, and marriage counseling ever put on film. (It was a big box-office success, but a critical failure.) Because of the violence and the car chases and the blowing up of buildings, many did not appreciate what a wonderful joke on marriage movies the film really was.

Movies such as *Roses* and *Smith* really were putting paid to the ideas of the original marriage-movie concept. Presumably, out of their mushroom clouds would come something new, even if slightly poisonous. What happened was a kind of death, and certainly a reconsideration of sorts, but not necessarily anything startlingly new. This has always been the problem of the marriage movie—how could its situation *really* be varied or made fresh?

Some movies solved the problem simply. Plots dropped the before and the after and just gave the ritual event. The movie showed the wedding planning and ceremony and nothing else—no real romantic-comedy prelude, and no discouraging issue-ridden aftermath. Movies started focusing on weddings. They became like issues of *Consumer Reports*. There were *Muriel's Wedding* (1995), *Four Weddings and a Funeral* (1994), *Betsy's Wedding* (1990), *Father of the Bride* (both parts, 1991 and 1995), *27 Dresses* (2008), *Bride Wars* (2009), *The Wedding Singer* (1998), *Wedding Crashers* (2005), *My Best Friend's Wedding* (1997), *Runaway Bride* (1999), *Bridesmaids* (2011), *Jumping the Broom* (a 2011 African-American variation), and a depressing list of others. Such movies put the wedding onscreen, and had everything in the plot linked to it, to its ritual, its wardrobe, its participants, its families, and its blatant consumerism. In her *New York Times* review of *Bride Wars* in 2009, critic Manohla Dargis wrote, "Do Hollywood studio executives think that women have a gene for tulle? Neural receptors for Vera Wang? . . . To judge from a clutch of recent titles, *License to Wed*, *Margot at the Wedding*, *Evening*, *Enchanted*, *The Heartbreak Kid*, *Sex and the City*, *Mamma Mia!*, *27 Dresses*, and *Maid of Honor*—the walk down the aisle has picked up increasing speed."*

The wedding ceremony on film has a curious history. Sometimes movies would begin with a wedding (*Our Betters*) or end with one (*It's a Great Feeling*, 1949), in which Doris Day gives up show business to return to her small home town and marry her high school sweetheart (Errol Flynn in a joke cameo). It was an opportunity for the costume department to blow the budget, and certainly one for lavishly adorning a beautiful female star. And yet, with notable exceptions, it was seldom lingered over in films.† Unless the bride was the young Elizabeth Taylor, whose beauty was worth stopping the show for (*Father of the Bride*, 1950), or the wedding was a grand state occasion with Marlene Dietrich as Catherine the Great (*The Scarlet Empress*, 1934) or a Ruritanian fantasy with a bride who looks like Madeleine Carroll or Deborah Kerr (the two versions of *The Prisoner of Zenda*, 1937 and 1952), weddings were often ignored, aborted, truncated, or used as a place for serious questions.

Brides are always running away. When Claudette Colbert comes down the aisle in *It Happened One Night* (1934), her father (Walter Connolly) tells her

---

* Dargis's review also mentions *What Happens in Vegas* and *Rachel Getting Married*. Her conclusion? "Die, Bridezilla, die!"

† World War II was a time in which there were exceptions, as in such films as *Thirty Seconds over Tokyo* or *The Clock*. Even then, however, Lana Turner questions herself at the altar in *Marriage Is a Private Affair*, and *The Clock*'s ceremony is in a crowded justice of the peace's office, with no family or friends. *Heartburn* (1986) is one of the few movies in which the actual marriage vows are fully spoken.

that Clark Gable is really a good guy—does she really want to marry the effete Sky King waiting at the altar? (She doesn't. She runs off.) When Rita Hayworth moves forward toward Lee Bowman in *Cover Girl* (1944), Otto Kruger shows her the little pearl Gene Kelly found for her. She, too, runs off, and is soon dancing joyously down the street with both Kelly and Phil Silvers. In *It Had to Be You* (1947), Ginger Rogers goes three times to the altar, in three spectacular wedding gowns, each time running away until she finds her true love, Cornel Wilde, a fireman.* The very march down the aisle is when the audience is shown where the future trouble will lie. In *Romance on the High Seas* (1948), as Janis Paige walks, holding the arm of S. Z. Sakall, she asks him to just look at the way her groom (Don DeFore) is ogling one of the bridesmaids. Meanwhile, DeFore himself is asking his best man to notice how his bride is flirting with one of the men she's passing by. It's all right there—movies have little faith in the wedding ceremony. It isn't even necessary to have the big dramatic *Jane Eyre* moment in which someone rushes in to warn the bride that the groom is already wed, or vice versa; it's enough to show the gown, the walk, the guests, the flowers, and to hear that ominous threat of a tune: "Here Comes the Bride."

Some weddings on film are really grim. Three film-noir movies present weddings in settings designed to indicate there will be no happily-ever-after. In *Gilda* (1946), Rita Hayworth weds Glenn Ford inside an office, and the audience watches through the window from the outside. It's pouring, and the ceremony is blurred through the ominously rain-streaked window. In *Angel Face* (1952), Jean Simmons and Robert Mitchum (both on trial for the murder of her stepmother and father) are wed in prison. They are serenaded by a motley group of female inmates, one of whom gushes through her toothless mouth, "We wish you two kids all the happiness in the world." Farley Granger and Cathy O'Donnell, the youthful stars of Nicholas Ray's first film, *They Live by Night* (1949), are introduced in the film before the credits. Underneath their images are the words: "This boy . . . and this girl . . . were never properly introduced to the world we live in." A thief on the run, Granger proposes to the lost-lamb O'Donnell, and as they disembark from a bus and look around for a place to wed, they see a neon sign flashing: Marriages Performed. They slowly walk across the dark street, burdened by coats and luggage, bathed in shadows. When they ring the doorbell of the house with the sign, it plays a mechanical "Here Comes the Bride." For twenty dollars, and another five for

---

* There are so many of these runaway-bride movies that Elizabeth Kendall titled her book on screwball comedy *The Runaway Bride*.

Movie marriage scenes come in all shapes and sizes. There's
the low-budget quickie ceremony for Farley Granger and Cathy
O'Donnell in *They Live by Night* . . .

the ring, a bald and sinister old man does indeed "perform" their ceremony.
"Marriages Performed" is a good slogan for movie marriages in general. They
are often acted with no real conviction, and with a sense of danger lingering in
the wording of the vows.

Movies presenting marriage boiled down to the ritual that initiates it—the
wedding—illustrate where audiences had arrived regarding marriage. It had
become like Valentine's Day or Halloween: we knew there was a reason behind
it, we knew something had triggered its celebration, we knew there was an
explanation—but exactly what that was had become a bit fuzzy. But, hey, who
cares? Let's put on the witch hat and go trick-or-treating. Couples began putting on the gown and the top hat and cutting the cake—it was the party that
mattered. Of course, a beautiful wedding had become a big box-office draw
before the late 1990s and early 2000s in movies like *Father of the Bride* (1950)
and *A Wedding* (1978). *Father of the Bride* was one of the great hits of the 1950s
(inspiring both its own sequel and the remake and sequel of the 1990s). It was
an amusing and loving story of family relationships, and of the father's confusion, consternation, and ultimate pride as he married off his only daughter at
great expense. *A Wedding,* on the other hand, was directed by Robert Altman,
and its focus was more cynical, its family all fighting with each other, and its
milieu definitely nouveau riche.

Centering everything in a film on the ritual of marriage, however, became
a phenomenon of later decades. In *Betsy's Wedding,* the two least important

. . . or the granddaddy of all the "let's put on a really big show" wedding movies, *Father of the Bride*, in which Spencer Tracy brings the exquisite young Elizabeth Taylor down the aisle in full regalia.

people are the couple being wed, but the most important event in the movie is their wedding, as it is being planned in opposite war camps by their parents. His, wealthy suburbanites, want things to be "correct"—as they define it—and her parents, mostly her Italian dad, just want to prove they can spend as much as anybody when it comes to their daughter's happiness. There is almost no screen story time given to the marrying couple (Molly Ringwald and Dylan Walsh)—who cares about them? But there's plenty of marriage on display. Betsy's father (Alan Alda, the Italian dad) is wed to Madeline Kahn (who's Jewish and just wants to make sure the groom stomps the wedding goblet). Kahn's sister (Catherine O'Hara) is unhappily wed to the adulterous Joe Pesci, and there are also the groom's parents and Alan Alda's mother and her dead husband, who's still complaining about her cooking. All the marriages are clichés: Alda and Kahn happy, happy, dancing in the kitchen, and happily bickering in clever Neil Simon–esque one-line zingers; O'Hara and Pesci, with him cheating on her with his blond secretary and her secretly buying up his business under an assumed name; and the mama remembering old grandpop while old grandpop himself (conveniently dead, appearing only to Alda) comments wryly on everything she says. In case this isn't enough to goose up the box office, there's an unwed daughter (Ally Sheedy) who's a cop. She hooks

Bruce Willis and Michelle Pfeiffer are the couple in *The Story of Us*, which contemplates once again the highs and lows of marriage. There's a Venetian getaway full of love and food and wine . . .

up with a courtly young wiseguy (Anthony LaPaglia) in what is essentially the main love story of the film, a mini-romcom.

The young couple just want a simple marriage, and as it balloons, Betsy says, "Everybody's got this emotional investment in this thing." Her statement is an explanation of how marriage is being depicted. The ritual wedding becomes an excuse to both deflect marital problems and define them sharply through the ritual event. "You marry each other but you have to worry about all these other people," says Betsy's mom. On the wedding day, it rains; Betsy (a student at FIT) has designed her own bizarre wedding outfit (white top hat, white cowboy boots, and a Vera Wang–style dress altered to show off her legs); the tent collapses, and everybody has a good time. Marriage isn't of enough interest to carry the plot, but it can be an excuse for a good party—and some new cowboy boots.*

As the millennium date was crossed, the poor marriage movie—always a challenge, always a chore—chugged forward, keeping itself afloat if the business

---

* Around 2001, a new ritual regarding the fashions of lavish weddings emerged: Trash the Dress. Instead of lovingly storing their wedding dresses in mothballs, brides began to hire photographers to record the all-out destruction of the gown. Visiting city dumps, beaches, wet fields, city streets, and abandoned buildings while dragging the dress behind her, a bride celebrated the end of her wedding and the stress it had caused by "trashing the

... and a depressed sense of defeat and alienation back home and in bed.

of movies felt a way to sell it could be found. In 1999, just before the millennium, the topic had stirred a bit. There was *Runaway Bride* (not really about marriage, but about avoiding it), *American Beauty* (another movie that told us that people in the suburbs were all idiots), *Eyes Wide Shut* (Stanley Kubrick's much-debated sexual adventure starring Tom Cruise and his then-wife, Nicole Kidman), *Me, Myself, and I* (an Australian film in which a single career woman, Rachel Griffiths, learns what her life would have been had she wed), *An Ideal Husband* (it's an 1895 comedy by Oscar Wilde but still had much to say about husbands, wives, marriage—and blackmail), and *The Story of Us* (1999).

The Story of Us affirms the arrival of a type of marriage movie that would now prevail: the therapy session. This format had begun to appear as far back as *Bob & Carol*, but now it dug in to stay. While the audience sits helplessly in their seats, an unhappy couple talk about their marriage. And talk. And talk. And talk. They talk to their friends about their problems. They talk to each other. They talk directly to the camera, both together and alone, as if they were facing a therapist. The only people they don't talk to about the death of their

dress." The resulting photographs, which featured the new wife ripping, tearing, mutilating, painting, smearing, and crushing her expensive wedding gown, were then placed in the traditional wedding album, a new-fashioned keepsake for the future. Various newspapers reported this phenomenon, with one reporter asking a bride who'd lain down across railroad tracks in her dress a simple question: why? She had no answer.

relationship, interestingly, are their children, who they agree must be spared the news. As a result, there's no dramatic climax in which someone, anyone (such as the children), has to face anything. They just talk. This *talking*—the constant analyzing and telling everything—becomes the new purpose to the marriage movie.

The Story of Us stars Bruce Willis and Michelle Pfeiffer as a couple who have been married for fifteen years.* While their children are away at summer camp, they decide to try a trial separation, since "fighting" has become "the condition, not the exception" and is now the "language of their relationship." In the first presentation of Willis and Pfeiffer with their two children, however, the family sits around the dinner table in their magnificent Craftsman home, happily playing word games together. The image is that of the typically happy sitcom family, but as soon as the children leave the table, Willis says, "Look, I don't really care what we do on our anniversary," and she adds, "Just as long as the kids see us leaving the house together." This inability to tell the children the truth will become what ends up holding them together, a shaky premise. As the movie moves slowly to this conclusion, it has a lot to say about marital misery: "Love is just lust in disguise, and lust fades" . . . "The loudest silences are the ones in which the silence is filled with everything that's been said" . . . "There are some hurts you can never really get over" . . . and "You love who we were—you couldn't possibly love who we've become"—all this and the usual "I love you" and "I hate you." After they decide to stay together, they conclude that "it's hard, much harder than I thought, but you don't just give up." The film tells us that they lived "mostly happily ever after." Although *The Story of Us* is couched in the cloak of honesty—marriage is miserable, hard to make work, burdened by kids, careers, daily life, and boredom, you stick together anyway—but that is essentially the message that marriage movies always provided. *The Story of Us* breaks no new ground.

In 2000, *The Family Man*, with Nicolas Cage and Téa Leoni, magically transports a ruthless exec into a married life. It was a smart movie that had three weeks on best box-office lists but then quietly disappeared.

In 2002, *Far from Heaven*, written and directed by Todd Haynes, caused a brief stir among critics who appreciated his aspirations to emulate Douglas Sirk, the genius of the 1950s filmed critique of America. *Far from Heaven* told the story of a couple living in Hartford, Connecticut, who undergo a severe marital crisis: he's gay and she falls in love with a black man. Well played by

---

* Paul Reiser plays a friend but is unbilled in the cast lists. In retrospect, that seems significant.

Dennis Quaid and Julianne Moore, and set in a Sirkian universe of heightened color and emotion, the movie inspired no imitations and could not really reach Sirk's level of honesty and informed sympathy. It did, however, bring the issues of homosexuality and racism out of the category of implied subtext.

After the millennium, throughout the following decade, pundits turned seriously toward the subject of marriage. The topic was evidently no longer a familiar old shoe but was suddenly new, a distanced concept worthy of intense scrutiny, possibly fueled by alienated times. Marriage became zeitgeist. These look-sees were the over-the-top sort of article that once appeared in marriage manuals or women's magazines, the let's-pull-up-our-socks-and-get-the-job-done approach. The new articles had statistics. Polls had been conducted. Testimonies were taken. Where once we had only been reminded of what we already knew, with a little reassurance thrown in, now we were being lectured, educated, informed. Carl Weisman, author of *Serious Doubts: Why People Marry When They Know It Won't Last*, said that people look at marriage as a way to solve a problem and then were inevitably disappointed. (He conducted a poll in which 79 percent of the people he queried indicated they felt it had been a mistake to marry their partner.) *Parade* magazine also conducted a poll to determine the major cause of problems in marriage. (The answer had long been available in the movies: money.) Stephanie Coontz, author of *Marriage: A History*, told an interviewer that "barely half of all adults in the United States are married." She added that "the median age at the time of a first marriage has never been higher, slightly more than 26 years old for women and almost 29 for men." She backed up her remarks with census-report statistics. In 1960, 72 percent of all adults over the age of eighteen were married; in 2000, only 57 percent were. In the year 2011, that number had already decreased to 51 percent, which meant that in 1960 three out of every five adults between the ages of eighteen and twenty-nine were married, but in 2011 only one in five were. Coontz drew a conclusion: "I think marriage is perceived as a very desirable good but no longer as a necessity." (Robert Thompson, an oft-quoted professor of television and popular culture at Syracuse University, disagrees. He says, "I think most Americans still love the idea that they will meet their soul mate and go into death together. I don't think we've gotten to the point where people have completely gotten so cynical about the notion of finding someone they can be happy with for the rest of their lives.")

Betsey Stevenson, an economist at the University of Pennsylvania's Wharton School, called the people who married in the 1970s "the greatest divorcing generation." Researchers from the University of Virginia's National Marriage Project defined *generosity* as a good source of happiness in marriage: "the virtue of giving good things to one's spouse freely and abundantly" was advocated, and suggestions were such things as simply making them coffee in the morning. (Gone was the movie dream of Gable putting a diamond bracelet in Loy's morning kippers.) Writing in the Sunday *New York Times Magazine*, Elizabeth Weil detailed evidence for her "I Have a Pretty Good Marriage" testimony. Lying in bed at night, she had begun to wonder "why I wasn't applying myself to the project of being a spouse." (She had been viewing her marriage "like the waves on the ocean.") Her written version of Bergman's *Scenes from a Marriage* provides details on the day-to-day of the project she and her husband, already happy enough, undertook to become more happy. Promising to have the courage and patience to grow, she concluded with what might be a cautionary note: "Maybe the perversity we all feel in the idea of striving at marriage—the reason so few of us do it—stems from a misapprehension of the proper goal." (She feels it's wish fulfillment, and every word she says could be a solid basis for a marriage movie screenplay from the past.)

Dan Savage, a sex-advice columnist, says we need to get over our American obsession with strict fidelity, because it gives people unrealistic expectations. Writing for *The Stranger*, an alternative weekly newspaper in Seattle, Savage thinks, "Monogamy is not natural, non-monogamy is not natural, variation is what's natural . . . people need the thrill that comes from the illicit rather than the predictable." Tara Parker-Pope, author of *The Happy Marriage Is the "Me" Marriage*, says, "For centuries, marriage was viewed as an economic and social institution, and the emotional and intellectual needs of the spouses were secondary to the survival of the marriage itself. But in modern relationships, people are looking for a partnership, and they want partners who make their lives more interesting."

Filmmaker Dana Adam Shapiro set out to interview a list of people he knew under the age of forty who were divorced, and ask them what happened. His Chekovian/Tolstoyan conclusion was, "All happy couples are the same, which is to say they are just boring." (The movies had long since understood this, which was why movie couples always had to mess things up: to become more interesting and thus more watchable.) In fact, when Shapiro presented descriptions of some of his interviewees, he handily labeled them as character types: The Adulteress. The Young Wife. The Two-Time Ex.

The Adulteress says when she first set eyes on her lover across the room at a party: "We were like magnets. I could have avoided it and probably should have, but I was weak, self-indulgent, disrespectful, and impulsive." Was she Greta Garbo in *The Painted Veil* or *Anna Karenina*?

The Young Wife says, "I thought he [her husband] was hot . . . but he began spending more and more of his time playing video games and watching television. I felt lonely." Was she Kim Novak in *Strangers When We Meet?*

The Two-Time Ex gets right to the nitty-gritty. "Halfway through any divorce the only thing you can think of is this: I hate this person, and I want this person to bleed." Was she Kathleen Turner in *The War of the Roses?*

Offscreen, marriage, once an inevitable social union for most people, had become a grab bag of movie plots, recycled as deep thinking. A kind of Reality Marriage Show.

Surveying the scene in early 2011, it's clear that marriage, no matter what, will always be a subject for comedies (see 2010's *It's Complicated* and 2011's *Newlyweds*—and 2012's *Celeste and Jesse Forever*, in which a couple splits up but can't bring themselves to let go and move on). It's familiar, it's always there, and it's tragic—three prerequisites for a good belly laugh. The subject is now largely treated by independent films seeking to give it intellectual credibility, literary cachet, or social relevance. Ironically, this hasn't brought it any great difference.*

Looking at four independent films that have been taken seriously in very recent years, it might be said that one can see something old, something new, something borrowed, and something blue—in other words, nothing we haven't heard or seen before. During the decade of 2000–2010, a number of dreary marital movies that offered no hope appeared, such as *Revolutionary Road* (2008) and *Blue Valentine* (2010). Marriage becomes a subject for high drama and deep-dish thinking. Everybody was doing *Who's Afraid of Virginia Woolf.* Suddenly marriage itself becomes the equivalent to crushing poverty during the Depression or drug addiction in the 1950s. It's hopeless, it's unfair, and it's a situation that can't sustain you, and that you can't sustain.

Revolutionary Road (something old) was based on an excellent novel by Richard Yates, but the film couldn't re-create the book's mournful tenderness or its tragic sense of loss. The movie was yet another presentation of the suburban world as a hopeless trap for clueless people who had wanted more out of life than marriage. The visual presentation of the 'burbs as the social wasteland of marital bliss had already been worked over for several decades, from the 1950s

---

* *Crazy, Stupid, Love* (2011) works a variation on 1937's *The Awful Truth*, in which Cary Grant was possibly a cheater, so Irene Dunne divorced him—right up front in the plot. This time it's the wife (Julianne Moore) who *definitely* has been having an affair and wants a divorce. The husband (Steve Carell) has to learn to date once again and cope with his busted life as well as his three kids. He's taught by Ryan Gosling (a "bar stud Henry Higgins," said critic Owen Gleiberman). This light romantic comedy has a streak of melancholy running underneath.

The married couple, Elizabeth Taylor and Richard Burton, act out
the definitive modern marriage disaster: Martha and George in *Who's
Afraid of Virginia Woolf?*

to the 1990s. There had been *The Man in the Grey Flannel Suit* and *No Down
Payment* (dramatic versions), *Rally 'Round the Flag, Boys* (the comic version),
The Stepford Wives (1975, the horror version, remade in 2004), *Bye Bye Birdie*
(1963, the musical version) and *The 'burbs* (1989, the inexplicable version), and
more. *Revolutionary Road* was tired, and died a quiet death at the box office.

Blue Valentine (something blue), like many marriage movies, is told out of
chronological order. This mode of storytelling has become extremely popular in the past two decades, perhaps fueled by filmmakers who watched *Citizen Kane* just once too often in college film classes.* The conceit of telling a
marriage story out of sequence keeps a constant reminder in front of viewers
about the pitfalls of monogamy. Critics loved *Blue Valentine*'s use of the form,
in particular praising the scene from the couple's past in which they share a
moment of musical improvisation, which tells audiences, or means to tell audiences, that they are emotionally right for each other. As Ryan Gosling strums
a ukulele, Michelle Williams executes a lumbering tap dance to "You Always
Hurt the One You Love." There's something contrived about the moment,

---

* *Kane* itself tells the story of three bad marriages: that of Kane's parents (his mother sends
  him away from his brutal father), his first marriage to a society belle (encapsulated by the
  famous breakfast-table sequence), and the dismal excess of his second marriage to the
  hapless mistress he encounters because she has a toothache.

New forms of marriage finally arrive onscreen: a happy, same-sex couple only temporarily derailed: Annette Bening and Julianne Moore in *The Kids Are All Right*.

a look-at-our-sweet-little-romance phoniness that illustrates the modern marriage movie's inability to really believe in such things. One has only to compare a similar scene from an old movie to note the difference. In *It Should Happen to You* (1954), Judy Holliday and Jack Lemmon are courting, and sitting around a neighborhood restaurant/bar where there's a piano. As he plays and they both sing "Let's Fall in Love," they also carry on an easy, natural conversation. The wedding of music, lyrics, piano, laughter, and natural dialogue, played by two incredible pros, masters of both comedy and tragedy, presents an audience with an honest look at a couple who are totally in sync and, as it were, made for each other. There are other examples. Jimmy Stewart and Donna Reed walk home together in *It's a Wonderful Life* (1946) improvising "Buffalo Gals," and Jean Harlow and Robert Williams make up their own lyrics in *Platinum Blonde* (1931). All of these films have authenticity. Gosling and Williams are talented, but their little song and dance is a self-conscious version of the earlier naturalistic ideas. It's postmodern—and unreal, like the marriage they inhabit. Married six years, he's a freelance house painter and she's an ambitious nurse, and the film is yet another that asks the question "What happened to us?"—but the audience is the first to wonder.

In 2011, one of the ten nominees for the Best Picture Oscar (along with *Blue Valentine*) was allegedly something new: a different take on the marriage film.

The Kids Are All Right presented a story in which two lesbian mothers have each borne a child by the same sperm donor. The two children, a son and a daughter, are now teenagers who search out their father and bring him home. One of the lesbian moms then has an affair with him, the other finds out, and the kids are no longer all right. The couple (lesbians) and the children (sperm donations) seem to be very new indeed, but the movie plot might easily have been concocted in 1935. It would have starred Kay Francis and George Brent as a happy couple with two adopted children (maybe Jackie Cooper and Bonita Granville) who decide to locate their birth mother (Gloria Stuart), who would then have an affair with old dad. The sexuality and the science give a "now" flip to what is essentially a set of marriage-plot issues from the past. In the endings of both films, the couples would be reunited around the importance of love and family life—even if *The Kids Are All Right* does it by having Annette Bening slam the door in the face of the sperm donor, yelling, "Get your own family."*

Unfaithful (2002) is something borrowed—from the French. It's a remake of Claude Chabrol's fabulous 1969 thriller *La Femme Infidèle*—a story of American adultery glacéed with French morality, ennui, and existential suspension of action. By 2002, it's time for the marriage movie to become an over-the-top, R-rated sexual experience, as indeed *Unfaithful* is. Nevertheless, the very first image of the movie is the traditional one of a fantastic white rambling colonial home set down a country lane—the dream setting of American movie marriages. What plays out later will be very European. For no real reason other than an accidental meeting, housewife Diane Lane, married to an adoring Richard Gere, begins an affair with—of course—a Frenchman (Olivier Martinez). She has met him very cute in an unseasonably high wind that's turned the streets of SoHo into a storm of flying papers, garbage-can lids, and debris. The couple simply bump into each other—a literal whirlwind courtship. The main emphasis of the movie is on their very steamy love scenes, stopping at very little where the censors are concerned.

There is almost no other action. Gere, a very sensitive man, quietly knows at once that something is strange about his wife, and he hires a detective to follow her. Once he learns the truth, he visits the lover, and after feeling slightly sick to his stomach and looking weak and beaten down, suddenly up and smashes the hapless Frenchman on the head with a snow globe, killing him very dead. (The snow globe is what set Gere off. He and his wife collect them, and she

* In his *Entertainment Weekly* "Final Cut" column of July 23, 2010, the perceptive critic Mark Harris made a positive point about the lesbian couple: "They're not intended to be role models for gay coupledom. They and their marriage are, however, recognizably human."

The modern adultery movie put the sex onscreen in new, steamier ways than the old films, but the results were the same: disaster. Diane Lane and Richard Gere play a married couple, but Lane threatens what they have when she starts a hot affair in *Unfaithful*.

has unforgivably presented one of their best ones to her lover as a gift. Spotting it beside their love bed, Gere is pushed over the brink.) The difference between this story of infidelity and earlier forms is that there's no real solution, no real forgiveness, no real sense of reconciliation, and certainly no future in it. Although the couple survive the police inquiries that inevitably occur, and reunite around their small son, they are trapped in an emotional limbo. They both have figured out what has happened. "What did you do? Did you hurt him? Tell me what you did," she demands. "No!" is his angry reply. "Tell me what *you* did." After they continue living as best they can, he says he will turn himself in, but she says not to: "No one will know." "*We'll* know," he reminds her. For one brief moment of release, Lane imagines the day she met Martinez. As he turns to her at the top of his steps, inviting her up to collect herself and tend to the knee she hurt in their collision, she smiles, says no, hails a cab, and drives away.

Driving home from the school auction, where Gere and Lane have happily interacted with friends, mingled socially, and she has danced with their son, they are tense and desperate in their car at a red light just in range of the police station. Their little boy is asleep in the backseat. They talk. Could they sell everything, go away, and live on the beach in Mexico? They lean toward each other, embrace, and kiss. It is late at night and there is no traffic. A cut takes viewers outside the car, to a position far behind them. As the light changes

Is it brother-to-brother, an affair, an after-work confrontation, an accidental meeting? Whatever it is, it's two men, but it's also exactly like a marriage, in *J. Edgar*, with Armie Hammer and Leonardo DiCaprio in the biopic about Clyde Tolson and J. Edgar Hoover.

to green, the car does not move. And it never moves. As the credits roll, the car just sits there in its position of suspension between right and wrong, marriage and divorce, prison and Mexico. Two people who've been wed for eleven years, and have known each other intimately, have learned that what they know about each other is only part of what there is to know. Who is he? Who is she? Who am I? What should we do? (As George Sanders says to his wife, Ingrid Bergman, in Roberto Rossellini's 1954 examination of marriage, *Voyage in Italy*, "Now that we're strangers, we can start all over again.") *Unfaithful*'s unresolved ending, borrowed from Chabrol, is indicative of where the marriage movie is headed: toward no resolution, no closure, no reassurance, and finally, no explanation. The denial of closure is a serious violation of earlier movie marriage stories, and it can be seen as emerging as a major change in all these films, *Revolutionary Road*, *Blue Valentine*, *The Kids Are All Right*, and *Unfaithful*. The movie business is beginning to accept that marriage is a story that somehow can't really be told. (They will, of course, try to tell it anyway.)

In late 2011, Clint Eastwood released a biopic called *J. Edgar*, the story of the man who built the FBI into a powerful political force in the United States. J. Edgar Hoover never married. His office was his home, and his home was his office. Yet contained within this film is one of the best portraits of a married relationship that has been seen in the motion picture. Hoover and his co-worker, Clyde Tolson, played by Leonardo DiCaprio and Armie Hammer, have a lifelong friend/companion/whatever relationship. It is a commitment between two men who are friends, colleagues, companions, and maybe lovers. (The film lets an audience decide.) Hoover and Tolson work together, play together, listen to each other, disagree and fight with each other, share joy and tragedy and challenge, and never lose their basic commitment from youth to old age. They are seen side by side at work, at the race track, at social events. They have their problems (they are both men, unable to wed or live openly as a gay couple, if you assume they're gay) and they have their frustrations (they function on different levels of self-awareness about their feelings). However, what an audience watches is a love story that deepens into marriage.

There are, in particular, three scenes of "married" domesticity. In one, they are in silken robes, sharing an "after party" gossip session, with champagne and delicacies, laughing happily and mocking their fellow guests. Married couples do this, and although the scene ends in a fistfight with an enforced kiss, it has the honesty of a marital end-of-the-day chitchat. In the second scene, they are in the kitchen after Tolson has had a stroke. Hoover is preparing breakfast, talking to Tolson with forceful optimism, cheering him up and urging him onward to recovery. Hoover speaks words his own mother used to keep *him* going forward in life. There is real pain and confusion in Tolson's eyes as he listens, and a grim determination to will his partner back to health in Hoover's as he fixes Tolson's eggs. The "I will give you strength" energy that flows between them is marital. In the third scene, just before Hoover dies, the two men speak obliquely about their feelings, remembering how and when they met. J. Edgar says the most he ever has to say in the film about his love for Clyde, touching him tenderly, but briefly, on the hand and shoulder. On the first day Tolson came to Hoover's office, he says, "You gave me a handkerchief." Quietly, Tolson again hands him one.

These scenes all show a couple alone together, in their private time, and reveal how they behave when not under scrutiny. They are about silent communication, years of shared experience, secret confidences, and common ideas. They are also about the one constant that can be found in the marriage movie: the inexplicable nature of any relationship between any two human beings that stands the test of time.

Married Life (2007) is a summarizing film. On the one hand, it's old-fashioned, concerning adultery, yearnings, disappointments in life, and strange marital loyalties that exist without the mates being fully aware of them. On the other hand, it's a bizarre mixture of what *Leonard Maltin's Movie Guide* calls "social commentary, soap opera, and noirish melodrama, set in 1949." It's a story in paralysis; it tells us the marriage film is right where it's always been.

Based on a novel by John Bingham (*Five Roundabouts to Heaven*), it presents marriage in a very low-key manner. Not much happens, but a lot *could* happen at any moment. Superbly acted by the quartet of Chris Cooper, Patricia Clarkson, Pierce Brosnan, and Rachel McAdams, it's about nothing but marriage and therefore is authentically representative of the modern attempt at the form. The story can be simply told: Pat (Clarkson) and Harry (Cooper) are happily married, an ideal couple, admired by their single womanizer friend, Richard (Brosnan). That's the surface. Underneath the surface, Harry is having a secret affair with Kay (McAdams), whom he plans to marry after dumping Pat, who is herself having a secret affair with a young neighborhood stud. When Richard meets Kay, he wants her, and sets about stealing her from Harry. Just before Harry learns of this, however, he has decided that he dreads hurting Pat too much. His leaving her, he assumes, would kill her, so he decides he should solve the problem by simply killing her himself, to spare her feelings. In the end, he arrives home in time to rescue her from her poisoned medicine, and Richard and Kay marry. All live—if not happily—apparently at least forever after.

The film is grounded in traditional marriage issues: adultery and murder. It uses a narrator (Brosnan's Richard) to contemplate the meaning of it all for the viewer. "This is my friend," he says at the beginning, about Harry. "He's married. He likes his wife. It can happen." However, Richard defines himself as a man who has always assumed that marriage was "a mild kind of illness, like the chicken pox or the flu, from which I was safely immune." In the hands of an Ernst Lubitsch, the film might have been a slyly sophisticated romp. Under a Billy Wilder, it could have been cynical but still romantic; and under a Preston Sturges it could have rocketed around the neighborhood like a chimpanzee on roller skates. But somehow, even with talented acting and skilled writing and directing (both by Ira Sachs), it just seems tired and bewildered.

Tired and bewildered, oddly enough, is the right approach for the marriage movie of 2007. As events unfold, Brosnan's comments, Cooper's sad face, McAdams's pulchritude, and Clarkson's obvious intelligence mesh to present something akin to truth. An audience can see that Harry wants romance, while Pat wants sex. Kay can only enjoy sex with Richard, and Richard can only believe in romance with Kay. In the end, the movie presents the mystery of marriage: why do people do it, and if they do it, why do they stay together? "And so Harry and Pat lived their lives together in the way that couples do," says Brosnan's narration. "A man who tried to poison his wife found out he'd be lost without her." The final scene shows the two couples, surrounded by a roomful of friends, happily playing charades while Pat's studly lover acts out

Married Life is always complicated. Pierce Brosnan loves and marries Rachel McAdams . . .

. . . who had an affair with Chris Cooper . . .

. . . who is married to Patricia Clarkson. They're all friends. There's no easy explanation. And that's marriage.

the word. "Whoever in this room knows what goes on in the mind of the person who sleeps next to you," says the narrator, "please raise your hand. I know you can't."*

It's the perfect ending to a movie that has nothing to tell us about marriage except what most of us already know: it can't be explained. The longer it lasts, the more committed people become, even if they've wanted to kill each other along the way. The difficulty of a movie presenting marriage in its honestly *misterioso* form—without any true action or resolution—is illustrated by the fact that *Married Life* actually had three other possible endings. Each of them concluded by having Harry and Pat's son marry, with everyone present as happy guests. In the first variation, on the drive home, Pat says "We're so lucky life's come to moments like this," and their sincere love is palpable. Harry then looks out the car window and sees a large highway sign advertising the brand of household poison he was going to give her. He runs off the road and crashes, killing her. He then asks Richard to kill him with the same poison ("You owe me") and Richard does so, ending up confessing in court to his mercy killing. In the second variation, Richard is also asked to perform the murder and does so, but the film ends with a memory shot of the past, with Pat and Harry from earlier in life, seen from the rear, holding hands as they walk toward their son's home. There is no court trial. In the third version, Harry observes the sign, looks momentarily puzzled or wary, and merely drives on by. Nobody dies.

The four endings show why movies about marriage are hard to make. After all, Harry did try to kill Pat, and shouldn't he be punished? And yet, why should Pat—merely the neighborhood adulteress—have to die to resolve the actions of these two guys? What's wrong with the three endings that are not used is that two of them are nothing but plot twists, and one offers an audience nothing. The ending that was chosen gets it right: "Who can explain what really goes on in a marriage?" it asks. Raise your hand. And that's why marriage movies are hard to make . . . and always have been.

After more than one hundred years of making movies about marriage, the American film business never really changed its formula, never *really* found new ways to tell the story, and varied its purposes only because of the changing social climate. There have been modifications, of course: currently, marriage movies are being treated as if they are romantic comedies. Where earlier films showed two people searching to find what they *might* have together, today we see two unhappy marrieds trying to find what they once had but have since

---

* It's not unlike the mystery of 1929's *Sunrise*. Who knows or can explain what really motivates any single marriage?

lost: *Hope Springs* (2012, with Meryl Streep and Tommy Lee Jones), for example. In older movies, sex was forbidden to unwed lovers, creating tension and excitement onscreen, but now sex is fully available, so that the big excitement comes from: can a couple rekindle the flame, and create a new kind of tension and excitement? Marriage—now an unnecessary status—is the new basis for "romcom." All the twists, all the will-they-or-won't-they-find-a-way-to-do-its, all the desire, the yearning, the sexual frustration lie *in* marriage rather than outside it.

Even so, despite new technologies like color and wide screen . . . despite the use of flashbacks and out-of-time sequences . . . despite Depression, war, and sexual revolution, despite international influences, despite brand-new topics such as same-sex marriage, sperm donors, and surrogate mothers, the marriage movie has remained the story the audience already knew. The bottom line of couple, situation, and problems, treated as comedy or caution (with clothes, bathrooms, and kitchens), stayed in place, too familiar and ordinary to even be recognized officially as a real genre. Over time, stories of marriage slowly grew less and less dramatic, slowing down to an almost cinema-vérité movement toward realism, with no resolution or explanation to be found, and certainly with no explanation of what kept any couple together. Real marriage remains a locked-room mystery, and the only people who hold the key to open it are the two people inside. In over one hundred years of filmmaking, the marriage movie flatlined . . . but somehow never died.

BIBLIOGRAPHY

In researching marriage movies for this book, I scoured old movie magazines and popular magazines (*Life, Look, Ladies Home Journal*, etc.) to find ads for motion pictures
and articles on marriage and divorce. I also read reviews of movies in *The New York
Times, Variety*, movie magazines, and other newspapers. The American Film Institute
Catalogs were an invaluable source for categories such as "marriage" and "divorce"
in silent films. For the past five years I have also been avidly reading advice columns
and articles in magazines and newspapers on marriage and divorce. What I learned
was pretty much what I already knew: marriage is a mystery. Some people can make it
work, some can't. As William Goldman famously said about the movie business itself,
when it comes to marriage, nobody knows anything.

Association of Motion Picture Producers, Inc. and Motion Picture Producers
    and Distributors of America, Inc. "Code: To Govern the Making of Talking,
    Synchronized and Silent Motion Pictures and the Reasons Supporting It," June 13,
    1934.
Barry, J. F., and E. W. Sargent. *Building Theater Patronage: Management and
    Merchandising*. New York: Chalmer's Publishing Co., 1927.
Basinger, Jeanine. *A Woman's View: How Hollywood Spoke to Women, 1930–1960*.
    New York: Alfred A. Knopf, 1993.
Bennetts, Leslie. "The Truth About American Marriage: A *Parade* Poll Special
    Report." *Parade*, September 21, 2008.
Cavell, Stanley. *Pursuits of Happiness: The Hollywood Comedy of Remarriage*.
    Cambridge: Harvard University Press, 1981.
Cherlin, Andrew J. *The Marriage-Go-Round: The State of Marriage and the Family in
    America Today*. New York: Alfred A. Knopf, 2009.
Coontz, Stephanie. *Marriage: A History*. New York: Viking Penguin, 2005.
"Divorce Rate in America," Style Section, *The New York Times*, August 29, 2010.
Douglas, Barbara. "Trash the Dress." *The Middletown Press*, June 23, 2011.
Eyman, Scott. *Empire of Dreams: The Epic Life of Cecil B. DeMille*. New York:
    Simon and Schuster, 2010.
Gallup, George, et al., *Gallup Looks at the Movies: Audience Research Reports, 1940–
    1950*. Wilmington, DE: Scholarly Resources, 1979.
Gilbert, Elizabeth. *Committed*. New York: Viking, 2010.
Graham, Katharine, *Personal History*. New York: Alfred A. Knopf, 1998.
Haag, Pamela. "The Future of Marriage." *New York Post*, May 29, 2011.
——. *Marriage Confidential: The Post-Romantic Age of Workhorse Wives, Royal*

Children, Undersexed Spouses & Rebel Couples Who Are Rewriting the Rules. New York: Harper Collins, 2011.

Haskell, Molly. *From Reverence to Rape: The Treatment of Women in the Movies.* New York: Holt, Rinehart & Winston, 1973.

Havrilesky, Heather. "A Joyful Kabuki Mask to Obscure the Anguish of Marital Bliss Gone Sour." *The New York Times Sunday Magazine,* July 10, 2011.

"Hometown USA, Wartime America Under the Microscope." *Look,* April 4, 1944.

Italic, Leanne. "On Current Census Figures," *Wisconsin State Journal,* December 21, 2011.

Itzkoff, Dave. "A Show About Something: Marriage." *The New York Times,* February 28, 2010.

Izod, John. *Hollywood and the Box Office, 1895–1986.* New York: Columbia University Press, 1988.

LaSalle, Mick. *Complicated Women: Sex and Power in the Pre-Code Hollywood.* New York: Thomas Dunne Books, St. Martin's Griffin, 2000.

"The Lonely Wife," *Life,* December 21, 1942.

Maltin, Leonard. *The Great Movie Shorts: Those Wonderful One- and Two-Reelers of the Thirties and Forties.* New York: Bonanza Books, 1972.

———. *Classic Movie Guide: From the Silent Era Through 1965,* 2nd ed. New York: Plume, 2010.

McBride, Joseph. *Searching for John Ford.* New York : St. Martin's Press, 2001.

Office of War Information, "Government Manual for the Motion Picture Industry," Summer 1942, Box 15, Files.

Oppenheimer, Mark. "Married, With Infidelities." *The New York Times Sunday Magazine,* July 3, 2011.

Parker-Pope, Tara. "Is Generosity Better than Sex?" *The New York Times Sunday Magazine,* December 11, 2011.

———. "Is Marriage Good for Your Health?" *The New York Times Sunday Magazine,* April 18, 2010.

———. "Scanning for Trouble." *The New York Times Sunday Magazine,* January 2, 2011.

Scherling, Carol Lynn, "Blondie Goes to the Movies." *Films of the Golden Age* 43 (Winter 2005).

Sternbergh, Adam, "Break It Up." *The New York Times Sunday Magazine,* March 13, 2011.

Swarns, Michael L. "More Americans Rejecting Marriage in 50s and Beyond." *The New York Times,* March 2, 2012.

Thomson, David. *The New Biographical Dictionary of Film.* New York: Alfred A. Knopf, 2002.

Weil, Elizabeth. *No Cheating, No Dying: I Had a Good Marriage, Then I Tried to Make It Better.* New York: Scribner, 2012.

Weisman, Carl. *Serious Doubts: Why People Marry When They Know It Won't Last.* Charleston. SC: Booksurge, 2009.

Wolfers, Justin. "How Marriage Survives." *The New York Times,* October 13, 2010.

Vieira, Mark. *Irving Thalberg: Boy Wonder to Producer Prince.* Berkeley: University of California Press, 2009.

INDEX

Page numbers in *italics* refer to illustrations.

PHOTOGRAPHIC CREDITS